The Science of

FICTION

GYVE BUSKIN

The Science of

FICTION

ISBN: 978-0-9853449-7-9

LIBRARY OF CONGRESS CONTROL NUMBER: 2019905705

Saint Grobian Press

Detroit - Umtata - Mumbai - Beijing

DOWNLOAD A FREE PDF OF THIS BOOK WITH LIVE LINKS AT:

www.UnionOfTruth.org/collections/books

The idea that the State originated to serve any kind of social purpose is completely unhistorical. It originated in conquest and confiscation - that is to say, in crime. It originated for the purpose of maintaining the division of society into an owning -and- exploiting class and a propertyless dependent class - that is, for a criminal purpose.

No State known to history originated in any other manner, or for any other purpose. Like all predatory or parasitic institutions, its first instinct is that of self-preservation. All its enterprises are directed first towards preserving its own life, and, second, towards increasing its own power and enlarging the scope of its own activity. For the sake of this it will, and regularly does, commit any crime which circumstances make expedient.

(Albert Jay Nock, "The criminality of the State", 1939)

The men of the higher circles are not representative men;

then - high position is not a result of moral virtue; their fabulous success is not firmly connected with meritorious ability.

Those who sit in the seats of the high and mighty are selected and formed by means of power, the sources of wealth, the mechanics of celebrity, which prevail in their society.

They are not men selected and formed by a civil service that is linked with the world of knowledge and sensibility.

They are not men shaped by nationally responsible parties that debate openly and clearly the issues this nation now so unintelligently confronts.

They are not men held in responsible check by a plurality of voluntary associations which connect debating publics with the pinnacles of decision.

Commanders of power unequaled in human history, they have succeeded within the American system of organized irresponsibility.

(C. Wright Mills, "The Power Elite", 1956. Page 361)

Despair is what happens when the wrong answers are questioned incorrectly. Anxiety is what happens when they aren't questioned at all.

A great man does not despair at having to eat excrement. He uses it to fertilize his mind.

True success is achieved when we stop asking permission to become what we yearn to be. The correct question *is* the answer.

(Raphael Sidelman, "Intrinsic limitations to the retention of power", 2005)

Welcome friend. You do know that history, philosophy, science, and religion all make startlingly clear the fact that truth is quite often counterintuitive, don't you?

Of course you do. So, what if someone were to prove through documented fact and simple logic that things of real importance are not at all what they are being presented as by the established shapers of public opinion? The innate power of reason would quickly and easily enable everyone to incorporate such information into their worldview, right?

Not quite. This book is going to prove with documented facts and logic that: **1-** in America documented fact and logical thought routinely take a back seat to that which promises at least some manner of instant gratification. **2-** Such folly continues to occur even when there is considerable incentive to act in accordance with fact and logic.

This book will also prove that, under such circumstances, it is completely outside the bounds of reason to refer to America as "The land of the free and the home of the brave".

You are familiar with Plato's "Allegory of the Cave", aren't you?

Well, in a nutshell, Plato has Socrates explaining the following to Plato's older brother, Glaucon. Imagine a group of people that have, since infancy, been shackled side by side within a cave. Imagine them shackled in a manner that keeps them from seeing anything but the back wall and each other. Surely those people would base much of their worldview on the following erroneous beliefs: **1-** any image appearing on the wall in front of them is, in fact, a primal entity rather than a mere shadow being cast from another thing by way of an artificial light behind them; **2-** any related sound they hear is a product of the primal entity/shadow, not that which actually caused it.

Of course, those who could best predict the occurrence of images, and/or seemingly explain the meanings of such occurrences and the images themselves, would be most highly regarded.

Furthermore, Socrates figures, if one of them were set free to discover the world outside and the primal entities from which the shadows and sounds originated, he would not immediately recognize what is real. He would be blinded by the light.

But what if, armed with an accurate worldview, he returned to tell his former roommates what he has learned? What if he offered to free them from their shackles so that they too could gain an accurate worldview?

According to Socrates, they would consider his message to be an outrageous lie. Their psychological investment in what they believe to be true is so great that they would try to kill him.

Counterintuitive though it may be, history has proven the validity of those concepts.

Honestly friend, would you like to become fully aware of the fact that physical chains are not requirements of shackled cave dwelling?

If you answered yes to my last question, you're in luck. This book was written as part of a wager that's been made regarding the average American's ability to gain an accurate worldview. It's a rather substantial wager, made with two of my colleagues. It will measure the effectiveness of the techniques that have been employed by the true powers that be to cognitively bankrupt the general population of the United States.

I'm betting on those techniques.

I'm betting they've been so effective that the average American is now incapable of doing anything appropriate to stop us; to stop the continuing purposeful deconstruction of those mechanisms that were put in place to keep their "Ship of State" in proper working order.

Even if I provide them with all of the proof that a rational human being could possibly need in order to clearly see what is happening. And, even if I explain exactly what they could do to thwart those plans and provide a $250,000 tax free cash incentive for each of them to do it.

That's right, **$250,000 tax free, in cash, for each person;** if they'll follow the simple, precise, completely lawful instructions to fix their "Ship of State" that are provided later in this book. Honestly. This is not a hoax. The $250,000 will be handed to them if they follow those instructions.

And, in keeping with the freed cave dweller motif, I've given full ownership of this book and full responsibility for disseminating its message to a guy that most people have never heard of. Oddly enough, he recently started a personal responsibility-themed t-shirt website which was brought to my attention through its noteworthy billboard campaign.

Be careful of what you wish for, right?

Suffice it to say that he's now been fully educated on all of the information contained in this book and all of the information that it links readers to.

And yet, he still doubts that the masses have been irreversibly conditioned in the manner that I detail repeatedly throughout this book. That is, that they've been rendered inert by instant gratification and an unshakable belief that the officially credentialed "experts" on "their side" of every "meaningful" issue are the sole arbiters of that which is correct.

I must admit, I'm genuinely interested in seeing how long he'll bear the thankless burden of his newfound responsibilities before realizing that my taking the bet was a no brainer and success was never in the cards for him.

Of course, our unlikely herald has very limited resources and no connections to anyone with a public platform, so he also created a YouTube channel to help spread the message this book presents (Union Of Truth). And with only thirty-two million other channels to compete against, plus a growing trend toward online censorship, it should be smooth sailing.

Then again, your having watched his show is most likely what prompted you to read this book. Clearly, you would not be one of the cognitively bankrupted Americans I've spoken of.

So, congratulations; you have defied the odds by willing yourself to put down the remote control for your ~~wall~~ television in order to ~~acclimate to the light~~ read and understand what I am presenting. It will soon be unmistakably clear to you that, for untold generations, the true powers that be have been making sure your family and your friends and neighbors families remain in and defend a shackled, delusional state.

As I bring to light the "unjust" plans that are successfully being carried out, I will even go so far as to regularly refer to the average American by way of unflattering characterizations *and prove that they fit*; while also sharing the actual instructions needed to thwart such plans and providing a **$250,000 tax free cash incentive** to do so.

And as you try to share this information with those around you, you will see that they are too far gone to entertain any alternative to their existing worldview; let alone experience any related, genuine indignation.

Note that *genuine* indignation is always expressed in heartfelt actions that are carried out in order to eliminate injustice. It is not expressed in mere words of dissatisfaction or attempts to ignore that which is deemed unjust.

Also note that losers substitute complaints for action and idiots substitute action for thought.

So how will you get them to act appropriately?

Now, in keeping with the spirit of my message, if you aren't absolutely sure of each of the precise - and possibly multiple - meanings of each of the words you have read thus far, I highly recommend that you grab a dictionary and learn them. Then re-read the sentences where those words were used, so you can fully understand my message.

Actually, if need be, look up the following words as well: coherent, symbol, valid, bereft, literate, vital, pyrrhic, emancipate, minion, sane, charlatan, flunky, trencherman, subjugate, footling, throng, condone, faux, sovereign, nomocracy, indolent, vigilance, dereliction, chatter, luxuriate, and voluble.

Such a need is nothing to be ashamed of.

Truth be told, if one cannot accurately and coherently explain the concepts that are merely being symbolized by a particular word, one does not actually know its meaning; which means that one's ability to effectively utilize ideas for their own benefit is limited.

Yet the fact remains that valid ideas and the actions they bring forth are the only valid currency on this planet. And to everyone who is capable of understanding the concepts it presents, this book will prove that fact beyond any logical doubt.

Relax; at no point does this book try to specifically appeal to any of the supposed intellectuals or other high-minded people in your midst. Their proven inability to fix any of the problems that it addresses clearly shows them to be as conceptually bereft as the other lost souls that populate your nation.

With the occasional aid of a dictionary and constant, careful consideration, even the barely literate among you can understand my message. Which is to say that, if what I have been sharing with you regarding America's planned cognitive bankruptcy is <u>not</u> correct, there can be no valid excuse for the majority of Citizens to not immediately begin acting appropriately.

Heck, there's even a $250,000 tax free cash incentive for the otherwise disinterested to do so.

But still, as you try to share this information with them, many of your fellow citizens will mock you. Others will say that the book is too long and asks too much of them (since it's not merely presenting *Barney and Friends*-level concepts in the brief fashion we've gotten them accustomed to).

Putting forth the effort required to understand accurate in-depth explanations of the techniques they're being manipulated by is outside of their pay grade. Moving their mouse to click on a link that provides information vital to their well-being will be seen as a pyrrhic endeavor.

And yet, the further you delve into this book the more you will understand this to be true: your inability to get those who you are in contact with to take proper actions regarding my message will result in *your* suffering. You will suffer in a manner similar to, but worse than, that which befalls those who try to disregard increasingly forceful knocks on the door from IRS agents whose paperwork says their employer is owed more than what has been submitted.

You see, our plans have progressed to the point that, unlike the enlightened former captive in Plato's allegory, to be free, *you* must also emancipate the shackled and delusional among you.

The time for living vicariously through the exploits of heroic figures has long since passed.

Now, just so you don't find the factual information I'm sharing with you too distasteful to be digested, click on the following link. Enjoy George Carlin's presentation of ideas that date back to the origins of informed sociopolitical commentary. Over four million people have already enjoyed it: http://www.youtube.com/watch?v=acLW1vFO-2Q

(After clicking on the above link and watching the three minute and fifteen second video it took you to…) Surely there's no question in your mind that George put forth the effort required to access what's beneath the thin, glossy surface that is all we present to you.

And yet, hardly any of the people who watch, read, or listen to him behave in a manner that's consistent with his sincere message. The vast majority act as though simply agreeing with and laughing at his message is action taken against the purposeful corruption of their lives.

And they continue to fill their "free" time with seemingly benign diversions that they cannot actually afford to be engaged in.

So, as per the terms of my bet, I'm going to prove beyond a reasonable doubt that the following statement is correct:

When it comes to <u>all</u> things of real importance, most of those whom you are surrounded by do not come anywhere near actually understanding their fundamental components, or their own existing relation to them, enough to act appropriately.

How could they? Those hypnotized minions do not engage in any real search for meaning.

The extent of their searching is limited to that of methodically mislabeled merchandise.

Consider the meaning of the word "Sane":

Of sound mind. **Having sound judgement; reasonable; rational. Manifesting or based upon reason; logical.** (Rational = having or exercising the ability to reason.) (Reason = to determine or conclude by logical thinking.) (Logic = reasoning conducted or assessed according to strict principles of validity.) (Validity = the quality of being logically or factually sound; soundness or cogency.)

After having carefully considered the above information, one who actually is sane must understand the disturbing, yet rationally undeniable significance of what I have merely begun to share.

You see, in actuality there are, and always have been, only three types of people on Earth:

1 - The very few who are worthy of power and who take it; "...hence the term for property, *mancipia* (manu capta), things taken by the hand of power." (Quoted from page 3 of the book "A manual of civil law" second edition, by Patrick Cumin, Barrister at Law; published in London, 1865.)

2 - The very few who are aware of the dangers of power being misapplied and who painstakingly strive to foster and live in a "just" society. Care for a sip of the hemlock?

3 - The 99.999% of the species who only resemble the other two types in a basic physical sense; the improperly educated masses who cannot act systematically without being given directions from their superiors (i.e., all of those who will mock you for having put forth the effort to read and understand this book and for taking the actions it prescribes).

There is no humor intended by the number printed above; it is a literal figure.

If anyone with even a somewhat accurate worldview were to do the math and then visualize the masses of incompetent, disinterested fools and assorted other charlatans they are surrounded by, that fact would be startlingly clear.

And if that same person were to read and re-read this book until they actually understood everything I am disclosing to you, they would also find the following facts to be startlingly clear as well.

We are in the late stages of a campaign to finally eliminate that second type of person from existence on this planet. It is being aided, often unwittingly, by the following people who <u>all</u> fall into the category of the third type of person listed above: **a-** your favorite "mainstream media" sponsored flunkies; **b-** the majority of your elected and appointed civil administrators; **c-** many highly credentialed "experts"; **d-** the masses of trenchermen surrounding you.

And it has been so successful that to an alien anthropologist devoid of the details involved, the results would be absolutely baffling.

Perhaps you've heard the following quote from the renowned thinker named Lao Tzu?

"True words are not necessarily beautiful. Beautiful words are not necessarily truthful."

Below is a list of topics whose truth I will begin to share with you. I'll do so by way of short introductions to your awful situation regarding those topics.

Each introduction is followed by links to articles and/or videos, books, and audio recordings. Once you put all of the clearly related pieces together, you will begin to see how we've been working to legally subjugate you through such means.

Note that links can become inoperative over time. If any listed links do not work, just go to: http://archive.org/web/web.php and paste the "URL" into the "Wayback Machine". All of the information is archived there – except for YouTube videos. (Perhaps a few concerned patriots will download those videos without delay and host them in another place with a simple page and link number index; so as to enable access to them in perpetuity. Of course, upon being provided with a link/links to those archived and indexed videos, they will immediately be added to this book).

I did not produce the information in the links. They do not include any groundbreaking inside information for the flag waving footlings to ignore.

Those who naively believe that your fellow citizens are capable of climbing out from the carefully crafted conceptual cave they are content to be confined in have produced some of these works. Other examples come from the main source of our being able to properly gauge exactly how far and how fast we can keep tightening our grip on you without having any meaningful backlash occur.

Indeed, I am referring to our wonderfully effective tool of misdirection known as the mainstream media.

I purposely keep each introduction as short as possible while providing an abundant, though not nearly exhaustive, list of links to such proof of our actions. This is done so that, should you miraculously be able to persuade any of your shackled and delusional fellow citizens to follow in your footsteps, they will not be overwhelmed.

Of course, in order to personally become aware of how badly they are being misled and abused by the actual powers that be, each reader must watch, read, and/or listen to the information presented in the links.

And, since the average American is incapable of perceiving value in anything that we don't first put some form of restriction on, I made sure to stipulate that electronic copies of this book must be offered free of charge: www.UnionOfTruth.org/collections/books

Take note: there are many supposed "experts" in your midst who hold impressive credentials that the "authorities" sanctioned. The credentials are a reward for their exceptional efforts in helping us to fully indoctrinate them with our perverted dogma; to the point that they can regurgitate it with an air of mastery. Thus, their specialty is disinformation.

These "experts" will, of course, claim as such to "debunk" what the "anti-establishment" sociopolitical commentators have been saying since antiquity; and what I am going to prove through documented fact and fundamental logic to be true.

So who will be believed? Who should be believed? The bottom line is this:

Throngs will continue to condone our conceptual cave. As an aspect of our faux feast, they have been taught by officially credentialed "experts" that their valid range of personal responsibility is limited. That is, limited to the particular areas of existence that have not been claimed with an air of mastery to be under the jurisdiction of officially credentialed experts.

Careful consideration is clearly not their responsibility, or of any interest to them. But how can freedom possibly be a part of such a limited, literally insane existence?

It can't. Ongoing freedom cannot exist without responsibility. And it is only by way of an accurate critical thinking process that one can act responsibly. Simple logic proves this.

And who can it possibly hurt if you and your friends and family are capable and desiring of having fact-based thoughtful conversation?

What's the danger in your figuring out if the institutions that have vast influence over each of your lives are acting in accordance with those concepts that are the foundation for the Declaration of Independence, The Constitution, and the Bill of Rights?

I'll give you a hint… ask those "experts" about the U.S. government "nationalizing" the Citizens personal holdings of gold, when, on April 5, 1933, President Roosevelt signed Executive Order 6102. Ask them why, in June of 1933, Congress passed the "Gold Repeal Joint Resolution", which outlawed the contractual demand for payment in gold or silver. Then ask them to tell you which Constitutional Amendment made forced usage of Federal Reserve notes bona fide law.

Also ask them to physically prove with authentic, dated documentation and the goods themselves, where all of the *precious* metal ultimately went and how and when it actually got there (both the amount that the public had once held and the government treasury's holdings). And vehemently insist that the "experts" fully explain both the public benefit that such actions brought forth, and the valid, lawful causes for such actions to have been taken.

But first, read these two short articles about the gold depository at Fort Knox. They'll provide you with a few topics worthy of fact-based thoughtful conversation with your friends and family: www.wallstreetdaily.com/2013/07/16/fort-knox-gold/

http://www.moneynews.com/Ed-Moy/Fort-Knox-gold-bar-audit/2014/06/06/id/575519/

(Oh, by the way, since the public schools in your nation do not teach anything that might impart upon their students an awareness of its actual meaning, allow me to clearly state the rationally undeniable fact of what your Declaration of Independence actually declares:

Public benefit, AS DEFINED SOLELY BY THE CITIZENS THEMSELVES, - *each of whom is inherently sovereign, having been endowed by their Creator with certain unalienable Natural Rights* - **is the one and only, singularly valid cause for the establishment and functioning of lawful government.**)

Then, when the "experts" simply cannot honor your requests, tell them pleasantly, though in no uncertain terms, to spew the perverted dogma elsewhere. Remind them of the term "Nomocracy".

 Now, here's another important fact that you were purposely <u>not</u> officially taught: devoted truth seekers are easily distinguishable from those who are content to remain in and defend a shackled, delusional state. How so?

A devoted truth seeker does not disregard documented fact, no matter who presents it.

Nor does a devoted truth seeker mockingly question the validity of information that is being shared with them, while at the same time declining to personally read, listen to, or watch what would quickly and unequivocally prove that their mockery is but a display of ignorance.

The faithful efforts of devoted truth seekers, which are properly defined as an allegiance to duty, lead to the following understanding: there are myriad techniques and players involved in the planned misdirection of one's awareness. As such, the identity of the messenger must not be allowed to influence one's ability to recognize and properly utilize factual information.

For instance, if, while chewing it over, the last two sentences tasted in any way like a conspiracy theory flavored offering, start reading Henry Kissinger's book "<u>Diplomacy</u>" without delay. When you've had your fill of "raison d'état"/"realpolitik", come right back to where you left off here.

Now, listen carefully as Thomas Sowell speaks about the current state of affairs regarding charter schools, public "education", and "the system": https://www.youtube.com/watch?v=9boQrCPwMws

Now listen to Sharyl Attkisson speak about numerous governmental techniques that have been employed to influence the news media and obscure facts that are in the public interest:
https://www.youtube.com/watch?v=9CgQ8wx-CXY&ebc=ANyPxKoIRQsmKOk3T1TiMzkUY_6P7vaCIVeQ_CMGaIfYjqzxqQF5v2XI3Ve94ASazJWlewnrmiWri6TwaxMLshiz46Btxx6zog&nohtml5=False

Now watch this presentation by Shiva Ayyadurai, Benny Smith and Phil Evans that explains the existence of coordinated election fraud: https://www.youtube.com/watch?v=Ztu5Y5obWPk

Now watch this enlightening Epoch Times interview with author Luke Rosiak:
https://www.youtube.com/watch?v=G0lhrzWtWMc

Now listen carefully as Bill Moyers interviews Mike Lofgren, a congressional staff member for 28 years: https://www.youtube.com/watch?v=EYS647HTgks&feature=youtu.be

Now listen carefully as Michigan State Senator Patrick Colbeck speaks about some scientifically proven dangers of the 5G technology that's coming very soon to the street you live on: https://www.youtube.com/watch?v=j-UEuOYOED4

Now check out exactly why James Corbett believes it's important to "#ExposeBillGates": https://www.corbettreport.com/exposebillgates/

Now listen carefully as Robert Kennedy junior shamelessly repeats numerous outlandish conspiracy "theorist" talking points: https://www.youtube.com/watch?v=QLi6ZrFp6vQ

Before I proceed to the following chapter listing, I'm going to refer you to three articles that will greatly benefit you if you read them at this point in this book. I recommend that you read these articles at this point because they will provide you with verifiably accurate prerequisite knowledge.

You see, unlike that of a sail, the wind that pushes you forward can be seen. It goes by the name of "past perception".

First we have excerpts from "Our Enemy the State", published in 1935 by a man named Albert Jay Nock. Mr. Nock diligently studied and rationally assessed both historical facts and current events. He then attempted to widely disseminate that which he learned from such study regarding the real meaning and purpose of the current events of his time. His insights and actions qualify him to be classified within the second category of the three types of people that have ever existed on this planet: www.panarchy.org/nock/state.html

The second is entitled "War is a racket". It was written by General Smedley Butler, who, at the time of his death, was the most decorated Marine in the history of your country. It's actually a pamphlet, but reading it in its entirety before going forward even one more sentence in this book will be a wise investment: www.panarchy.org/butler/war.html

The third article consists of excerpts from the book "Obedience to Authority", by Stanley Milgram. It does a fine job of explaining how we are always able to have your fellow countrymen willingly abuse whomever we tell them to, whenever it suits our interests: www.panarchy.org/milgram/obedience.html

I also recommend that you put forth the relatively minor effort required to remain, at all times, consciously aware of the ideas being presented in these two quotes:

"It is the common fate of the indolent to see their rights become prey to the active. The condition upon which God hath given liberty to man is eternal vigilance; which condition if he break, servitude is at once the consequence of his crime and the punishment of his guilt."

(John Philpot Curran, "Election of Lord Mayor of Dublin speech" given on July 10th, 1790)

"If there is any slight crookedness of being, or even a slight deviation or separation from pure law and reason, the being is immediately downgraded to the realm of duality and subjected to the control of the two laws of *energy response* and *pure law and reason*, he is the servant of these two masters. The further the being is downgraded, the more physical law is imposed. The further the downfall of a person, the more forces he is subjected to and bound by in the form of laws..."

(Lao Tzu, as translated and elucidated by Hua-Ching Ni. Note that Hua-Ching Ni's exact presentation does not utilize the above words I have presented in italics, but rather the words "Chi" and "Li".)

"Where the old initiated, the new merely 'conditions'. The old dealt with its pupils as grown birds deal with young birds when they teach them to fly; the new deals with them more as the poultry-keeper deals with young birds— making them thus or thus for purposes of which the birds know nothing. In a word, the old was a kind of propagation—men transmitting manhood to men; the new is merely propaganda...

The task of the modern educator is not to cut down jungles but to irrigate deserts. The right defence against false sentiments is to inculcate just sentiments. By starving the sensibility of our pupils we only make them easier prey to the propagandist when he comes..."

(C.S. Lewis "The Abolition of Man", 1943)

SECTIONS:

I - **The Two-Party System** – Are Republicans and Democrats really two different well-educated ideological groups whose members in government are upholding their sworn oath to defend the Constitution/Bill of Rights?

If so, why have your rights and prosperity been disappearing faster than free tickets to the Super bowl? Try to comprehend what I am about to explain.

The following holds true in the lifetime of anyone you can speak with.

A fundamentally honest, meaningful public debate has yet to take place between any candidates for the Presidency of your country. Not once have you been able to listen to two or more Presidential candidates' challenge each other and those in the audience to delve deeply into any true underlying causes. This holds true for all of the problems that your country has faced and is currently facing. This is not a result of programming-related time restraints.

In order to "promote the general welfare" they need not sacrifice principle to expediency; unless the general welfare they are promoting is that of their big donors. How familiar are you with the infamous bank bailout? http://www.rollingstone.com/politics/news/secret-and-lies-of-the-bailout-20130104

Yet, not one single time have you had any Presidential candidate thoroughly explain to you the fundamental error in the thought process of their opponent. Never have they thoroughly explained to you, from the locations of both that error and its counterpart in correctness, the reason-based solution to that which ails you.

Not once has there been a debate that brought forth that clear, unbiased presentation.

***Logical question: If it is not such candidates' duty to do so, upon what valid conceptualization does your vote get cast?

Yet, not for a fleeting moment have even one percent of the people around you had any conscious awareness of the facts that I just presented. (But then again, in all fairness, I do see how such an oversight could easily occur. *The candidates' always wear their American flag lapel pins.*)

Forget not seeing the forest for the trees; their entire conceptualization of basically every aspect of their existence is but a purposely-designed aspect of someone else's purposely-destructive agenda.

Take a minute to consider the word "leader". Try to be fully aware of the fact that the word is used for the purpose of identifying those people whose influence causes others to go to the places that such influence intended to cause them to go.

Then, while maintaining such an awareness, look around at the current state of affairs in your country regarding the following: **1**- your lack of buying power; **2**- your oppressive system of taxation; **3**- your staggeringly high national debt; **4**- your polluted air, water, and food; **5**- your failing education system; **6**- illegal immigration; **7**- the constant *legal* confiscation of your supposed rights; **8**- the ever-expanding for-profit prison industry business model; **9**- the ever-increasing "need" for governmental/police/military/ surveillance/intrusion in all areas of personal and public affairs, etc. And understand exactly how it is that you got to this place.

Understand that the rights of the indolent have become prey to the active. Understand that because of such indolence there is now what amounts to a private interest owned and operated, exclusive system in place that controls the ability to hold any manner of meaningful public office.

Understand that such office is what empowers those people whose *direct* influence causes others to go to the places that such influence intended to cause them to go.

Then Google the terms "ALEC exposed", "gerrymandering", "omnibus bill", "Federal debt", "defense department cannot account for funds", "government cost overruns", "words of art", "legal fiction", "surreptitious", "rationale", "deference", and "quisling".

Then look at what the "leaders" who have created the miserable quagmire you've been led into have repeatedly done regarding the legal ability to confront those hazards. They've done their best to make sure that such power remains in the hands of the same group of traitors who brought forth the mess and who are continually crafting legislation that will enable it to flourish.

Does my usage of the word "traitors" seem unjustified to you? Does it seem as though I'm being overly critical or perhaps even exhibiting a "dangerous political ideology"?

Well, just in case anyone answered yes to either - or both - of the previous questions, let's see how the Merriam Webster dictionary defines the words "Treason", "Insurrection", and "Rebel".

Treason: the offense of attempting to overthrow the government of one's country or assisting its enemies in war.

Insurrection: an act or instance of revolting against civil authority or an established government.

Rebel: To resist the authority of one's government. To act in or show disobedience. To feel or exhibit anger or revulsion. (Revulsion: a feeling of complete distaste or repugnance)

The last time I checked, the Declaration of Independence, the Constitution, and the Bill of Rights expressed and still define both the lawful purpose of government in general and the lawful scope of the federal government specifically. The last time I checked, functionaries of a government are not *the* government; they merely *work for* that government.

So, rationally speaking, aren't "official" actions that are in violation - or not in pursuance - of the concepts and procedures that the above-mentioned documents (and state constitutions) express, and in certain cases specifically instruct, actions taken against the government they officially established and whose scope they define? Are those not acts of breaking the law?

And when such actions are taken repeatedly, by way of methods that evince designs to circumvent and undermine said established government through: **1**- outright deception; **2**- the elimination of meaningful public oversight; **3**- the inability of the average person to interpret statutes, codes, and regulations, let alone find recourse in the law (recourse neither in the law that Article VI of the Constitution proclaims "under the Authority of the United States" to be the "supreme Law of the Land", nor in the Law that Aristotle, Cicero, Edward Coke, William Blackstone and James Wilson all state to be the actual Foundational Law of existence, - and thus the only valid foundation for manmade law - the same law that the Declaration of Independence refers to as the "Laws of Nature and of Nature's God"); how can such actions not constitute attempts to overthrow and revolt against one's government?

Furthermore, rationally speaking, how can such actions <u>not</u> be aiding said government's enemies? And regardless of their job title, aren't those who repeatedly commit such acts correctly defined as said government's enemies as well? In truth, how can it not be so? (Think "Nomocracy")

And why should the definitions of "war" and "force" be limited to the use of "conventional" weapons and techniques? Upon what matter of fact would such a determination be made?

("If an unfriendly foreign power had attempted to impose on America the mediocre educational performance that exists today, we might well have viewed it as an act of war." National Commission on Excellence in Education, "A Nation At Risk: The Imperative For Educational Reform", April, 1983 (2nd paragraph): http://www2.ed.gov/pubs/NatAtRisk/index.html)

Do you recognize the fact that Article V of your nation's Constitution was not inserted on a lark? Are you aware of the acknowledgment in your nation's founding documents of Natural Rights and Common Law? How about your nation's longstanding practice of Jury Nullification? Indeed; there comes a point in the honest search for truth when, regardless of how conceptual roadblocks are artfully administered in an attempt to disguise it, truth becomes plainly evident.

I dare you to find an actual example of government officials *in any government* being understood, by the highly educated men who founded your nation, as trusted arbiters of truth.

And while you're at it, I dare you to find an actual example of employees *in any other field* **literally controlling the lives of their employers** – and regularly telling them bald-faced lies without any meaningful negative consequence.

Google the following terms and examine the many examples of outright bald-faced lying that you will be presented with: "Bush Sr. lies", "Bush Jr. lies", "Bill Clinton lies", "Obama lies", "Hillary Clinton lies", "Mc Connell lies", "Pelosi lies", "Reid lies", "Cheney lies", "IRS Commissioner lies", "Attorney General lies", etc.

Then carefully consider the <u>fact</u> that you and everyone you know, and pretty much everyone you know of, are the combined host organism for a relatively small group of my smug, ruthless, parasitic front men. Indignation? Anyone?

1 - A **MUST WATCH** video from the Hillsdale College "Public Policy from a Constitutional Viewpoint" online course. Discover how current "government regulation" actually functions: https://youtu.be/z3lqBaKFUB4

2 - A **MUST WATCH** video by Bill Moyers. It exposes certain "questionable" actions that are routinely practiced by those who have been elected to craft legislation that's in your best interests: http://www.youtube.com/watch?v=IyTU9RbOEJo

3 - A **MUST READ** article from Forbes entitled "Obama's Disdain for the Constitution Means We Risk Losing Our Republic": http://www.forbes.com/sites/realspin/2013/11/19/obamas-disdain-for-the-constitution-means-we-risk-losing-our-republic/

4 - A FREE pdf download of the Cato institute's **MUST READ** white paper entitled "Power Surge: The Constitutional Record of George W. Bush". (Scroll down for the free pdf button): http://www.cato.org/publications/white-paper/power-surge-constitutional-record-george-w-bush

5 - A **MUST WATCH** conversation between Chris Hedges and John Ralston Saul. Compare their viewpoints to the constantly reinforced "official narrative": https://www.youtube.com/watch?v=GOWYfZtgimI

6 - A **MUST WATCH** 1957 Mike Wallace interview with Senator Wayne Morse. Listen to what the Senator says about the reasons for his actions. Also, see if you can detect any of the subtle advertising that was seamlessly blended into the broadcast: www.hrc.utexas.edu/multimedia/video/2008/wallace/morse_wayne.html

7 - A **MUST WATCH** video that talks about the purposeful exclusion of third party candidates in Presidential debates: http://publish.dvlabs.com/democracynow/ipod/dn2008-1002.mp4?start=1873&end=2743

8 - Part one of a **MUST WATCH** video interview on C-span with George Farah, author of the book "No debate": http://www.youtube.com/watch?v=6fGtY1-pw1M

9 - A **MUST WATCH** five minute video entitled "Why can't Chuck get his business off the ground?" It will help even the most dedicated patriots see how their "leaders" in "government" are working to insure their "prosperity": www.youtube.com/watch?v=YQscE3Xed64

10 - A report *from 2009* that explains how, of 2,737 lobbyists hired to promote the interests of drug companies, health professionals, industry groups, business organizations, insurers, and hospitals, 1,418 (or 52 percent) had worked for Congress, the White House or federal agencies. That included 55 former members of Congress: file:///C:/Users/Admin.HP-Win7/Downloads/Feb%2010%20Finalist%20Files.pdf

11 - A video that talks about the incredible amounts of money that health care lobbyists spent to make sure that health care reform was done to their liking: http://money.cnn.com/video/news/2009/10/15/n_healthcare_lobby.cnnmoney/

12 - A video that shows how lobbyists are really running your Congress: http://www.youtube.com/watch?v=m17VkNIbymA&feature=PlayList&p=4D15D1E50A27637A&index=29

13 - A video that shows how your congressmen are consistently selling you out rather than representing what is in your best interest: http://www.youtube.com/watch?v=-U6PafLNLzo&NR=1

14 - An article that shows how congressmen get rich by working for the destructive concerns that they had supposedly sworn to protect you from: http://www.thenation.com/article/166809/when-congressman-becomes-lobbyist-he-gets-1452-percent-raise-average#

15 - An article about lobbying that gives the reader an accurate idea of how things really work inside their "government": http://www.huffingtonpost.com/bill-moyers/delay-abramoff-and-the-pu_b_16534.html

16 - An article that talks about how your "representatives" in "government" have sold out your best interests to their corporate buddies for big profits and future employment: http://www.corpwatch.org/article.php?id=13780

17 - A few articles that will shed some light on the actuality of how well your "government" "representatives" have been representing you: http://cafr1.com/ThePuzzle.html

18 - An article that explains the history, and many techniques of "Gerrymandering": http://en.wikipedia.org/wiki/Gerrymandering

19 - An article explaining how "Gerrymandering" makes many votes completely ineffective: http://www.davidbrin.com/gerrymandering1.htm

20 - A **MUST VISIT** webpage that provides boatloads of information from expert sources on electronic voting machines and "government" plans to fully implement their use: http://www.notablesoftware.com/evote.html

21 - An article about problems associated with electronic voting machines: http://www.commondreams.org/news/2008/10/29/vote-grab-voting-machines-are-unreliable-and-inaccurate

22 - Part one of a five-part video on electronic voter machine fraud. Watch all five parts: http://www.youtube.com/watch?v=JSe24deOpUY

23 - An interview with Russel Ramsland of Allied Security Operations. Russel explains electronic voter fraud techniques and provides examples of recent election fraud: https://www.youtube.com/watch?v=ficae6x1Q5A&feature=youtu.be

24 - An article that talks about how "both" political parties of your "government" are on the same team when it comes to undermining what is in the best interests of the general public: http://www.conspiracyarchive.com/Articles/Seizing_Power_and_Property.htm

25 - A free preview of a book entitled "The Best Democracy Money Can Buy"; it's a good introduction to some of the valid documentation available that proves how badly the public is getting abused by their loyal "representatives" in "government": http://www.amazon.com/Best-Democracy-Money-Can-Buy/dp/0452285674/ref=pd_sim_b_2#reader_0452285674

26 - A video from Public Television that explains the story of some swell guys who were major lobbyists in Washington D.C.: http://www.pbs.org/wgbh/pages/frontline/video/flv/generic.html?s=moyj06p2fe

27 - A free preview of the book entitled "Shadow Elite". It describes some of the process through which you are getting shafted by those who were supposed to look out for your best interests: http://www.amazon.com/Shadow-Elite-Undermine-Democracy-Government/dp/0465091067#reader_0465091067

28 - Watch a former U.S Attorney General - *the top law enforcement officer in your country* - present an obvious and unabashed command performance in the act of obfuscation: https://www.youtube.com/watch?v=FUaw_Z6sjmw

29 - Two articles that provide a brief, yet valuable, introduction to a man who was born southeast of Rome and is now known simply as "Cicero": http://www.nlnrac.org/classical/cicero

https://fee.org/articles/marcus-tullius-cicero-who-gave-natural-law-to-the-modern-world/

II - Education

II - **Education** – Fact: the continuing purposeful deconstruction of those mechanisms that were put in place to keep your "Ship of State" in proper working order is made possible by our continuing ability to cognitively bankrupt the general population.

Our ability to insidiously nurture and encourage an overwhelming lack of interest in putting forth the energy required to learn anything of real value is the guarantee of your nation's ruin. Indeed, if history teaches any lesson worth the effort of its application, it's that there's absolutely no way for any group of people to remain free unless they are properly educated.

Yes, historically speaking, the general public of the world has been poorly educated, if educated at all. That is why, historically speaking, the general public of the world have been anything but free people.

The majority of Americans believe that their "Constitutional rights" are something the "government" grants to them and guarantees them, regardless of their action or inaction. Yet those supposedly overhyped things are actually "constitutionally protected" **Natural Rights.**

So why do so many people hold such an erroneous belief? The simplest correct answer is that, for decades, your "leaders" have been working on all fronts to craftily delegitimize the concept of unalienable Natural Rights; even though it is inarguably the conceptual foundation of both the Declaration of Independence and the Bill of Rights.

Why else would the vast majority of American citizens who received High School and College diplomas be incapable of providing a well-articulated, in-depth explanation of the rationale which underlies the deference that was paid by your nation's founders to the concepts of unalienable Natural Rights, Dominion, Agency, and Possession?

Can you even approach such a task? Read this right now: http://teamlaw.net/Sovereignty.htm. Now (I'll presume that you've read and understood the article that the link takes you to), put forth your finest effort to understand this fact: whether or not you believe in the God of the bible, in this context it remains the bedrock of law upon which your exercisable rights exist. The *legal* bastardization of that bedrock, the absence of such lessons in classrooms, and the elimination of its overt presence in courtrooms are crucial cracks in the hull of your "Ship of State".

Tell me friend, without there having been concerted acts of subversion committed by large numbers of Democrats and Republicans, how exactly is it that the conceptual foundation of the "supreme Law of the Land" came to be legally categorized as "terrorist ideology"? Ask yourself, was it members of the United States Marijuana Party that instructed law enforcement agencies and the Pentagon to train their employees to view sovereign minded citizens as violent extremists? (Fear not freedom lovers, such instruction is documented in this book)

Where were all of the honest and in-depth, highly publicized and widely broadcast prime time debates regarding the illegitimacy of that now "dangerous", demonized conceptual foundation? (Or those regarding "destructive" acts of biological-based gender differentiation? Read this to gain insight into the real agenda: http://www.thepublicdiscourse.com/2016/10/17811/)

The price of believing that it is someone else's job to know about anything that really matters is slavery. And - surprise - only those who have failed to personally invest the time and effort required to earn a proper education get stuck with that bill.

Yes, only bamboozled people believe they can actually afford to spend all of their time and "money" on the limitless diversions/misbranded merchandise we present to them.

Anyone with even the slightest inclination to think would be aware of this fact: we have been systematically destroying the market value of your nation's "money" and the structural integrity of your families, communities, school systems, and manufacturing industries for decades. And they would be outraged.

Like you, they would be busy properly directing the same considerable effort and energy toward fixing the problem that most citizens reserve for very rare occasions; such as when their cable or phone company mistakenly disconnects them from the chief sources of mental stimulation they desire and are capable of processing.

Unlike most Americans, they would not be wasting an amount of time equivalent to a full-time job seeking entertainment by way of fluff filled magazines and novels, watching movies and "reality" television, playing video games, and attending faithfully to both their favorite real and "fantasy" sports; while spending the rest of their "free" time playing around on the internet and/or shopping with a high interest credit card for unneeded trinkets and gadgets that certain of our operatives told them they needed.

Nor would they constantly be ingesting all of the other poisons that are successfully being passed off as medicine, food, beverage, and news. Are you familiar with the word "ethos"?

Try to get those around you to take a look at the facts regarding the downward spiral of your country's general levels of education and prosperity. Can they be made to realize that, in the midst of such a downward spiral, only a deranged creature could be compelled to regularly supplement their already hours long fantasy inspired interest in the plainly obvious diversions from reality known as collegiate and professional sports, with their own "fantasy leagues" that are simply based upon the statistical details of such diversions? (Can you luxuriate in such voluble sentences?) Can they be made to realize that such actions amount to a dereliction of duty?

Can they be made to realize that such actions are equivalent to those of a fat, sweaty, severely unhealthy instant gratification junkie, who happens to be on high cholesterol, high blood pressure, gout, diabetes, and erectile dysfunction medications, regularly eating pounds and pounds of greasy French fries that've each been wrapped in bacon before being fried again in hydrogenated oil and then covered with a few pounds of liquid cheese, and washing it all down with pancake syrup... Such actions are clearly insane, right?

Now let me remind you that later on in this very book there are detailed, easy to follow instructions on how to personally, lawfully, peacefully earn $250,000 completely tax free! Just for carrying out one's Declaration of Independence-mandated duty to repair the damage that has been inflicted upon your "Ship of State" and prevent it from happening again!

("But when a long train of abuses and usurpations, pursuing invariably the same Object evinces a design to reduce them under absolute Despotism, it is their right, it is their duty, to throw off such Government, and to provide new Guards for their future security." **FYI, the Declaration of Independence and the Constitution/Bill of Rights are in the back of this book.**)

Do you believe that you'll be able to get your fellow citizens to follow such instructions, or at least fully read and understand them in order to verify their validity?

Of course you believe that such an incentive will help win them over. But I know better. Don't get me wrong; those instructions <u>are</u> in this book. I just know, for numerous soon to be shared reasons, that you don't have a shot at getting them to make the investment required to understand exactly how - and why - to get that money into their pockets.

1 - A **MUST HEAR** recorded lecture on the importance of philosophy, given at West Point in 1974 by Ayn Rand. It will influence the entire way that you view the world (clearly she never read "War is a Racket", but don't let that take away from her otherwise logical presentation): http://aricampus.s3-website-us-east-1.amazonaws.com/media/MP3s/11/Philosophy-Who%20Needs%20It.mp3

2 - A **MUST WATCH** video that presents a thought provoking conversation between Chris Hedges and Alain de Botton. If you carefully consider the ideas they present, the resulting thoughts and feelings you will have are sure to positively influence the entire way that you experience the world: https://www.youtube.com/watch?v=XivXmrnBpf8&nohtml5=False

3 - A **MUST READ** article entitled "Are You a Thug?" written by the long time freedom activist and criminal law attorney, Mark J. Victor. Why aren't these concepts the official party line? https://www.lewrockwell.com/2015/11/marc-j-victor/thug-2/

4 - A **MUST HEAR** presentation, given by former New York City Teacher of the year John Taylor Gatto, of historical facts regarding the planning and development of public schooling in the United States and the identities of the architects and financial sponsors behind such activities: https://www.youtube.com/watch?v=1KZvOWrT9h4&nohtml5=False

5 - In light of what the previous link (#4) offered, doesn't the "Common Core" curriculum smell like the next stage of that long-term plan? https://www.youtube.com/watch?v=-htDV60CjkA&nohtml5=False

6 - A **MUST READ** article that explains what the proper role of government is. It will help you understand that being properly educated is a fundamental requirement of the safeguarding of one's rights. As you read it remember that it was written in 1963: http://www.aynrand.org/site/PageServer?pagename=ari_ayn_rand_the_nature_of_government

7 - A **Free** pdf of the **MUST READ** book entitled "The underground history of American education". It presents the true nature of public education in your country and the people behind its planning and implementation. At the very least you should read all of **chapter two** (the link brings you there): http://www.johntaylorgatto.com/chapters/2a.htm

8 - A **Free** pdf of the **MUST READ** book entitled "The deliberate dumbing down of America": http://www.deliberatedumbingdown.com/MomsPDFs/DDDoA.sml.pdf

9 - A **Free** pdf of the **MUST READ** book entitled "The closing of the American mind". It explains that the higher education system in America has been helping to bring about widespread conceptual bankruptcy: http://archive.org/details/ClosingOfTheAmericanMind

10 - A **MUST READ** article that explains how your "government" is working to remove the constitutionally protected right of parents to choose the education that their own children will receive: http://www.hslda.org/docs/news/2013/201302110.asp

11 - A **MUST READ** article that provides important information about your nation's public school curriculum: http://www.whatwouldthefoundersthink.com/the-sucker-list

III - **Propaganda** – Friend, you are on a mission of utmost importance. It entails your needing to help others see that we constantly subject them to gross injustices that are generally undetectable, and literally unbelievable when detected. So how could I not include any mention of the practice of "propaganda"?

Due to, and in conjunction with, the widespread and varied derelictions of duty that are a hallmark of the American people, for many generations we've been able to take advantage of each successful model of control that has been used throughout history.

We've accomplished this by employing some of the finest minds available to study the methods of the art of effective, purposeful misdirection and every form of salesmanship and theory of psychology that has ever existed.

We've extracted and co-opted every useful aspect of every method ever used by religious authorities, psychiatric professionals, "benevolent" monarchs, tyrants, demagogues, hypnotists, magicians, street peddlers, carnival vendors, and other predatory organisms.

And we are constantly improving upon what is now the science of how to control the mind of a simpleton. You see, our high-tech weapons can do much more than directly physically injure their victims.

The technologies at our disposal, and our unlimited ability to utilize and almost instantaneously morph them to our advantage, enable us to continue our scam. We constantly bathe you in and feed you with the exact ideas, images, and sounds at the exact frequencies that prompt most people to "think" and act however it suits us best.

Contrary to what most Americans are unaware of having been programmed to believe, freedom is <u>not</u> correctly defined as the ability to watch and/or record your choice of whatever television shows are being offered, while simultaneously being able to buy without ready cash whatever you have been told that you want from whichever name brands have long since conquered your otherwise barren mental landscape.

  As I've said, having those Grobianites (that's Saint Grobian) sink to that level was both an art form and a science. Numerous examples of such are offered in the links below. But before I conclude the introduction to such information, I have a few simple questions for you to ponder. As a matter of fact, I recommend that you continue to ponder them as you read the remainder of this book and investigate the supporting information that I'll link you to.

Is your nation filled to the brim with completely self-modeled, uninterested bums and/or loathsome cowards? Bums and cowards who <u>are</u> aware of the fact that arsonists have been torching their entire societal structure but are too lazy and/or fearful to learn how it has actually been done, in order to properly do anything about it?

If what I have just told you about our methods of control were <u>not</u> true, how else could we have possibly gotten away for so long with all of the other corrupt things that this book is providing clear proof of?

Is what I just told you about our methods of control true?

Or are you somehow surrounded by a multitude of completely self-made, uninterested bums and loathsome cowards?

Keep reading and investigating. You will soon come to understand that you are, in fact, surrounded by living, breathing tools that we are using with precision to help bring about our desired ends.

They believe only what we tell them. We tell them only what serves our best interests.

1 - A **MUST WATCH** 1958 Mike Wallace interview of Aldous Huxley:
www.hrc.utexas.edu/multimedia/video/2008/wallace/huxley_aldous.html

2 - A **MUST READ** article that talks about a propaganda technique being used by your "government" that is known as the "video news release":
http://www.nytimes.com/2005/03/13/politics/under-bush-a-new-age-of-prepackaged-tv-news.html

3 - A **MUST WATCH** presentation by Sharyl Attkisson regarding certain media manipulations and deceptions: https://www.youtube.com/watch?v=-bYAQ-ZZtEU

4- A **MUST WATCH** glimpse into an important piece of our high-tech weapon arsenal:
https://www.youtube.com/watch?v=rQmIPK7DQh8

5 - A **MUST READ** article by Glenn Greenwald that presents a tiny portion of the information in whistleblower Edward Snowden's vast archive of previously secret "national security"-related documents. Its title, "How Covert Agents Infiltrate the Internet to Manipulate, Deceive, and Destroy Reputations", should give you a pretty good idea of what it's about:
https://firstlook.org/theintercept/2014/02/24/jtrig-manipulation/

6 - A **MUST READ** article that will help you to fully appreciate the information provided by way of link #4 above. Make sure to follow the numerous links provided in this article:
http://www.washingtonsblog.com/2014/02/secret-playbook-social-media-censors.html

7 - Some **MUST READ** excerpts from the book "Media Control" by Noam Chomsky:
http://www.thirdworldtraveler.com/Chomsky/MediaControl_excerpts.html

8 - A New York Times article **exposing the <u>fact</u> that your own "government" was paying former high-ranking military and intelligence officials to tell you what the Bush Administration wanted you to hear regarding the invasion of Iraq after 9/11 and the ongoing military operations there**. Strangely enough, *nothing* was ever done about it. And the story was never shoved down your throats by all forms of media, like the things we want everyone to be "thinking" that they're actually thinking about. Hmmm…
http://www.nytimes.com/2008/04/20/us/20generals.html

9 - An in-depth report about the "Pentagon military analyst program"; it offers many links to official documents and other important information:
http://www.sourcewatch.org/index.php?title=Pentagon_military_analyst_program

10 - An excellent article that explains what propaganda is, and its history and use. The article offers many informative links: http://www.sourcewatch.org/index.php?title=Propaganda

11 - An article that documents many examples of the use of propaganda by "government" and lobbyists: http://hope.journ.wwu.edu/tpilgrim/j190/vnrandfaking.html

12 - An article that gives numerous examples of "covert propaganda" used by the "United States government" toward the citizens of your country: http://www.sourcewatch.org/index.php?title=Covert_propaganda

13 - An article that talks about the Pentagon's plan to have an official agency called the "Office of Strategic Influence" set up a few months after 9/11, to spread misinformation to foreign news media outlets that would have then been reported upon in the U.S.: https://web.archive.org/web/20050205071531/http://www.fair.org/index.php?page=1103

14 - An article that reports on the Bush administration using "Manufactured Journalism": http://www.sourcewatch.org/index.php?title=Manufactured_journalism

15 - An article that talks about the many ways the powers that be use, and have used, propaganda to further contort all aspects of the average American's worldview: https://web.archive.org/web/20070314150228/http://oldthinkernews.com/Articles/oldthinker%20news/humanity_under_attack.htm

16 - An article whose name says it all, "Why propaganda trumps truth": http://www.informationclearinghouse.info/article23498.htm

17 - Don't worry; this would never happen in America: https://www.youtube.com/watch?v=rSmqOf_HOnU

18 - A website that is dedicated to educating people about how to recognize and avoid becoming trapped by propaganda. **Take the short amount of time required to read each article that's offered through the links on the landing page**: http://www.propagandacritic.com/

19 - Another webpage dedicated to educating people to recognize propaganda, so that they might not continue being fooled by it (click on the little boxes in the middle of the page to read the lessons. Start with the one that says "Introduction" and work your way down. Yes, the vast majority of potential readers need these instructions): http://www.learntoquestion.com/resources/lessons/propaganda/

20 - A **MUST WATCH** BBC video documentary about propaganda, entitled "The century of the self": https://www.youtube.com/watch?v=eJ3RzGoQC4s&nohtml5=False

21 - A **MUST READ** short book from 1928 entitled "Propaganda", written by the master, Edward Bernays. You'll be amazed at how much of today's reality could have been foreseen in 1928: http://www.historyisaweapon.com/defcon1/bernprop.html

22 - An article that explains how your "government" distorts the facts in order to shape popular opinion to be exactly what the "leadership" wants: http://www.salon.com/2010/03/27/wikileaks/

23 - A video introduction to the movie entitled "Constructing public opinion"; it shows how the media actually use polling to get its victims to "think" about and want what they want them to "think" about and want: http://www.youtube.com/watch?v=DvodhsMc2QM

24 - An article that gives introductions into the admissions of many top journalists that cover-ups in the media are happening all the time:
https://web.archive.org/web/20030801072944/http://www.wanttoknow.info/mediacover-up

25 - A **MUST READ** article that talks about how "Globalization" is undermining your national security, and how it is being done for profit. I included it here so that you might wonder why the "mainstream media" has not force fed such information to you for the last decade and a half:
https://web.archive.org/web/20130306010133/http://www.augustforecast.com/2006/03/07/globalization_the_final_demise_of_national_security/

26 - An article from 2004 that talks about the book "Into the Buzzsaw", which exposed the myth of a free press in the United States:
https://web.archive.org/web/20051020040649/http://www.buzzflash.com/reviews/05/rev05032.html

27 - The **MUST READ** transcript of an interview by "Truthdig" with Elliot D. Cohen, co-author of the book "The Last Days of Democracy":
http://www.truthdig.com/report/item/20070802_last_days_of_democracy?/interview/item/20070802_last_days_of_democracy

28 - A **FREE PDF** of the 2003 book entitled "Bias"; written by the eight-time Emmy Award winner Bernard Goldberg, who spent almost thirty years working as a reporter for CBS. The insolent Mr. Goldberg wrote about how media outlets give the public a distorted presentation (liberal bias) of the news that they report on. Do you think he might have been on to something?
https://archive.org/details/pdfy-W6bvevEK4W3tQ38a

29 - "We begin this multi-part series by stepping way back, because the scale of corruption is so vast and so extensive that your vote might have been stolen years before the election." That quote is the actual description for this video by Bill Whittle about election fraud in the 2020 election:
https://www.youtube.com/watch?v=M7hqtcnDehE

30 - Now compare all of the information that I've presented you with so far in this book, to the "authoritative content" I'm presenting you with in the following articles:

https://www.cnn.com/2020/11/10/tech/biden-lost-pennsylvania-fact-check/index.html

https://www.theguardian.com/us-news/2020/nov/10/whoa-fox-news-cuts-off-kayleigh-mcenany-for-votes-spiel

https://www.cnn.com/2020/11/10/politics/trump-biden-transition-of-power-delay/index.html

https://www.cnn.com/2020/11/10/politics/transition-teams-biden/index.html

https://nypost.com/2020/10/14/if-unreliable-is-the-issue-why-did-social-media-never-block-anti-trump-stories/

https://www.theguardian.com/us-news/2020/nov/11/can-donald-trump-stay-in-office-second-term-president-coup

https://web.archive.org/web/20201111154749/https://www.nytimes.com/2020/11/10/us/politics/voting-fraud.html

IV **- Diversions -** Roman leaders understood that the average human was a complete idiot. They knew that their legitimate complaints would be quickly forgotten if they were presented with regularly scheduled diversions based on one or more of their primal urges for sex, slaughter, slander and sport.

Those leaders wisely created the "Circuses" for people to go to. A scheduled feeding of such primal desires was used to overshadow reason-based "government" related dissatisfaction. In other words, that feeding helped prevent the masses from expressing such dissatisfaction in any meaningful manner.

The Roman leaders did the best they could with what they had, to keep their gravy train of corruption rolling.

Today, seamlessly blended with our aforementioned tools of cognitive bankruptcy, we have tools of diversion at our disposal that the Roman leaders could not have possibly even dreamed of.

In Rome, the people had to make the effort of going to the "Colosseum" or other stadiums where the planned diversions were held.

Surely that need to put forth effort kept some people from getting there; from having those reason-based complaints drowned out by the mass feeding frenzy that their conscious and unconscious primal desires would have been allowed to engage in.

Not to mention that Roman arenas included plenty of third rate seats.

Today we have taken their concept to a whole new level. As a matter of fact, we have perfected it.

This is one reason why I'm fully confident in my bet.

The average American is so lost within the combination funhouse and horror show we've constructed that they are simply incapable of recognizing and acting upon the truth.

Of course, those with whom I've made my aforementioned bet believe I'm overconfident:

"But you'll need to explain exactly how such enslavement is legally being brought about!" "You must provide the correct instructions to follow to thwart our plans and you must include a $250,000 tax free cash incentive for each citizen who will follow said instructions!"

Yawn.

We have constructed a system of diversions from truth that is so instantaneously gratifying, so shiny, so tasty, so interwoven and all-encompassing that a great effort must be made in order for anyone to *not* be fully immersed in it.

You see, whereas in Rome the people had to go to the circus, now the average person's entire life experience actually takes place within it.

And even the "unemployed" have plush, front row, fully interactive seats.

(There are quotations around the word unemployed since it should be obvious to everyone but isn't, that, in light of the fact that we are carefully engineering your demise, everyone is being purposely employed.)

The average person's entire existence is an aspect of the circus we have created and are continually modifying. Why? To keep them from being able to formulate, let alone properly act upon, their own reason-based complaints regarding our theft of everything that is needed in order to prosper while being independent of us.

And our system is so well-designed that it also prevents almost everyone from being able to recognize the validity of anything that anyone might say which is not in agreement with what we tell them.

Most people are incapable of properly investigating *any* idea, let alone one that is not our own. One that they were introduced to and had continually reinforced upon them within the circus we have created for everyone to fully exist within.

Which aspects of what they've been taught and which aspects of what they are seeing and hearing weren't purposely presented to them by us as part of our ongoing effort to keep them from properly formulating and acting upon their own reason-based "government" related dissatisfaction?

Do you know what happens to most swimmers who get caught in a riptide?

What information source will he or she trust when there are many other "credible" sources that state the opposite of what your source claims is true?

What symbols or symbolism will they look toward as guideposts for proper direction - which we haven't already begun to manipulate for our purposes?

How long will they be able to try to "think" outside the box before we offer up some sexy bodies for them to drool over?

How long will it be before one of their favorite television shows comes on, or one of their favorite teams has a game they *need* to watch?

How long will it be before the media, or someone they know, starts telling them the juicy details involved in the mess that some other schmo is making of their life?

How long will it be before we remind them that they are too hungry and too thirsty to possibly "think" about anything but getting some of our ~~toxic~~ tasty food and drink - *which they so deserve* - into their mouth?

How long will it be before the next holiday or birthday that they **need** to buy gifts for is so close that they **need** to start taking care of it?

How long will it be before we alert them to the incredibly important fact that some of the newest stuff we've convinced them that they **need** to buy is on sale for a limited time?

How long will it be before we introduce another must have gadget that they **need** to continually download new must have "apps" for?

How long will it be before the next urgent warning of a possible terrorist attack or deadly flu-like virus is constantly broadcast everywhere? (How long after that will it be uniformly considered unpatriotic to "think" or talk about the "unalienable rights" they've been endowed with by their Creator?)

The list is endless, so I ask you this:

How will you ever pull anyone to a safe shore when they are caught in the middle of a constant, all-encompassing rip tide that they've been taught *is* the safe shore?

And don't forget the fact that any prolonged lack of our intellectual, ecological, economic, and nutritional poison will cause them to suffer from the pain of mental and physical withdrawal.

Am I exaggerating? Try getting some friends to head <u>deep</u> into the woods with you for an enjoyable, fun-filled vacation lasting four or more weeks. Go without anything but the items for which you are the sole power source and that you can each carry on your back; as you hike fifteen or so miles a day.

Go ahead; I'll even let you pick the time of year.

Oh, is that too extreme of an example? Well then, get them to join you for an enjoyable month with the Amish while fully taking part in that unadulterated, wholesome way of life.

Admit it friend, the average American would be hard pressed to name a dozen people they know between the ages of three and sixty who would even enjoy staying in a luxury resort for that same amount of time without being able to play around on a computerized device, flip through some fluff filled magazines and novels, watch television/movies, and chatter at length on the phone. Not to mention eating and drinking some other types of methodically mislabeled, packaged poisons.

1 - A **MUST WATCH** 1958 Mike Wallace interview with Erich Fromm. Listen to what Erich Fromm says, and remember how long ago he said it: www.hrc.utexas.edu/multimedia/video/2008/wallace/fromm_erich.html

2 - The farewell speech of President George Washington. Take some time to read and reflect upon what he said (if nothing else, at least read the second half): http://avalon.law.yale.edu/18th_century/washing.asp

3 - An article that explains the technique of "Distraction": http://www.sourcewatch.org/index.php?title=Distraction

4 - A **MUST READ** article from the Wall Street Journal entitled "Does the Internet Make You Dumber?": http://www.wsj.com/articles/SB10001424052748704025304575284981644790098

5 - An article that speaks about the users of certain technologies being in a constant state of distraction: http://www.theguardian.com/media-network/media-network-blog/2014/dec/15/distraction-economy-technology-downgraded-attention-facebook-tinder

6 - A graph that shows the <u>incredible</u> amount of time Americans have been wasting watching television every month (in 2010). Grab a calculator and divide the numbers by both four (4) and thirty (30) in order to see those numbers in a weekly and daily context:
http://www.marketingcharts.com/television/more-viewers-watch-timeshifted-tv-15093/nielsen-tv-usage-q2-2010-monthly-time-spent-by-age-nov10gif/

7 - A news report that shows the amount of time the average American is spending daily on the internet (in 2013) , in addition to showing the amount of time they *aren't* spending doing other things:
http://www.businessinsider.com/how-much-time-people-spend-online-2013-10

8 - A short article that reports on the increase in time spent playing video Games: http://content.usatoday.com/communities/gamehunters/post/2009/08/nielsen-time-spent-playing-games-up/1

9 - An article that tells us how many hours have been spent so far playing a particular, popular video game (in 2014). After reading the article, imagine how many useful things could have been done with that amount of time:
http://numbers.kotaku.com/when-we-talk-about-a-franchise-as-popular-as-halo-some-1648423502

10 - An illustrated graph that shows how much "money" is spent on sports and where it is spent. Realize that ultimately, even indirectly involved consumers help to pay every single penny of it:
http://www.sportsbusinessjournal.com/images/random/SportsIndustry.pdf

11 - "The American Delusion: Distracted, Diverted And Insulated From The Grim Reality Of The Police State", by John Whitehead of the Rutherford Institute:
http://www.mintpressnews.com/american-delusion-distracted-diverted-insulated-grim-reality-police-state/196171/

12 - An article that will introduce you to some patents that have been granted for the purpose of behavior modification. Be sure to scroll down to the bottom of the page:
https://web.archive.org/web/20050419005137/http://www.wanttoknow.info/050331behaviormodificationtv

V – **The Pharmaceutical-Industrial Complex** – Speaking of methodically mislabeled, packaged poisons... where else, but within the pharmaceutical industry, can we find companies with endless budgets who are constantly working to have their poisonous concoctions pushed into your mouth and veins by way of mandatory, "governmental" decree?

Were it not for the fact that you have been groomed since birth to accept the claims from our credentialed "experts" that you are not qualified to question anything they do, or that they tell you to do, what could possibly be more astounding than these two issues: **1**- the pharmaceutical industry's extremely successful, relentless attack on the sovereign right of each human to personally regulate which substances will be put into their body; **2**- the absolute, unquestioning servitude that the average American exhibits toward the agenda of those companies who are chemically engineering their destruction?

In exchange for the lie that someone else would look after everyone's best interests while they were busy mindlessly supporting their favorite brands, Americans have given away the power of accurately informed choice.

Their mindless support of those brands has allowed thousands of years' worth of discoveries regarding **1**- the healing powers of the body in conjunction with certain naturally occurring substances; **2**- proper diet and exercise; **3**- proper body mechanics and the methods to maintain and make corrections toward them, to be bastardized by a group of profit-driven corporate shills. And since they're protected from lawsuits, those companies care less about adverse effects to their products than your neighbors care about what happens to the dead batteries they replace in their TV remote controls.

The noose around the public's neck keeps getting tighter. But an array of ~~toxic~~ terrific tasting vittles and thirst-inducing flavorful beverages are always available within mere steps of anywhere they ever are. And the cost of our newest high-definition televisions and other assorted gadgets is always within their price range; *especially when they make the minimum monthly payment*. In other words, the really important stuff is always there to unconsciously reassure most people that they can continue to avoid the hassle of due exercise of the faculty of logical thought (i.e., reason). Oh, did I fail to mention the profusely prescribed psychoactive pills that promote the pathology?

Pose the following questions to those who would mock you.

After discovering that it is literally impossible for the following to occur because of a mistake (due to the mandatory protocols which are in place to protect the public from ever mistakenly being exposed to a dangerous pathogen), what sane creature would willingly get injected with any drug which was manufactured by a company that was found to have shipped over 18,000 units of a "vaccine" that had the deadly, live, full-strength disease in it that the vaccine was being sold as a cure for?

How about taking drugs from a company that patented the "cure" for a type of flu-like deadly disease that supposedly was <u>not</u> developed in a lab, but hadn't even been publicly known to exist at the time the patent was filed for? Would logic permit such action?

Do you know that doctor approved legislation has been written to force people in certain industries to submit to mandatory vaccinations with products from the above-mentioned companies?

The proof of everything I've just claimed is only a few keystrokes away.

And yet, since I didn't make it more accessible than a gas station snack shop, by offering you clickable links to it, you will never get anyone to personally verify those facts. They'll either stick with their current opinion, which someone else supplied, or if their opinion changes it will be a result of their simply believing what someone else told them about it…

But here are some clickable links to a few other examples of how well your nation's populace is being looked after by those companies with endless budgets who are constantly working to have their poisonous concoctions pushed into your mouth and veins:

This **MUST READ** article is titled "Drug companies drive the Psychiatric drugging of children": http://www.huffingtonpost.com/dr-peter-breggin/psychiatric-drugs_b_1693649.html

This **MUST READ** article is titled "The wave of evil: New report on ADHD drugs blowback": http://www.huffingtonpost.com/bruce-e-levine/the-wave-of-evil-new-repo_b_235232.html

This **MUST READ** article is titled "Shrinks for Sale: Psychiatry's Conflicted Alliance": https://www.cchrint.org/issues/the-corrupt-alliance-of-the-psychiatric-pharmaceutical-industry/

This **MUST READ** article, entitled "Psycho-Pharma Front Groups", will introduce you to a little known technique that's used quite successfully by the pharmaceutical industry (but are they the only one?): http://www.cchrint.org/issues/psycho-pharmaceutical-front-groups/

This is a **MUST READ** article from the vaccine awareness website named Vactruth.com: http://vactruth.com/2012/04/29/monkeys-get-autism/

This is a **MUST READ** article explaining that the product Gardasil, whose use officials in "government" have been trying to make mandatory, has been proven in numerous tests to have some VERY bad things in it: http://www.naturalnews.com/033585_Gardasil_contamination.html

This is a **MUST WATCH** documentary film about vaccines/pharmaceuticals called "The Greater Good": https://www.youtube.com/watch?v=o_nWp6ZHA2Q&nohtml5=False

So why exactly are those goldbricks pimping out their genetically modified, drug-addicted children?

Is it because they have been completely engulfed by our methods of control? Or is it somehow possible that they've each earned the shameful distinction of becoming a noteworthy incompetent all on their own?

Oh, and not that it's of any consequence, but how many people do you know who are aware of the fact that <u>at least</u> 31 school shootings and/or school-related acts of violence have been committed by those taking or withdrawing from psychoactive drugs?

READ THIS RIGHT NOW: http://www.cchrint.org/2012/07/20/the-aurora-colorado-tragedy-another-senseless-shooting-another-psychotropic-drug/

No, no, the guns were not on psychoactive drugs. The people who used the guns were taking psychoactive drugs, or withdrawing from them.

So why aren't the outraged members of "government" who are writing legislation to hold gun manufacturers liable for such atrocities, instead writing legislation that will enable victims of psychoactive drug-induced shootings to sue the doctors that prescribed them and the pharmacies that dispensed them?

Bartenders and wait staff are legally held liable for enabling motor vehicle operators to drive drunk. Yet there is no legislation in effect that enables the victims of alcohol-induced motor vehicle accidents to sue the manufacturers of the motor vehicle whose use enabled the crime to occur. And the occurrence of alcohol-induced motor vehicle homicides' is much greater than those that are gun-related. And when used properly, guns do not exhibit any negative side effects. Subtle deception abounds.

Common sense tells me that those well-educated "law" makers are deeply aware of the well-documented concerns that caused the inclusion of the second amendment to your nation's Constitution, which proclaims that "A well regulated automobile fleet, being necessary to the ongoing convenience of a flippant state, the right of the people to keep and drive cars shall not be infringed."

Or was it, "A non-regulated pharmaceutical industry, being necessary to the security of a criminal syndicate that has hijacked an entire nation, the right of the 'government' to legislate that people keep baring their arms so that they can be injected with known poisons and other questionable substances shall not be infringed."

Take your pick. The fact is that the average American is not ever going to go anywhere we haven't already led them to believe they've independently decided to go.

1 - The **MUST WATCH** documentary film, "BIG BUCKS, BIG PHARMA Marketing Disease & Pushing Drugs": https://www.youtube.com/watch?v=lAzh28nEoWU&nohtml5=False

2 - A book review of "The truth about the drug companies", taken from the *New England Journal of Medicine,* that reveals how corrupt the pharmaceutical and health care industries have become. **The book was written by the former editor in chief of the Journal**: http://www.wanttoknow.info/healthcoverup

3 - An article that reports on the fact that *at least* 25 former federal officials and legislative aides who helped draft the 2003 Medicare Part D drug benefit are now working as lobbyists for pharmaceutical interests: http://www.prwatch.org/node/8677

4 - A **MUST READ** article from Psychology Today entitled "In Bed with Big Pharma":
http://m.psychologytoday.com/blog/therapy-matters/201107/in-bed-big-pharma

5 - An article whose title says it all, "Report condemns swine flu experts' ties to big pharma":
http://www.guardian.co.uk/business/2010/jun/04/swine-flu-experts-big-pharmaceutical

6 - An article that highlights some of the many stories of Pharmaceutical industry related corruption that are presented in the three books mentioned at the top of the landing page this link will take you to: http://www.nybooks.com/articles/22237#

7 - An article that will help you to understand the truth about many "clinical trials" for drugs:
http://www.naturalnews.com/028194_Scott_Reuben_research_fraud.html

8 - An article that sheds a bit of light on the character of those Pharmaceutical companies that the American public is mindlessly putting their lives and the lives of their children in the hands of:
http://www.citizen.org/pressroom/pressroomredirect.cfm?ID=3239

9 - An article that talks about how "...the whole system of incentives encourages doctors and researchers to serve the interests of the medical industry":
http://www.nytimes.com/2005/12/16/opinion/drugs-devices-and-doctors.html

10 - A free preview of the book entitled "**The truth about the drug companies**":
http://books.google.com/books?id=snVR0YW2yQYC&dq=pharmaceutical+industry+corruption&printsec=frontcover&source=in&hl=en&ei=S-_jSoiOCs-m8Aaw8piIBw&sa=X&oi=book_result&ct=result&resnum=13&ved=0CCcQ6AEwDA#v=onepage&q=&f=false

11 - An article exposing the "government" cover-up of a study from 1974 that showed Marijuana to be useful in curing cancer, and which talks about a recent study in Spain that showed the same results: http://www.alternet.org/story/9257/?page=entire

12 - Jane Burgermeister files lawsuit against Baxter AG, Baxter International and Avir Green Hill Biotechnology AG, "for manufacturing, disseminating, and releasing a biological weapon of mass destruction...": http://birdflu666.wordpress.com/2009/04/

Why not Google Jane Burgermeister, to see for yourself if she's just a conspiracy kook?

13 - Information regarding the patenting of a swine flu virus two years before the outbreak:
http://birdflu666.wordpress.com/2009/07/17/baxter-team-patents-the-swine-flu-vaccine-two-years-before-swine-flu-outbreak-austrian-baxter-scientist-involved-in-h1n1-vaccine-patent-also-advises-who/

14 - A thought provoking article titled "The mandatory vaccination of health care workers":
http://www.americanbar.org/publications/law_practice_today_home/law_practice_today_archive/april11/the_mandatory_vaccination_of_health_care_workers.html

15 - Two **MUST READ** articles that provide important information about the extremely powerful Pharmaceutical industry, vaccines, and your ability to avoid taking such products:
http://vaccinationcrisis.com/avoiding.html

http://articles.mercola.com/sites/articles/archive/2010/11/04/big-profits-linked-to-vaccine-mandates.aspx

VI – **The Agricultural-Industrial Complex** – Surely you recall that in the last section I asked the question, "Where else, but within the pharmaceutical industry, can we find companies with endless budgets who are constantly working to have their poisonous concoctions pushed into your mouth and veins by way of mandatory, 'governmental' decree?". You remember that, right?

Well, there isn't *yet* a lobby pushing for mandatory regulations regarding school children having to mainline Cheese Whiz™. So, technically, you would only be partially correct if your answer was "every one of the major commercial aspects of the food industry".

Yes, these wolves in sheep's clothing have also been working tirelessly to eliminate any ability that anyone *had* to personally regulate that which they eat and drink.

If one really is that which they eat, most people are a laboratory created toxic mess that has little or no resemblance to the human beings who lived just one hundred years ago.

Indeed, for some time now, Americans have quietly been getting served every bizarre concoction of waste product-based, genetically modified, chemically manipulated and/or irradiated ingredients that the industry's ingenious minds can dream up.

Not that you'll get anyone to do anything constructive with the information, but those supposedly healthy fruits and vegetables being displayed at the grocery store are actually covered and/or filled with known toxic chemicals; without there being any warning to you of that fact.

A short list includes oranges, grapefruits, tangerines, lemons, and other fruits such as apples that have been treated with yummy sounding known toxic chemicals called "Imazalil" and "Thiabendazole".

And the Imazalil actually seeps into the fruit so that washing it cannot remove the toxin.

Yes, your well-informed nation is sold meat from animals that have had cancer. And how would you feel about also legally being sold meat from cloned animals without there being any warning to you of that fact? http://www.dailymail.co.uk/sciencetech/article-3673926/Are-eating-cloned-meat-common-think-20-years-Dolly-sheep-born.html

Check out these two clips of the well-known British chef Jaime Oliver explaining how a once popular meat product is made (for some strange reason all of the high quality, full length clips seem to have vanished from the web…):

http://www.takepart.com/video/2015/05/14/jamie-oliver-shows-you-whats-really-pink-slime

https://www.youtube.com/watch?v=uEe6UzlQVJ0&index=2&list=PLUnXSms9ZpQViPVc3isASntvvte60zy3D&nohtml5=False

And who was selling it before the uproar? http://abcnews.go.com/m/blogEntry?id=15491602

Bad taste in your mouth? Relax; you're still only at the point of sale. Really, how effective is even the best example without some background to help you put it into proper perspective?

http://www.nationofchange.org/how-pink-slime-industry-buys-influence-government-1334325098

www.billmoyers.com/2013/07/10/alec-activists-and-ag-gag/

The cows Americans eat are fed chicken feces and feathers as a source of protein (i.e., "Chicken Litter").

The GMO corn you eat is patented as an insecticide and has been shown to cause sterility in the second generation offspring of those who ingest it.

The DNA of numerous plants has had the DNA of assorted creatures, such as flies, fish, and **viruses** spliced into them.

And contrary to the "myth debunkers" claims, researchers' safety concerns regarding GMO crops that have virus derived genetic codes inserted into their seeds have <u>not</u> been definitively answered: http://www.gmofreeusa.org/research/gmo-science-research/

But fear not; this **MUST READ** article/video will reinforce your trust in those flag lapel pin wearing, officially credentialed "experts" who are the sole arbiters of that which is medically correct:

http://articles.mercola.com/sites/articles/archive/2015/03/08/altered-genes-twisted-truth-gmo.aspx?e_cid=20150308Z1_SNL_NB_art_1&utm_source=snl&utm_medium=email&utm_content=art1&utm_campaign=20150308Z1_SNL_NB&et_cid=DM69481&et_rid=868596127

Ooops... the FDA and the USDA, who are legally in charge of protecting your best interests regarding that which you eat, insure that these insane and unlawful practices continue *and* flourish!

Well, if it's any consolation, at least they've been fulfilling one constitutionally mandated responsibility; you know, the one that directs them to regularly carry out, *with extremely intimidating shows of deadly military force*, the confiscation of non-irradiated, non-genetically modified, non-toxic, organically produced raw foods that have been cultivated by unpatriotic, criminally minded domestic terrorists who are attempting to pass themselves off as health conscious sovereign Citizens. ☺

How could this happen?

The majority of your neighbors are relaxing on the couch, wishing that their local cable company would add a few more comedy and sports channels to their monthly subscription package. Huge corporations are busy having their operatives in "government" allow known poisons to be served up daily *and* mandate that it happens without any notification of their presence.

And included in the full product price are <u>all</u> of the costs involved in the governmental lobbying that ensures the implementation and continual growth of such plans (which also includes many generous "government" subsidies).

But hey, "servitude is at once the consequence of his crime", right?

It is a known fact that few people care about what they actually physically ingest as long as it's plenty sweet and salty, and microwavable if eaten hot. And it is a known fact that even fewer people possess the tools needed to properly consider the validity and far reaching consequences of that which they mentally ingest.

Should I be concerned that the average adult American might begin to fathom just how absurd it is that the following statement from page <u>28</u> remains equally true when the words "pharmaceutical industry" are replaced by the words "commercial food industry"?

"Were it not for the fact that you have been groomed since birth to accept the claims from our credentialed "experts" that you are not qualified to question anything they do, or that they tell you to do, what could possibly be more astounding than these two issues: **1**- the commercial food industry's extremely successful, relentless attack on the sovereign right of each human to personally regulate which substances will be put into their body; **2**- the absolute, unquestioning servitude that the average American exhibits toward the agenda of those companies who are chemically engineering their destruction?"

No. Regardless of the fact that there are numerous industries it can rightfully name, and regardless of how many times you might attempt to have them understand it, your audience will never see the previous statement as indicative of the actual state of affairs in your country.

Do anomalies currently exist?

Yes. Watch this well-informed fourteen year old hold her ground against a disingenuous corporate shill: https://www.youtube.com/watch?v=HIXER_yZUBg

Don't pin your hopes on that anomaly.

 In sincere appreciation of the monumental task ahead of you regarding your need to pull the shackled, delusional masses from an all-encompassing rip tide that they've been taught *is* the safe shore, I'm going to lighten up the mood a bit.

With few exceptions, the rest of this book is going to be presented as though I was speaking directly to those hapless creatures.

Just make note of the fact that, since your well-being depends upon me <u>not</u> winning my bet, you are strongly advised against presenting your case to them in such a manner. A wise man once told me that one should not vilify their audience.

Of course, since I'm not actually attempting to engage your audience, I'm going to vilify them (Just picture me speaking directly to them; I won't be using quotation marks. Here goes…).

By the way, what exactly is your personal plan to avoid being trapped in the coming worldwide reliance on genetically modified "terminator" seeds?

Yes, I'm referring to the patented new type that are eventually going to be the only seeds anyone is <u>legally</u> allowed to plant, and which need to be bought from their manufacturer every single planting season.

http://www.globalresearch.ca/the-seeds-of-suicide-how-monsanto-destroys-farming/5329947

Yes, poo poo pants, all of the non-animal foods that you eat come from seeds. And before you eat them, all of those tasty animals eat food that also comes from seeds.

Seafood? Sure, which pesticide poisoned pond or oil spill filled or nuclear waste ridden body of water do you prefer to have us drop our ecosystem defiling, stadium sized catch-all nets into for you?

Yes, poo poo pants, the "farm raised" varieties are essentially just animated underwater versions of those "terminator" seeds.

And how about a little third day o'creation (Genesis 1:11, 1:12): "And God said, 'Let the earth sprout vegetation: seed bearing plants, fruit trees of every kind on earth that bear fruit with the seed in it'. And it was so. The earth brought forth vegetation: seed bearing plants of every kind, and trees of every kind bearing fruit with the seed in it. And God saw that this was good."

Now check out day six regarding such plants and trees (Genesis 1:29).

Then tell me if you've read anything that could rationally be construed as a restriction placed upon the ability to possess and/or personally cultivate any of those seeds. Or any mention of exclusive rights to the "intellectual property" otherwise known as the DNA of any of God's creations.

By the way, what have your trusted news sources been telling you about Codex Alimentarius?

1 - A **MUST READ** article entitled "What's Even Grosser Than Pink Slime?"
http://m.motherjones.com/tom-philpott/2012/04/pink-slime-vilsack-USDA-poultry

2 - A **MUST READ** article entitled "Four Things Grosser Than Pink Slime". Be sure to follow all of the links offered: http://m.motherjones.com/tom-philpott/2012/04/things-are-grosser-pink-slime

3 - A **MUST READ** article entitled "Cattle Futures?"
http://www.nytimes.com/2004/01/11/magazine/11WWLN.html

4 - A **MUST READ** article entitled "3 New Studies Link Bee Decline to Bayer Pesticide:
http://m.motherjones.com/tom-philpott/2012/03/bayer-pesticide-bees-studies

5 - The website for the "GMO Verification Project". If you take the time to search all of the information that they offer, you will not only become informed on matters related to genetically modified foods, but you will also discover what brands and products offer certified alternatives to GMO's and where you can buy them: http://www.nongmoproject.org/learn-more/what-is-gmo/

6 - An article that provides more information, and links to documentation about its claims, than the average American can handle: http://www.raw-wisdom.com/genetically_modified

7 - An article that talks about how companies are using public relations efforts to disguise their real agenda with genetically modified foods: http://www.corpwatch.org/article.php?id=2228

8 - An article about Monsanto being fined for getting caught bribing a government official in Indonesia, in an attempt to have their genetically modified cotton used there despite opposition from activists: http://news.bbc.co.uk/2/hi/business/4153635.stm

9 - A **MUST WATCH** film entitled "The world according to Monsanto". It explains quite a bit about a company whom most American's are unwittingly entrusting a huge portion of their health and wellbeing to: https://www.youtube.com/watch?v=87qrTXZaXkk&nohtml5=False

10 - The official website for the **MUST WATCH** film entitled "The future of food": http://www.thefutureoffood.com/

An in-depth interview with the film maker: http://www.youtube.com/watch?v=XPFk4S1Q6vo

11 - A **MUST WATCH** film by Gary Null entitled "Seeds of Death: Unveiling the Lies of GMO's": https://www.youtube.com/watch?v=dKXqiS7PILs&nohtml5=False

12 - The official website for the **MUST READ** books "Seeds of Deception" and "Genetic Roulette". Scroll to the bottom of the landing page in order to view the **MUST WATCH** video entitled "Everything you HAVE TO KNOW about Dangerous Genetically Modified Foods": http://www.seedsofdeception.com/

13 - A free preview of a book entitled "Stolen Harvest". It explains how large corporations are forcing the people all over the world to use only their products, and how they are putting independent farmers out of business: http://www.amazon.com/Stolen-Harvest-Hijacking-Global-Supply/dp/0896086070#reader_0896086070

14 - A **MUST READ** webpage that talks about the history of Codex. It has links to many important articles that will enable you to become well-informed about Codex: http://www4.dr-rath-foundation.org/PHARMACEUTICAL_BUSINESS/health_movement_against_codex/index.htm

15 - An important article entitled "Codex and Health Freedom – Be Wary of the 'Instant Experts'": http://www4.dr-rath-foundation.org/THE_FOUNDATION/Events/codex-beware.htm

16 - An important video documentary on the dangers of Aspartame entitled "Sweet Misery": http://www.personalgrowthcourses.net/video/aspartame_dangers

17 - And be sure to watch each of the following highly educational documentary films: **"Farmageddon"; "Food Beware"; "Food, inc."; "Food Matters"; "Forks over Knives"; "Ingredients: The Local Food Movement Takes Root"; "King Corn"; "Our Daily Bread"; "Simply Raw; Reversing Diabetes in 30 Days"**. (FYI, you can watch all of them on Netflix.)

VII - **The Military-Industrial Complex** – Speaking of the actual state of affairs in your country, see if the following information finally causes any of your dormant self-preservation-related instinctual alarms to go off:

Your former President, Dwight D. Eisenhower, felt a need to specifically warn the Citizens of the United States about something during his farewell address. Do you recall what it was?

He warned that there was a real danger inherent in their allowing the military, and the related industries with which it is interwoven, to continue to grow without their absolute, ever-vigilant scrutiny.

He personally, specifically gave this warning to the public. Not to Congress or the Judiciary or the next President.

He did <u>not</u> share his message as a mere passing suggestion in the manner that someone might recommend a particular flavor of ice cream or variety of donut to fellow shoppers.

He gave this important message as a stated warning.

He was a former Five-Star General who just served as President of the United States.

And he specifically, in no uncertain terms, warned the American people that there would be grave violations to their ongoing liberty if they were not constantly being fully attentive to the operations of their "government". He did this in the year nineteen hundred and sixty-one (1961).

   The bet that prompted me to begin writing this book was made on the Fiftieth (50th) Anniversary of President Eisenhower issuing his warning.

Since that warning was issued, the vast majority of the people in your country have been getting their news from a fourth estate that's been co-opted by the fifth column.

Like I've said, it was an easy bet.

So how much more toxic is the structure that has been left unchecked to determine all-manner of your governance?

Well, imagine a fire that was constantly being fed massive amounts of specifically directed fuel for sixty years. Now imagine the fire taking place on a ship that was made of parchment.

Yes, poo poo pants, that ship is your "Ship of State".

Almost the entire population of your nation consists of cognitively shackled oarsmen aboard that burning, sinking, ruined craft.

Everything you see around you is a thin, poorly constructed facade.

Why else would the powers that be forbid anyone from examining it in an unhampered, straightforward and meaningful way?

How else could it have come to be that the economically disadvantaged young adults in your country who obviously have some level of ambition and a desire to work (but have no other shot of ever "legitimately" "making it" in the "real world"), would go overseas in the name of freedom to kill other people and things for what are, unbeknownst to them, nothing but proven, paid-"expert"-hyped pretenses that have been manufactured by the powers that be?

How else could "the homeland" be getting rapidly remodeled in the form of a technologically advanced police state? How else could it be that anyone who is vocal about their recognition of it is placed on a "government" watch list? How else would a self-regulating growth industry that's repeatedly caught with its hands in the cookie jar get away with telling you that documented proof of its being caught as such is unhinged "conspiracy theory"?

Rather than conveniently doubting what I've said, fully investigate these links:

http://www.longislandpress.com/2013/05/14/u-s-military-power-grab-goes-into-effect/

http://www.washingtonsblog.com/2012/09/in-america-journalists-are-considered-terrorists.html

http://www.foxnews.com/politics/2009/03/23/fusion-centers-expand-criteria-identify-militia-members/

http://www.infowars.com/secret-state-police-report-ron-paul-bob-barr-chuck-baldwin-libertarians-are-terrorists/

http://www.nytimes.com/2008/04/20/us/20generals.html

http://www.youtube.com/watch?v=lO6yQvODZjI

https://www.youtube.com/watch?v=TN6InTMWt7Q&nohtml5=False

http://www.washingtonsblog.com/2011/12/explaining-to-a-5-year-old-why-the-indefinite-detention-bill-does-apply-to-u-s-citizens-on-u-s-soil.html

http://www.washingtonsblog.com/2011/12/the-indefinite-detention-bill-does-apply-to-american-citizens-on-u-s-soil.html

http://www.longislandpress.com/2013/07/02/22024/ (make sure to watch the short video that's included)

http://thenewspaper.com/news/39/3904.asp

And do you recall that the founders of the United States of America specifically stated in the Declaration of Independence that government derives its just power from the consent of the governed? Well, guess what?

Power does not reside in a ballot. It resides only in the ongoing actions of those to whom the elected official must be accountable.

When there is no fully informed and organized public action, there is no public power; "government" is accountable only to the well-informed and well-organized commercial industries that keep those elected tholes/oarlocks in their misused positions of power.

That form of "government" is not even a lowly democracy. It is a corporatocracy.

Now, take a break from rowing in order to open a dictionary to discover the meanings of the words "oarsman", "thole", "oarlock", "corporatocracy", "fourth estate", and "fifth column".

And make no mistake about it; there's only one meaningful difference between a corporatocracy and the brand of "liberal" collectivism, supposedly born of compassion, that for decades we have been slowly, quietly, unlawfully replacing so many of the mechanisms of the Constitutional Republic of the United States of America with.

The former acts overtly while the latter works covertly.

Can you say "Affordable Care Act"? How about "Social Security"?

And so, like the "two-party" political perfidy that oversees the implementation of the above-mentioned *de*construction project, they both arrive at the same ruinous end. It's achieved by way of the public being led to believe that the empowerment of what are actually parasitic entities is, in fact, needed to protect that public from all potential threats.

1 - A **MUST READ** article by law professor Jonathan Turley, entitled "Big Money Behind War: the Military-Industrial Complex": http://www.informationclearinghouse.info/article37361.htm

2 - A **MUST READ** New York Times article entitled "One Man's Military-Industrial-Media Complex": http://www.nytimes.com/2008/11/30/washington/30general.html?pagewanted=all&_r=0

3 - A **MUST WATCH** PBS documentary made in the late 1980's by Bill Moyers entitled "Secret Government". It will give you some idea of what President Eisenhower was warning you about. Remember that it was made over twenty years ago:
http://www.youtube.com/watch?v=qJldun440Sk

4 - A free electronic copy of a small book/pamphlet that might seem vaguely familiar, entitled "War is a racket". It was written by General Smedley Butler, who at the time of his death was the most decorated Marine in the history of your country. www.panarchy.org/butler/war.html

5 - A **MUST WATCH** documentary entitled "Kill the Messenger". Learn the heartwarming story of an FBI translator who did all she could to bring national security-related factual information to interested ears in "government":
https://www.youtube.com/watch?v=kn10itGL5iM&nohtml5=False

6 - President Eisenhower's farewell speech. I highly recommended that you **WATCH THE ENTIRE SPEECH**: http://www.c-spanvideo.org/program/15026-1

7 – A FREE pdf download of the **MUST READ** book entitled "The Power Elite". It was written by a Professor of Sociology at Columbia University named C. Wright Mills, and published in 1956. For an extra special treat, read it with the mindset of it being the relatively unknown "prequel" to the book 1984; the impact of both books will be greatly enhanced: http://www.watchmenfaithministries.com/images/The_Power_Elite_-_New_Edition__first_full-scale_study_of_structure_and_distribution_of_power_in_USA___2000_.pdf

8 – A documentary film entitled "Why we fight". It looks into the real reasons why America is continuously involved in armed conflicts: http://www.ustream.tv/recorded/1330231

9 – A documentary film entitled "War made easy". It looks into the ways that war is sold to the public, and how all opposing voices are discredited. Most importantly, make sure to watch and listen to the words of a former Senator starting at the running time of 1:05:11, and follow closely until the end of the film. If you do nothing else, at least go right to that point in the movie and re-watch it a few times: http://www.ustream.tv/recorded/1397760

10 – An article that talks about the U.S. army illegally ordering psychological operations to be run on senators visiting Afghanistan in order to manipulate them into providing more troops and funding for the war: www.rollingstone.com/politics/news/another-runaway-general-army-deploys-psy-ops-on-u-s-senators-20110223

11 – An article that shows how the Military-Industrial Complex is working to make money for corporations rather than working for what's in the best interests of the Citizens of the United States of America: http://www.corpwatch.org/article.php?id=7856

12 – A website that exists to keep a record and tally of contract information released by the United States Department of Defense. Look around the site to see the amounts of money that many companies are being paid for contracts they have with your "government's" defense department, it will boggle your mind: http://www.militaryindustrialcomplex.com/

13 – An article that talks about the Military-Industrial Complex; it goes on to list certain ideas about how liberals and conservatives opposed to war can collaborate to rein-in the industry: http://original.antiwar.com/utley/2009/03/31/left-and-right-against-the-military-industrial-complex/

14 – An article that gives a quick overview of the company "Halliburton" that your former Vice President Dick Cheney used to run. There are numerous informative links at the bottom of the article: http://www.corpwatch.org/article.php?list=type&type=15

15 – A review of the book entitled "Halliburton's Army: How A Well-Connected Texas Oil Company Revolutionized The Way America Makes War"; it's quite interesting and informative: http://www.corpwatch.org/article.php?id=15287

16 - A **MUST READ** webpage filled with all sorts of interesting information about Halliburton: http://www.endgame.org/halliburton.html

And still, no self-preservation-related instinctual alarms going off.

VIII – "Law" Enforcement

VIII – **"Law" Enforcement** – The founders of your nation established a Constitutional Republic. As such, properly functioning law enforcement agencies cannot be tools used to protect and serve a criminal governing body that is constantly working on all possible fronts to deprive you of your constitutionally protected rights while they bankrupt you.

They cannot be tools used by international business interests to shut down whole sections of *your* cities and deprive you of your right to free speech. But that's exactly what happens whenever groups who are working to eliminate your national sovereignty show up to hold a meeting.

I dare you to read the Declaration of Independence and the Constitution/Bill of Rights and then, using sound logic, answer this question: How, in the midst of a peaceful demonstration, can there be *anything* lawful about a bunch of police dressed in black riot gear, with their badge numbers covered up, forcibly dispersing the crowd?

I dare anyone to sensibly explain what aspects of the Declaration of Independence and the Constitution/Bill of Rights such actions are upholding and protecting.

Who exactly is it that is being protected and served in such a situation?

What exactly is it that is being protected and served in such a situation?

Don't just nod your head in agreement or shake it in disbelief or disgust. Answer those questions rationally, based upon a firsthand study of: **1**- the Declaration of Independence; **2**- the Constitution/Bill of Rights; **3**- the concepts that inspired and informed those documents; **4**- the many documented instances of the above-mentioned "law enforcement" being carried out under the guise of having the legitimate authority to do so.

Go ahead; prove to yourself beyond any shadow of a doubt whether or not those documents grant anyone the legitimate authority to act as such or to direct such actions.

How, the victims all ask without a clue, can the law abiding Citizens of a country whose "leaders" advertise it as *Earth's official defender of freedom*, now be living in fear of the machine that was originally created to insure their own ongoing freedom?

Well, the basic answer is quite simple:

Just government cannot ever become a self-regulating growth industry. For the purposes of its Citizens freedom, **which are the only purposes that bestow upon it any validity**, just governance cannot ever become a self-regulating growth industry.

Just governance is merely an ongoing process of enacting and enforcing the minimum amount of restrictions which are required to equally safeguard the unalienable rights of all Citizens from whatever <u>actual</u>, credible threats or trespasses may emerge.

The proper determination of such things requires an ongoing, accurately informed discourse among the entire population.

Emotion-based perspectives <u>cannot</u> accurately inform you of such things.

Such credible threats or trespasses can only be gauged through logical, objective investigation.

Now allow me to explain why the claimed need for protection from "potential" threats is a farce.

You see, the meaning of the term "potential threat" is literally no different than that of the terms "the potential for the indication of potential harm", "possible expression of intent to do harm", and "the possibility of the indication of possible harm".

Feel free to look up the meanings of the words "potential" and "threat".

(But really, besides a robust "civil asset forfeiture" program and the militarization of local police, what else is a self-regulating growth industry to do when it's out of actual domestic threats to scare people into willing submission with?

And how else can that self-regulating growth industry justify the annual issuance of **billions** of "dollars" of hand-in-glove contracts for weapons and surveillance equipment and pseudo-governmental, supra-Constitutional security personnel that are helping to cause every possible manner of bankruptcy? Psst... Dwight D. Eisenhower was a conspiracy kook...)

The "*expression of intent to do harm*" (known by a certain popular dictionary as a threat) is but an indication of the *possibility* of harm actually being done.

So, upon what rational notion can a claimed need for the restriction of Citizens rights which is based merely on "the *possibility* of the indication of *possible* harm", be founded?

That's the act of seeking protection from "the potential for the indication of potential harm" (behold; we've spotted the full grown offspring of a "trigger warning" protected "safe space").

If ever there has been a more ridiculous or empty display (farce), I'm not aware of it.

Newsflash: the justification for restrictive actions based upon such a conceptualization <u>cannot</u> possibly exist within a system of governance that is actually upholding the concepts presented in the Declaration of Independence and the Constitution/Bill of Rights.

You do know that such a conceptualization is the completely accurate picture of a dictatorship asserting its claimed right to convict *anyone* for crimes that have <u>not</u> been committed. Don't you?

You do know that such a conceptualization is none other than the completely accurate picture of a "police state". Don't you?

It is the <u>legal</u> right to claim that a crime exists merely because the de facto rulers of those subjects imagine that there *might* be an *expression of potential* for it to come to fruition.

Do you understand that the exact situation I have explained above is the exact situation you are already actually in, thanks to years old legislation you may have heard of, some of which goes by the name of "The Patriot Act"?

Watch this video from the 14:28 mark: https://www.youtube.com/watch?v=oJhkJVH13bE

And if the Patriot Act (whose name sums up the Orwellian State that you fierce freedom fighters have battled valiantly to establish) **doesn't show you that the Declaration of Independence and the Constitution/Bill of Rights do not apply to you...**

Then certainly the National Defense Authorization Act of 2012 (which was signed in to "law" by a supposed Constitutional scholar who is the poster child for the fifth column, and which "authorizes" the "United States government" to legally abduct and indefinitely detain or assassinate United States citizens on U.S. soil simply because, for some unidentified reason, they are considered, by some unidentified functionary, to be a potential threat to the "United States government") **won't do it either**.

Yet such facts cannot be rationally denied.

As with any situation, it is the responsibility of a creation's creators and heirs to insure that the creation exists/functions in a manner that always serves their actual best interests.

Unlike you frivolous footlings who have squandered your estimable inheritance, those of us who are the creators of, and heirs to, the above-mentioned duplicitous acts of genius know the meaning of personal responsibility.

But since I have a bet to win:

1 - "Law" enforcement agencies are a creation of government. Government is a creation of the People. The "Supreme Court" is a part of - not apart from - the creation.

2 - The sole purpose of those creations in the United States of America was that they serve the public according to the concepts of just governance.

Those concepts were expressed in the Declaration of Independence and in the individual State documents that ratified the Constitution for the United States. They were collectively formulated into a framework of Organic Law.

That framework was designed to be capable of enabling the creation of statutory law as needed based upon those concepts, while simultaneously preventing the enactment of any statutory law which is in opposition to such concepts. Google the term "Organic Law".

3 - The powers delegated to such creations can **never** rightfully supersede those of their creators who are merely entrusting them with such power in order to serve what said creators and their heirs believe is their best interest; which was the purpose of the creation taking place to begin with. The Declaration of Independence declares this. Simple logic proves it.

As does jury nullification. You do know what jury nullification is, don't you?
http://www.fija.org/docs/JG_Jurors_Handbook.pdf

As does Article V of the Constitution. Through it the founders specifically left the ultimate power to control the federal government in the hands of the People, by way of their state legislatures.

The states can lawfully subdue an oppressive federal government by convening an "Article V Convention" for proposing Amendments to the Constitution that will, upon ratification, definitively modify those aspects of the federal government that have become cancerous.

And, *for now*, there is nothing the feds can do about it (other than covertly orchestrating "runaway" ratifying conventions in at least three-fourths of the states or having their moles positioned as a majority of the legislators in at least three-fourths of the states. In which case a properly educated and unified populace would immediately "throw the bums out" and start the process over – "runaway" ratifying conventions and traitorous state legislators cannot invalidate the Declaration of Independence).

Are the feds overreaching by way of the "general welfare clause"? Amend it so that its language will no longer allow it to be misapplied.

Are they doing the same by way of the "commerce clause" and the "necessary and proper clause"? Amend them so that their language will not allow misapplication.

There is literally no aspect of oppressive federal governance that cannot be lawfully rectified through this inarguably valid process.

Those people calling for state secession are not thinking clearly.

What about the people who deny that states have the inherent right of nullification, are they thinking clearly? In this case, "nullification" being that a particular state or numerous states refuse to enforce federal dictates that are not "in pursuance" of the concepts expressed in the Constitution (similar to jury nullification, but here it's the states versus the federal "government").

To see just how serious of a matter this was to the framers of the Constitution, read what more than one state ratifying resolution specifically stated in regard to the conditional limitations of the powers they were delegating to their creation, the federal government.

For instance, why not read the ratifying documents of New York, Rhode Island, and Virginia?

http://avalon.law.yale.edu/18th_century/ratny.asp

http://avalon.law.yale.edu/18th_century/ratri.asp

https://www.usconstitution.net/rat_va.html

And while you're at it, I highly recommend that you read these *enlightening* articles as well:

https://www.thenewamerican.com/culture/history/item/18620-lessons-from-the-colonial-declarations-of-independence

http://www.nlnrac.org/american/scottish-enlightenment

http://tenthamendmentcenter.com/2017/07/14/nullification-defending-liberty-from-federal-tyranny/

http://tenthamendmentcenter.com/2017/05/31/james-madison-did-not-reject-nullification/

Now take some time to logically investigate the following scenario:

A group of people are demanding that you join them in breaking a law.

In order for you to act lawfully, by not breaking the law, should some of the people in that group first have to grant you permission to not break the law?

Can the claim that you would need their permission to <u>not</u> break the law have a logical basis?

And would such a completely absurd claim not somehow appear even more absurd if you discovered the following facts?

1- Said group was comprised mainly of people who became members because they each spent vast amounts of time and "money" trying to convince you that they, more than anyone else, were committed to upholding the law.

2- The rest of the group became members only because the existing members decided to let them in, based upon the claims that: **a-** such people have a superior understanding of the law; **b-** their expertise would be used for the purpose of making sure that the group was, in fact, always upholding the law (*just disregard <u>Dred Scott v. Sanford</u>; <u>Buck v. Bell</u>; <u>Korematsu v. U.S.</u>; etc...*).

3- Prior to being made a member of the group, each of those people willingly took a sworn oath to uphold the law.

Is it apparent to you that known words and phrases fail to express the depth and breadth of certain affronts to reason?

Or do you feel as though an organized media campaign that positively presents the group's constant, uncorroborated claims should prompt a "yes" answer to the following questions?

Do they have the legitimate authority to do and/or make you do whatever they decide among themselves?

Is such flag waving sophistry a valid substitute for simple logic and the personal and state sovereignty that the Declaration of Independence and the state ratifying resolutions clearly recognized and reserved?

Can the Declaration of Independence ever be lawfully altered in a manner that would invalidate the following lines?

"We hold these truths to be self-evident, that all men are created equal, that they are endowed by their Creator with certain unalienable Rights, that among these are Life, Liberty and the pursuit of Happiness.

—That to secure these rights, Governments are instituted among Men, deriving their just powers from the consent of the governed, --

That whenever any Form of government becomes destructive of these ends, it is the Right of the People to alter or to abolish it, and to institute new Government, laying its foundation on such principles and organizing its powers in such form, as to them shall seem most likely to effect their Safety and Happiness."

If you answered yes to any of those questions, an exciting future might await you as the U.S Attorney General, or in Congress, or in the NSA, the CIA, or the FBI; or even as President!

But just so there can be no mistaking the severity of the situation that everyone else is in, I'm going to re-word something of great importance that I already mentioned on page 5 of this book:

Your entire life experience and the future of your nation are dependent upon the outcome of a nearly completed battle.

The battle is between those who agree with the previous quote, and those whose actions are based upon the idea that every aspect of everyone's life (*but theirs and their family and friends*) must be regulated by an incredibly small unit of power whose actions and dictates are not to be questioned or reviewed by anyone outside of that small unit (*which happens to be comprised of them, their family, and their friends*).

It's a fact that such a battle was already fought and won. Remember the guys who declared their beliefs by signing the document known as the Declaration of Independence? They then formulated them into a framework of governance known as the Constitution/Bill of Rights.

So how can the actions of those who are working from within your "government" to undermine the concepts outlined in those essential documents, *after taking an oath of office that lawfully binds them to defend those documents*, not be publicly seen as acts of sedition, insurrection, and rebellion?

(By the way, have you read Section 3 of the fourteenth amendment?)

The simple, correct answer is this:

Those whose actions are based upon the idea that every aspect of everyone's life (*but theirs and their family and friends*) must be regulated by an incredibly small unit of power whose actions and dictates are not to be questioned or reviewed by anyone outside of that small unit (*which happens to be comprised of them, their family, and their friends*), have already maneuvered their way into all of the positions of power that get to direct the manner in which everything is officially portrayed to the public.

By the way, have you ever pondered the following facts?

At the time of the writing and signing of your nation's founding documents, many of the colonists were living under the actual threat and fairly regular occurrence of "terrorist attacks" by the indigenous people of North America.

Yet, the founding documents of your nation do not make exceptions for those in power to eliminate the "God given" "unalienable" Rights of the People by way of assertions that such actions are being taken as a precaution, to protect them from potential threats.

And does the following line from the Declaration of Independence ring a bell?

*"...and to assume among the powers of the earth, **the separate and equal station** to which the Laws of Nature and of Nature's God entitle them..."*

Yes, it declares that each man is sovereign. When is the last time you heard of a king relinquishing his rights because of a potential threat?

"There is danger from all men. The only maxim of a free government ought to be to trust no man living with power to endanger the public liberty." (John Adams, notes for an oration at Braintree; spring 1772. http://www.john-adams-heritage.com/quotes/)

Dictionary time: de facto, incomparable, homeostasis, duplicity, diametric, estimable, delegated, supersede, rescind, exponential, corroborate, ideology, ramification, indigenous, assertion, cartel, tender, usurpation, legalese, pernicious.

I hear you, screw the dictionary. Screw all of this non-gratifying, paranoia-based law and logic mumbo jumbo. I hear it loud and clear:

It's the echo of that which we have instructed you to "think".

1 - A video that shows a woman who is simply holding a sign in protest getting shot twice with rubber bullets by police. The video then shows the police laughing about it and making fun of other protestors: http://www.youtube.com/watch?v=G63FEamhpA0&NR=1

2 - A video that shows undercover police officers getting caught for dressing up as protestors and trying to cause problems: https://www.youtube.com/watch?v=D5RaaM3-YYk&nohtml5=False

3 - **A video that proves that the men arrested in the above video (#2) were police officers**. The police actually admit that the guys were police officers: https://www.youtube.com/watch?v=22yqoDs1_TE&nohtml5=False

4 - An article, with ABC News video (channel 7 New York City), entitled "NJ Cops Indicted After Video They Hid Reveals They Beat Innocent Man & Filed False Charges" (after reading the article and watching the video, be sure to investigate all of the information that is offered in the sidebars of the landing page):http://informationliberation.com/?id=46569

5 - A **MUST READ** article from the New York Times that tells you about what happened when police officers from Rialto, California, started wearing video cameras as a part of their uniform: http://mobile.nytimes.com/2013/04/07/business/wearable-video-cameras-for-police-officers.html?pagewanted=all&_r=5

6 - A **MUST READ** report by the Cato Institute entitled "Overkill: The Rise of Paramilitary Police Raids in America": http://www.cato.org/publications/white-paper/overkill-rise-paramilitary-police-raids-america

7 - An article from the ACLU "BLOG OF RIGHTS" entitled "10-Hour SWAT Raid of Organic Farm? Just Another Day in the War on Drugs: https://www.aclu.org/blog/criminal-law-reform-free-speech-technology-and-liberty/10-hour-swat-raid-organic-farm-just

8 - An eye-opening article entitled "The absurdly dangerous militarization of America's police": http://www.salon.com/2014/01/09/the_absurdly_dangerous_militarization_of_americas_police_partner/

9 - A few **MUST READ** articles highlighting the pathetic state of affairs that have been allowed to happen in your country: http://www.thenewspaper.com/news/11/1138.asp

http://www.thenewspaper.com/news/28/2893.asp

http://www.thenewspaper.com/news/28/2894.asp

http://www.thenewspaper.com/news/29/2900.asp

http://www.thenewspaper.com/news/25/2597.asp

10 - A **MUST READ** report by the Justice Policy Institute entitled "RETHINKING THE BLUES: HOW WE POLICE IN THE U.S. AND AT WHAT COST": http://www.justicepolicy.org/mobile/research/3906

11 - A webpage with many articles that document how you are actually living under a police state. Read the short explanation of a "police state" near the top of the page, and then scroll down to find many articles that *should* help to awaken everyone from their trance: http://www.freedomsphoenix.com/Standard-Page.htm?EdNo=001&Page=00083

12 - A video that will show you the privacy-free near future that awaits all of you: http://www.youtube.com/watch?v=SKZm34jsNHY&feature=player_embedded

13 - A **MUST READ** article entitled "HSBC, too big to jail, is the new poster child for US two-tiered justice system": https://www.theguardian.com/commentisfree/2012/dec/12/hsbc-prosecution-fine-money-laundering

14 - A webpage that will help you to understand the concept of nullification. **Make sure to watch the videos that are embedded toward the bottom of the page**. As you scroll down the page, look at the right hand column to see a listing of the *anti-American* faculty at LibertyClassroom.com; and make sure to look into the *dangerous* classes they offer through the website: http://www.libertyclassroom.com/nullification/

15 - A **MUST READ** article, with audio, that provides important, accurate information on the Bill of Rights: http://tenthamendmentcenter.com/2011/12/15/bill-of-rights-ftw/

16 - Two **MUST READ** articles that explain nullification and the "supremacy clause": http://tenthamendmentcenter.com/2015/03/26/refuting-objections-but-nullification-isnt-in-the-constitution/

http://tenthamendmentcenter.com/2013/03/11/state-nullification-and-the-supremacy-clause/

17 - "The Kentucky Resolutions of 1798", by Thomas Jefferson. Take note of how his resolutions can correctly be applied to the current state of affairs in your ~~hijacked~~ justly governed nation; and vehemently insist to anyone who dismisses their validity, that they fully document their basis for such belief: http://www.constitution.org/cons/kent1798.htm

IX **- Your Rights** – Fact: because of your inability to understand and properly manage your relationship with the criminal syndicate that's widely known as your "government", you effectively have no rights.

Obviously, all you've got are a few conditional concessions that may or may not be granted to you when you request the favor from those who are legally in control of your entire life.

Or are you a "well-informed" reader/watcher of "mainstream media" news offerings who "knows" that the above statements are based on nothing but "alternative news" spawned "conspiracy theories" or frivolous anomalies?

Do you have an unshakable faith in the purely patriotic intentions of the parentally compassionate, constitutionally-bound, trustworthy governmental operatives who are at the helm of your nation's "Ship of State"?

If so, click on the following links to learn about the highly profitable, *legal* theft that's being carried out by police forces all across the Land of the Free.

Tell me, where exactly are your "rights" when the "government" can seize your assets without charging you with a crime? Does the term "civil asset forfeiture" ring a bell?

https://www.washingtonpost.com/news/wonk/wp/2015/10/01/most-americans-dont-realize-its-this-easy-for-police-to-take-your-cash/?tid=a_inl&utm_term=.414d1cb6b67d

http://www.newyorker.com/magazine/2013/08/12/taken

https://www.washingtonpost.com/news/wonk/wp/2015/11/23/cops-took-more-stuff-from-people-than-burglars-did-last-year/?utm_term=.d5e56c25e61c

http://endforfeiture.com/

Friend, if you weren't caught in the middle of the constant, all-encompassing rip tide that you've been taught *is* the safe shore, you would now be aware of the <u>fact</u> that you effectively have no rights.

Where are your rights when your "government" has claimed the authority to secretly abduct you and deprive you of your supposed rights to: **1**- Have your family notified of your whereabouts; **2**- be informed of the exact nature of the crime you are being charged with; **3**- receive a fair and speedy trial; **4**- face your accuser.

Where are your rights when it is now a documented fact that your "government" has been monitoring all of <u>everyone's</u> communications and working to destroy the lives of those who exposed their actions?

Check out this speech to the EU Parliament committee on Civil Liberties, Justice and Home Affairs by NSA whistleblower Thomas Drake: https://www.youtube.com/watch?v=q8lV9awduUI

Where are your rights when it has already been judicially declared that: **1**- "government" law enforcement agents can forcibly enter and search your home without a warrant; **2**- "government" law enforcement agents can arrest you, or legally kill you, if you make any attempt to stop what is defined by the Constitution/Bill of Rights (and logical thought) as an unlawful trespass.

Where are your rights when the Executive branch of your "government" has (without a peep from Congress or the mainstream media) given itself the authority to declare non-congressionally reviewable martial law for any reason? (NSPD-51)

Where are your rights when the Pentagon has already instructed its employees to regard citizens as "low level terrorists" if they speak out about actions taken by your "government" that are in contradiction to the Constitution/Bill of Rights? (Of course there is a link with proof of this below.)

Now couple that with the 2012 NDAA and you have the exact scenario that the eighth resolution of The Kentucky Resolutions of 1798 warned about - **OVER 200 YEARS AGO**. (The Kentucky Resolutions of 1798 happen to be what link #17 on page <u>48</u> takes you to)

Where are your rights when the Supreme Court has upheld the decision of a local "government" to claim the right of eminent domain in order to take property from a Connecticut resident for the purpose of selling it to a for-profit company?

Now, jointly ponder these two examples of "government" decree and see if you're able to identify and coherently explain why they are not compatible with the Declaration of Independence: 1- Numerous courts have ruled that the police have no legal requirement to physically protect you unless you are being detained by them. 2- A group of self-styled militiamen were recently rebuked for detaining people who were **illegally** crossing the border from Mexico. (Stumped? Hint: The Declaration of Independence clearly states that your "government" cannot force you to purchase their product – regardless of how majorities vote.)

Where are your supposed rights when the following statement is a rationally undeniable fact?

If I were legally acknowledged to have the same pathetic legal status as you, the act of my having authored this book - which numerous social media, "mainstream" media outlets and tech companies will likely construe as an aid to "terrorists" - could qualify me to be legally subject to undocumented, undeclared, unsubstantiated, unreviewable, indefinite detainment and/or assassination by unannounced, unmarked, unknown operatives who are being directed by certain "civil administrators" acting under the "color of law".

Feel that heat? Seems like it's near four hundred and fifty-one degrees in this joint.

02558102910291581516518197815157815029158341131769182541120112477796210

IXA - In the glorious tradition of your plankton-like parents and grandparents, you pusillanimous plebs have literally enabled your worst enemies to **LEGALLY** complete their long planned **LEGAL** takeover of your country.

So, what's it to you that the Supreme Court recently took away your supposed right to be informed of your "Miranda Rights" whenever you are being interrogated by law enforcement agents after having already been incarcerated?

You don't even know what I'm talking about.

And many of the other protections you once had from "the State" are now gone because **YOU** didn't protect them from all enemies, both foreign and domestic.

No sweat; Batman and the ghosts of George Washington and Andrew Jackson are sure to show up just in time. Right?

Hardly; if either of those former Presidents did show up they might pistol whip your apparently drunken arse and then deport you. Why? For aiding and abetting those who have been craftily, maliciously bastardizing the rational, equitable ideas that they both put their lives on the line to establish and maintain as law.

Google "Andrew Jackson Central Bankers", since you don't know anything about him. Or did you already know that putting his face on the "twenty dollar" Federal Reserve note was the equivalent of urinating on his grave? (FYI, with a proper knowledge of the criminal cartel that's known as the Federal Reserve, Harriet Tubman wouldn't want her face on it either.)

Your supposed rights are not mystical material objects that watch over and protect the weak and the stupid.

Those rights are *ideas* based on the idea of universally equivalent justice for all people; which is itself based on immutable Natural law and the idea of an equivalent inherent worth of all human beings (all humans who don't already inhabit the land you want, or who aren't your slaves, of course. Yet such atrocities do not invalidate those logic-based concepts!).

Those ideas became accepted as law only after interested people formulated them in a coherent manner and then <u>continually</u> fought for them to be lawfully acknowledged.

Unfortunately for you, rights only protect those who understand them and who refuse to let anyone infringe upon them. What good is Article V if enough people aren't smart enough to properly utilize it? What good is the Bill of Rights if you don't understand it?

Indeed, the price of liberty is eternal vigilance. But we trained you to believe that the function of vigilance is limited to your fantasy sports waiver wire and the ability to view the latest celebrity beaver shot before any of your friends or co-workers can surprise you with any news relating to either of them.

As such, you are constantly being laughed at by those of us who have groomed you into the apparently drunken buffoon that George, Andrew, and Harriet would each take you to be.

Don't believe me? Hire someone who has the writing skills you lack and tell them your version of your life story. You can sell it as the screenplay for a new "Twilight Zone" movie.

1 - A **MUST WATCH** Mike Wallace interview from 1958 with Supreme Court Justice William Douglas. Pay close attention to the entire interview and see if anything the judge said in **1958** sounds like anything that resembles the actions of your current "government": www.hrc.utexas.edu/multimedia/video/2008/wallace/douglas_william.html

1a - You probably won't take the time to watch the interview. But perhaps you'll read a few quotes from the former Supreme Court Justice that, in relation to your nation's current state of affairs, will let you know how pathetic you people have become: http://quotes.liberty-tree.ca/quotes_by/william+o.+douglas

2 - A **MUST WATCH** interview/expose´ with Paul Craig Roberts entitled "How The Law Was Lost". Mr. Roberts was the Assistant Secretary of the Treasury in the Reagan Administration and is a former editor and columnist for the Wall Street Journal, Business Week, and Scripps Howard News Service: http://www.youtube.com/watch?v=Ct9J_0ZKqH0&feature=related

3 - A **MUST WATCH** documentary based on the book by Naomi Wolf, "The end of America". It explains how your "government" is working to undermine the Constitution/Bill of Rights: https://www.youtube.com/watch?v=C5c99jLHp9o

4 - A video news report of police abusing a woman in a jail cell for six hours after stripping her of all of her clothes: https://www.youtube.com/watch?v=kBOGOzCDRD4

5 - An article about the woman in the video above (#4). It also has links to more video footage of what the police did to her. Take a few minutes to follow all of the links to additional video of the ordeal at the bottom of the article: http://www.tulanelink.com/tulanelink/policemisconduct_08a.htm

6 - An article that illustrates how the insanity outlined in the previous two links (#4 and #5) is not an isolated instance: http://www.paulcraigroberts.org/2017/04/20/freedom-democracy-tyranny/

7 - An article that reports on former attorney general Gonzales saying to Congress that the Constitution of the United States of America does not guarantee the right to Habeas Corpus: http://www.sfgate.com/cgi-bin/article.cgi?f=/c/a/2007/01/24/MNGDONO11O1.DTL

8 - An article that reports on a released "secret" memo from the Bush white house lawyers that was not condemned by the administration for over seven years; which stated, among other things, that "First Amendment speech and press rights may also be subordinated to the overriding need to wage war successfully": http://www.nokilling.org/extraordinary/index.html

9 - The **MUST READ** transcript of a "Truthdig" interview with Matthew Rothschild, author of the book "You Have No Rights": http://m.truthdig.com/report/item/20070814_rothschild_transcript

10 - An article that talks about the "MIAC" report from Missouri law enforcement. The report instructs law enforcement officials to consider constitutionally aware Americans **potential terrorists**: http://www.foxnews.com/politics/2009/03/23/fusion-centers-expand-criteria-identify-militia-members/

11 - An article that lets you read the actual pages of the "MIAC" report by clicking on the pictures of each page of the report:
http://www.infowars.com/secret-state-police-report-ron-paul-bob-barr-chuck-baldwin-libertarians-are-terrorists/

12 - Two MUST READ articles that will explain to you how the police have no legal requirement to protect you from harm - even if they are standing two feet away, watching you being attacked: https://nypost.com/2013/01/27/city-says-cops-had-no-duty-to-protect-subway-hero-who-subdued-killer/

https://www.barneslawllp.com/blog/police-not-required-protect

13 - An article about self-styled militiamen detaining people who were illegally entering the United States through Mexico. Logically consider the statement by the ACLU that the militia is operating without state or federal authority to arrest or detain "migrants": https://thehill.com/latino/439681-new-mexico-militia-group-detained-hundreds-of-migrants-at-gunpoint-report

14 - An article that explains the true nature of "Rights". It shows how yours have been consistently taken away by way of false claims from your "government" and international governing bodies: http://aynrandlexicon.com/ayn-rand-ideas/the-objectivist-ethics.html

15 - An article that talks about "free speech zones", a tool that you rugged patriots have allowed your government to use against those of you who wish to speak out against things they are doing: http://baltimorechronicle.com/052704FreeSpeechZones.shtml

16 - An article about "free speech zones" that would put any non-delusional brain on high alert. It shows how "government" is purposely, methodically taking away your "right" to speak out against whatever it cares to subject you to: http://www.amconmag.com/article/2003/dec/15/00012/

17 - An article that gives a basic history and explanation of why "free speech zones" are a serious threat to actual freedom: http://en.wikipedia.org/wiki/Free_speech_zone

18 - A video that should look familiar to you. It explains "NSPD-51", a Presidential directive that gives the President the authority to assume complete dictatorial control of the United States of America for pretty much any reason he feels is necessary. Note that the Obama administration did not cancel the directive. Will the current administration cancel it? https://www.youtube.com/watch?v=6pM1vPPKnRI

19 - This article talks about the department of defense teaching its employees that protestors are "low level terrorists". The article also has links to some interesting stories that the mainstream media must have forgotten to shove down your throats like they do with celebrity scandals, sports reports, and the newest prefabricated, hip trends: http://www.wnd.com/2009/06/101473/

20 - An article that reports on the Pentagon removing the "low level terrorist" question mentioned in the above article link from its testing after receiving complaints about it: http://www.foxnews.com/story/0,2933,527181,00.html

21 - An article about the "government" use of eminent domain to take property from its owner in order to give it to another for the purpose of monetary gain. Note that the article fails to mention that the pharmaceutical company Pfizer was the party that wanted and got the land. Also note that Pfizer has since moved its operation from that all important property to a different location: http://en.wikipedia.org/wiki/Kelo_v._City_of_New_London

22 - The dissent written by Justice Sandra Day O'Connor regarding the Supreme Court case in the above article (#21). Anyone with a properly functioning brain would consider this to be VERY important: http://www.law.cornell.edu/supct/html/04-108.ZD.html

23 - The dissent written by Justice Clarence Thomas regarding the court case in link #21 above. Of particular importance to a patriot like you is section "IV" near the bottom of the page: http://www.law.cornell.edu/supct/html/04-108.ZD1.html

24 - An article about a poor bastard from Canada who was wrongly accused of being a terrorist. He was abducted by your "government", taken to Syria, and tortured. I put this link in so that you might read it and "think" about the **FACT** that the same exact thing can just as easily happen to you or a member of your family; and there is literally nothing that you will be able to do about it. If you don't believe me, just read what the "2012 NDAA" allows your "government" to do to anyone they choose: http://ccrjustice.org/ourcases/current-cases/arar-v.-ashcroft

25 - An article that provides another example of the Constitution being gutted - a 2007 Presidential order that was authorized by the International Emergency Economic Powers Act (IEEPA), a statute that delegates vast legislative powers over national security affairs: http://www.washingtontimes.com/news/2007/aug/07/our-orphaned-constitution/

26 - This article talks about a bill in Congress that could make it even easier for your "government" to crush lawful dissent by making the dissenters disappear. Click on the link in the article that will show you the actual bill: http://www.prisonplanet.com/dissenters-to-be-detained-as-enemy-belligerents.html

27 - This article does a pretty good job at quickly summing up many of the ways we are abusing you through the mechanisms of established "government" that are in clear opposition to the Constitution/Bill of Rights and the Declaration of Independence: http://www.activistpost.com/2010/09/debunking-department-of-justices-hit_4518.html

28 - President Obama gives Interpol immunity from the laws of your country. Try to understand how that "Constitutional scholar" just completely backed up my claim that you no longer have any constitutionally protected rights: http://threatswatch.org/analysis/2009/12/print/wither_sovereignty/

29 - A website that has been set up to get your "government" to pass laws that will force food companies to tell the public what's actually in the products they buy. Where is your "right" to know what you are actually buying? Where is your "right" to know what you are actually ingesting and/or having your children ingest? http://justlabelit.org/

30 - A **MUST WATCH** video that explains the **outrageous legal theft** known as "Civil Asset Forfeiture": http://www.cato.org/events/policing-profit-abuse-civil-asset-forfeiture

31 - More about civil asset forfeiture, from Forbes. Click on each link in the article: http://www.forbes.com/sites/georgeleef/2014/09/12/time-for-civil-asset-forfeiture-laws-to-meet-the-same-fate-as-jim-crow/

32 - A **MUST READ** article entitled "Ignorance Is No Excuse for Wrongdoing, Unless You're a Cop":
https://www.rutherford.org/publications_resources/john_whiteheads_commentary/ignorance_is_no_excuse_for_wrongdoing_unless_youre_a_cop

X **– The Prison-Industrial Complex** – Outside of the Twilight Zone, how much freedom can exist in a country that has private companies doing the following: **1-** building and running the jails for profit; **2-** bribing judges to unnecessarily lock people up; **3-** lobbying Congress to enact laws which will guarantee that their business continues to be very profitable.

If America really is the land of the free and the home of the brave, why is more of your population in prison than any other country in the world?

Actual freedom-loving independent thinkers make damn sure that the "money" they fund government with is being spent on nothing but that which ensures the overall well-being of their society.

They do not allow anyone to get paid for locking them up in a for-profit, privately-owned prison that's guaranteed a 90% occupancy rate by the "government".

They do not allow any of their pay to be spent on keeping huge numbers of people in jail so that multinational corporations can also utilize inmate labor for massive profit.

And yet, as usual, the "land of the free and the home of the brave" is getting legally robbed by a bunch of traitors who are scheming to take as much of your "money" and freedom as they possibly can in the name of promoting the general welfare.

But they're not merely making sure that all of your "money" and energy is spent by "government" operatives in ways that work against your best interests.

Those turncoats have accustomed you to also having private companies be in on the act.

Hmmm… private companies in positions of power that should only be granted to closely monitored, completely transparent, publicly supervised governmental agencies. What could go wrong?

In stark contrast to the misguided masses, those who are interested enough to be properly informed and empowered are aware of this fact: when private companies are merged with their "government", the country they live in has become an outright corporatocracy.

In a corporatocracy the "government" is, despite unsubstantiated slogans claiming otherwise, controlled by private interests solely for the long-term benefit of those people who personally profit from increases in their company's sphere of influence.

Other than the decoration of its thin veneer, it's the same mechanism as: **1-** fascism; **2-** socialism; **3-** communism; **4-** democracy; **5-** every other distinctly named manifestation of the fundamental consolidated power that exists parasitically by way of: **a-** currency control; **b-** legal disguise; **c-** all other manner of constant dissemination of officially sanctioned misinformation.

In a corporatocracy the judges, the legislators, the President, the military, the police, and the prison guards are simply the enforcement branches/oarlocks of certain private interests that dictate "government" policy.

In a corporatocracy, the military, the police, and the prison guards are not directed by the President, the legislators, or the judges to uphold the spirit or the substance of your nation's "outdated" founding documents (i.e., the actual Law).

In a corporatocracy, the public is nothing but a host organism that those on the different rungs of power each use to extract the fuel for their extravagant way of life; until their rung is no longer needed, and they too are devoured by the system they abetted.

Interesting path that your "leadership" has you freedom-loving patriots on, no?

The architects of your *former* republic understood that, in this world, where the "unalienable" rights of others will always be forcefully oppressed whenever the opportunity arises, **exercisable rights are merely the fruit of ongoing duty.**

They officially declared that whenever any form of government "*...evinces a design to reduce them under absolute Despotism, it is their right, it is their duty, to throw off such Government, and to provide new Guards for their future security.*" And they made sure to put in place the Constitutional mechanisms by which a properly educated, ever-vigilant populace would retain the lawful ability to act as such.

Yet, *somehow*, the nation they established based upon such logically sound ideas has become the fully supportive environment for a thriving "Prison-Industrial Complex". Ooops!

1 - An article about two judges who were caught getting millions of dollars in kickbacks for sending juveniles to privately-run detention centers: http://www.cnbc.com/id/29355276

2 - Three articles that will give you some idea of what the "Prison-Industrial Complex" is doing to help me win my bet: http://www.theatlantic.com/magazine/archive/1998/12/the-prison-industrial-complex/4669/

http://www.forbes.com/sites/erikkain/2011/09/01/texas-and-the-prison-industrial-complex/

http://www.globalresearch.ca/the-prison-industry-in-the-united-states-big-business-or-a-new-form-of-slavery/8289

3 - A **MUST READ** article that offers a video report and a slideshow. Enjoy **must read** quotes from numerous annual reports and letters to shareholders of your country's largest private prison company:
http://www.huffingtonpost.com/2013/04/11/cca-prison-industry_n_3061115.html?ref=topbar

4 - A webpage filled with **MUST SEE** information that helps expose the Prison-Industrial Complex for the destructive construct that it actually is. Make sure to click your way through the entire presentation (i.e., each chapter in the "corrections study guide" and the "prison maps print-outs): http://www.correctionsproject.com

5 - A **MUST READ** article from the American Civil Liberties Union entitled "Banking on Bondage: Private Prisons and Mass Incarceration". **Be sure to click the "Download" link at the bottom of the article, so that you can read the entire fifty-seven page pdf that the article is based upon**: https://www.aclu.org/prisoners-rights/banking-bondage-private-prisons-and-mass-incarceration

6 - A **MUST READ** report from the website of the Comprehensive Resource Center on Privatization and Responsible Contracting **(InThePublicInterest.org)**. The report is named "Criminal: How Lockup Quotas and 'Low-Crime Taxes" Guarantee Profits for Private Prison Corporations" (Note that their entire website is a treasure trove of important information regarding the practice of "privatization". You will be well-served to fully investigate all of the information they provide.):
http://www.inthepublicinterest.org/criminal-how-lockup-quotas-and-low-crime-taxes-guarantee-profits-for-private-prison-corporations/

7 - A webpage filled with **MUST READ** information about the extortion racket known as the Prison Telephone Industry: http://www.prisonpolicy.org/phones/

8 - A **MUST READ** article that explains how a widespread education regarding the usage of jury nullification would be of great benefit to Americans'; particularly the racial minorities who populate your nation's prisons in disproportionately high numbers:
http://www.longislandpress.com/2013/04/02/hang-the-jury/

9 - An article from **1998** about certain realities of private prison companies. Have you asked yourself yet why the mainstream media made such a huge deal over the "reprehensible", congressional hearing-worthy actions of athletes taking steroids - but never made any meaningful effort to bring this industry under a prolonged, intense public scrutiny?
http://prop1.org/legal/prisons/980105.htm

10 - An article written in **1993** about the privatization of the prison industry. Make sure to keep in mind that it was written over **twenty years ago** and that the continued growth of the industry has been tremendous. Make sure to click on the links with the company names near the bottom of the page to read about the private companies mentioned: http://mediafilter.org/MFF/Prison.html

11 - A webpage with numerous articles about the private prison industry. Keep in mind that the articles were written almost **twenty years ago**: http://prop1.org/legal/prisons/970317itt.htm

12 - An article from New Zealand about a protest to stop their government from allowing privately-run prisons. The protestors were trying to stop the industry from ever getting started. Why aren't more of your nation's citizens doing anything to stop the already huge industry in your country? https://web.archive.org/web/20091020183026/http://blog.labour.org.nz/index.php/2009/10/18/join-the-protest-against-private-prisons/

13 - An article about the high court of Israel outlawing private prisons for numerous reasons related to human rights. How come that hasn't happened in your country?
http://www.jurist.org/paperchase/2009/11/israel-supreme-court-bans-for-profit-20.php

14 - The Wikipedia post for the term "Prison-Industrial Complex". Though it's a fairly short post, there are numerous interesting bits of information offered that - shockingly - tie into other areas of our all-encompassing methodology of bringing about your complete legal subjugation:
http://en.wikipedia.org/wiki/Prison%E2%80%93industrial_complex

XI - **The Environment** – In regard to the environment, we are only interested in one thing: control. But I'll present it as two separate things for ease of understanding.

1 - Gaining and maintaining control of natural resources that we can extract and refine/modify/manipulate so as to control markets and related legislation in order to then force them back on to you at a premium to help further our ends.

2 - Gaining and maintaining control of as much land, sea, air, and consciousness as possible so as to <u>legally</u> begin herding you vassals into the extremely limited areas we have allocated for your coming confinement; in order to most efficiently, completely control those of you who are left after your numbers have been drastically reduced.

We do not care about a "sound ecological balance" or any other concept relating to the "health" of the environment. Not even a tiny bit.

Nor is our exploitation of your resources about making "money". We can create as much of that as we care to, whenever we like. It is about continually manufacturing costly things that we are able to convince everyone that they need.

And those costly things are both products *and* regulations.

Remember that all things manufactured are not necessarily tangible products.

Catastrophes and the methods that are needed to be saved from them are some of the most effective products that we manufacture. Can you say "Cap and Trade"?

How about "Attention Deficit Disorder"? What about "Ten Million Illegal Aliens"?

Our manufacturing process is about making you powerless and poor; in ways that are generally, gradually implemented and that go mostly undetected by the masses of nitwits like you and your neighbors and children.

I'll say it again: We do not care about a "sound ecological balance" or any other concept relating to the "health" of the environment.

We know that there will be plenty of what we need left over for those of us who control the cards. That is, after the majority of you dodos' have allowed us to cast your genetic material alongside that of the other misbegotten misfits who couldn't continue anteing up enough of the right currency to remain at the table.

And you're still trying to reassure yourself that your favorite news personalities on your favorite news channels would be warning you of such terrible things if they were actually true.

I know that your maliciously manipulated mind is doing everything it has been trained to do, to avoid any manner of truth. That's no secret.

I know that what I'm saying sounds like "groundless conspiracy theory". So take a very close look at our stellar track record regarding environmental conservation and related responsibilities. Be sure to Google "great pacific garbage patch" and "fertilizer runoff".

By the way, have you ever heard of "fracking"?

Take a close look at what fracking is and then try to figure out how such actions could possibly be taking place if, in fact, the powers that be cared at all about their supposed ward, Mother Nature. And while you're at it, try to correctly answer these two questions:

Who keeps clouding the sky every day with aluminum, barium, and strontium particles?

Is it being done by criminal gang members from the projects or Al Qaeda operatives?

Well, thanks to years of ongoing, yet officially denied, "Geoengineering" that the vast majority of you are too whacked out to have noticed, there's no longer such a thing as "fresh air". There's no longer such a thing as "blue skies" either. Nowadays an apparently cloudless sky is merely a bluish white, while the landscape is imbued with a whitish haze.

A simple method of recognizing this is to hold your hands up over the sun and look at the area of sky just outside of your hands; you'll quickly notice that the sky is filled with a whitish haze. And if you're in an area where you can see off into the distance, if you're conscious of it you will notice that objects in the distance are shrouded in that same whitish haze. This is not even taking into account otherwise cloudless days when the sky is filled with lingering, expanding "contrails" that literally blot out the sun.

https://www.newscientist.com/article/dn21873-geoengineering-would-turn-blue-skies-whiter/

http://harvardmagazine.com/2013/07/buffering-the-sun

Regardless of the preposterous precedents that might be cited, any court that would rule in favor of that covert scheme being lawful is by far a greater danger to the public welfare than any gang member from the projects or any Al Qaeda operative. "Think" about it.

Were you asked by any of the civil administrators who gave such action the green light, if it was ok with you to have massive quantities of known toxins systematically dumped into the very air upon which your Life, your Liberty, and your pursuit of Happiness literally depend?

I didn't think so. I guess they've been too busy protecting you from raw dairy products to have put aside the time to ask.

But hey, maybe the continual worldwide rise in respiratory problems and cancers really has nothing to do with the continual dispersal of poisons into the air, the water, and the soil. It could just be a coincidence. Things like that happen. Look at what happened to the price of gold after its ~~legal confiscation~~ nationalization in 1933.

Know this as you continue to hide from the conscious awareness of what we are actually doing:

I - You are hiding within shoddy, poisonous constructs. They achieve only the precise minimum requirements we needed to manufacture them to so dregs like you would embrace them for such purposes.

And make no mistake about it; such minimum requirements have been steadily *decreasing* with increasing frequency for numerous generations.

II - Like all other bottom feeders, you are filled with and surrounded by nothing but the garbage that those of us at the top drop down onto you.

1 - The website for a couple of **MUST WATCH** movies about fracking. The names of the movies are "Gasland" and "Gasland 2": http://www.gaslandthemovie.com/whats-fracking

2 - "What Is Fracking And Why Should It Be Banned?" Follow all of the links offered at the end of the article: http://www.foodandwaterwatch.org/water/fracking/

3 - An article about soil depletion entitled "Sick Soil". Be sure to take a long, hard look at the graph that shows how a decrease in foodborne minerals has caused an increase in mineral deficiency diseases: http://www.ecoorganics.com/sick-soil/

4 - A **MUST READ** excerpt from the book "Toxic Sludge is Good for You": http://www.organicconsumers.org/articles/article_17035.cfm

5 - A **MUST READ** webpage that has a bevy of information about "Biosolids" (i.e., TOXIC SEWAGE SLUDGE). It's important that you read and/or watch all of the information provided on the page and that you follow the links offered. Take special note of the many products that are listed in the section near the bottom of the page that is headlined, "Warning: Toxic Sludge Products. Toxic Sludge Is Good For You!": http://www.sourcewatch.org/index.php?title=Portal:Toxic_Sludge

6 - An article from the **Environmental Protection Agency's website regarding Biosolids**. Contrast what these supposed defenders of the public have to say about Biosolids, with what the above articles are telling you; then decide on which party has your best interests in mind. Then carefully consider what that means in relation to the central premise of this book: http://water.epa.gov/polwaste/wastewater/treatment/biosolids/

7 - A **MUST WATCH** video entitled "Global Warming or Global Governance". Watch it and then "think" about who is really looking out for your best interests and who is consistently working really hard to divert your attention from what's really going on: https://www.youtube.com/watch?v=_u81qXOYfKg

8 - Part one of a **MUST WATCH** documentary about **Geoengineering**, named "What in the world are they spraying?" http://www.youtube.com/watch?v=jf0khstYDLA

8a - The recently released **Must Watch** follow up to the above **Geoengineering** documentary: http://www.infowars.com/why-in-the-world-are-they-spraying-full-length-documentary-hd/

9 - A Colbert Report segment on **Geoengineering**: http://thecolbertreport.cc.com/videos/lv0hd2/david-keith

10 - An article from the U.N. News Centre entitled "Outdoor air pollution a leading cause of cancer, say U.N. health experts": http://www.un.org/apps/news/story.asp?NewsID=46276&Cr=cancer&Cr1=#.Us-GSTe2XvQ

11 - An article that talks about the President's Cancer Panel, which stated in its 240 page report that chemical pollution is causing preventable cancer: http://www.mnn.com/health/fitness-well-being/blogs/chemical-pollution-is-causing-preventable-cancer-says-presidents-can

12 - A short video that will introduce you to what "Agenda 21" is about: https://www.youtube.com/watch?v=govL-fUAwMA

13 - An in-depth presentation about the nefarious "Agenda 21": http://www.youtube.com/watch?v=CEHWsdimVO4&feature=related

14 - A link to a PowerPoint slideshow of the United Nations plan for "sustainable development" (click on the page where it says "Freedom advocates PowerPoint"): http://www.freedomadvocates.org/powerpoints/

15 - A webpage with articles about an aspect of the coming doom we have in store for you. On the right hand side of the page there are links for you to get inexpensive pamphlets that explain the "Agenda 21" plan in-depth. Will you order any of the cheap hard copies to share with people you know? http://www.freedomadvocates.org/category/articles/illegitimate-government-articles/

16 - An article that talks about the value of your unalienable rights versus our plans to take away everything that you "think" you own - under the guise of certain "global needs": http://www.freedomadvocates.org/unalienable-rights-versus-globalism/

17 - The **MUST WATCH** "Big Oil" documentary by James Corbett. Watch both parts, "How Big Oil Conquered The World" and "Why Big Oil Conquered The World". James pulls the veil back on the real players and agenda behind the formation of the "sustainable development" scam: https://www.corbettreport.com/bigoil/

18 - A full length major policy address by a former FCC chairman regarding "5G technology" and how it is going to be implemented nationally: https://www.youtube.com/watch?v=tNH35Kcao60

19 - A **MUST WATCH** alternative viewpoint to the wildly enthusiastic 5G policy address that the previous link (#18) takes you to: https://www.youtube.com/watch?v=ZqM4y8hPhic

20 - A **MUST WATCH** video that will introduce you to some people who claim to be achieving success against false claims of authority regarding smart meters, etc… by properly applying the laws that govern commerce: https://inpowermovement.com/

XII - **Immigration** – Although we do occasionally direct operations that cause immediate, drastic changes in your routine way of life, the way we usually like to do things is by having aspects of our plans slowly introduced in stages. It gets most voters used to seeing certain things that would otherwise be shocking to them if we were to push the entire plan upon them at once.

Each time we are able to gauge that the majorities needed to justify such actions in the name of public sentiment have become fully accepting of the last stage, we introduce a new one.

As I said in the last section, our manufacturing process is about making you powerless and poor; in ways that are generally, gradually implemented and that go mostly undetected by the masses of nitwits like you and your neighbors and children.

That reminds me; do you know and understand the meaning of the word "ethos"?

Yes friend, many influential "think tanks" and "elite universities" are modern sophist temples. We fund them to legitimize, defend, and make into public policy the methods we've been using to eventually bring about the U.S. Gulag.

I'd say that those highly credentialed ~~traitors~~ "experts" are doing a fine job. Do you know and understand the meaning of the word "sophistry"? How about the word "subvert"?

Where exactly do you believe that the corrupt ideas which are made into legislation first get fitted with the facade of beneficial, and possibly even compassionate, public policy?

Statement of fact: by allowing <u>millions</u> of Spanish speaking illegal aliens to invade the United States, we have succeeded in manufacturing a huge cultural division and a heck of a lot of underlying tensions between large segments of the population.

Sophist temple retort: "Your usage of the word 'invade' incites irrational fear!" **Hmmm…**

Entering and remaining in a country in defiance of its established framework of law? (✓)

Not striving to embody the host nation's values? (✓)

Not learning the native language? (✓)

Not adjusting to existing local customs and norms? (✓)

I queried Google. Here are their definitions for the words <u>invade</u> and <u>invasion</u>. "**Invade:** enter (a place, situation, or sphere of activity) in large numbers, especially with intrusive effect." "**Invasion:** an unwelcome intrusion into another's domain." (Domain=Ownership)

We've also simultaneously guaranteed a large workforce that's happy to fill all of the low paying "service" and "primary" sector jobs that no-one can actually afford to take. That is, no-one who isn't living with numerous other wage earners in one apartment or a very small house, and who isn't receiving some "government" supplementation of the pay being offered.

Imagine the drain on your economy that such an agenda causes. Significant amounts of your tax "money" gets funneled into various social welfare and health benefit/medical treatment programs that have been created without your actual consent. Not for wounded or homeless veterans; for the benefit of those millions of "underprivileged" people who are in your country illegally.

Do you see the real cost of the goods you buy from the companies we're having you subsidize?

Now picture another related drain on your economy: this one occurs when the "underprivileged" people who are in your country illegally send what amounts to <u>tens of billions</u> of Federal Reserve notes out of your country every year. But really, can you blame them? They do it so that their families will ascend the socioeconomic structure in their own poverty-stricken countries. Why shouldn't they live more comfortably than you patsies who are covering their healthcare costs?

And speaking of subsidies *and* being surrounded by nothing but the garbage that those of us at the top drop down onto you… such anti-xenophobic compassion causes an additional drain on your economy through the funneling of significant amounts of tax "money" into the ~~Profit Centers~~ prisons. They're needed to protect you from hundreds of thousands of ~~jailed criminals~~ misunderstood, "underprivileged" people that are in your country illegally.

And don't forget to add hundreds of thousands of Sharia law following Middle Eastern "refugees" into the equation – they'll be shipped into a "Welcoming City" near you faster than your child can get suspended from school for wearing an American flag t-shirt.

Are you still with me? Try to imagine exactly how far up the United States' "career ladder" anyone is going to be climbing if they cannot speak English. For decades we've been consistently restricting and/or eliminating the middle to upper rungs from registered Republicans and Democrats like you who do speak the language. **Remember the saying "divided we fall"?**

XIIA – Let's see if you can figure this one out:

When most of the technologically skilled labor that's needed is being taken care of by robots or extremely low paid workers overseas who have skills that are superior to yours…

And the majority of the low paying, low to medium skilled jobs are being taken care of domestically by robots or your new neighbors who procreate at much higher rates than you and who have no desire or incentive to read or speak English or to blend in culturally with the other residents of the neighborhoods they've essentially invaded…

To what heights of that career ladder do you "think" you and your poorly educated children are going to be ascending?

Since you are not actually capable of independently supporting yourself, the law of cause and effect makes me feel completely confident that you are going to be living just *below* the bottom rung; like the hungry, diseased creatures in undeveloped third world nations.

Their abysmal education levels, marketable job skills, and opportunities for educational and economic advancement are comparable to what deep-thinking social activists like you and your neighbors and children are on schedule to have in the near future.

When perceived with any amount of sharp discernment, that "career ladder" looks like a slippery, magnetic inlet to a deep dark pit. Not a tool used for climbing. Give it your full attention and see if you don't agree. Did you look up the word "Gulag" yet?

1 - A **MUST WATCH** video on "Immigration from a Constitutional perspective" from the esteemed patriots at Hillsdale College: https://youtu.be/iya0eNlu9D0

2 - A **MUST WATCH** take on using the words "invade"/"invasion" to describe the influx of illegal immigration, by Bill Whittle and Scott Ott: https://www.youtube.com/watch?v=ryGuBUN1peg

3 - A **MUST WATCH** five minute video of Michigan State Senator Patrick Colbeck explaining some inconvenient facts about the real agenda of the Muslim Brotherhood and CAIR: https://www.youtube.com/watch?v=TpyfE1cNmCM

4 - A **MUST WATCH** video by the infamous "hate monger", Pat Condell. Compare what he says to historical fact and the reality around you: https://www.youtube.com/watch?v=6K7YXaNw2CU

5 - Are you familiar with the Federal "government" refugee resettlement program? Read this letter written by U.S. Rep. Trey Gowdy of South Carolina regarding "… the lack of notice, information, and consultation afforded to me and my constituents about this issue." https://gowdy.house.gov/media-center/press-releases/gowdy-requests-information-spartanburg-refugee-resettlement-program

6 - A **MUST READ** article that will help rational minds appreciate the fact that the information in the links that follow, which outlines a long range-insurrectionist plan to circumvent the Constitution and destroy your nation by way of undisclosed, unlawful "partnerships", is based on factual data: http://mobile.wnd.com/2015/04/how-to-know-when-migrant-gravy-train-arrives-in-your-town/

7 - A **MUST READ** article that will give you some insight into the fact that the same techniques which resulted in the gradual coming into being of the European Union are being employed for the purpose of quietly bringing about a "North American Union". Make sure to follow both links regarding the "TPP" agreement that are offered in the last sentence of the article: http://www.thenewamerican.com/world-news/north-america/item/16345-north-american-union-from-nafta-to-the-nau

8 - A **MUST READ** article entitled "Wikileaks: 'North American Initiative' no 'theory'": http://www.wnd.com/2011/05/301325/

9 - An article that explains how the "North American Union" is coming to your country, and the basics of how it happened: https://web.archive.org/web/20130306021947/http://www.augustforecast.com/2006/08/18/toward_a_north_american_union/

10 - An article that talks about how the coming "North American Union" has slowly and quietly been being put in place by policy makers: https://web.archive.org/web/20131019142758/http://www.augustforecast.com/2007/07/16/conquering_canada_the_elite_re_configuration_of_north_america/

11 - An article that explains a few noteworthy things about the coming North American Union: https://web.archive.org/web/20160107085234/http://www.augustforecast.com/2007/12/18/the_north_american_union_and_the_larger_plan/

12 - A webpage that explains some of the history behind the planning and implementation of the North American Union; there are many useful links throughout the page: http://www.channelingreality.com/NAU/NAU_Main.htm

XIII - Conspiracy Theorists

XIII - Conspiracy Theorists – The act of labeling someone a "conspiracy theorist" is arguably the most effective tool of State-sponsored propaganda ever devised. It allows the establishment to instantaneously cause the ~~brand loyal~~ meritocratic-minded masses to utterly disregard any challenge to any official explanation of events.

The moment we label anyone as a "conspiracy theorist", or anything as "conspiracy theory", we have effectively taken away all of their credibility. The level of public trust and respect someone might have held even one second prior is completely irrelevant.

But I'll tell you what makes all of this especially laughable. Outside of the realm of UFO's, the "conspiracy theorists" are usually able to present much better evidence to support their case than the establishment can produce to defend its bogus position. **These people do actual research**; a task we work very hard to persuade you from becoming engaged in.

And of course we expertly lead you to believe that they are just uncool losers who can't get a date or otherwise interact in any of the social activities that we have had our false incarnations of coolness co-opt and sanction. Nope; they really have nothing better to do than spend their time entertaining utterly implausible explanations for that which is or isn't being widely reported on, and what it all actually means. **FORGO RATIONAL THOUGHT**.

Rational thought is slavery. It prevents the enjoyment of our instantly gratifying circus.

What can history teach us about many of the official claims that brought nations into economic turmoil, a police state, or war?

It teaches that they were nothing but covers for actual conspiracies, concocted by a few power hungry people. And yet, such lessons have never become ingrained in the collective consciousness of the general public. It will soon teach the same thing for "Multiculturalism".

Our myriad tools of propagandized censorship, diversion, and bogus educational instruction obstruct the "conspiracy theorists" presentation of the facts. They can't get the amount of mainstream media coverage and genuine public scrutiny that would quickly cause our bogus cover story to be exposed as fraud. How else could we build an enduring invisible empire?

Come to think of it... if a house fire is reported, rather than insisting that both the identity and the motive of the party who caused it be proven before any meaningful action is taken, all fire departments immediately allocate every means available to extinguish the blaze and provide medical attention to anyone who's been injured. The same holds true for *most* police departments in regard to *most* crimes. So, why does the average American do the exact opposite when they are alerted to the fact of far reaching criminal atrocities that may have been institutionally sponsored?

As soon as you've finished pondering the average American's mode of mental malfunction and their resulting twisted perspective, explore these three links and "think" about their core message:
https://www.corbettreport.com/interview-1570-james-corbett-on-derailing-the-gates-agenda/
http://www.unz.com/runz/american-pravda-how-the-cia-invented-conspiracy-theories/
http://www.unz.com/runz/american-pravda-john-mccain-jeffrey-epstein-and-pizzagate/

Then watch this video about World Trade Center building 7 that's narrated by the infamous conspiracy theorist Ed Asner: https://www.youtube.com/watch?v=_nyogTsrsgI

Then force yourself to follow each of the links below. They'll introduce you to some people who most likely can get a date, and who definitely have friends and acquaintances of a much higher moral stature than you, who've been wasting tons of time and energy attempting to spread the truth about all sorts of dirty dealings that the powers that be have quietly been up to until now.

And realize that, on a fundamental level, what they're telling you only differs with what George Carlin has told you in that their message includes the detailed facts he was smart enough to leave out; so that you would listen to him. Perhaps you should re-watch the video of him that I offered a link to on page 4: http://www.youtube.com/watch?v=acLW1vFO-2Q

Here's a theory for you: unlike most of these truth tellers, George knew what made the American public tick. He knew that he was dealing with conceptually aborted, instant gratification junkies; whose only shot at taking their proper medicine was to have each ounce of it presented with a twelve pound coating of sugar - or high fructose corn syrup, or aspartame, etc. He knew that you could only face yourselves from a seemingly safe distance.

So here you are friend, a **MUST WATCH** video that will help you do just that:
http://www.youtube.com/watch?feature=endscreen&v=QljOYU6uFto&NR=1

The concerned patriot who's speaking works for a major public policy "think tank". Is he shamelessly admitting that events which have long been claimed by "conspiracy theorists" to be "false flag events" were exactly that? And is he saying that he believes such criminal actions should again be taken, this time in order to justify an attack on Iran?

He's definitely not saying that he, or his own children, should personally be involved in the accompanying bloody ground assault that will cause every surviving soldier and civilian in the battle zone to suffer long lasting anguish that can only be fully appreciated by those who experience it firsthand. Nor is he volunteering himself or his children to be the victims of the sickness that befalls those who are exposed to the depleted uranium laden ammunition that your "Global Force for Good" has been doing their best Johnny Appleseed impression with.

http://www.bandepleteduranium.org/en/faq

http://www.globalresearch.ca/depleted-uranium-pernicious-killer-keeps-on-killing/4867

http://www.globalresearch.ca/explaining-how-depleted-uranium-is-killing-civilians-soldiers-land/6009

The following is in no particular order, nor is it anywhere near a complete listing of those who have wasted, and are wasting, vast amounts of their time and energy trying to awaken you.

And - *although the methodology I will soon share with you to rectify the problems that your nation is in do not require any knowledge of such fields of study* - since much time and honest effort has gone into their presentation, and since those in the tin foil hats might otherwise feel slighted, I've also included links to some classics of the conspiracy canon and certain less-known, yet thought provoking, works of "hard core conspiracy theory" (numbers 42 - 80).

The links numbered 82 and 83 will bring you to articles from your friends at "TeamLaw.org". I give this information special mention because I have yet to see anyone in "government" fully address it and authoritatively and unequivocally disprove it. The last link offered here is my special treat to everyone who is compelled to question "authority" as if their life depends on it.

1 - A **MUST WATCH** investigative report by James Corbett which will help you visualize how large scale criminal conspiracies that are designed to shape the "World Order" are actually orchestrated: https://www.corbettreport.com/episode-297-china-and-the-new-world-order/

2 - A **MUST READ** article/report from the Wall Street Journal that shows how the legal profession is, in fact, a cartel that imposes its self-serving dictates on the public: http://online.wsj.com/public/resources/documents/barton.pdf

3 - A **MUST READ** article that documents a major corporate conspiracy to keep the public in the dark regarding the dangers of an agricultural chemical that your country uses close to fifty million pounds (50,000,000) a year of: http://100r.org/2013/06/pest-control-syngentas-secret-campaign-to-discredit-atrazines-critics/

3a - A related **MUST LISTEN** report by David Icke: https://www.youtube.com/watch?v=zpKAov8rgZM

4 - A **MUST READ** article by Naomi Wolf that explains how a high-level Bank/FBI conspiracy was actually implemented in order to destroy the "Occupy" movement: http://www.theguardian.com/commentisfree/2012/dec/29/fbi-coordinated-crackdown-occupy

5 - This article is from the "Dissenter" blog on the independent news site Firedoglake.com. The name of the article is "CIA Had Propaganda Campaign Which Involved Leaking Classified Information To Sell Torture": http://dissenter.firedoglake.com/2014/12/10/cia-had-propaganda-campaign-which-involved-leaking-classified-information-to-sell-torture/

6 - A **MUST READ** article by Julian Assange entitled "Google Is Not What It Seems". Allow Mr. Wikileaks himself to school you on a conspiracy of truly epic proportions: https://wikileaks.org/google-is-not-what-it-seems/

7 - A couple of **MUST WATCH** videos that feature the Soviet defector Yuri "I have a crystal ball" Besmenov: https://www.youtube.com/watch?v=Y9TviIuXPSE&t=371s https://www.youtube.com/watch?v=AhAzGLb1j40

8 - A **MUST READ** essay by the arch advocate of anarchy, Lysander Spooner. Join him on an absolutely logical journey into the rarely examined concept of assumed governmental jurisdiction: http://www.freedomforallseasons.org/TaxFreedomEmail/LysanderSpoonerNoTreason.pdf

9 - A **FREE pdf** copy of the **MUST READ** book "Commentaries on the Laws of England in Four Books", by William Blackstone. **Understanding the information it provides is a requirement of personal liberty**: http://files.libertyfund.org/files/2140/Blackstone_1387-01_EBk_v6.0.pdf

10 - A **FREE pdf** copy of a **MUST READ** book that was published in 1850: "The Law", by Frederic Bastiat. Consider it another fine example of how some things never change… http://www.lawfulpath.com/ref/the-law1.shtml

11 - A **MUST READ** introduction to George Seldes, the best investigative reporter that you've never heard of. This man was speaking truth to power through every major event of the twentieth century. Follow all of the links offered: http://brasscheck.com/seldes/

Click on the following link to watch the Academy Award nominated film about him, "Tell the Truth and Run": https://www.youtube.com/watch?v=j9qZ5jE_yMw

12 - A **MUST READ** article by Greg Palast. It'll show you how the International Monetary Fund and the World Bank are actually glorified mobsters:
http://www.guardian.co.uk/business/2001/apr/29/business.mbas

13 - The **MUST READ** Grace Commission report to President Ronald Reagan, which clearly states that <u>none</u> of the money taken in by the IRS is used to fund government:
http://famguardian.org/Subjects/Taxes/Research/GraceCommissionReports.pdf

14 - A **MUST READ** article about personal responsibility, entitled "A Nation of Cowards". Take the time to deeply process the message: http://www.lawfulpath.com/ref/ntncwrds.shtml

15 - Did you see the German TV interview with Edward Snowden? This article explains why most Americans don't even know that the interview took place:
http://jonathanturley.org/2014/02/01/edward-snowden-speaks-us-blackout-of-interview/

Click here if the video of the interview didn't play: https://archive.org/details/snowden_interview_en

16 - A FREE pdf download of the **MUST READ** Council on Foreign Relations report entitled "Building a North American Community" (yes, *the* "CFR"). This report will be especially interesting to those of you who actually followed the links offered at the end of the "Immigration" section: www.cfr.org/canada/building-north-american-community/p8102

17 - An article that explains some of the history and workings of the "**Trilateral Commission**". The website has many interesting and informative articles that explain different aspects of how your country has been getting sold out to international corporate interests: https://web.archive.org/web/20130819184626/http://www.augustforecast.com/2007/08/03/the_trilateral_commission_usurping_sovereignty/

18 - A **MUST READ** article from Salon.com entitled "Elites' strange plot to take over the world": http://www.salon.com/2013/09/20/elites_strange_plot_to_take_over_the_world/

An essay by George Orwell written in 1939 that addresses **the same exact subject matter**, while highlighting absurd hypocrisy: www.orwell.ru/library/articles/niggers/english/e_ncn

19 - A **MUST READ** webpage that provides a wealth of information about the ultra-secret "Trans-Pacific Partnership" that's been pushed by certain members of the "fifth column" within your "government": http://www.citizen.org/TPP

20 - "You are not to inquire how your trade may be increased, nor how you are to become a great and powerful people, but how your liberties can be secured; for liberty ought to be the direct end of your government." (Patrick Henry - Virginia ratifying convention, June 5th, 1788. (1st, paragraph)): http://teachingamericanhistory.org/library/document/patrick-henry-virginia-ratifying-convention-va/

21 – An interview by the Real News Network with award winning writer Kris Newby, author of the book "BITTEN The Secret History of Lyme Disease and Chemical Weapons": https://www.youtube.com/watch?v=t7lbkyGPPcw

21a - An interview by the Real News Network with investigative reporter Carey Gillam, author of the book "WHITEWASH: The Story of a Weed Killer, Cancer, and the Corruption of Science": https://www.youtube.com/watch?v=HcCp1PhYjdw

22 - A FREE pdf of the **MUST READ** book "Tragedy and Hope 101". It consolidates most of the comments which were made by Professor Carroll Quigley that are relevant to "The Network" that controls the entire world (clickable links to the locations of the source material are always provided): www.tragedyandhope.info

23 - More lunacy from Domestic Terrorist Number One, Patrick Henry: "Are we at last brought to such an humiliating and debasing degradation that we cannot be trusted with arms for our own defense? Where is the difference between having our arms under our own possession and under our own direction, and having them under the management of Congress? If our defense be the real object of having those arms, in whose hands can they be trusted with more propriety, or equal safety to us, as in our own hands?" (Virginia ratifying convention, June 9th, 1788. http://www.constitution.org/rc/rat_va_07.htm (27th paragraph))

24 - Watch these two episodes of "Reality Check" from the award winning news reporter Ben Swann. **Watch them right now**. It will only take up about seven minutes of your time: http://www.youtube.com/watch?feature=player_embedded&v=cf0MO55kMsI

https://www.youtube.com/watch?v=ONqcBKhikfk

25 - A FREE pdf of the **MUST READ** book "**Listen, Little Man!**" (Make sure to investigate the rest of this website): http://www.arvindguptatoys.com/arvindgupta/listenlittleman.pdf

26 - John Taylor Gatto's acceptance speech for the New York City Teacher of the Year Award - this is a **MUST READ.** Be sure to note that this article is but one of many important articles relating to education and law that are offered on the website for the "Quaqua Society", which was founded by Daniel E. Witte: http://www.quaqua.org/Gattoteach.htm

27 - A **MUST READ** article entitled "Do You Own Yourself?" written by professor Butler Shaffer of the Southwestern University School of Law: http://www.lawfulpath.com/ref/ownyourself.shtml

28 - A **MUST READ** article on the origins of hate-speech laws. It's also an excellent example of how the ability to think logically is absolutely necessary in order to be free. And it'll help you appreciate Eleanor Roosevelt: www.hoover.org/research/sordid-origin-hate-speech-laws

29 - The **MUST WATCH** Corbett Report Podcast Episode #228, focusing on Bill Gates, "How to Become a Billionaire (and what to do with it)": https://www.youtube.com/watch?v=DwEb623d7kA

30 - A **MUST READ** Bill Moyers interview with Susan Crawford, Author of the book "Captive Audience: The Telecom Industry and Monopoly Power in the Gilded Age":

http://www.alternet.org/bill-moyers-why-us-internet-access-slow-costly-and-unfair

31 - Both parts of the **MUST READ** article "'Smart meters' - the new silent killer", written by an outspoken critic of the entire power structure in your country, Devvy "the dynamite redhead" Kidd: http://www.fourwinds10.net/siterun_data/health/harmful_products/news.php?q=1324748592

32 - The **MUST WATCH** Corbett Report Podcast Episode #238 - "Meet the Corporatocracy". Learn some interesting American history: https://www.youtube.com/watch?v=lw5rQkXqL5w

32a - A **MUST LISTEN** podcast that outlines a short list of private interests that receive "government" welfare (i.e. your "money"). Investigate the related links that are offered on the website of the broadcast: https://www.youtube.com/watch?v=PS2IpBRiRVM

33 - An article that highlights a few of the many "radical", "un-American", "unpatriotic" and "dangerous" ideas put forth by an unconscionable domestic terrorist from your nation's past who went by the name "H. L. Menken": http://www.quebecoislibre.org/08/080915-11.htm

34 - The "About us" page for Endgame Research. Click on the link for "Taking back our land" and **read the entire essay**: http://endgame.org/about.htm

35 - A **MUST WATCH** interview/expose´ about the **Rand Corporation** with their archive researcher Alex Abella, author of the book "Soldiers of Reason: The Rand Corporation and the American Empire, a study of the world's most influential think tank": http://www.youtube.com/watch?v=mYrkLwLTrIg&feature=related

36 - A **MUST READ** article that will help to educate you on certain facts regarding the funding of terrorists by your "government": http://www.washingtonsblog.com/2012/09/sleeping-with-the-devil-how-u-s-and-saudi-backing-of-al-qaeda-led-to-911.html

37 - An article explaining that the "underwear bomber" was actually allowed on the plane by State Department operatives in your "government": http://www.pacificfreepress.com/news/1/5568-letting-the-underwear-bomber-slip-through.html

38 - An article that was written by an eyewitness to the "underwear bomber" events. After reading this article, Google the author and watch video interviews with him: http://archive.lewrockwell.com/pr/haskell-truth-flight253.html

39 - A very interesting article entitled "How Bush's grandfather helped Hitler's rise to power". Make note of the fact that such criminal activity did not prevent Prescott Bush from becoming a U.S. Senator: http://www.theguardian.com/world/2004/sep/25/usa.secondworldwar

40 - Click on the following links for **FREE pdf** downloads of two **MUST READ** classic works of conspiracy research. Just don't forget to remember that a devoted truth seeker does not disregard documented fact, no matter who presents it - which, in this case, is to say that the fact that the author of the following two books was, to put it mildly, not a fan of a certain group of people should not cause anyone who seeks truth to discount the factual information that he shares in these books - since, both in the search for truth and buried treasure, one must discard much of what they dig up: http://www.archive.org/details/TheSecretsOfTheFederalReserve_294

http://www.archive.org/details/EustaceMullins-TheGreatBetrayalTheGeneralWelfareClauseOfThe

41 - An article that explains how Social Security funds are actually used and how the system is quickly going completely broke: http://web.archive.org/web/20120104092531/http://mises.org/daily/3469

42 - A **FREE** electronic copy of the **MUST READ** book "None dare call it conspiracy": http://govtslaves.info/wp-content/uploads/2014/04/none-dare-call-it-conspiracy1.pdf

43 - Excerpts from the 1991 underground classic "Behold a Pale Horse" read by the author, legendary conspiracy researcher and outspoken critic of the United States "government", William "Bill" Cooper. The first hour and twenty-two minutes are interesting. (FYI, at the end of June, 2001, Bill Cooper actually predicted that Osama Bin Laden would soon be blamed for a terrorist attack on America. Bill was shot to death by Arizona Sheriffs on 11/05/2001; two months after his prediction came true): http://archive.org/details/BeholdAPaleHorse-WilliambillCooper

44 - "The Report From Iron Mountain". Lost among the controversy surrounding this report is the fact that, like certain other cherished works of the conspiracy canon, this classic has been keeping many of those among you in the tin foil hats from doing the type of meaningful research that would lead them to see that there are, in fact, many proofs of State criminality to be found that will serve them much better in their quest for the kind of slam dunk information that would - in theory - help to fully awaken their fellow prisoners and enable the institution of just governance: https://archive.org/details/ReportFromIronMountain

45 - The controversial document known as "Silent Weapons for Quiet Wars". As legend has it, this Top Secret masterpiece of manipulation, dated May, 1979, was accidentally uncovered on July 7th, 1986 by a Boeing Aircraft employee who found it sitting inside of a used copying machine that they had recently purchased at a surplus sale. Had it been written earlier, Stymie probably would have baked it into the cake along with Spanky's copy of the "Protocols of the learned Elders of Zion". Do yourself a favor, put forth the effort required to read and fully understand all of the other information that I am sharing with you and then act accordingly; all machinations of the wicked will be suppressed: http://www.lawfulpath.com/ref/sw4qw/index.shtml

46 - A website that's full of high-ranking professional military and intelligence officers from the U.S. and other countries, and professional engineers and architects, who are each convinced that 9/11 was a false flag event. Scroll down and click any of the numerous links on the page to check out their impressive credentials and what they each have to say: http://patriotsquestion911.com/

47 - A **very interesting** video of Richard Gage explaining how the official 9/11 explanation is not merely implausible, but in defiance of the laws of physics: https://www.youtube.com/watch?v=IRETskj4mio

48 - A few web pages that relate to a couple of extremely well-researched books on the subject of taxes. They might have caused their author to become the target of ongoing "government" harassment and lies, jury tampering, and false imprisonment. Be sure to take the time required to follow, and read and understand, the entirety of these links:

http://www.losthorizons.com/comment/WasGrandpaReallyaMoron.pdf

http://www.losthorizons.com

http://www.losthorizons.com/Intro.pdf

http://www.losthorizons.com/comment/archives/WhyItMatters.pdf

FREE pdf of the book "Cracking the code": http://www.1215.org/lawnotes/misc/ctcforfree.pdf

49 - A **MUST LISTEN** interview by Curt Linderman with Dr. Russell Blaylock. The interview covers topics such as Geoengineering, Vaccines, and their environmental and medical implications: http://m.youtube.com/watch?v=X3lW-TGGlk0

50 - A thought provoking documentary about Geoengineering and the ways in which it is covertly being pushed upon the public: https://www.youtube.com/watch?v=31JFDGHs5bQ

51 - How could there be pools of molten metal simmering under all three Trade Center towers for many weeks after they fell? Building 7 wasn't even hit by a plane?! Can burning jet fuel even cause molten metal? http://911research.wtc7.net/wtc/evidence/moltensteel.html

52 - False flag events carried out by placing Anthrax inside letters and sending them to certain well-known people so that the media reports will scare the pants off of the public? http://www.youtube.com/watch?feature=player_embedded&v=j0Bu-0-eKJI#!

53 - "Accidentally" releasing a lab-created "bird flu" and having the media constantly report on how the potentially deadly virus is spreading like wildfire across the entire planet, causing the public to hand away their conditional privileges as quickly as any thieving traitor will collect them? http://www.inquisitr.com/1418566/cdc-accidentally-shipped-a-deadly-avian-flu-virus-to-department-of-agriculture/

54 - An article that will tell you about a plan called "Operation Northwoods" (it was actually presented to President Kennedy for his approval by the Joint Chiefs of Staff). It called for, among other things, the killing of many American civilians. **(FYI**, JFK became President *three days* after Eisenhower delivered his foreboding farewell address.) : http://whatreallyhappened.com/WRHARTICLES/northwoods.html

55 - A **MUST WATCH** documentary by the BBC about "Operation Gladio". Watch the entire documentary and see if you can detect that its ingredients are strikingly similar to those of the latest brand of industrial cleanser being used in the Middle East by the CIA: http://www.youtube.com/watch?v=GGHXjO8wHsA

56 - The **MUST WATCH** documentary film "A Noble Lie". This film exposes the Oklahoma City federal building bombing as a false flag event: https://www.youtube.com/watch?v=vHDIhxeMOcI

57 - A **MUST WATCH** video report by James Corbett on the **extremely suspicious death** (supposed suicide) **of a police officer**, Sgt Terrance Yeakey, who was one of the first-responders at the scene of the **Oklahoma City federal building bombing**: https://www.corbettreport.com/requiem-for-the-suicided-terrance-yeakey/

58 - A brief "Summary of False Flag Operations and False Flag Terrorism" that offers plenty of links to documentation of its claims: http://www.wanttoknow.info/falseflag

59 - An article that talks about the lie that started the official, declared U.S. involvement in the Vietnam War; the "Gulf of Tonkin incident": http://www.fair.org/index.php?page=2261

60 - An article that offers interesting information about operation Fast and Furious: http://www.forbes.com/sites/realspin/2011/09/28/fast-and-furious-just-might-be-president-obamas-watergate/

61 - An interesting article entitled "President Obama lies to Univision about Operation Fast and Furious". Make sure to watch the videos it offers: http://townhall.com/tipsheet/katiepavlich/2012/09/21/president_obama_lies_to_univision_about_operation_fast_and_furious

62 - An interesting article entitled "Americans Are Finally Learning About False Flag Terror": http://www.globalresearch.ca/americans-are-finally-learning-about-false-flag-terror/5359234

63 - A wealth of information regarding the actual legislation that's being proposed by the **U.N. small arms treaty**: http://www.infowars.com/foreign-troops-to-confiscate-american-guns-under-un-treaty/

64 - An article that explains how your second amendment "rights" are under attack by powerful interests whose opinion on the nature of rights differs greatly from the men who founded your country: http://www.thenewamerican.com/usnews/constitution/item/14912-bizarre-interpretation-of-second-amendment-is-obstacle-to-un-gun-grab

65 - A **MUST READ** article that shares many interesting facts about gun control. Make sure to read the entire article and then go to the end of the bibliography where it says "For further information read". Then read what the next nine lines of text have to say. Then see if you "think" anything fishy is going on: http://www.lawfulpath.com/ref/notesOnGunControl.php

66 - The first part of a long article that explains how your "government" has been operating in order to get you supremely aware citizens ready for further enslavement. Make sure to follow all of the links that are offered: https://web.archive.org/web/20080511183605/http://www.thepeoplesvoice.org/cgi-bin/blogs/voices.php/2008/04/14/bush_s_conspiracy_to_create_an_american

67 - An article that shows how your congressional "representatives" are working hard to keep the small number of you who are seeking the light, in the dark: https://web.archive.org/web/20100105064447/http://www.keepandshare.com/doc/view.php?id=1505703&da=y

68 - A **MUST READ** article about the California Senate passing "SB.649", despite massive opposition. They are *legally* forcing constant, hazardous radiation on the public: http://www.businesswire.com/news/home/20170602005869/en/California-Senate-Passed-SB.649-%E2%80%94-Unconstitutional-Bill

69 - See if you "think" this sixteen minute video is merely a paranoia filled rant against wonderful, liberating technology: https://www.youtube.com/watch?v=4PekRuzMpFk

70 - A **MUST READ** article entitled "This is what it feels like to have your life savings confiscated by the global elite": http://www.infowars.com/this-is-what-it-feels-like-to-have-your-life-savings-confiscated-by-the-global-elite/

71 - A **MUST READ** article by Ellen Brown that the article above (#70) has quoted and offers links to: http://webofdebt.wordpress.com/2013/03/28/it-can-happen-here-the-confiscation-scheme-planned-for-us-and-uk-depositors/

72 - An article that, *in theory*, should wake any semi-conscious "person" back into full consciousness: http://jonrappoport.wordpress.com/2013/03/28/top-10-excuses-for-obama-signing-the-monsanto-protection-act/

73 - A **highly recommended** video called "The biggest game in town". It explains the truth about a method being used by your "government" to help make your "money" quietly disappear: https://www.youtube.com/watch?v=jkwjtbTjTsE

74 - The response by Walter Burien to a letter from someone who doubted the actuality of the scam that is exposed in the previous video (#73). Scroll down the landing page for a listing of links to the reviews of state "comprehensive annual financial reports" for 2003 prepared by Gerald Klatt, a thirty-year federal Auditor - FBI and CIA trained. Then click on the link that says "Silence is golden": http://cafr1.com/ShowMeTheMoney.html

75 - An interesting article relating to the **deleted thirteenth amendment** to your nation's Constitution. That is <u>not</u> a typo. Read it: http://www.lawfulpath.com/ref/13th-amend.shtml

76 - A **FREE pdf** of the book entitled "Echoes from the cabinet", from 1855. Go to the 38th page of the book and read Article XIII: http://archive.org/details/echoesfromcabine00newy

77 - **"Know Your Constitution"** with Carl Miller (part 1 of 3). These videos explore fundamental concepts of Constitutional Law and attempt to educate you on how to safeguard your unalienable rights: https://www.youtube.com/watch?v=1s-zHrNPfkQ

78 - A **free pdf download** of Carl Miller's Constitutional Law instruction – it includes case law and law journal citations: www.privateaudio.homestead.com/carltext.pdf

79 - A **MUST WATCH** video wherein Eddie Craig explains a few methods by which your "government" might be circumventing your unalienable rights, scamming you into acquiring unneeded licenses and trapping you in a false legal construct. I like to start watching it at the 12:57 mark and finish at the 2:28:10 mark: http://www.youtube.com/watch?v=V9kVCQ0y5Ec

80 - A very interesting video that features Robert Menard, a Canadian man. He claims to have done the work required to become free from his country's version of certain bogus legal constructs that most human beings are unwittingly trapped in. **Research the concepts he presents**: https://www.youtube.com/watch?v=ohiyO-IcqG8

81 - The text of Public Law 97-280, approved on October 4^{th,} 1982. Congress officially recognized that the bible is the word of God. After clicking on this link, you should re-read page 17: https://www.gpo.gov/fdsys/pkg/STATUTE-96/pdf/STATUTE-96-Pg1211.pdf

82 - A **MUST READ** article that explains the ongoing process of re-seating what is known as the "Original Jurisdiction Government of the United States of America": www.teamlaw.org/Government/usmap.htm

83 - A **MUST READ** article that *should* cause you to question some very important aspects of your life that you probably haven't spent much time thinking about (I'm not speaking about the article's quick reference to certain things that may or may not have happened at the Pentagon): http://teamlawforum.net/viewtopic.php?f=2&t=577

And now, since this is the "Conspiracy Theorists" section of the book, here's my special treat to everyone who is compelled to question authority…

FACT: I personally cut the three definitions below directly from the "United States board on geographic names" "feature class definitions" webpage using the web address printed below:

http://geonames.usgs.gov/pls/gnispublic/f?p=154:8:2447449967582945

The above web address no longer works. The "Wayback Machine" on Archive.org cannot access the archived page because their webcrawlers have been blocked by the website. Bookmarking the updated web address will not allow you to access this information, so I could not provide you with an updated link to it. This information can be accessed by way of a Google search for the words "http://geonames.usgs.gov definitions", and clicking on the result at the top of the page: Definitions - US Board On Geographic Names - the USGS.
(**Click here to view screen shots of the actual webpages:** https://unionoftruth.org/pages/screenshots-for-the-science-of-fiction)

Populated Place	Place or area with clustered or scattered buildings and a permanent human population (city, settlement, town, village). A populated place is usually not incorporated and by definition has no legal boundaries. However, a populated place may have a corresponding "civil" record, the legal boundaries of which may or may not coincide with the perceived populated place. Distinct from Census and Civil classes
Census	A statistical area delineated locally specifically for the tabulation of Census Bureau data (census designated place, census county division, unorganized territory, various types of American Indian/Alaska Native statistical areas). Distinct from Civil and Populated Place.
Civil	A political division formed for administrative purposes (borough, county, incorporated place, municipio, parish, town, township). Distinct from Census and Populated Place.

Fasten the chinstrap on your tin foil hat. Keep in mind all of the information I've presented thus far in this book and through the links I've shared with you. And carefully consider this:

Every single inch of space within the United States is legally classified within the two legally unrelated categories of "Census area" and "Civil political division formed for administrative purposes". So how can a "Populated Place" have a permanent human population, by definition have no legal boundaries, *and* not necessarily have a corresponding "civil" record?

Since the fundamental purpose of such "administrative purposes" happens to be the continual expansion of every conceivable aspect of every conceivable definition of the "Civil legal boundaries" of your "government"…

And since "…a populated place *may* have a corresponding 'civil' record, the legal boundaries of which may or may not coincide with the *perceived* populated place"…

And since "the tabulation of Census Bureau data" and "Civil administrative purposes" are not stated to be directly related to the actual humans that populate the "Populated Place"…

And since a "legal fiction" is also legally recognized as a "person" and an "individual", and as a "taxpayer"…

Are you wondering if you've unwittingly been living within some "Matrix"-like, specious "Civil legal boundaries"?

Are you wondering if those boundaries were established for "administrative purposes" that relate merely to "legal fictions/creatures of the state", though they simultaneously seamlessly coexist with the places in which human beings live?

If you aren't, why aren't you? Exactly what documentation of such a thought definitively being incorrect have you been made privy to?

Consider the sizable amount of almost unbelievable, though fully documented, corruption that this book has already shared with you.

Do the definitions I pasted above corroborate what links #79, 80, 82, and 83 claim to be true? What are you going to do in order to be absolutely sure? Wouldn't you rather be watching TV?

(Did you Google "legal fiction" and "creature of the state"? After doing that, go back to link #9 of this section and click on it. Then read sections I and II of the introduction, and chapter XVIII of "Book the First" and chapter I of "Book the Second". Such an education will equip you with *some* of the tools that are required in order to have a properly informed viewpoint.)

  Clearly, <u>everyone</u> should logically question what prompted their decision to accept as valid, the claims of authority that are made by "the State". *Regardless of the actual legal meaning of each definition I pasted above.*

Clearly, <u>everyone</u> should logically question the validity and legitimacy of force being used against them by the "Political divisions formed for administrative purposes".

And, clearly, <u>everyone</u> should conduct their analysis from the standpoint of a documented sovereign human being who has been endowed with documented "unalienable" rights by their creator. You've heard of the Declaration of Independence, haven't you? Have you read it?

From what authority would the <u>legal</u> ability of "Civil administrators" to infringe upon those "unalienable" rights arise? Logic dictates that these questions are of fundamental concern.

A good place to begin one's analysis would be with an understanding of the difference between the "Laws of Nature and of Nature's God" and "statutory law"; and then the difference between "statutory law" and "case law". Then understand the term "color of law". Then dig deep to see if you can discover any valid difference between the terms "legal" and "lawful".

To have ongoing success in any endeavor, one's efforts must be in positive accord with the "Laws of Nature and of Nature's God". Unfortunately for the American public, those whose influence directs the creation of statutory law, regulations, codes and public education standards onerously disregard such immutable fact. Or do they?

How exactly is it that a human who is choosing to exercise their sovereignty (or should I say "...assume among the powers of the earth, the separate and equal station to which the Laws of Nature and of Nature's God entitle them..."), can instead, without committing a trespass or causing injury to another human, be forcefully compelled to abide by someone else's brand of authority?

XIV - The "Federal" Reserve System – Do you know what a cartel is?

Do you know that the "Federal" Reserve System is a banking cartel that has de facto control over the entire societal structure of your country?

Everything having anything meaningful to do with the creation, regulation, usage, and official value of Federal Reserve notes is decided upon in private, by a private group of "economic experts".

The Federal Reserve is <u>not</u>, and has not ever been, an agency of the government of the United States of America. How does that resonate with what's left of your inherent sense of right and wrong?

Their policies, in conjunction with those of the Republicans and the Democrats, have enabled dishonest gain on a scale that was simply not possible before the legalization of the Federal Reserve System.

(Indeed, the Republicans and the Democrats are their lackeys. So, yes, the entire production is a farce. And it works to keep the shackled cave dwellers from recognizing that they are, in fact, just that.)

Ok, now put forth the effort required to wrap your mind around these facts:

The "Federal Reserve note" is <u>not</u> a freely available and completely safe substance. Pretty much everyone's life does, in fact, depend on it and revolve around it. Yet most people do not have any idea of what it actually is, or how it became "legal tender". Or what the proper methods of its creation, regulation, valuation, and usage should be.

Nor have even one percent of your fellow countrymen ever spent more than one full minute considering such things.

Most people never perceive of anything but what their superiors have purposely guided them toward. And then they conceptualize such things only in the ways they were taught to.

Most people simply accept, as fact, that everything to do with money is outside of their valid range of responsibility. That is, unless it directly relates to their "discretionary spending".

Guess what? Being in such an ignorant state automatically qualifies one to be correctly referred to as a shackled cave dweller.

Answer this my fettered friend: why would free people ever use a completely unregulated cartel to control the production and distribution of their country's "money" supply, and to regulate their country's interest rates?

Why would free people ever allow their constitutionally mandated money (which was, generally speaking, highly valued worldwide) to be phased out by way of "government" force?

Why would they allow it to be replaced without recompense by a new currency which, without the use of force, would have no purchasing power anywhere in their own country, let alone the rest of the world?

Why would free people ever allow that profit-seeking banking monopoly to operate without any meaningful public scrutiny?

What if an order of business was the further creation and regulation of their own self-serving designs regarding the production, distribution, usage, and valuation of their uniquely sanctioned official brand of currency?

Why would free people ever need to surrender such incredibly far-reaching power to someone else? Would it not then become an immensely profitable, supremely influential product?

Why would free people ever contract with such an organization to begin with?

Carefully consider the following question in relation to money, religion, and legislation and/or adjudication of law: why would anyone who isn't conceptually corrupted ever allow a scam artist, who has been falsely promoting himself as a legitimately empowered authority, to completely rule them?

That's right, they wouldn't.

So now it's time for you to carefully consider these selected passages from pages <u>235</u> and <u>236</u> of the book "<u>The Economic Consequences of the Peace</u>" by the famed economist John Maynard Keynes. Here he shares with the reader his take on a few ideas that the Marxist, Vladimir Lenin, reportedly had in regard to the best way of destroying the capitalist system:

"By a continuous process of inflation, governments can confiscate secretly and unobserved, an important part of the wealth of their citizens...

Lenin was certainly right. There is no subtler, no surer means of overturning the existing basis of society than to debauch the currency.

The process engages all the hidden forces of economic law on the side of destruction - and does it in a manner in which not one man in a million is able to diagnose."

Speaking of confiscation, few people realize that on April 5, 1933, the "United States government" went way beyond the bounds of that quote by John Maynard Keynes.

As per the recommendation of the Federal Reserve, they graduated from the minor league game of confiscating secretly and unobserved, an important part of the wealth of their citizens by way of manipulating the currency through inflation.

What did the "government" do on April 5, 1933? President Roosevelt signed Executive Order 6102. It legally required every citizen to turn in all of their privately held gold to the "United States government" for a set price. Not criminal enough for you? Ok...

They also replaced the existing paper currency. The currency that got replaced had claimed on its face that it was redeemable for gold on demand. The new one was redeemable for another piece of similar-looking paper with a different serial number on it. But the "authorities" artfully legitimized such theft by way of legislating that the new counterfeit currency would henceforth be "legal tender for all debts public and private".

And what did the "government" do two months later, on June 5, 1933? Congress passed the "Gold Repeal Joint Resolution", which outlawed the contractual demand for payment in gold or silver and forced the public to accept payment for debts in the new currency (see link #15 below).

But why, besides the simple fact that criminals always steal when they know they'll get away with it, would they have taken such actions, you ask? Hold that thought until you finish reading the article that this link will take you to: http://www.moonlightmint.com/bailout.htm

Now, while taking into account all of the other lamentable information that this book has provided, ask yourself this question:

Is it possible that Executive Order 6102 was enacted, *in part*, to bail the Federal Reserve out of a HUGE shortfall of gold? Had they circulated a massive quantity of "U.S. paper currency" that, while claiming on its face to be redeemable for gold, actually had as much gold backing it as cantaloupes have fish?

(Hint: read the information provided in the rest of this section; read the third paragraph of section 16 of the Federal Reserve act of 1913; read the fourteenth paragraph in link #17 below; any truth seeker with the ability to follow a clearly delineated path will see that it is highly probable. Also note that the gold was owed chiefly to their associates. If the shortfall was not planned, it would prove that the "experts" were as short sighted and outright stupid as any people who had ever lived.)

And did I mention what happened soon after the above-mentioned ~~confiscation~~ nationalization?

The price of gold just happened to be increased by a rather generous measure. It went from $20.67 an ounce to $35.00. Considering what that 84.6% increase would be equal to in relation to today's price for an ounce of gold, would you call that generous?

Now I highly recommend that you read the entire Coinage Act of April 2, 1792 before going any further into this book. It won't take a slow reader more than five minutes to complete the task: https://www.usmint.gov/learn/history/historical-documents/coinage-act-of-april-2-1792

Then try really hard to find the exact Constitutional amendment that invalidated your nation's Constitutional firewall against confiscation of wealth by way of a debauched currency - i.e., the requirement that **"No State shall... coin Money; emit Bills of Credit; make any Thing but gold or silver Coin a Tender in Payment of Debts;",** as stated in Article I, section 10.

Notice that the Constitution does <u>not</u> say "No State shall... Tender any Thing but gold or silver coin in Payment of Debts;"

Notice that the Constitution <u>does</u> say "No State shall... coin Money; emit Bills of Credit;".

One cannot logically construe the meaning in the Constitution of **"No State shall... make any Thing but gold or silver Coin a Tender in Payment of Debts;"** as anything other than a simple, clear prohibition against legally considering anything but gold or silver coin a tender in payment of debts, *regardless of who tenders the payment*.

Or do you believe that the framers of the Constitution made sure to insert that phrase so as to prevent the individual states from attempting to pay their debts with mud pies?

"Think" about it; by placing such a prohibition on the individual states, the Constitution was simultaneously protecting the Citizenry from having their money debased by criminals within state *and* federal government.

Without amending the Constitution (or having criminals sit on the Supreme Court), how could criminal factions that might infiltrate the federal government now force a debased currency on the People?

Hmmm… it appears as though we must investigate the idea of having criminals sit on the Supreme Court in order to force a debased currency on the People and to interpret the Constitution in a manner that grants unlimited powers to the federal government.

Do you remember the following lines from page <u>45</u>?

"A group of people are demanding that you join them in breaking a law.

In order for you to act lawfully, by not breaking the law, should some of the people in that group first have to grant you permission to not break the law?

Can the claim that you would need their permission to <u>not</u> break the law have a logical basis?

And would such a completely absurd claim not somehow appear even more absurd if you discovered the following facts?

1- Said group was comprised mainly of people who became members because they each spent vast amounts of time and "money" trying to convince you that they, more than anyone else, were committed to upholding the law.

2- The rest of the group became members only because the existing members decided to let them in, based upon the claims that: **a-** such people have a superior understanding of the law;

b- their expertise would be used for the purpose of making sure that the group was, in fact, always upholding the law (*just disregard Dred Scott v. Sanford; Buck v. Bell; Korematsu v. U.S.; etc…*).

3- Prior to being made a member of the group, each of those people willingly took a sworn oath to uphold the law.

Is it apparent to you that known words and phrases fail to express the depth and breadth of certain affronts to reason?"

Well, now let's imagine that the people who are mentioned in point **#2** went on to claim that, since the Constitution did not specifically tell them otherwise, they and the other members of their group had the authority to dictate what the official legal meanings of the words "money" and "lawful money" were.

And let's imagine that they also went on to say that their group had the authority to remove inherent value from the nation's official currency, at their whim, even if such an adjustment would cause lenders to effectively be repaid a smaller amount of value than what their loan contract stipulated they would be repaid, or perhaps even less than what they had loaned out.

I'll ask you again, is it apparent to you that known words and phrases fail to express the depth and breadth of certain affronts to reason? Even one of meager cognitive capabilities would easily recognize that such claims are clearly subversive and criminal.

And yet, the U.S. Supreme Court effectively ruled in *Juilliard v. Greenman* (1884) that the "U.S. Government" has the authority to do just that. The following quoted material highlights the opinion of the Court (there is a link to the full decision below, #21):

"So, under the power to coin money and to regulate its value, Congress may (as it did with regard to gold by the Act of June 28, 1834, c. 95, and with regard to silver by the Act of February 28, 1878, c. 20) issue coins of the same denominations as those already current by law, but of less intrinsic value than those by reason of containing a less weight of the precious metals, and thereby enable debtors to discharge their debts by the payment of coins of the less real value. A contract to pay a certain sum in money, without any stipulation as to the kind of money in which it shall be paid, may always be satisfied by payment of that sum in any currency which is lawful money at the place and time at which payment is to be made. 1 Hale, P.C. 192-194; Bac.Abr. "Tender, B. 2;" Pothier, Contract of Sale, No. 416; Pardessus Droit Commercial, Nos. 204, 205; Searight v. Calbraith, 4 Dall. 324 [omitted]. As observed by Mr. Justice Strong in delivering the opinion of the Court in the Legal Tender Cases,
'Every contract for the payment of money simply is necessarily subject to the constitutional power of the government over the currency, whatever that power may be, and the obligation of the parties is therefore assumed with reference to that power.'"

Because of the importance of this subject matter, as it relates to your freedom and the valid limitations on authority granted to the government by the Constitution, I was compelled to print the dissenting opinion of Justice Field for the above mentioned case, rather than merely offer you the link to it (#21).

While the following dissent will seem a bit lengthy for many readers, the information it presents is of utmost importance to you and your family and friends.

In other words, YOU MUST READ AND UNDERSTAND THIS ENTIRE DISSENT.

"MR. JUSTICE FIELD, dissenting.

From the judgment of the Court in this case and from all the positions advanced in its support I dissent. The question of the power of Congress to impart the quality of legal tender to the notes of the United States, and thus make them money and a standard of value, is not new here. Unfortunately, it has been too frequently before the Court, and its latest decision previous to this one has never been entirely accepted and approved by the country. Nor should this excite surprise, for whenever it is declared that this government, ordained to establish justice, has the power to alter the condition of contracts between private parties and authorize their payment or discharge in something different from that which the parties stipulated, thus disturbing the relations of commerce and the business of the community generally, the doctrine will not and ought not to be readily accepted. There will be many who will adhere to the teachings and abide by the faith of their fathers. So the question has come again, and will continue to come until it is settled so as to uphold, and not impair, the contracts of parties, to promote and not defeat justice.

If there be anything in the history of the Constitution which can be established with moral certainty, it is that the framers of that instrument intended to prohibit the issue of legal tender notes both by the general government and by the states, and thus prevent interference with the contracts of private parties. During the Revolution and the period of the old Confederation, the Continental Congress issued bills of credit, and upon its recommendation the states made them a legal tender, and the refusal to receive them an extinguishment of the debts for which they were offered. They also enacted severe penalties against those who refused to accept them at their nominal value, as equal to coin, in exchange for commodities. And previously, as early as January, 1776, Congress had declared that if any person should be "so lost to all virtue and regard for his country" as to refuse to receive in payment the bills then issued, he should, on conviction thereof, be "deemed, published, and treated as an enemy of his county, and precluded

Page 110 U. S. 452

from all trade and intercourse with the inhabitants of the colonies."

Yet this legislation proved ineffectual; the universal law of currency prevailed which makes promises of money valuable only as they are convertible into coin. The notes depreciated until they became valueless in the hands of their possessors. So it always will be; legislative declaration cannot make the promise of a thing the equivalent of the thing itself.

The legislation to which the states were thus induced to resort was not confined to the attempt to make paper money a legal tender for debts, but the principle that private contracts could be legally impaired and their obligation disregarded being once established, other measures equally dishonest and destructive of good faith between parties were adopted. What followed is thus stated by Mr. Justice Story in his Commentaries:

"The history, indeed," he says,

"of the various laws which were passed by the states, in their colonial and independent character, upon this subject is startling at once to our morals, to our patriotism, and to our sense of justice. Not only was paper money issued and declared to be a tender in payment of debts, but laws of another character, well known under the appellation of tender laws, appraisement laws, installment laws, and suspension laws, were from time to time enacted, which prostrated all private credit and all private morals. By some of these laws the due payment of debts was suspended; debts were, in violation of the very terms of the contract, authorized to be paid by installments at different periods; property of any sort, however worthless, either real or personal, might be tendered by the debtor in payment of his debts, and the creditor was compelled to take the property of the debtor, which he might seize on execution at an appraisement wholly disproportionate to its known value. Such grievances and oppressions and others of a like nature were the ordinary results of legislation during the Revolutionary War and the intermediate period down to the formation of the Constitution. They entailed the most enormous evils on the country, and introduced a system of fraud, chicanery, and profligacy which destroyed all private confidence and all industry and enterprise."

2 Story on the Constitution § 1371.

Page 110 U. S. 453

To put an end to this vicious system of legislation which only encouraged fraud, thus graphically described by Story, the clauses which forbid the states from emitting bills of credit or making anything but gold and silver a tender in payment of debts, or passing any law impairing the obligation of contracts, were inserted in the Constitution.

"The attention of the convention therefore" says Chief Justice Marshall,

"was particularly directed to paper money and to acts which enable the debtor to discharge his debt otherwise than was stipulated in the contract. Had nothing more been intended, nothing more would have been expressed, but, in the opinion of the convention, much more remained to be done. The same mischief might be effected by other means. To restore public confidence completely, it was necessary not only to prohibit the use of particular means by which it might be effected, but to prohibit the use of any means by which the same mischief might be produced. The convention appears to have intended to establish a great principle that contracts should be inviolable."

Sturges v. Crowninshield, 4 Wheat. 122, 17 U. S. 206. It would be difficult to believe even in the absence of the historical evidence we have on the subject that the framers of the Constitution, profoundly impressed by the evils resulting from this kind of legislation, ever intended that the new government, ordained to establish justice, should possess the power of making its bills a legal tender, which they were unwilling should remain with the states, and in which the past had proved so dangerous to the peace of the community, so disturbing to the business of the people and so destructive of their morality.

The great historian of our country has recently given to the world a history of the convention, the result of years of labor in the examination of all public documents relating to its formation and of the recorded opinions of its framers, and thus he writes:

"With the full recollection of the need or seeming need of paper money in the Revolution, with the menace of danger in future time of war from its prohibition, authority to issue bills of

Page 110 U. S. 454

credit that should be legal tender was refused to the general government by the vote of nine states against New Jersey and Maryland. It was Madison who decided the vote of Virginia, and he has left his testimony that 'the pretext for paper currency, and particularly for making the bills a tender either for public or private debts, was cut off.' This is the interpretation of the clause made at the time of its adoption, alike by its authors and by its opponents, accepted by all the statesmen of that age, not open to dispute because too clear for argument, and never disputed so long as anyone man who took part in framing the Constitution remained alive. History cannot name a man who has gained enduring honor by causing the issue of paper money. Wherever such paper has been employed it has in every case thrown upon its authors the burden of exculpation under the plea of pressing necessity."

Bancroft's History of the formation of the Constitution of the United States, vol. 2, p. 134.

And when the convention came to the prohibition upon the states, the historian says that the clause "No state shall make anything but gold and silver a tender in payment of debts" was accepted without a dissentient state. "So the adoption of the Constitution," he adds,

"is to be the end forever of paper money, whether issued by the several states or by the United States, if the Constitution shall be rightly interpreted and honestly obeyed."

Id., 137.

For nearly three-quarters of a century after the adoption of the Constitution and until the legislation during the recent civil war, no jurist and no statesman of any position in the country ever pretended that a power to impart the quality of legal tender to its notes was vested in the general government. There is no recorded word of even one in favor of its possessing the power. All conceded, as an axiom of constitutional law, that the power did not exist.

Mr. Webster, from his first entrance into public life in 1812, gave great consideration to the subject of the currency, and in an elaborate speech on that subject, made in the Senate in 1836, then sitting in this room, he said:

Page 110 U. S. 455

"Currency, in a large and perhaps just sense, includes not only gold and silver and bank bills, but bills of exchange also. It may include all that adjusts exchanges and settles balances in the operations of trade and business; but if we understand by currency the legal money of the country, and that which constitutes a legal tender for debts, and is the standard measure of value, then undoubtedly nothing is included but gold and silver. Most unquestionably there is no legal tender, and there can be no legal tender in this country, under the authority of this government or any other, but gold and silver, either the coinage of our own mints or foreign coins at rates regulated by Congress.

This is a constitutional principle, perfectly plain and of the highest importance. The states are expressly prohibited from making anything but gold and silver a legal tender in payment of debts, and although no such express prohibition is applied to Congress, yet as Congress has no power granted to it in this respect but to coin money and to regulate the value of foreign coins, it clearly has no power to substitute paper or anything else for coin as a tender in payment of debts and in discharge of contracts. Congress has exercised this power fully in both its branches; it has coined money and still coins it; it has regulated the value of foreign coins, and still regulates their value. The legal tender, therefore, the constitutional standard of value, is established and cannot be overthrown. To overthrow it would shake the whole system."

4 Webster's Works 271.

When the idea of imparting the legal tender quality to the notes of the United States, issued under the first act of 1862, was first broached, the advocates of the measure rested their support of it on the ground that it was a war measure, to which the country was compelled to resort by the exigencies of its condition, being then sorely pressed by the Confederate forces, and requiring the daily expenditure of enormous sums to maintain its army and navy and to carry on the government. The representative who introduced the bill in the House declared that it was a measure of that nature, "one of necessity and not of choice;" that the times were extraordinary, and that extraordinary measures must be resorted to in order to save our government and preserve our nationality. Speech of Spaulding

Page 110 U. S. 456

of New York; Cong.Globe, 1861-62, pt. 1, 523. Other members of the house frankly confessed their doubt as to its constitutionality, but yielded their support of it under the pressure of this supposed necessity.

In the Senate also, the measure was pressed for the same reasons. When the act was reported by the committee on finance, its chairman, while opposing the legal tender provision, said:

"It is put on the ground of absolute overwhelming necessity; that the government has now arrived at that point when it must have funds, and those funds are not to be obtained from ordinary sources, or from any of the expedients to which we have heretofore had recourse, and therefore this new, anomalous, and remarkable provision must be resorted to in order to enable the government to pay off the debt that it now owes and afford circulation which will be available for other purposes."

Cong.Globe, 1861-62, pt. 1, 764.

And upon that ground, the provision was adopted, some of the senators stating that in the exigency then existing money must be had, and they therefore sustained the measure although they apprehended danger from the experiment. "The medicine of the Constitution," said Senator Summer, "must not become its daily food." Id., 800. A similar necessity was urged upon the state tribunals and this Court in justification of the measure when its validity was questioned. The dissenting opinion in Hepburn v. Griswold referred to the pressure that was upon the government at the time to enable it to raise and support an army, and to provide and maintain a navy.

Chief Justice Chase, who gave the prevailing opinion in that case, also spoke of the existence of the feeling when the bill was passed that the provision was necessary. He favored the provision on that ground when Secretary of the Treasury, although he had come to that conclusion with reluctance, and recommended its adoption by Congress. When the question as to its validity reached this Court, this expression of favor was referred to, and by many it was supposed that it would control his judicial action. But after long pondering upon the

Page 110 U. S. 457

subject, after listening to repeated arguments by able counsel, he decided against the constitutionality of the provision and, holding in his hands the casting vote, he determined the judgment of the Court. He thus preferred to preserve his integrity as a judicial officer, rather than his consistency as a statesman. In his opinion, he thus referred to his previous views:

"It is not surprising that amid the tumult of the late civil war, and under the influence of apprehensions for the safety of the republic almost universal, different views, never before entertained by American statesmen or jurists, were adopted by many. The time was not favorable to considerate reflection upon the constitutional limits of legislative or executive authority. If power was assumed from patriotic motives, the assumption found ready justification in patriotic hearts. Many who doubted yielded their doubts; many who did not doubt were silent. Some who were strongly averse to making government notes a legal tender felt themselves constrained to acquiesce in the views of the advocates of the measure. Not a few who then insisted upon its necessity or acquiesced in that view have, since the return of peace and under the influence of the calmer time, reconsidered their conclusions, and now concur in those which we have just announced. These conclusions seem to us to be fully sanctioned by the letter and spirit of the Constitution."

8 Wall. 75 U. S. 625.

It must be evident, however, upon reflection that if there were any power in the government of the United States to impart the quality of legal tender to its promissory notes, it was for Congress to determine when the necessity for its exercise existed; that war merely increased the urgency for money; it did not add to the powers of the government nor change their nature; that if the power existed, it might be equally exercised when a loan was made to meet ordinary expenses in time of peace, as when vast sums were needed to support an army or a navy in time of war. The wants of the government could never be the measure of its powers. But in the excitement and apprehensions of the war, these considerations were unheeded; the measure was passed as one of overruling

Page 110 U. S. 458

necessity in a perilous crisis of the country. Now it is no longer advocated as one of necessity, but as one that may be adopted at any time. Never before was it contended by any jurist or commentator on the Constitution that the government, in full receipt of ample income, with a Treasury overflowing, with more money on hand than it knows what to do with, could issue paper money as a legal tender. What was in 1862 called the "medicine of the Constitution" has now become its daily bread.

So it always happens that whenever a wrong principle of conduct, political or personal, is adopted on a plea of necessity, it will be afterwards followed on a plea of convenience.

The advocates of the measure have not been consistent in the designation of the power upon which they have supported its validity, some placing it on the power to borrow money, some on the coining power, and some have claimed it as an incident to the general powers of the government. In the present case, it is placed by the Court upon the power to borrow money, and the alleged sovereignty of the United States over the currency. It is assumed that this power, when exercised by the government, is something different from what it is when exercised by corporations or individuals, and that the government has, by the legal tender provision, the power to enforce loans of money because the sovereign governments of European countries have claimed and exercised such power.

The words "to borrow money," says the Court,

"are not to receive that limited and restricted interpretation and meaning which they would have in a penal statute or in an authority conferred by law or by contract upon trustees or agents for private purposes."

And it adds that

"The power, as incident to the power of borrowing money and issuing bills or notes of the government for money borrowed, of impressing upon those bills or notes the quality of being a legal tender for the payment of private debts, was a power universally understood to belong to sovereignty, in Europe and America at the time of the framing and adoption of the Constitution of the United States. The governments

Page 110 U. S. 459

of Europe, acting through the monarch or the legislature, according to the distribution of powers under their respective constitutions, had and have as sovereign a power of issuing paper money as of stamping coin,"

and that

"the exercise of this power not being prohibited to Congress by the Constitution, it is included in the power expressly granted to borrow money on the credit of the United States."

As to the terms "to borrow money," where, I would ask, does the Court find any authority for giving to them a different interpretation in the Constitution from what they receive when used in other instruments, as in the charters of municipal bodies or of private corporations, or in the contracts of individuals? They are not ambiguous; they have a well settled meaning in other instruments. If the Court may change that in the Constitution, so it may the meaning of all other clauses, and the powers which the government may exercise will be found declared not by plain words in the organic law, but by words of a new significance resting in the minds of the judges. Until some authority beyond the alleged claim and practice of the sovereign governments of Europe be produced, I must believe that the terms have the same meaning in all instruments, wherever they are used;

that they mean a power only to contract for a loan of money upon considerations to be agreed between the parties. The conditions of the loan, or whether any particular security shall be given to the lender, are matters of arrangement between the parties; they do not concern anyone else. They do not imply that the borrower can give to his promise to refund the money any security to the lender outside of property or rights which he possesses. The transaction is completed when the lender parts with his money and the borrower gives his promise to pay at the time and in the manner and with the securities agreed upon. Whatever stipulations may be made to add to the value of the promise or to secure its fulfillment must necessarily be limited to the property, rights, and privileges, which the borrower possesses. Whether he can add to his promises any element which will induce others

Page 110 U. S. 460

to receive them beyond the security which he gives for their payment depends upon his power to control such element. If he has a right to put a limitation upon the use of other persons' property or to enforce an exaction of some benefit from them, he may give such privilege to the lender; but if he has no right thus to interfere with the property or possession of others, of course, he can give none. It will hardly be pretended that the government of the United States has any power to enter into an engagement that, as security for its notes, the lender shall have special privileges with respect to the visible property of others, shall be able to occupy a portion of their lands or their houses, and thus interfere with the possession and use of their property. If the government cannot do that, how can it step in and say, as a condition of loaning money, that the lender shall have a right to interfere with contracts between private parties? A large proportion of the property of the world exists in contracts, and the government has no more right to deprive one of their value by legislation operating directly upon them than it has a right to deprive one of the value of any visible and tangible property. No one, I think, will pretend that individuals or corporations possess the power to impart to their evidences of indebtedness any quality by which the holder will be able to affect the contracts of other parties, strangers to the loan; nor would anyone pretend that Congress possesses the power to impart any such quality to the notes of the United States, except from the clause authorizing it to make laws necessary and proper to the execution of its powers. That clause, however, does not enlarge the expressly designated powers; it merely states what Congress could have done without its insertion in the Constitution. Without it, Congress could have adopted any appropriate means to borrow, but that can only be appropriate for that purpose which has some relation of fitness to the end, which has respect to the terms essential to the contract, or to the securities which the borrower may furnish for the repayment of the loan. The quality of legal tender does not touch the terms of the contract; that is complete without it; nor does it stand as a security for the loan, for

Page 110 U. S. 461

a security is a thing pledged, over which the borrower has some control, or in which he holds some interest.

The argument presented by the advocates of legal tender is in substance this: the object of borrowing is to raise funds, the addition of the quality of legal tender to the notes of the government will induce parties to take them, and funds will thereby be more readily loaned.

But the same thing may be said of the addition of any other quality which would give to the holder of the notes some advantage over the property of others -- as, for instance, that the notes should serve as a pass on the public conveyances of the country, or as a ticket to places of amusement, or should exempt his property from state and municipal taxation, or entitle him to the free use of the telegraph lines, or to a percentage from the revenues of private corporations. The same consequence -- a ready acceptance of the notes -- would follow, and yet no one would pretend that the addition of privileges of this kind with respect to the property of others, over which the borrower has no control, would be in any sense an appropriate measure to the execution of the power to borrow.

Undoubtedly the power to borrow includes the power to give evidences of the loan in bonds, Treasury notes, or in such other form as may be agreed between the parties. These may be issued in such amounts as will fit them for circulation, and for that purpose may be made payable to bearer, and transferable by delivery. Experience has shown that the form best fitted to secure their ready acceptance is that of notes payable to bearer, in such amounts as may suit the ability of the lender. The government, in substance, says to parties with whom it deals: lend us your money, or furnish us with your products or your labor, and we will ultimately pay you, and as evidence of it we will give you our notes, in such form and amount as may suit your convenience, and enable you to transfer them; we will also receive them for certain demands due to us. In all this matter there is only a dealing between the government and the individuals who trust it. The transaction concerns no others. The power which authorizes it is a very different one from a

Page 110 U. S. 462

power to deal between parties to private contracts in which the government is not interested, and to compel the receipt of these promises to pay in place of the money for which the contracts stipulated. This latter power is not an incident to the former; it is a distinct and far greater power. There is no legal connection between the two -- between the power to borrow from those willing to lend and the power to interfere with the independent contracts of others. The possession of this latter power would justify the interference of the government with any rights of property of other parties, under the pretense that its allowance to the holders of the notes would lead to their more ready acceptance, and thus furnish the needed means.

The power vested in Congress to coin money does not, in my judgment, fortify the position of the Court, as its opinion affirms. So far from deducing from that power any authority to impress the notes of the government with the quality of legal tender, its existence seems to me inconsistent with a power to make anything but coin a legal tender. The meaning of the terms "to coin money" is not at all doubtful. It is to mould metallic substances into forms convenient for circulation and to stamp them with the impress of the government authority indicating their value with reference to the unit of value established by law. Coins are pieces of metal of definite weight and value, stamped such by the authority of the government. If any doubt could exist that the power has reference to metallic substances only it would be removed by the language which immediately follows, authorizing Congress to regulate the value of money thus coined and of foreign coin, and also by clauses making a distinction between coin and the obligations of the general government and of the states. Thus, in the clause authorizing Congress "to provide for the punishment of counterfeiting the securities and current coin of the United States," a distinction is made between the obligations and the coin of the government.

Money is not only a medium of exchange, but it is a standard of value. Nothing can be such standard which has not intrinsic

Page 110 U. S. 463

value, or which is subject to frequent changes in value. From the earliest period in the history of civilized nations we find pieces of gold and silver used as money. These metals are scattered over the world in small quantities; they are susceptible of division, capable of easy impression, have more value in proportion to weight and size, and are less subject to loss by wear and abrasion than any other material possessing these qualities. It requires labor to obtain them; they are not dependent upon legislation or the caprices of the multitude; they cannot be manufactured or decreed into existence, and they do not perish by lapse of time. They have, therefore, naturally, if not necessarily, become throughout the world a standard of value. In exchange for pieces of them, products requiring an equal amount of labor are readily given. When the product and the piece of metal represent the same labor, or an approximation to it, they are freely exchanged. There can be no adequate substitute for these metals. Says Mr. Webster, in a speech made in the House of Representatives in 1815:

"The circulating medium of a commercial community must be that which is also the circulating medium of other commercial communities, or must be capable of being converted into that medium without loss. It must also be able not only to pass in payments and receipts among individuals of the same society and nation, but to adjust and discharge the balance of exchanges between different nations. It must be something which has a value abroad as well as at home, by which foreign as well as domestic debts can be satisfied. The precious metals alone answer these purposes. They alone therefore are money, and whatever else is to perform the functions of money must be their representative, and capable of being turned into them at will. So long as bank paper retains this quality it is a substitute for money; divested of this, nothing can give it that character."

3 Webster's Works 41.

The clause to coin money must be read in connection with the prohibition upon the states to make anything but gold and silver coin a tender in payment of debts. The two taken together

Page 110 U. S. 464

clearly show that the coins to be fabricated under the authority of the general government, and as such to be a legal tender for debts, are to be composed principally, if not entirely, of the metals of gold and silver. Coins of such metals are necessarily a legal tender to the amount of their respective values, without any legislative enactment, and the statute of the United States providing that they shall be such tender is only declaratory of their effect when offered in payment. When the Constitution says, therefore, that Congress shall have the power to coin money, interpreting that clause with the prohibition upon the states, it says it shall have the power to make coins of the precious metals a legal tender, for that alone which is money can be a legal tender. If this be the true import of the language, nothing else can be made a legal tender. We all know that the value of the notes of the government in the market, and in the commercial world generally, depends upon their convertibility on demand into coin, and as confidence in such convertibility increases or diminishes, so does the exchangeable value of the notes vary.

So far from becoming themselves standards of value by reason of the legislative declaration to that effect, their own value is measured by the facility with which they can be exchanged into that which alone is regarded as money by the commercial world. They are promises of money, but they are not money in the sense of the Constitution. The term "money" is used in that instrument in several clauses -- in the one authorizing Congress "to borrow money;" in the one authorizing Congress "to coin money;" in the one declaring that "no money" shall be drawn from the Treasury, but in consequence of appropriations made by law, and in the one declaring that no state shall "coin money." And it is a settled rule of interpretation that the same term occurring in different parts of the same instrument shall be taken in the same sense unless there is something in the context indicating that a different meaning was intended. Now to coin money is, as I have said, to make coins out of metallic substances, and the only money the value of which Congress can regulate is coined money, either of our mints or of foreign

Page 110 U. S. 465

countries. It should seem, therefore, that to borrow money is to obtain a loan of coin money -- that is, money composed of the precious metals, representing value in the purchase of property and payment of debts. Between the promises of the government, designated as its securities, and this money the Constitution draws a distinction which disappears in the opinion of the Court.

The opinion not only declares that it is in the power of Congress to make the notes of the government a legal tender and a standard of value, but that under the power to coin money and regulate the value thereof, Congress may issue coins of the same denominations as those now already current, but of less intrinsic value by reason of containing a less weight of the precious metals, and thereby enable debtors to discharge their debts by payment of coins of less real value. This doctrine is put forth as in some way a justification of the legislation authorizing the tender of nominal money in place of real money in payment of debts. Undoubtedly Congress has power to alter the value of coins issued, either by increasing or diminishing the alloy they contain; so it may alter at its pleasure, their denominations; it may hereafter call a dollar an eagle, and it may call an eagle a dollar. But if it be intended to assert that Congress can make the coins changed the equivalent of those having a greater value in their previous condition, and compel parties contracting for the latter to receive coins with diminished value, I must be permitted to deny any such authority.

Any such declaration on its part would be not only utterly inoperative in fact, but a shameful disregard of its constitutional duty. As I said on a former occasion:

"The power to coin money, as declared by this Court, is a great trust devolved upon Congress, carrying with it the duty of creating and maintaining a uniform standard of value throughout the Union, and it would be a manifest abuse of this trust to give to the coins issued by its authority any other than their real value. By debasing the coins, when once the standard is fixed, is meant giving to the coins by their form and impress a certificate of their having a relation to that standard different from that which in truth

Page 110 U. S. 466

they possess -- in other words, giving to the coins a false certificate of their value.

- 91 -

Arbitrary and profligate governments have often resorted to this miserable scheme of robbery, which Mill designates as a shallow and impudent artifice, the

"least covert of all modes of knavery, which consists in calling a shilling a pound, that a debt of one hundred pounds may be cancelled by the payment of one hundred shillings."

No such debasement has ever been attempted in this country, and none ever will be so long as any sentiment of honor influences the governing power of the nation. The changes from time to time in the quantity of alloy in the different coins has been made to preserve the proper relative value between gold and silver, or to prevent exportation, and not with a view of debasing them. Whatever power may be vested in the government of the United States, it has none to perpetrate such monstrous iniquity. One of the great purposes of its creation, as expressed in the preamble of the Constitution, was the establishment of justice, and not a line nor a word is found in that instrument which sanctions any intentional wrong to the citizen, either in war or in peace.

But beyond and above all the objections which I have stated to the decision recognizing a power in Congress to impart the legal tender quality to the notes of the government is my objection to the rule of construction, adopted by the Court to reach its conclusions -- a rule which, fully carried out, would change the whole nature of our Constitution and break down the barriers which separate a government of limited from one of unlimited powers. When the Constitution came before the conventions of the several states for adoption, apprehension existed that other powers than those designated might be claimed, and it led to the first ten amendments. When these were presented to the states, they were preceded by a preamble stating that the conventions of a number of the states had at the time of adopting the Constitution, expressed a desire, "in order to prevent misconception or abuse of its powers, that further declaratory and restrictive clauses should be added." One of them is found in the Tenth Amendment, which declares

Page 110 U. S. 467

that

"The powers not delegated to the United States by the Constitution, nor prohibited by it to the states, are reserved to the states respectively, or to the people."

The framers of the Constitution, as I have said, were profoundly impressed with the evils which had resulted from the vicious legislation of the states making notes a legal tender, and they determined that such a power should not exist any longer. They therefore prohibited the states from exercising it, and they refused to grant it to the new government which they created. Of what purpose is it then to refer to the exercise of the power by the absolute or the limited governments of Europe, or by the states previous to our constitution?

Congress can exercise no power by virtue of any supposed inherent sovereignty in the general government. Indeed it may be doubted whether the power can be correctly said to appertain to sovereignty in any proper sense, as an attribute of an independent political community.

The power to commit violence, perpetrate injustice, take private property by force without compensation to the owner, and compel the receipt of promises to pay in place of money, may be exercised, as it often has been, by irresponsible authority, but it cannot be considered as belonging to a government founded upon law.

But be that as it may, there is no such thing as a power of inherent sovereignty in the government of the United States. It is a government of delegated powers, supreme within its prescribed sphere but powerless outside of it. In this country, sovereignty resides in the people, and Congress can exercise no power which they have not, by their Constitution, entrusted to it; all else is withheld. It seems, however, to be supposed that as the power was taken from the states, it could not have been intended that it should disappear entirely, and therefore it must in some way adhere to the general government notwithstanding the Tenth Amendment and the nature of the Constitution. The doctrine that a power not expressly forbidden may be exercised would, as I have observed, change the character of our government. If I have read the Constitution aright, if there is any weight to be given to the uniform teachings of our great jurists and of commentators

Page 110 U. S. 468

previous to the late civil war, the true doctrine is the very opposite of this. If the power is not in terms granted, and is not necessary and proper for the exercise of a power which is thus granted, it does not exist. And in determining what measures may be adopted in executing the powers granted, Chief Justice Marshall declares that they must be appropriate, plainly adapted to the end, not prohibited, and consistent with the letter and spirit of the Constitution. Now all through that instrument we find limitations upon the power both of the general government and the state governments so as to prevent oppression and injustice. No legislation, therefore, tending to promote either can consist with the letter and spirit of the Constitution. A law which interferes with the contracts of others and compels one of the parties to receive in satisfaction something different from that stipulated, without reference to its actual value in the market, necessarily works such injustice and wrong.

There is, it is true, no provision in the Constitution of the United States forbidding in direct terms the passing of laws by Congress impairing the obligation of contracts, and there are many express powers conferred, such as the power to declare war, levy duties, and regulate commerce, the exercise of which affects more or less the value of contracts. Thus, war necessarily suspends intercourse between the citizens or subjects of belligerent nations, and the performance during its continuance of previous contracts. The imposition of duties upon goods may affect the prices of articles imported or manufactured, so as to materially alter the value of previous contracts respecting them. But these incidental consequences arising from the exercise of such powers were contemplated in the grant of them. As there can be no solid objection to legislation under them, no just complaint can be made of such consequences. But far different is the case when the impairment of the contract does not follow incidentally, but is directly and in terms allowed and enacted. Legislation operating directly upon private contracts, changing their conditions, is forbidden to the states, and no power to alter the stipulations of such contracts by direct legislation

Page 110 U. S. 469

is conferred upon Congress. There are also many considerations, outside of the fact that there is no grant of the power, which show that the framers of the Constitution never intended that such power should be exercised. One of the great objects of the Constitution, as already observed, was to establish justice, and what was meant by that in its relations to contracts, as said by the late Chief Justice in his opinion in Hepburn v. Griswold, was not left to interference or conjecture. And in support of this statement he refers to the fact that when the Constitution was undergoing discussion in the convention, the Congress of the Confederation was engaged in framing the ordinance for the government of the Northwest Territory, in which certain articles of compact were established between the people of the original states and the people of the territory "for the purposes," as expressed in the instrument,

"of extending the fundamental principles of civil and religious liberty, whereon these republics [the states united under the Confederation], their laws and constitutions, are erected."

That Congress was also alive to the evils which the loose legislation of the states had created by interfering with the obligation of private contracts and making notes a legal tender for debts, and the ordinance declared that in the just preservation of rights and property, no law

"ought ever to be made or have force in the said territory that shall in any manner whatever interfere with or affect private contracts or engagements bona fide and without fraud previously formed."

This principle, said the Chief Justice, found more condensed expression in the prohibition upon the states against impairing the obligation of contracts, which has always been recognized "as an efficient safeguard against injustice," and the Court was then of opinion that

"It is clear that those who framed and those who adopted the Constitution intended that the spirit of this prohibition should pervade the entire body of legislation, and that the justice which the Constitution was ordained to establish was not thought by them to be compatible with legislation of an opposite tendency."

Soon after the Constitution was adopted, the case of Calder v. Bull came before this Court, and it was Page 110 U. S. 470

there said that there were acts which the federal and state legislatures could not do without exceeding their authority, and among them was mentioned a law which punished a citizen for an innocent act, and a law which destroyed or impaired the lawful private contracts of citizens. "It is against all reason and justice," it was added, "for a people to entrust a legislature with such powers, and therefore it cannot be presumed that they have done it." 3 Dall. 3 U. S. 388. And Mr. Madison, in one of the articles in the Federalist, declared that laws impairing the obligation of contracts were contrary to the first principles of the social compact and to every principle of sound legislation. Yet this Court holds that a measure directly operating upon and necessarily impairing private contracts may be adopted in the execution of powers specifically granted for other purposes because it is not in terms prohibited, and that it is consistent with the letter and spirit of the Constitution.

From the decision of the Court I see only evil likely to follow. There have been times within the memory of all of us when the legal tender notes of the United States were not exchangeable for more than one-half of their nominal value. The possibility of such depreciation will always attend paper money.

This inborn infirmity no mere legislative declaration can cure. If Congress has the power to make the notes a legal tender and to pass as money or its equivalent, why should not a sufficient amount be issued to pay the bonds of the United States as they mature? Why pay interest on the millions of dollars of bonds now due when Congress can in one day make the money to pay the principal? And why should there be any restraint upon unlimited appropriations by the government for all imaginary schemes of public improvement if the printing press can furnish the money that is needed for them?"

Now tell me friend, do you believe that what the framers of the Constitution really meant to insure was:

That while the governments of the individual states would be restricted from making "...any Thing but gold and silver Coin a Tender in Payment of Debts", the federal government - in spite of that quote and in spite of everything that Justice Field mentioned in his dissent - should *somehow* actually have the authority to contract with a banking cartel that would, in a nutshell:

1 – *somehow* have the authority to purchase unlimited amounts of government debt with specious collateral;

2 - regulate the nation's interest rates and the amount of official currency in general circulation;

3 - pay the U.S. Treasury only the exact cost of producing said currency (said currency happens to be that cartel's own brand of intrinsically worthless bearer notes/bank notes that have debt as collateral). And what exactly is it that they pay the U.S. Treasury with?

4 - loan/rent those notes to the federal government, at interest, so the federal government can mandate that those worthless notes are "legal tender for all debts public and private";

which is to say that the federal government can lawfully force the Citizens to use those bearer notes under the guise of it being the nation's "lawful money"; and then tax their wages in order to pay off *some* of the government debts that have accrued by way of the cartel being allowed to assist the government in running up mind-boggling amounts of debt.

Does that sound plausible to you?

Don't get me wrong, I can see how after taking the time to fully understand what was said in the previous fifteen pages, and extensively researching the writings of your nation's founding fathers and studying the reasons that the Revolutionary War was fought, and reading the Coinage Act of 1792, and personally experiencing anything even remotely similar to the mental, physical, and economic hardships that said war and its prelude inflicted upon the Colonists, one who was equipped with such insight into the mindset of those men would have no objections to the scenario put forth in the earlier part of this paragraph - or not really care much about stuff like that anyway.

Ok, well, actually I can't.

But let's look at exactly what the U.S. department of the Treasury has to say about Federal Reserve notes.

The following information has been cut directly from the Treasury Department's website (http://www.treasury.gov/resource-center/faqs/currency/pages/legal-tender.aspx):

What are Federal Reserve notes and how are they different from United States notes?

Federal Reserve notes are legal tender currency notes. The twelve Federal Reserve Banks issue them into circulation pursuant to the Federal Reserve Act of 1913. A commercial bank belonging to the Federal Reserve System can obtain Federal Reserve notes from the Federal Reserve Bank in its district whenever it wishes. It must pay for them in full, dollar for dollar, by drawing down its account with its district Federal Reserve Bank.

Federal Reserve Banks obtain the notes from our <u>Bureau of Engraving and Printing</u> (BEP). It pays the BEP for the cost of producing the notes, which then become liabilities of the Federal Reserve Banks, and obligations of the United States Government.

Congress has specified that a Federal Reserve Bank must hold collateral equal in value to the Federal Reserve notes that the Bank receives. This collateral is chiefly gold certificates and United States securities. This provides backing for the note issue. The idea was that if the Congress dissolved the Federal Reserve System, the United States would take over the notes (liabilities). This would meet the requirements of Section 411, but the government would also take over the assets, which would be of equal value. Federal Reserve notes represent a first lien on all the assets of the Federal Reserve Banks, and on the collateral specifically held against them.

Federal Reserve notes are not redeemable in gold, silver or any other commodity, and receive no backing by anything This has been the case since 1933. The notes have no value for themselves, but for what they will buy. In another sense, because they are legal tender, Federal Reserve notes are "backed" by all the goods and services in the economy.

Does that sound reassuring to you?

Does the above explanation make you feel as though the usage of those "legal tender currency notes" is a fair swap for the currency that Article I, section 10 of the Constitution specified as the only officially authorized tender of debt in your nation?

Actually, it amounts to an indirect admission that the currency laws enacted by your nation's founders have been nullified by insurrectionists. Unsurprisingly, the usurpation of power was enabled by a cunning employment of falsity expressed in legalese.

But I don't want you to lose interest in the subject at hand, so I won't point out the chicanery being employed in each of those lines of text.

Instead, I'll just sum it up quickly for the layman:

A criminal cartel has effectively eaten your lunch. They then took a dump in the empty bag and convinced you and everyone else to make do with the new contents of the bag.

Everything with officially declared "inherent value" has long since vanished.

Feel free to read section 16 of the Federal Reserve act.

Discover firsthand what is deemed acceptable as the tender of collateral required in order for a bank to receive Federal Reserve notes.

In actuality that supposed collateral is nothing but IOU's.

As a matter of fact, it is debt that the citizens of your nation are legally, collectively being held responsible for. Remember the bank bailouts?

In other words, standardized and measured gold and silver coin was originally being used, *by way of Constitutional mandate.*

It was used so as to insure that none of any Citizen's monetary wealth and unalienable rights could be confiscated secretly and unobserved in a manner in which not one man in a million is able to diagnose.

But that money and those rights were confiscated openly, through the use of unlawful "government" force being justified by patently absurd judicial decree.

And the thieves replaced the money with paper notes that are admittedly worthless, if not for the fact that the threat of force is printed on their face!

"Federal Reserve notes are not redeemable in gold, silver or any other commodity, and receive no backing by anything. This has been the case since 1933. The notes have no value for themselves, but for what they will buy. In another sense, because they are legal tender, Federal Reserve notes are "backed" by all the goods and services in the economy."

Reality Check: the Federal Reserve System blatantly contradicts the concepts expressed in your Declaration of Independence and your Constitution/Bill of Rights.

It is nothing other than an elaborately disguised counterfeiting operation.

It was designed to legally force its victims to reward Federal Reserve operatives and lackeys for committing Munchausen syndrome by proxy.

Read this article about debt monetization:
http://www.peakprosperity.com/martensonreport/shell-game-how-federal-reserve-monetizing-debt

It is an absolute affront to reason. Yet, even after a full examination of everything I have just shared with you, not one man in a million is able to diagnose the parasitic affliction.

Honestly, can you coherently explain what the real crux of the matter is?

Can you see how your nation's constitutionally mandated currency laws have been hijacked?

Do you understand that said constitutionally mandated currency laws insured each prudent Citizen that their monetary wealth was individualized and fully secure from the negative consequences that anyone else might suffer as a result of their own imprudent or miscalculated actions?

Can you see that everyone in your nation is now, by way of deception and force, part of a legally mandated collective?

Do you understand that your entire social structure is dependent upon policies cooked up in private by an unlawful banking cartel?

Their very existence was decried by the founders of your nation.

Even so; is *that* the real crux of the matter?

"There is no subtler, no surer means of overturning the existing basis of society than to debauch the currency."

So, have you come to a point in the search for truth when, regardless of how conceptual roadblocks are artfully administered in an attempt to disguise it, truth becomes plainly evident?

Well, either way, take a deep breath. What you have read thus far is only the beginning of this twisted tale. Follow the links below to learn much more about the alternate reality you're stuck in.

Then ask yourself these two questions: **1**- What role has the legal profession been playing in the subversion of the Organic Laws of the United States of America? **2**- What role has the legal profession been playing in keeping everyone on Earth from realizing that the Federal Reserve is a pernicious counterfeiting cartel?

I will soon provide you with the concepts and methodology that must be widely understood and employed in order to establish and maintain actual freedom and prosperity.

Patience friend, I haven't forgotten about the **$250,000 tax free cash incentive** mentioned earlier. The details are provided a bit later in the book.

I want you to be able to incorporate the knowledge you'll acquire on your way there into the message you'll be spreading about it to all of your otherwise uninterested friends, family, and neighbors.

1 - A free electronic copy of the **must read** book entitled "The Money Manipulators" by June Grem: https://archive.org/details/pdfy-XAH1KjQvs6DgnuRr

2 - A **must read** webpage that offers a clear, easy to follow summary of important information about the Federal Reserve. There are plenty of links to related information and videos: http://wanttoknow.info/financialbankingcoverup

3 - A video that explains many aspects of the formation and ongoing existence of the Federal Reserve: https://www.youtube.com/watch?v=lu_VqX6J93k

4 - A short, **must watch** video clip of a well-known former Fed chairman explaining some important truth about the Federal Reserve:
http://m.youtube.com/watch?v=zV0MyMpcSp4

5 - The Federal Reserve act of 1913:
https://fraser.stlouisfed.org/docs/publications/books/fract_iden_1914.pdf

6 - An informative article from the Forbes website entitled "How the fed is helping to rig the stock market". It happens to mention how the Fed conjures "money" out of thin air:
http://www.forbes.com/sites/investor/2013/01/30/how-the-fed-is-helping-to-rig-the-stock-market/

7 - A **must read** article that will give you accurate insight into the minds of those whose "expert" influence directly affects your life.

This is not a parody. The CFR sponsored authors of the article that's reprinted therein are admitting that the entire monetary system is a farce; a sham; bogus; fraudulent; corrupt: http://www.zerohedge.com/news/2014-08-26/it-begins-council-foreign-relations-proposes-central-banks-should-hand-consumers-cas

8 - A **must read** essay by Murray Rothbard that details the methods employed and the players involved in creating the Federal Reserve:
http://www.deepblacklies.co.uk/rothbard.pdf

9 - An article from Rolling Stone magazine that points out some very shady dealings:
http://m.rollingstone.com/politics/news/everything-is-rigged-the-biggest-financial-scandal-yet-20130425

10 - A fun calculator. It will introduce you to some of the real effects of the scam being run by the Federal Reserve on the purchasing power of the worthless paper that you call "money": http://www.usinflationcalculator.com/

11 - An article that explains the basic process of "Fractional Reserve Banking". Be sure to think back on these concepts after following the next two links: http://en.m.wikipedia.org/wiki/Fractional_reserve_banking

12 - An article that explains the basic process of "Debt Monetization" (legally creating currency by way of backing it with debt) by which the general population of the world is being completely fleeced: http://en.m.wikipedia.org/wiki/Monetization#Monetizing_debt

13 - A Forbes blog article on debt monetization with numerous graphs that help to illustrate the damage being done to you. Be sure to understand what each graph shows: http://blogs.forbes.com/michaelpollaro/us-government-debt-monetization/

14 - Read the actual text of Executive order #6102: www.presidency.ucsb.edu/ws/index.php?pid=14611%26st=%26st1=#axzz1MVgxSNnO

15 - The "Gold Repeal Joint Resolution": https://web.archive.org/web/20190102212324/https://en.wikisource.org/wiki/Gold_Repeal_Joint_Resolution

16 - Some important information about President John F Kennedy's misunderstood, myth inspiring Executive order #11110: www.youtube.com/watch?v=HrWgi6JVsd0

17 - A **must read** speech given by a previous Fed chairman, in which he admits that the Fed caused the Great Depression. (The admission is at the end of the speech. Readers with a working brain will find it quite interesting that, while he clearly insinuates that the gold standard was a mistake, the legal crime of "fractional reserve banking" is never mentioned as a factor in the collapse.): http://www.federalreserve.gov/BOARDDOCS/SPEECHES/2002/20021108/default.htm

18 - An article that <u>must</u> be read in its entirety. It highlights some of the speeches given to Congress by former Congressman Louis T McFadden, Chairman of the Banking and Currency Committee for more than 10 years and an outspoken critic of the Federal Reserve: http://hiwaay.net/~becraft/mcfadden.html

19 - A **FREE pdf** of the highly informative book "The Creature from Jekyll Island". Note that the video in link #3 above is based upon this book: http://www.pdfarchive.info/pdf/G/Gr/Griffin_G_Edward_-_The_Creature_from_Jekyll_Island.pdf

20 - An article that provides some very interesting information about the "Brettonwoods Agreement" and the U.S. Government. It would serve you well to discover firsthand if the claims it makes are valid: http://teamlaw.org/history.htm

21 - The full majority opinion and dissent of the Supreme Court in the above mentioned case of *Juilliard v. Greenman*: https://supreme.justia.com/cases/federal/us/110/421/case.html

22 - A **FREE pdf** of "History of the formation of the Constitution of the United States of America", book I and book II, by George Bancroft. Published in 1882: https://ia600209.us.archive.org/28/items/historyofformati01banc/historyofformati01banc.pdf

And since no meaningful exploration of the "Federal" Reserve can be properly conducted without including at least a brief educational journey into the **"Bank of International Settlements"**, make sure to follow all of the links below:

1 – A **MUST READ** article that talks about the history, the functions and the members of the BIS. Make sure to read the section near the bottom that talks about the 1998 bank bailout in Brazil, and the section following it that talks about how the BIS no longer uses gold as a unit of account – there is no currency in the world that is backed by gold anymore:
https://web.archive.org/web/20140918094048/http://www.augustforecast.com/2005/10/14/global_banking_the_bank_for_international_settlements/

2 – A **MUST READ** article that tells of the history and function of the IMF (international monetary fund), and how it and the World Bank are tied together with the BIS:
https://web.archive.org/web/20130819102817/http://www.augustforecast.com/2005/12/29/global_banking_the_international_monetary_fund/

3 – A **MUST READ** article that tells the history and function of the World Bank. After reading the prior two articles, one of the major ways we've been leading you toward your doom should be coming into focus:
https://web.archive.org/web/20140331063911/http://www.augustforecast.com/2006/02/01/global_banking_the_world_bank/

4 – A **MUST READ** article that explains how the BIS is taking control of sovereign government functions in your country by way of President Obama's commitment to their "financial stability board": http://www.webofdebt.com/articles/big_brother_basel.php

5 – A two-part article that explains the dangers to national sovereignty from the "financial stability board" of the Bank of International Settlements. Read both parts of the article: http://www.newswithviews.com/Veon/joan165.htm

6 – An article that talks about how the "financial stability board" of the Bank of International Settlements directly undermines the sovereignty of the United States: http://www.newswithviews.com/Barnewall/marilyn103.htm

7 – An article that outlines some of the functioning of the BIS. It also explains some of the "special" advantages given to those who own its stock and/or are employed by the bank: http://www.libertyforlife.com/banking/bank_for_international_settlemen.htm

8 – A **MUST READ** article entitled "One Bank to Rule Them All: The Bank for International Settlements": http://www.globalresearch.ca/one-bank-to-rule-them-all-the-bank-for-international-settlements/5480852

9 – An article that gives a little background history and information regarding the functionality of the BIS: http://www.globalresearch.ca/index.php?context=va&aid=13239

XV – The Map, the Keys, and the Instructions for Redemption

Since the average American has no knowledge of history, or of the useful insight that such an education provides, they can't see our plans unfolding in broad daylight.

I'm talking about a more subtle, more dangerous, more widespread and more technologically advanced reenactment of the situation that Winston Churchill unsuccessfully tried to wake Europe to in the early 1930's.

Try to stay focused here, so that you can share in the awareness I am imparting:

Winston Churchill saw that the Germans were rebuilding their military strength - in clear violation of the Treaty of Versailles. And he spoke out to have their efforts stopped cold before they could successfully invade any of the other countries in the region.

The Treaty of Versailles is what the Germans were forced to sign after their loss of the First World War (In which they admitted full blame for the war, and which forbade them from rebuilding a substantial military, etc.).

According to the Treaty of Versailles, France and England had the specified right to act exactly as Churchill was urging.

Yet in response to his keen insights and considerable efforts to share them, he was laughed at and called a "warmonger".

History shows that he was quite the conspiracy theorist...

So the German military continued to grow, finally marching into the Rhineland, in clear violation of the Treaty of Versailles.

Churchill kept warning of the coming storm, but none of the powers in Europe did a thing. They all said that Hitler would be content with what he had just done.

But the Nazis kept invading other countries and increasing their military might.

And what did the career politicians of England and the other European countries yet to be invaded do?

They kept telling the ignorant citizens of their countries that everything was fine.

They knew from the polling data of their time that those citizens wanted nothing to do with another armed conflict anyway.

(Might they have felt that way because there was no-one but the "warmonger" Churchill prompting their poorly equipped, poorly functioning minds to conceive of it being in their best interests to pursue such a course of action?)

On this went until German troops finally had control of the continent; they were soon building fortifications along the shore of the English Channel in France. Why were they doing that? They were doing it in order to protect their position from the English as they prepared for their vicious aerial assault on the island nation.

If you don't know the rest of the story, look into it. There's more than enough death and suffering at a seemingly safe distance to keep you entertained:

An unimaginably widespread physical destruction of irreplaceable architecture and art; almost sixty million people dead (60,000,000), with countless more wounded, tormented, and tortured; plus a couple of atomic bombs being dropped. You'll love it.

(Of course, you should note that my mention of 60,000,000 dead people does <u>not</u> include the additional 90,000,000 people that died after the war, at the hands of Stalin and Mao)

So you're wondering why this little history lesson is important?

I'll keep it real simple: try to imagine your Declaration of Independence and Bill of Rights as the European continent, and your top "government" operatives and their corporate partners as the National Socialist German Workers Party, pre-World War Two.

They intend to take much more of it than you are willing to believe they want, and that they are willing to admit to wanting.

And the more of it that you keep *letting* them take, the more entrenched and powerful they are becoming; in clear opposition to the concepts of personal freedom and just government that are expressed in your Declaration of Independence.

This means that the ability to eliminate the poisonous constructs you have been helping them wall you in with will soon be gone. Large numbers of you must immediately become fully aware of what's really happening, and of what needs to be done to stop it.

The German generals admitted after World War Two that if Churchill had simply been listened to from the start, the Nazi menace never would have amounted to anything.

Funny that they should have said that; contrast their words with something Lao Tzu said:

"Tackle difficulties when they are easy. Accomplish great things when they are small. Handle what is going to be rough when it is still smooth. Control what has not yet formed its force. Deal with a dangerous situation while it is safe. Manage what is hard while it is soft. Eliminate what is vicious before it becomes destructive. This is called attending to great things at small beginnings."

XVA - It's going to take courage for you to act on what I am about to explain. A strong sense of honor will also be needed.

It will <u>not</u> require a single shot to be fired, and I am going to explain what must be done in enough detail that a group of fourteen year old children could actually carry out the plan if they were given permission to do so by their parents. But many among you will be completely overwhelmed. The amount of personal responsibility and resolve that is required to redeem yourselves and your nation will not appeal to the indolent masses we've cultivated.

Unfortunately for your children, less than a handful of their elders possess even a spark of noble spirit. Most of you don't even know what honor is. **You are a lost flock.**

Yet you do not have even one day to waste before doing the following things:

1 – You and everyone you know must form local, regional, state, and national branches of a coalition. It must bring together every other related activist group in your country, in order to organize the widespread presentation of the message and concepts offered in this book.

Such presentations must be made in every single college, public library, union hall, church, synagogue, mosque, volunteer fire house, private home, public park, and drinking establishment in your country. The number of people involved must overwhelm any "governmental" opposition to the completely lawful actions and demands you must all take and make (yes, they are outlined in the following sections of this book). And everyone must be informed of the **$250,000 tax free cash incentive** that is being offered.

The coalition must utilize the internet via a central website, continuous email, and a social media campaign in order to keep everyone properly informed of all happenings. The mainstream media will surely distort the facts. They will lie about the peaceful nature of the coalition. They will not accurately describe its size and strength, its true purpose, or its Constitutionality. They will demonize its Declaration of Independence-mandated ideology.

The coalition must direct everyone to immediately purchase as many heirloom fruit and vegetable seeds as they can. Heirloom seeds will produce more seeds with which to grow more food in the future. And everyone must begin planting their seeds as soon as the growing season for what they have arrives.

Everyone must learn of the techniques required to: **1**- grow those fruits and vegetables; **2**- properly "can" them: **3**- dehydrate and store them; **4**- harvest and store the new seeds for future use; **5**- construct an inexpensive, simple greenhouse.

There are many books on the subject and many related videos on YouTube. Any local garden center will set you on the right course.

You **NEED** to forget the idea of green lawns, empty rooftops, and vacant lots.

You **NEED** to plant a "Victory garden" http://en.m.wikipedia.org/wiki/Victory_garden#section_1

I cannot possibly overstate the **NEED** for everyone everywhere to grow such gardens on every single inch of available space in your nation. **Your lives literally depend on this**.

But, before any of you conceptual casualties consider committing to the cause, take notice. You <u>must</u> act in accordance with the following fact:

2 – Your success will absolutely depend upon the full-scale, fervent participation of the youth in your country. (Fervent = marked by great intensity of feeling.)

Unlike most of the adults, they have not yet had their spirit and the voice of reason fully ground down and shut out by their inability to genuinely, honorably succeed in the "real world" we have constructed.

Yes, we do constantly work to undermine their inherent positive attributes and capabilities with poisonous chemical compounds and by instituting their "real world" "education" and "personal interests"; but they have not yet been fully, personally beaten down by the endless maze of bureaucracy and innumerable socioeconomic roadblocks we've crafted.

Unlike most adults, they've not yet completed our doctorate-level courses in being discouraged from believing they have any intrinsic worth.

They don't yet believe that even a truly concerted effort to change the world would be absolutely futile and thus not worth the hassle of any serious consideration, conversation, or action.

Those victims in training must be made fully aware of these facts: **1**- literally every aspect of their future is dependent upon this. **2**- They cannot, in-any-way, depend upon the adults to see to it that the needed work will get done.

It must be made crystal clear to them that you mental and moral weaklings have allowed a highly intelligent, extremely creative, supremely patient small group of thieves whose purpose is your destruction, and whose goal is that you suffer along the path to that end, to ensnare you in an intricate system of slavery that is nothing other than a highly evolved method of forcefully controlling your actual being - in order to steal from you as they have you gather whatever it is that they value; while they simultaneously, effectively force false ideas upon you through myriad misleading claims whose constant, clever presentation leads to your believing that the actions taken by them are needed for your own benefit.

In other words, make sure, since *your* life does depend on it, that all of the youth in your country immediately tune out and turn off our mind melting gadgets. Make sure they read, re-read, and understand every single word in this book.

See, unlike their completely beaten down predecessors, those youth might get a clear picture of the horrible future that awaits them.

And enough of them just might do the work required to get that tax free $250,000 plus, that I mentioned earlier, into their own pockets. How's that for incentive?

3 – Once it is formed, the coalition must immediately begin recruiting volunteers for what will culminate in an enormous, long-term peaceful rally in Washington D.C.

All of the details needed to insure the success of the rally are provided below.

The coalition will have a name and its members will promote it *almost* as if it were a new political party. It will not be a new political party.

The name of the rally will be the "United Sovereign's Absolution" / "USA" rally.

Note that this will not be a protest rally. If you haven't noticed, they don't actually get much done.

No, this is a comeback rally that will be announcing the end of the status quo.

This rally is <u>not</u> about asking those in power to make concessions. It's about telling them and the rest of the world that you've come to collect your rightful inheritance.

Constitutional amendments will be made soon after the 2024 elections (that is to say, as soon as all of the steps required to ratify new amendments have lawfully been accomplished).

The rally must not disperse *for any reason* until the Constitutional amendments have been ratified and all of the associated changes in your governance that are outlined below have been instituted.

I cannot possibly overstate your need to make this rally happen as directed below.

You must begin laying the proper groundwork for such a rally now.

Otherwise you will eventually, when it is already far too late, find yourselves trying to hold ill-fated protest rallies with no "Official Authorization" to do so, no planning or organization, and no comprehensive, rational set of demands to actually fix all that is wrong.

Such actions will be even less successful than the dismal failure of the 1960's mass masturbation sessions that got certain competent people killed, and which failed to address 99% of the fundamental institutionalized criminality that was eroding your societal structure.

Don't get me wrong; those sessions did have a silver lining. They enabled the powers that be to make heroes and cultural icons out of numerous incompetent daydreamers who were capable only of artfully expressing complaints without any rational plans for change.

Did that seem a bit harsh? Is such seeming blasphemy actually uncalled for regarding those *absolute failures* who you chumps so admire, and who helped us cause you to believe that simply complaining about injustice with a bit of finesse is an act worthy of adulation?

If so, please point out exactly what part of the Promised Land they've led you to. Why are you valetudinarians in the life threatening mess that this book has been pointing out?

***trigger warning: my usage of the term "life threatening" is <u>not</u> inclusive of the myriad "microaggressions" that are finally being astutely recognized and bravely eradicated from those "safe spaces" which once callously championed the safe exchange of logic-based ideas and were oppressively called "Institutions of Higher Learning", "Intellectual Journals", "News Networks", and "Newspapers".

Seriously; just look at your latest laughable attempts to pout and whine yourselves into the driver's seat of our intricate, remotely operated vehicle that has been precision engineered to slowly crush you, and that at best you can only faintly recognize; even though, ironically enough, you'd quickly perish without it.

The puerile attempts I'm referring to are:

1- The thoroughly infiltrated "Occupy Wall Street" movement;

2- The completely co-opted "Tea Party" movement;

3- The blind rage and professional rabble-rouser fueled marches, riots, and outright armed insurrections that began under the pretense of being a response to the unchecked excessive use of force by police, and then *diversified* to include the unchecked excessive use of "privilege" that's been enabled and encouraged through "systemic racism".

Yet, many of you conceptually corralled creatures believe that the best possible attempts at rectifying the injustice we've crafted were brought to fruition by those childish trick or treaters with the "brave patriot" and "indignant citizen" costumes on who "took their message to the streets".

Since you can't tell, **NONE OF YOU** have so much as a vague clue about the actual details and functionality of the vehicle whose tread marks are the insignia of everything you proudly wear and desire. The system is broken? **NOT**. That vehicle *is* the system.

"Also note that losers substitute complaints for action and idiots substitute action for thought."

In actuality, the only message that you and the well-meaning idiots and thug rioters at those protest rallies, political rallies, and marches/disruptions have made loud and clear is the same one made by the wankers of the 1960's:

Those who do not even occupy their own minds cannot possibly effectively occupy any area outside of an amusement park, an arena with professionally planned entertainment, the outskirts of a mechanized assembly line, a church/temple/mosque, a shopping mall, a waiting room, a drinking establishment/drug den, a sex shop, a jail cell, a toilet seat, or a couch near a television (ok, today you can also throw in an internet portal).

And the extent to which you professional victims can even effectively occupy such places is limited to your simply being there, following the instructions and having the resulting experiences that are issued to you by your superiors.

As of yet, you have been incapable of occupying in the manner of taking hold or possession of. Do you see it?

As of yet, the only thing any of you have actually been capable of is the consumption of the poison that is consuming you.

For once you must find the courage to act with FORESIGHT and RESOLVE.

By the way, you can be rest assured that some catastrophe (e.g., economic collapse, a pandemic, or an act of terrorism) will be engineered within or outside of the rally to force the issue at hand to be put on a back burner.

This cannot be allowed to happen under <u>any</u> circumstances.

You will each finally have to discover, within yourselves, the same insight-based resolve that freed your country in the first place.

Here's some food for thought on the subject at hand from Dr. Martin Luther King (the following are excerpts from a letter he wrote <u>while sitting in jail</u>. Bold emphasis is mine):

"I submit that an individual who breaks a law that conscience tells him is unjust, and willingly accepts the penalty by staying in jail to arouse the conscience of the community over its injustice, is in reality expressing the very highest respect for law.... **We can never forget that everything Hitler did in Germany was "legal" and everything the Hungarian freedom fighters did in Hungary was "illegal"....** Actually, we who engage in nonviolent direct action are not the creators of tension. We merely bring to the surface the hidden tension that is already alive. We bring it out in the open where it can be seen and dealt with. Like a boil that can never be cured as long as it is covered up but must be opened with all its pus-flowing ugliness to the natural medicines of air and light, injustice must likewise be exposed, with all of the tension its exposing creates, to the light of human conscience and the air of national opinion before it can be cured."

Read the entire letter: http://mlk-kpp01.stanford.edu:5801/transcription/document_images/undecided/630416-019.pdf

And, speaking of insight-based resolve, are you going to take it upon yourself to discover the meanings of the following words? Absolution, concession, emulate, dismal, artful, puerile, blasphemy, finesse, adulation, valetudinarian, resolve, inane, insignia, underling, omnibus, bevy, sessile, acquiescence, scrupulous, lucrative, thenceforth, contemptible, renounce.

3A – The groundwork for meaningful, coordinated planning of the rally must begin by July 4th of the year 2021. And it will, **IF** enough of you react to these insights as their being the valid testimony that they are.

You must immediately take the COMPLETELY PEACEFUL actions that are required of you to end the long running, concealed invasion and occupation of your country.

(A country whose creation was enabled by its founders willingness to engage in all-out war in order to establish as law the concepts that are expressed in the Declaration of Independence and the Constitution/Bill of Rights; which, besides the "Laws of Nature and of Nature's God", happen to be the only valid basis for any statutory law by which the country is to be governed. Judiciary reference to English Common Law can be expounded upon elsewhere.)

Or do you believe that by waiting to act on what must be done right now, until the next Presidential election cycle, the chances of your success will somehow be any better than they currently are?

Even though the stated policy agendas of "either" political party make absolutely no mention of a plan to rectify any of the far-reaching fundamental problems that, by way of dereliction of duty and deceit, have become institutionally woven into the fabric of your nation's systems of education, commerce, media, and governance?!

Do you finally see that the current **absolute disregard** for any pretense of a logic-based legitimacy within the "mainstream media", "big tech"/social media, the banking and investment industry, k-12 "education" and numerous other branches of "government" are nothing other than the outputs of a system that's been working exactly how it was designed to work?

If you do, good luck. You've got your work cut out for you. Try to name even a handful of people who you personally know that share your logic-based insight.

How else could tens of millions of your fellow Citizens believe in the legitimacy of the most blatant, ongoing Coup attempt against a duly-elected President to ever occur in your nation? (Click on these links to access a bevy of related documentation)

How else could they believe in the legitimacy of the most widespread and obvious election fraud that's ever been attempted outside of a military dictatorship? (Did anyone else notice that as of 11/7/2020, in regard to the search term "list of examples of election fraud 2020", the first nine pages of Google did not show any of the many documented examples of recent election fraud that have surfaced across your nation?)

And how else could those on either side of the arguments not know that, while real, they're really just surface-level diversions? (You're wearing a mask as you read this, right?)

Friend, regardless of which party's candidates' win, with each passing day the number and type of obstacles placed in your path will continue to grow at an increasing rate.

But make no mistake about it; many people throughout the history of your country have sacrificed much more, and have suffered much greater discomfort than will be required of anyone during this event.

Have you ever heard about those troops that George Washington led across the icy Delaware River, in a snow storm, on Christmas night in 1776, so they could then march nine (9) miles through the snow into Trenton New Jersey - *without any boots on their feet* - and win a battle that changed the entire course of the Revolutionary War?

3ʙ - Organizers of this event must effectively present it to all American Citizens and the rest of the world as a peaceful, properly organized, constitutionally protected, Declaration of Independence-mandated effort to thwart an outright invasion of your country. No effort can be spared to make sure that all of the goals of this campaign are achieved.

But there must not be any celebrity meet and greet going on at the rally.

Unless they wish to fully join in with the actual rugged, freedom-loving patriots who volunteer, those plaster saints can get stroked elsewhere. This rally is not a photo op.

Just imagine the level of public interest that a star's full participation would spark!

Good luck! If the lack of your beloved stage and screen stars' widespread involvement does not prove to you that an absolute disrespect exists within them for those whose stupidity supports their lavish lifestyle, then nothing short of the outright physical enslavement that's coming to all of you will ever wake you or them from your lives of delusion.

I mean, this is not an invitation to a low end keg party.

No, it is quite the opposite. And their disinterest will be undeniable proof that they too are unaware of the fact that they are nothing but disposable hired hands being employed in the Colosseum to keep you gorging on the sex, slaughter, slander, and sport that aids in the diversion of your awareness from the actuality of your enfeebled existence.

But maybe I'm wrong.

Maybe they really are a bunch of fine patriots who, although they certainly aren't going to get down in the trenches with the common folk during the rally, will actually help finance it by presenting an omnibus type of continuous nationwide tour (music, stand-up comedy, theatrical sketches, readings of pertinent historical speeches, etc.).

It can begin previous to the culmination of the rally in Washington D.C. and run daily for over a year, while featuring different entertainers in different cities in order to accommodate their schedules.

The full proceeds can then be <u>loaned</u> to fellow patriots who wish to do their part to insure the rally's success, but are lacking the funds required to fully participate as outlined later on.

Such actions certainly would NOT diminish any of their star power.

Really, what would those fine patriots have to lose by undertaking such an endeavor?

They'll all get paid for their work. Such "money" would be <u>contractually loaned out</u>.

And their patriotic performances would be protected by the first amendment; right?

Golly, those fine patriotic entertainers sure would raise a whole lot of dough if they were to do something like that.

They would also be able to raise a whole lot of consciousness too.

Not to mention the fact that the first major star who officially announces their plans to act as such will be immortalized with Paul Revere-like status. **Good luck!**

And speaking of sport, will the lack of your beloved professional athletes' widespread involvement prove to you that the highly promoted "show of respect" they gave to the memory of a fellow professional named Pat Tillman was really just a circus routine?

If not, then nothing short of the outright physical enslavement that's coming will ever wake you or them from your lives of delusion.

In case you aren't aware of it, Pat Tillman was an actual rugged, freedom-loving patriot who put his life and considerable fortune on the line for what he thought was a noble cause.

He turned down a multi-million dollar renewal of his NFL contract in order to join the military in 2002 and go overseas to try to do his part in securing the safety and freedom of his fellow countrymen. Did I mention that he was happily married?

Is that not the height of putting your money where your mouth is?

But he ended up getting murdered because of his plans to report on all of the wrongdoing he was personally witnessing.

And the details of his murder were then covered up at very high levels of "government".

Why not Google him and look into it?

Since Pat Tillman attempted to do much more for the cause of freedom than:

Wear a t-shirt with a "trending" tagline: http://www.chicagotribune.com/sports/breaking/chi-lebron-james-eric-garner-protest-20141208-htmlstory.html

Or "Tweet" a "socially conscious message": http://www.foxsports.com/buzzer/story/athletes-react-to-ferguson-news-via-twitter-112414

Or sport a "patriotic" tattoo and complain about some players on the other side of the field not putting their hand over their heart during a performance of the overhyped diversionary jingle that you all robotically get out of your seats to show a passionate false reverence to: http://profootballtalk.nbcsports.com/2011/12/19/jeremy-shockey-texans-disrespected-america-during-national-anthem/

Isn't it completely reasonable to believe that the genuine, meaningful show of respect for the memory of Pat Tillman (and the many other victims of corrupt "government" operatives and institutions), by those athletes would be nothing less than:

Making the comparably insignificant personal sacrifices needed in order to participate fully in what will bring about that which every soldier and civil-rights activist who has ever died in the name of freedom believed they were fighting for. That makes sense, no?

Good luck! Don't those articles just highlight what a lost flock you really are!

You sessile stooges must finally learn that you do _not_ need help or permission to do this from any of the current representatives in our varied line of the false incarnations of power, beauty, intellect, talent, or virtue that we created long ago and still use with precision to convince you that you are incapable of worthwhile success without first being molded into some commercially available likeness of their well-crafted image, and then receiving their blessings and assistance.

Yes, it's true, we actually cause you to believe that a properly functioning human existence is one which, unbeknownst to you, happens to be equivalent to that of an opiate addict whose only method of survival is to be employed by us so that you can seemingly afford to continually pay us huge fees in order to exist within the all-encompassing den we have constructed for the purpose of doing great harm to you.

Indeed, U.S.A. actually stands for _United State of Acquiescence._

Can you _not_ be made aware of the fact that all of the insights I am sharing with you are valid testimony? Are you thoroughly lost within the labyrinth of the elaborate scam being run on you?

I'm betting big that you are.

Perhaps Ben Franklin was on to something when, as legend has it, in response to a question regarding the type of government that would be implemented in the United States of America he replied, "A republic, if you can keep it".

Or has the time come that the entire world will witness the massive, properly organized, peaceful, _lawful_ act of the alteration of oppressive "government"?

The Declaration of Independence declares it to be your unalienable right and _duty_.

Currently, you do not have any idea of what an effect on your own consciousness, and the consciousness of your fellow citizens and the rest of the world, that an enormous and conceptually sound, long-term act of solidarity as I am about to detail would have.

How could you? There's never been an attempt, or a suggestion, to accomplish anything even remotely similar. Not even in a work of fiction.

Yet, rationally speaking does that mean it can't happen?

Ponder the following line as you picture but a fraction of the discoveries, inventions, and events that have shattered popular notions of the limits of possibility:

"Winners' situations are created by viewpoint. Losers' viewpoints are created by situation."

I assure you that if you actually make this rally happen, as per my forthcoming scrupulous directions, there will be a nationwide abundance of honest, capable candidates who would each gladly guarantee in writing, their votes to bring forth the reform that is this rally's purpose.

Like I said, this rally is <u>not</u> about asking those in power to make concessions. It's about telling them, and the rest of the world, that you've come to collect your rightful inheritance.

I do hate to put you on the spot; but are you going to wait for someone else to light the fuse?

Will you do anything more than buy a rally-related, sweat shop produced knock off hat or t-shirt and lie to everyone that you support the cause?

I'm betting that, at best, you would check out what's happening at the event during the commercial breaks of the instantly gratifying diversions that you'd still be immersed in.

Fact: if you do not prove me wrong, you are proving me right.

So where are all of the rugged, freedom-loving patriots who are each willing to go outside of their comfort zone and earn $250,000 plus, tax free, in this desperate time of need?

4 – Since very few of you can act systematically without guidance, let me explain in detail how this event is going to have to be organized and carried out in order to insure unity, efficiency, and success.

These instructions can easily be followed by a fourteen year old child. But, in order to *understand* the remaining contents of this book, you will be forced to expand your current conceptual limit.

Are you ready to do the extremely lucrative work that's required in order to discover and master the techniques that enable proper self-determination?

Starting within each school district in each state, volunteers will have to begin forming two groups ("Home" and "Away") that will each be comprised of two thousand (2000) **d**ivisions.

There will be fifty (50) **v**olunteers in each "Away" **d**ivision and at least that amount of volunteers in each "Home" **d**ivision.

In other words, each state will have a total of at least 200,000 volunteers.

50(**v**) x 2,000(**d**) = 100,000. 100,000 x 2(**g**) = 200,000 volunteers per state.

Each school district should be represented by as many people as possible; so that, within each division, as many people as possible already know one another.

This will be a measure of insurance against infiltration by "governmental" agent provocateurs.

Each volunteer will need to commit themselves to a <u>minimum</u> sixteen (16) month "tour of duty". Yes, that's approximately one and one half years. Yes, that's $250,000 plus, tax free.

Too long for ya?

Tell it to the soldiers who have spent more time than that recovering from the wounds they suffered during tours of duty in hostile lands, in the name of your country.

Prove to them how much you appreciate their "having your back".

Tell it to your children and grandchildren - whose outright slavery is the actual price for your current way of life.

The "Home" group will be comprised of both male and female volunteers who are at least fourteen (14) years old or entering the ninth (9th) grade at the start of the upcoming school year. Such volunteers will be working strictly on the local and state level.

They will, in fact, be the nervous system of the rally. The "Home" group will be responsible for the following:

1 - Spreading the word about the rally's purpose and goals from person to person on the most local levels and through constant well-planned efforts to have such information accurately announced daily through all forms of established news media.

2 - Coordinating the efforts of each of its divisions and constantly sharing information regarding every successful technique that is employed.

3 - Building, maintaining, and constantly updating the official website and social media accounts for the rally; and constantly increasing the amount of quality traffic they all receive.

4 - Coordinating qualified personnel to conduct the many tasks that will be required in order for there to be a successful, engaging, continual broadcast of all aspects of the rally.

5 - Coordinating all of the many deliveries of goods that will be needed by the "Away" group.

6 - High level managerial interactions with the companies that will be making those deliveries. The need for such interaction will be explained in further detail later in this book.

Needless to say, a great deal of the success for both the "Away" group and *all essential operations* will be dependent upon the well-planned, ongoing efforts of the "Home" group.

The "Away" group will be comprised strictly of males who are at least eighteen years old (18) and without any mental or physical handicap that would prevent them from being able to complete any of the tasks that are outlined in the following paragraphs. **They will each be required to leave home for a minimum of sixteen months, for training and deployment.**

Such volunteers must all be male because of:

1 - The otherwise unavoidable physical attraction and intimacy which will occur and severely distract the volunteers if males and females are intermingled in this aspect of the operation. http://www.washingtonpost.com/wp-dyn/content/article/2007/02/12/AR2007021201657.html

2- The fact that even a single, unconfirmed case of sexual misconduct being reported upon in the news would instantaneously cast the entire nationwide effort in a negative light.

3 - The fact that, under the circumstances that will be present, the many special allowances that would be required to accommodate both sexes hygienic needs, their privacy, and their safety would be unreasonable when compared to any arguable advantage that a female presence might provide in terms of the success of the operation.

Rational minds will not view this as a humiliating discourtesy.

No-one whose opinion is worth listening to doubts the female ability to stand toe to toe with the men here.

Those of you who are inclined to challenge these directions must not allow yourselves to act out upon misinformed emotions.

In the name of reason, carefully consider how your efforts can be most helpful in eliminating the traitorous parasites that are working to bankrupt you in every possible way under the flag waving guise of legitimate governance.

Carefully consider the fact that you are, in effect, trapped within a structure that is engulfed in flames. Under such circumstances it is not in your best interest to do anything other than attempt to leave the premises in the quickest, most orderly fashion possible.

In consideration of both the scenario I just illustrated and the literal object of this rally effort, can it be deemed wise to also make this an attempt at a superfluous, long-term, large scale group mastery over what is arguably our most powerful biological impulse?

Does a lack of mutual interest necessarily extinguish the literally intoxicating sexual desires one might have?

Understand that this is not a military operation where constant disciplinarian supervision and the imminent threat of danger are often sufficient means to prevent the occurrence of actions that would be detrimental to a stated end.

Is it possible that the "Away" group could achieve its stated end, which you haven't even read yet, with the inclusion of females?

Of course it is; **but does a reasonable human being add any level of complexity and difficulty to an already difficult, utterly important task?**

If everyone shares their unique talents and full efforts in accordance with these directions, the wholesome object of this rally effort will be achieved. Make no mistake; this is sound advice.

Note that this topic <u>will</u> be seen by those who are in opposition to the success of the rally as a potential powder keg and an extremely targetable weak spot upon which to stage a disruptive and possibly fully destructive attack.

As such, a well-organized preemptive educational campaign must be implemented as soon as possible. It must discredit any of the divisive actions and claims which are sure to be made by the opposition. It must be based upon the previous sixteen sentences and the fact that such an arrangement is in no way advocating or even insinuating the preposterous idea of a female inability to succeed here.

The campaign must initially be carried out by the female members of the "Home" group.

I'm talking about those females who understand the above explanations; those who understand the fact that such divisive action and claims are but one of the techniques we have long been using with great success to destroy the family unit and increase the number of those who unwittingly ensure that we employ them for our nefarious purposes.

To find the right emotional hook go with proven success.

For instance, look toward a couple of those brands who have conquered your otherwise barren mental landscape:

Aim for a well-balanced mix between that iconic, old television commercial run by the supremely popular cola company from Atlanta who was recently successfully sued by some of their employees for being **racially discriminatory**, which said something along the lines of wanting to teach the world to "sing in perfect harmony": http://abcnews.go.com/US/story?id=94989

And the long running advertising campaign by the Italian clothing company/massive conglomerate (that has been, among other shady dealings, looking to unjustly profit from you through the **privatization of many thousands of miles of highway in your country**) that cleverly ties simple visuals into their usage of the otherwise ambiguous statement "United colors": https://web.archive.org/web/20071008132002/http://www.santarosarecuperada.com.ar/english/benetton_empire.html

Make no mistake about it; this recommendation is as serious as a heart attack.

And make no mistake about this: <u>all</u> of the actual sources of the opposition's funding and direction must be quickly discovered and widely broadcast and discredited.

As I've already stated, a great deal of the success of the "Away" group will ultimately be in the hands of the "Home" group.

So there will be plenty of pride and glory to be had by everyone if they are each dedicated to their assigned tasks.

4_A – During training, the entire "Away" group will be stationed on the outskirts of their respective state capitals for four (4) months. **That training begins March 1st 2024, at 12pm.**

This gives willing volunteers ample time to secure the funds they will need to participate, as outlined a little later, and to get their affairs in order before "shipping out".

It will also allow every division enough time to be fully trained and to arrive at their exact deployment location in Washington D.C. by the morning of **July 2nd, 2024**. (Why July 2nd? It'll give the men two days to prepare, on location, for their epic Fourth of July shindig.)

Being without air-conditioning during the summer will be uncomfortable, and the following winter in Washington D.C. will surely bring plenty of rough weather.

So make sure to read up on your nation's history a.s.a.p. in order to become aware of the fact that plenty of women and children have survived worse conditions in the land of the free and the home of the brave.

Not to mention that no-one will be required to march nine miles through snow without boots on; let alone doing so in order to then engage in an actual chaotic battle to the death.

Each of the two thousand divisions of fifty men in each state will be made up firstly of men from the same school district. And whenever necessary, divisions will be assembled with men who live in adjoining school districts.

Volunteers will be bumped out of divisions comprised wholly of men from their own school district before anyone is placed in a division whose members are not all from adjoining school districts.

If no-one is willing to volunteer to get bumped into another division, numbers will be blindly pulled from a box until someone picks the number "one". That guy gets bumped. That guy will survive.

He is not going to be shipped to a different theater of war. At worst, he will ultimately be deployed about one or two miles away from everyone in his home school district.

And, he'll be spending his time with fellow Citizens who will become some of his closest friends for life.

Divisions will be identified by their state name and a number that will be blindly pulled from a box after each group has been assigned a temporary number from one to two thousand.

The first group whose temporary number is picked will be named the 2,000th division from that state, the second group picked will be named the 1st division from that state, the third group picked will be named the 1,999th division, and the fourth group picked will be named the 2nd division, etc.

They will learn to become extremely efficient, interchangeable work units. And each individual will learn to act appropriately in all situations which may arise. They will each learn first aid, CPR, and proper hygiene protocols.

They will each learn how to start and maintain a fire, and how to quickly assemble and disassemble their tent in the dark.

They will each learn how to expertly construct and blindly assemble, disassemble, utilize, and even repair numerous fairly simple mechanical devices (to be mentioned later) which will be crucial to their success.

They will each perform numerous types of exercise, such as fully loaded hikes, for two hours per day. And they will each help setup and maintain what will amount to vast vegetable gardens, with fruit trees, that will continue to be cultivated by the "Home" group when the men leave the area.

For at least five hours per day, each man will study the following vital information:

1- The Declaration of Independence;

2- "Commentaries on the Laws of England, Book the First, Chapter 1 – Of the Absolute Rights of Individuals" by William Blackstone;

3- The pamphlet "No Treason" by Lysander Spooner;

4- The Constitution/Bill of Rights;

5- Their own state Constitution;

6- All of the concepts brought forth in this book and all of the information it links readers to.

Each man will discover the value of his estimable inheritance and gain the tools necessary to reclaim it.

They will each learn to precisely and persuasively express the facts relating to all of the above-mentioned material and the fundamental concepts upon which such material is based - regardless of the beliefs, opinions, or distractive techniques used by anyone they might speak with.

They will each come to be expertly aware of every inch of the area they'll ultimately be deployed in.

This, of course, includes knowledge of every fire hydrant, sewer, sewer cap, gas line, train line, bus line, and public bathroom facility (and their full schedule of availability), within two and a half miles of the mall in Washington D.C..

Furthermore, since that area is surrounded by water, they will also learn the tide table and carry a printed chart of it upon being deployed.

And, of no less importance, they will each learn to maintain peaceful, positive interactions within each division of fifty men and within the entire two thousand divisions in each state;

without there being any definitively empowered hierarchy of leadership.

Each division will become a precisely run machine that is fully capable of operating indefinitely without direction from any "superiors" or the loss of any part causing detriment to the whole

They will also be able to instantaneously fully integrate with the full number of other divisions nationwide.

When every man realizes that every other man is literally putting it all on the line for the same exact reasons, they will begin to form unbreakable lifelong bonds of friendship and mutual admiration.

And that last point being accomplished will be the final link in the chain that's going to ensure the success of the rally and the future success of every concerted effort that the Citizens of your nation decide to undertake.

Within the first twenty-four (24) hours of their arrival at "camp", all of the volunteers in each division will work together to establish basic guidelines and scheduling for individual and group responsibilities relating to exercise, mechanical training, group study, and numerous daily duties, etc., which will be mentioned a little later.

After that, a new volunteer will assume the leadership of their fifty man division each day. The order in which such leadership will occur will be worked out in the same manner as the numbering of divisions.

They'll each get to lead twice, so he who goes first also goes last.

After each man has led twice, the entire division will vote for the five men they feel are best qualified to represent them as spokesmen in their dealings with other divisions when they are deployed.

Each of those five men will then have an additional four (4) day period as division leader, after which time another vote will be held to choose a single division spokesman from among those five men.

Once chosen, the official division spokesman will be the sole communications contact with the home group.

This spokesman is not anyone's boss.

He is simply the person responsible for all of the coordination of his division's required activity, and the liaison that is needed between divisions to insure efficient communication and coordination between large groups of men.

Unfortunately, his job will also include being a petty dispute arbitrator.

The best spokesmen will figure out how to manage such problems with wisdom and grace, and they will be rewarded for their efforts.

Weekly competition relating to efficiency in mechanical tasks and group preparedness will be held between divisions.

Winning divisions will have their accomplishment and their picture posted on the official website of the rally.

4B – When deployed to their exact pre-planned location point in Washington D.C., each state division will join all of the other state divisions that have been given the same identifying number as themselves.

This will make each division into a 2,500 man "platoon" that will function as such and which will be identified by the same number that identifies each of its divisions.

Within **one hour** of every division having arrived at their destination point in Washington D.C., each division spokesman will address their entire 2,500 man platoon with a speech that is approximately three minutes in length, and which:

1- Summarizes his beliefs on why it is important that they are all there.

2- Explains how he thinks the country should move forward after the event has achieved its goals.

3- Explains what he thinks they can do to most effectively share their message with the tourists who will be in the area.

All speeches will be videotaped and uploaded to the official website of the event and to "YouTube".

The order of delivery will be decided upon by assigning each leader with a number from one to fifty, and then blindly picking numbers from a box.

The first man whose number is picked will be the first to go.

To insure that the order doesn't enable plagiarization, a copy of each speech will be submitted to the group of men who actually picked the numbers from the box.

After hearing all of the speeches, the men will vote for their ten favorites. After a short break, those ten division leaders will then re-read their speeches; when they have all been re-read, the men will vote for their favorite single speech.

Those division leaders whose speeches were voted in the top ten will become "squadron" spokesmen. (Regarding squadron matters, each will be the spokesman for the five divisions that comprise it.)

The divisions that will make up each squadron will be chosen by way of each squadron spokesman blindly picking a number from one to ten from a box, and then having the state name of each division whose spokesman was <u>not</u> picked as a squadron leader put into the now empty box (His division will automatically be in his squadron.).

The first division that is blindly picked from the box will be assigned to the squadron spokesman who was designated as number one. The second division that is blindly picked from the box will be assigned to the squadron spokesman who was designated as number two, etc., until all divisions are assigned to a squadron.

Those ten groups of five divisions of 250 men will then be referred to as "squadrons" and temporarily numbered from one to ten by way of assigning each squadron with a number from one to ten, and then blindly picking numbers from a box. The first squadron picked is permanently referred to as number ten. The second is number two, etc.

Each division will always be stationed directly next to those other divisions that are part of their squadron. And whenever needed, each 250 man squadron will function as a single unit.

The division leader whose speech was voted as the best of those ten squadron spokesmen will also become the spokesman for their entire 2,500 man platoon.

Within **seven hours** of arriving at their destination point in Washington D.C., and in the presence of all 2,500 men, the ten squadron leaders that make up the platoon will establish a system for all of the duties that need to be carried out among the men.

Such duties will include water gathering and distribution, food distribution, garbage removal, waste removal, mail collection and distribution, "toilet kit" rotation scheduling, and surveillance duty, etc.

The men will all be absolutely familiar with every aspect of every duty mentioned.

They will have been carrying out the same exact duties every single day for the previous four months. The only thing that will have changed for them is the location.

The entire meeting will be videotaped and uploaded to the official website of the event and to "YouTube".

Within **nine hours** of arriving in Washington D.C., each of the spokesmen from the 2,000 platoons will meet with those spokesmen from the twenty platoons whose numbers are closest to it.

(Meaning that the spokesmen from platoons numbered one through twenty will meet, while spokesmen from platoons numbered twenty-one through forty will meet, etc.)

The entire meeting process will be videotaped and uploaded to the official website of the event, and to "YouTube".

Each group of twenty platoons will form a "company".

Each group of twenty platoon spokesmen will listen to each other's speech that earned them their current position as platoon spokesman, and they will then vote on a singular spokesman for their company.

They will then work out a schedule of daily duties for their 50,000 man company which will include, among other things:

Water gathering and distribution; food distribution; garbage removal; waste removal; mail collection and distribution; surveillance duty; and the company relocation that will occur every three (3) days.

Each company will be assigned an identifying number from one to one hundred, and the lowest number will be assigned to the company made up of the lowest numbered platoons. (Meaning that the company which is made up of the platoons numbered one through twenty will be named "company one", etc.)

Within **twelve hours** of arriving in Washington D.C., each of the one hundred company spokesmen will meet, and the spokesmen will form ten groups of ten men with each group based upon the identifying number of their company.

(Meaning companies numbered one through ten will meet with each other, while companies numbered eleven through twenty will meet with each other, etc.)

The entire meeting will be videotaped and uploaded to the official website of the event and to "YouTube".

Each ten-company group will form a "battalion".

Each of those ten battalions will then choose a singular spokesman based upon the same procedures that were used in the previous votes.

The battalions will identify themselves based upon a number from one to ten which will be decided upon by the identifying numbers of the companies it is made up of.

(Meaning that the group of companies numbered one through ten will be named "battalion one", and the group of companies numbered eleven through twenty will be named "battalion two", etc.)

The ten men who will each be the official spokesman for a single battalion (totaling 500,000 men) will be responsible for coordinating all battalion movements (which will occur every fifteen (15) days), and for all-manner of coordination with the people who will be their "Home" battalion counterparts and contacts.

Within **fourteen hours** of arriving in Washington D.C., each "Away" battalion spokesman will personally meet their "Home" battalion counterparts whom they are now teamed with. The entire meeting will be videotaped and uploaded to the official website of the event and to "YouTube".

The people who hold such positions within the "Home" group will have earned their rank in a manner similar to their "Away" counterparts, but such rank will have been established one (1) month earlier than that of the "Away" group.

And each "Home" division, squadron, platoon, company, and battalion will have five (5) spokespeople. Thus, "Home" division leaders will, from the start, always be working together in teams of five.

And each of the five spokespeople for each "Home" battalion will be from a different state. With the technology in existence, this will not cause any inconvenience.

"Home" battalions, companies, platoons, and squadrons will have been formed with regard to physical proximity.

Eight of those ten battalions will be formed by combining five connected states:

1 - Rhode Island, Massachusetts, Vermont, New Hampshire, Maine;

2 - Delaware, Pennsylvania, New Jersey, New York, Connecticut;

3 - Maryland, Virginia, West Virginia, Ohio, Michigan;

4 - North Carolina, South Carolina, Georgia, Alabama, Florida;

5 - Tennessee, Kentucky, Missouri, Arkansas, Mississippi;

6 - Indiana, Illinois, Iowa, Wisconsin, Minnesota;

7 - Louisiana, Texas, Oklahoma, Kansas, Nebraska;

8 - Colorado, New Mexico, South Dakota, North Dakota, Wyoming.

The other two will be formed by combining "closely" situated and connected states:

9 - Montana, Idaho, Oregon, Washington, Alaska;

10 - California, Arizona, Nevada, Utah, and Hawaii.

Each state will be represented by two (2) companies. Each company will obviously be made up of platoons that are all from the same state and whose squadrons are made up of divisions that are in closest proximity to each other.

During this meeting, each "Away" battalion spokesman will receive a fully charged "smart" phone and a solar battery charger.

The phone will be used <u>solely</u> for immediate twenty-four (24) hour contact with the "Home" battalion spokespeople that they are teamed with.

They will be the only people who are in contact with each other regarding any type of "Home" and "Away" coordination and planning.

Usage of the phone for any unauthorized purpose will result in the battalion spokesman's immediate dismissal from their position.

Such contact and coordination will determine which roads are taken by drivers for their delivery of food, mail, etc., and for the actual timing and location of such deliveries and certain pickups.

Obviously they will occur very late at night so as to avoid traffic. But such coordination is also important because half of each battalion's men will need to be in the proper position to quickly unload/load the trucks, and to distribute the goods to every man in every division of the battalion.

"Away" battalion spokesmen will always immediately share all such information, in writing, to each of the other battalion spokesmen and with the nine "company" spokesmen that serve with them directly.

This can certainly be done by way of email when possible. Each "Home" battalion can send the finalized information to their "Away" counterpart in an email that they will each personally proofread for accuracy and then forward to their above-mentioned partners who will each verify receipt.

Company spokesmen will then pass such information on to their platoon spokesmen who will do the same in regard to their squadron spokesmen, etc. They can also use email.

If an "Away" battalion spokesman is ever incapacitated in any way, the nine company spokesmen that serve with him directly will immediately vote for his replacement.

The replacement will be given the phone. Should his incapacitation be projected as long-term, such replacement will occur as far back down the line as needed.

In such an event, the other nine battalion spokesmen will each immediately contact their "Home" battalion teammates to let them know that the person who will be calling the "Home" battalion teammates of the incapacitated person is, in fact, who they say they are.

That phone call will not be made until this procedure has been completed, but it will be made immediately thereafter.

In the case of a "Home" battalion spokesperson being incapacitated, the other company spokespeople from his or her state will immediately vote for his or her replacement.

Immediately after the vote, each of the other battalion spokespeople will be informed of the result and operations will carry on as planned.

Take note: a large portion of the details which need to be understood for the successful operation of the rally to occur are located in what would appear to be an addendum in the back of this book. Although such information is <u>absolutely vital</u>, it has been relegated to the back of the bus so as to not push the boundaries of the famously fleet American attention span (page <u>257</u>, sections **4C** through **4H** can be found there).

4_I - **During the day, the "Away" group will look like the biggest parade route of all time.**

Everywhere around and within the mall, and on both sides of the main streets for quite some distance, there will be multi-layered groups of ten (10) men occupying a 25ft wide area.

Each will be stationed at each other's end, almost shoulder to shoulder; so that from above, or from the middle of the street, it will be apparent that there are many extremely long columns of men.

Each group will be packed as deep with the volunteers as they need to be, in order to have the maximum amount of men in place for the rally without blocking the way of anyone walking by.

The groups of men will <u>always</u> have only other groups of their fellow volunteers behind them; so that the long walls they form are always facing out, both forward and back.

This will enable the creation of standard sized corridors between each "wall" being formed by the men on the mall, so that there is always a clear pathway for people to walk; and so that no-one who is not a volunteer would be able to simply blend into the crowd to possibly cause a problem without being identified and detained until the police came to take them away.

Each group of ten men will have a 25ft x 2ft banner in their "toilet kit" that will be hung daily between two poles from the kit.

When tarps are put up in bad weather, the banners will be hanging against the front and back of the enclosure; so that people walking by will easily be able to see and read them.

Each banner will be made of red plastic sheeting that can be rolled up. And it will have a reinforced hole near the center of its top long edge and in each top corner. Each top hole will accommodate a carabiner, and at both bottom corners there will be two twelve-inch long, Velcro-covered ties made from the same sheeting material.

The words on each banner will have been printed in white paint in a standard font.

Each banner will have a different message on it relating to either an aspect of the injustice that this book and the links it offers points out, or one of the things that are explained in the final section of this book that you need to do to redeem yourself.

Each group of men under each banner will always be wearing the same colored clothes and cap so that their appearance is uniform, enabling the entire rally to be presented in both a visually pleasing manner and as a fully integrated and properly organized effort.

Regardless of the season, they will be wearing long-sleeved t-shirts and pants made of a suitable weighted fabric that is loose fitting and very comfortable.

This will also help keep them from getting eaten alive by bugs in warm weather.

All of their clothing will be navy blue; so as to create a red, white, and blue effect in conjunction with the banner and the white baseball cap they will each be wearing.

As the men stand under their banners they will offer all interested parties a friendly, well-articulated explanation of that topic, with plenty of examples to support their claims.

All non-interested parties will receive a warm greeting with a smile, but they will not get bothered in any way by the men.

Each man will always have a number of business cards on him that will have the web addresses of both the official website of the campaign and this book on one side, and a powerful quote regarding freedom, justice, education, the proper role of government, etc., by one of the founding fathers of your country on the other side.

4ⱼ - During the day, as many of you who are active or retired policemen or military who volunteer for the rally will always be dressed in an official-looking white and gold outfit that clearly lets everyone know who you are and exactly what position you currently or previously serve/served in law enforcement and/or the military.

And you will be stationed at certain intervals throughout the open corridors and on all street corners (depending on how many of you there are), so as to project an atmosphere of order and safety to all of the people who are watching the event on television and the internet; and to actually maintain that atmosphere on location without causing any feeling of tension in the people who are in the area, but not officially involved in the rally.

In the event that the "government" sends a martial force of police and/or military into the area, surveillance units will alert you in advance of their arrival. You will need to quickly assemble to present yourselves united, though unarmed, as a barrier of "white knights" between the traitors in black riot gear and the rest of your fellow volunteers.

In other words, you will be demonstrating to the world what a law enforcement presence whose functionality is fully consistent with the Declaration of Independence and Constitution/Bill of Rights looks like.

At night, you will be doing the same work as every other volunteer in your division.

All active and retired police and military who are not able to volunteer for the rally full-time, but who wish to lend their presence for certain shorter lengths of time, will be welcome to participate on a part-time basis. Yes, "all" means both men and women.

All such people will be utilized only on the outermost perimeters of the rally, having limited actual contact with the full-time volunteers.

All such people will be subject to eating and sleeping accommodations that are separate from the rest of the men. In other words, you will basically be out of actual contact with the full-time volunteers; other than those who are battalion and company leaders. Unless the fit hits the shan.

Those of you who wish to participate will have to contact members of the "Home" group who will be coordinating such participation and the training it will require. Should those people not be personally known to you, a link to their contact information will be clearly posted on the home page of the official website of the rally.

Now, don't forget the section in the back of this book that offers many details which need to be taken into account in order to ensure proper function and procedure for the "Away" group. What you have read thus far is a mere outline that, on its own, will insure as much success as the infamous screen door on a submarine; or voting Republican or Democrat.

And don't believe for a second that holding the rally is any guarantee that the changes you need to make to your "government" will ever actually be made.

You need to have Constitutional amendments passed.

You folks are going to have to have two-thirds (2/3) of both houses of Congress vote for the needed amendments to be proposed, or have at least two-thirds (2/3) of the states call for a Constitutional convention to be held.

And then at least three-fourths (3/4) of the states of the Union will have to ratify the proposed amendments by way of either the state legislators or ratifying conventions. Either route will require dedication to the cause.

And though it's not mandatory, electing Governors who are committed to the cause in the states that will be holding such elections in 2022, and 2023 really wouldn't be a bad thing.

Filling the vast majority of the House of Representatives, the thirty-four (34) Senate seats that will be up for grabs in 2022 if no-one retires, and, of course, the Presidency in 2024 wouldn't hurt the cause either.

4ₖ – What's the greatest obstacle to the implementation and success of this plan? Your inability to understand and believe in the practicality of the method I am about to provide for the funding and supply of the food and other goods that will be needed.

Well, that *and* your unwillingness to get off of your behinds to make it happen.

The explanation for your inability to understand and believe in the practicality of the method I am going to provide is quite simple and is as follows:

In concert with the fact that your mental capacities have been chemically and psychologically weakened, you sharecroppers have purposely never been educated in the ways that truly large scale operations are actually brought to fruition.

Simply stated, our methods of control prevent you from surpassing the "bake sale" mentality.

We keep you from ever gaining the courage and brains needed to be able to formulate a plan with truly far-reaching capabilities.

You have been forced into a situation where all of your plans must be quite limited in order to accomplish any type of goal that appears even remotely independent of our self-serving involvement.

Without having us loan you "money", your only option is to appeal to whatever limited aspects of your community might be willing to provide you with donations and/or direct voluntary assistance.

The method I am going to provide is radically different because it is based upon certain of the economic concepts that have been used to gain and maintain our control over you.

And because of our propaganda and strict usage of esoteric terminology regarding this field of endeavor, the simplicity and stated far-reaching effects of this method will cause you to doubt its validity.

But if you are able to logically examine this method, you will see that it is absolutely valid.

You will also see that it utilizes some of the same basic techniques that we have been successfully controlling you with; the main difference being the fact that we never actually need to "raise capital".

   Without scaring anyone off by getting into too much detail, here is what must be done:

Each of the five million men who volunteer for the "Away" group of the rally must invest exactly four ounces (4) of gold, or two hundred and thirty-five and one-half ounces (235.5) of silver, or the equivalent amount of Federal Reserve notes.

Whether they do this by way of their own "money" or by way of begging and/or borrowing from one hundred people is up to them. As you'll soon see, they'll each get back way more than what they put in.

Individuals who volunteer for the "Home" group and those human individuals who do not volunteer at all will also be able to invest that exact amount, no more and no less.

Investors will each be issued one share of a "stock" that no-one can ever lawfully own more than one share of and that can only be owned by Citizens of the United States of America.

And wealthy individuals and businesses would be wise to sponsor/loan needed funds to as many volunteers as they possibly can. As you'll soon see, such loans will easily be paid back.

Such action would be wise since it is the only way to protect what they've got.

Though they will not lawfully gain interest on such loans, it is the only true safe haven left for them to invest in. If you haven't already figured it out, in keeping with the history of tyranny, everything else is on schedule to be drastically devalued and legally stolen.

Not to mention the fact that if you poseurs make sure the rally succeeds, no-one will be paying income tax or numerous other taxes ever again. Re-read that last sentence.

I would just make sure that my loans were given directly to the trustees of the rally fund, and that it was contractually stipulated that I get my investment back before any volunteer I sponsored was able to get any monetary payout from the rally. But that's me.

Now imagine if that nationwide entertainment tour I spoke of earlier were to happen…

Patriots using their star power to raise, and eventually bank, tons of "money" in order to help the public finally do what's needed for everyone to leave the cave.

Should they do this for free? **NO WAY.**

FYI, looking for handouts is what caused the mess you're in.

What a simple, easy to execute, mutually-beneficial method of making sure that every qualified person who desires to be a member of the "Away" group can afford to do it.

What a simple, easy to execute, mutually-beneficial method of making sure that those star powered patriots have the perfect platform to help educate the public and prepare them to take proper action. Actually, solo tours with the same purpose probably wouldn't hurt…

If no-one but the "Away" group volunteers decide to contribute, there will be the equivalent of about twenty-five and a half **billion** "dollars" ($25,500,000,000) in the rally fund.

Those funds must be contributed in the manner stated above so that the further purposeful devaluation of Federal Reserve notes will not be able to thwart this plan.

4L - Are you an actual rugged, freedom-loving patriot who is willing to ante up? Do you believe that enough of your fellow citizens are actually going to join you, to make this rally happen? If so, you should run out immediately after reading the next sentence and buy gold and/or silver.

The kind of gold or silver that you can actually put in your pocket and hold onto; not a *supposed* investment for which you will merely be handed a receipt that claims to be proof of your *supposed* purchase which is "being held in a vault" somewhere.

This should be done so that, when the "dollar" drops even more, you will be able to hand in your share of precious metal.

It will have cost you way less than it will be costing those who might eventually be willing to contribute, but who will wait to act until the rally is starting to attract large numbers of volunteers.

And if this rally never occurs, you will have still made a wise investment. Doesn't the idea of getting your hands on something that's guaranteed to retain a heck of a lot more buying power than the Federal Reserve's "legal tender" make sense?

Of course, whether or not there will be anything to buy with that gold and silver is another story; as is your ability to protect it from seizure, legal or otherwise.

A portion of the accumulated metals will be used to strategically buy companies that produce certain goods needed by the men during the rally. And some of it will be used to buy and strategically stockpile needed fuel for the delivery of the goods.

Who knows, as doubtful as it is, you might even get a few highly qualified people to volunteer to help insure that those companies are going to be run as efficiently as possible.

Companies being purchased will be those that produce toilet paper, wet wipes, copy paper, paper to separate slices of cheese, poster board, large envelopes, ink and toner; bread, cheese, whey protein powder, the raw materials for those foods; fruit, vegetables, vitamins, and "raw super green food tablets"; t-shirts, sweatshirts, socks, shorts, underwear, and lounge pants; screen printing for those products, the "cloth" materials needed to make those items and micro-fiber towels; recyclable plastic packaging with printing for those products and those that follow; plastic bags and tarps, plastic containers such as five-gallon water bottles and toilet kit buckets, solar heating bags, spray bottles, latex gloves, large rubber bands, poles, pole holders, etc.

(Fear not, this is not an omnibus bill. The actual legitimate need for each of the above-mentioned items is fully explained in the easily understandable, detailed instructions for success that are in the addendum-like section located at the back of this book.)

Though the upfront cost will be more than starting from scratch, well-vetted existing companies will be bought because of time restraints and the fact that their business models will have already been proven to work as needed.

(e.g., supply chains, production and distribution methods, **existing market share**, etc.)

Then again, in this rigged economy there might be some serious bargains to be had.

Either way, those companies will be ready to deliver the goods yesterday.

One of the many considerations to be made before any purchases occur is that of location.

The companies purchased should ultimately result in there being volunteer-owned production facilities in numerous regions of the country, so as to minimize all delivery costs and to maximize on future market share.

As you'll find out if you read the aforementioned detailed instructions for success, no less than 2,000,000 loaves of bread will be needed every single day; at least 40,000,000 slices of cheese will be needed every single day; over 20,000,000 scoops of whey protein powder will be needed every single day; millions of multi-vitamins and related tablets will be needed every single day; at least a dozen pieces of fruit will be needed every day; more than one million rolls of toilet paper will be needed every day; tens of millions of plastic bags for the packaging of such goods and for use in toilet kits will be needed every day.

And tens of millions of t-shirts, pants, and socks will be needed; more than one million five-gallon water containers will be needed; more than one million toilet kit buckets will be needed; millions of square feet of tarp will be needed; millions of highly absorbent, quick drying micro-fiber towels will be needed; millions of poles and pole holders will be needed, etc.

Trust me friend; if they actually invest the time required to read and understand it, and they're honest, those whose word you're going to take regarding such information will say that it all makes perfect sense.

The businesses that are purchased will <u>not</u> only produce and deliver their products to the men at the rally.

They will aggressively increase their market share and profitability by way of their new, shared brand name being clearly tied into the rally (while also temporarily still producing under their previous name).

That shared brand name will be "Responsibility".

It has now been trademarked for this exact purpose, to help prove that you will not act in the manner required to redeem yourself.

If you intellectual dead beats can somehow get your act together, you can use the name for free to help promote one of the core concepts *responsible* for the success of this rally.

There are many pressing reasons why **YOU** must immediately begin to understand the need for personal responsibility.

And until each of you discovers what they all are, and learns to act accordingly, this rally and the just governance it will bring forth are as likely to occur as the IRS not ruining your life if you've failed to hand over in a timely manner the full portion of their self-regulated, generous cut of the fruits of your labor.

The brand name and the entire combined effort of the rally are quickly going to be made extremely clear, near, and dear to everyone in your country and the rest of the world.

The way it will happen is quite simple actually.

Literally every aspect of the rally is going to be presented to the general public by way of the latest highly successful method in use to keep you from gaining awareness of anything meaningful:

"Reality television".

That's right; there will be continuous, *twenty-four (24) hour a day* programming successfully presenting every emotionally exploitable angle of everything that has anything to do with the efforts being made to ensure that the rally achieves its purpose.

Truly, this will bring the seamless blending of irresistibly gripping entertainment, worthwhile education, and commercial advertising to a level that could not otherwise possibly be achieved.

It will be the most compelling, action-packed and drama-filled line up of entertainment that has ever been presented on television.

It will be the greatest documentary of all time.

School children of all ages will be encouraged to show their support by writing essays about the rally that will win the best of them "Responsibility" brand prizes, and by writing letters to a particular volunteer who will become their pen pal; and by instituting a simple, one minute routine of exercise into their day at twenty minute intervals.

All of this will of course be filmed, edited to perfection, and broadcast in high-definition for everyone's viewing pleasure.

FYI, regardless of where their work is accomplished, each person who will be doing said filming, editing, and broadcasting full-time will lawfully be considered a member of the "Home" group.

The "rally fund" will be incorporated as a trust ("United Sovereign's Absolution") that will be the sole owner and lawful claimant of all rights relating to the "Responsibility" brand name and products, and of all rights relating to any and all aspects and functions of the rally that can possibly be protected.

Those who invest in the "rally fund" will be its beneficiaries.

Though the readers of this book will have to alert them of the fact, the following people will be offered the combined trusteeship of the fund - which will also have the final word on all procedural and otherwise irreconcilable rally-related disputes.

If you aren't familiar with anyone listed below, click on their name for an introduction:

Heather Mac Donald, Cornel West, Richard Grove, Eric Thomas, Camille Paglia, Scott Ott, Chris Hedges, Rocio Munoz, Dan Bongino, Tom Woods, Candace Owens, Charlie LeDuff, Mark Steyn, Richard Epstein, KrisAnne Hall, Jan Jekielek, Dave Rubin, Camila Chávez, Sharyl Attkisson, Larry Elder, Katharine Birbalsingh, Josh del Sol, Rosa Koire, Jason Riley, Erin Brockovich, Paul Craig Roberts, Chris Chappel, Victor Davis Hanson, Shiva Ayyadurai, Shelby Steele, Douglas Murray, Glenn Laury, Kira Davis, Steve Green, John McWhorter, Michael Malice, John Lovell, Chloe Valdary, Andrew Klavan, Tom Fitton, Carol M. Swain, Ayaan Hirsi Ali, Josephine Mathias, Jon Stewart, James Corbett, Sara Carter, Tammy Bruce, Brigitte Gabriel, Ben Swann, Jordan Peterson, John Solomon, James O'Keefe, John Stossel, James Lindsay, Les Brown, Tucker Carlson, RFK Jr., Bill Whittle, Scott Adams, Ben Shapiro

Through an initial advertising campaign (that will be spread locally and online by the families and friends of volunteers and all of their investors), the general public will quickly begin tuning in and becoming completely captivated.

Businesses that sponsor volunteers will be officially authorized by said trust to post and distribute rally-themed announcements of exactly how they've contributed.

So that from then on, the public will know exactly where to shop.

And since they will not be asked to make donations to the rally, the general public will be emotionally compelled to eagerly seek out the "Responsibility" brand as a way of supporting the cause whenever they are in the market for the types of goods being sold.

As the brand's market share increases (it will happen quickly) a massive, paid advertising campaign through select forms of media will begin.

By the time the men are deployed to Washington D.C. there will hardly be anyone on the planet who is unaware of the rally and its purpose.

And you can rest assured that people of all ages, worldwide, will be wearing graphic t-shirts, shorts, hats, and lounge pants with product names and/or the name of a division, squadron, platoon, company, or battalion on it - all of which will be sold exclusively through the official website of the rally, to minimize the sale of knock offs.

And do you "think" that a fair portion of the highly lucrative sneaker market would not be ripe for the taking (and keeping for generations to come) if a few well-designed, extremely affordable, super-sturdy, <u>American made</u> styles that were being worn on TV, and strategically promoted by men in the "Away" group, were made widely available to those school children and the rest of the public?

Do you "think" that if a bunch of well-known "patriotic tough guys" and professional or former professional athletes were to volunteer to be involved in the rally's on air operations, while also "roughing it" regarding their accommodations, the rally's appeal wouldn't be that much greater?

And imagine what the effect on sales would be if it were common knowledge that such heroic figures were wearing those snazzy sneakers, and other official merchandise, without getting any royalties just for doing so. WOW.

I'll even say that backwards: WOW.

Note that only men will be involved in any of the aspects of filming the "Away" group.

4ₘ – After the "Home" and "Away" groups have each chosen (on camera of course) volunteers from their respective group to represent them in each local, state, and national government office that will be up for grabs in the November election, the following will occur on September 3rd, 2024:

Each "Home" and "Away" candidate who is vying for the same position will have a debate, in person, near their home location.

The debates will be broadcast live in every media outlet possible, in addition to the official website of the rally. And they will be uploaded immediately to "YouTube".

Then, on September 7th, <u>regardless of their age</u>, each volunteer from each group will vote for their respective candidates of choice.

The candidate who receives the greatest total number of votes for that position will get the nomination.

The entire process in each location will be videotaped and uploaded to the official website of the rally and to "YouTube".

The platform that they will all be running on is described in the final section of this book.

So, in other words, the only criteria any of the volunteers should use, to decide upon the candidate they prefer, is that they believe a particular candidate will be more effective than their opponent in accomplishing the tasks which make up the platform.

On September 11th, during simultaneous live broadcasts at 3pm Eastern Standard Time, from the foot of each state capital and the Lincoln memorial in Washington D.C., each of the candidates will sign a lawfully binding contract which states the following:

"In the event that I am elected, but it is widely believed that I am not following through with my commitment to immediately do all that is lawfully and realistically possible from that post to bring all aspects of the platform into effect, a three-fourths (3/4) majority vote by my constituents who volunteered for the rally, which calls for me to step down from my post, will cause me to do so immediately."

All of the volunteers from both groups will then announce their full support for those candidates, and they will begin doing all they can to help ensure their election.

The infrastructure that has already been put in place for the support of the rally is what will be used to ensure that each person gets elected to the office they have chosen to serve.

In mid-September, certain of the "shows" will begin being broadcast with a focus on the candidates and their particular messages.

And the advertising campaign for the rally will begin to include messages about, and from, the volunteers who are candidates for office.

From then on, the ads will focus more and more on the election and the importance of making sure everyone is registered to vote.

A listing of candidates by state, and the localities within each state, will be presented on the official website of the rally.

And each candidate's name will be a link that will take voters to videos of their debate and any earlier speeches they may have made, and of them being interviewed about numerous important issues.

Included in those web pages will be a summary of their duties during the rally and any other pertinent information they may wish to include.

While all of the steps required to enable each of the candidates to become a valid write-in candidate will be taken in a timely fashion, not one attempt will be made to get any candidate's name on the official ballot.

On Election Day, as many members of the "Home" group and as many other supporters of the rally as possible will work in the voting locations as outlined below.

Certain volunteers will be videotaping the scene.

Others will be handing out a pre-printed sticker sheet and a photocopy of a template that has every governmental position that voters can vote for in the election printed on it.

There will be a blank space next to each such position, wherein voters will be able to quickly and easily print the name of the candidate who they will have ultimately voted for.

Previous to the vote, through every lawful means possible, all voters will have been instructed to vote for the rally's write-in candidates by simply pasting those candidate's names directly on the ballot in the appropriate spot (s), in every voting location that such action is not prohibited.

Every sticker sheet will have each candidate's properly spelled name on it with their future job title printed next to it, and a colored ring around them both to prevent any mistakes; so that interested voters can simply place the sticker with their preferred candidate's name on it in the proper area of a paper ballot.

The glue on that sticker will not allow it to be removed from the ballot without clearly damaging the ballot.

Previous to the actual vote, and again on Election Day, voters will be constantly reminded of the following:

1- All voting locations will have numerous people on hand who are each a notary public. Each notary public will be available, free of charge, to certify with their official seal and signature that they witnessed the voter making the exact selections for write-in candidates that is shown on their completed template.

2- To walk directly to a designated volunteer who has a video camera as soon as they leave the voting booth (regardless of the type of voting machine they used), so they can hold up their completed template with the notary public seal and signature on it, while stating their full name.

They need not necessarily show their exact selections.

Can enough of you figure out the rest of the details needed to ensure proper function and procedure for the "Home" group and everything that has been mentioned regarding the election?

The information I've provided has fulfilled the related terms of the bet that prompted me to write this book.

So I'll leave it up to you to leave an in-depth analysis up to someone else who will mislead you for their own gain.

Oh, did I forget to mention that I've just offered up an opportunity to line the pockets of those who would like to prove that they're members of the second category of the three types of people that exist in this world?

You just read the first part of the detailed, easy to follow instructions on how to personally, lawfully earn more than $250,000 completely tax free.

Such payment is explained a little later on in this book.

Such payment has nothing to do with any proceeds from the rally fund.

Had enough of our flag waving rump riving yet?

5 - One last thing, before I introduce the actual concepts that will enable your ongoing freedom:

A nationwide educational campaign regarding the proper application of the information outlined below must also go into effect immediately in all localities and through all possible institutions and forms of media, including the internet.

This must be done in order to prepare everyone for the responsibilities they will each have if the following concepts ever go into effect.

Not a single one of you is currently prepared to properly utilize such power. And the widespread chaos that will result from its misuse will cause as many problems for you as any scheme we have ever cooked up.

Those of you who have talent and imagination must create simple, effective methods of transmitting the ideas below to the masses of mental vagrants in your midst who will not otherwise do the work required of them.

The majority of the population (whose gross stupidity is a very real threat to your freedom) will otherwise inevitably screw everything up because they are improperly educated, and thus uninterested in the far-reaching consequences of their actions.

As always, they will act irrationally and will be expecting someone else to clean-up their mess; while they indulge themselves in mindless entertainment and complain to each other about the cost of the coming clean-up efforts. Oblivious that finally there will be no such effort, and that the cost will be their brutal enslavement.

If those of you with talent and imagination do not step up to the plate here, your lives will be completely ruined by the ignorant hordes that are in desperate need of your skillful guidance.

You must first lead them to the understanding of the concepts of personal responsibility and community involvement.

You must then lead them to the further awareness of how only an understanding of those concepts enables the ability to understand and properly act upon the concepts contained within each of the subsections below.

You must not mistake actions which are needed for your own redemption as an unfair sacrifice being made merely for the benefit of the disinterested masses.

You must understand that the only alternative to your doing what I have just explained is *your own* absolute enslavement.

Call it unfair if you'd like, but you need their help just as badly as they need yours.

There is no alternative. And the clock is ticking.

Below are the basic explanations of the concepts that must be fully understood, continually acted upon, and in certain cases enacted into law by way of Constitutional amendments.

Differences of opinion regarding the need for a particular concept to be enacted into law must not be allowed to grow into factions that will prevent the ultimate success of the rally.

Debate them honestly, respectfully, and in-depth while participating in the rally.

Every available method will be used to keep you misinformed, divided, and impotent.

But make no mistake about it, regardless of what anyone in "government" or the private sector tells you to the contrary, if any of the following concepts are not widely and properly acted upon, you and your offspring will eventually be fully enslaved.

This means that **YOU** must re-read every line of every subsection below until you fully understand the reasoning behind each concept presented, and are thus able to clearly recognize their far-reaching consequences and the absolutely vital need for them to be implemented.

Ensuring your ongoing freedom

1 – Let's start with the fact that you must establish a just monetary system.

Since literally none of you have any idea how to even approach such a thing, I am going to clearly explain what needs to be done.

If the method I am going to explain is put into effect, it will be the only method of institutionalized money creation and supply in the entire history of the world that did not rip off the average ~~patsy~~ citizen, while granting those in charge more wealth and power.

Of course, the average American's maliciously manipulated mind could not possibly, on its own, understand how there is nothing invalid about the method of money creation and supply that I will instruct you to implement.

So, before I introduce that method I will first enable everyone to be able to recognize the validity of what would otherwise appear to be an invalid plan.

I will do this by exposing the purposely hidden truth of what "money" is first and foremost being used for and by explaining how the powers that be have been able to legally, completely control the masses through our complete control of the world's monetary systems; which was made possible by expertly hiding the truth of what "money" is actually being used for.

Once you are able to understand the truth of the matter, the just method I'll be presenting will not appear invalid. Its simplicity, validity, and legitimacy will be obvious.

What will also be obvious at that point is that your entire conceptualization of basically every aspect of your existence has been a purposely-designed aspect of someone else's purposely-destructive agenda.

So now let's see exactly how a criminal cartel is legally looting and defiling the "land of the free and the home of the brave" through their own completely invalid system of currency creation and control.

1A - Contrary to what many improperly educated "experts" will tell you, money does <u>not</u> need to be made of precious metal.

Make no mistake; prior to the advent of high-powered computers and the internet, the usage of "precious" metals in money as a reliable store of value was the best option available for conducting large-scale/widespread commerce. But it had many limitations.

There's never been a government that did not eventually debase their gold and silver coins or print more "precious metal backed" paper currency than there was precious metal backing it.

Even if a nation's government did not debase their currency, how could they protect their stores of value in international trade with nations whose governments did? Or with nations whose official currency was admittedly worthless "legal tender" paper notes? And how would they protect that store of value while issuing credit, etc...

Furthermore, by claiming to base the value of a currency on a precious metal, or some other inanimate physical object, what is actually being accomplished is that a class-based, resource controlling, physical and conceptual wedge is placed between the plebeians who have very little or none of those *supposedly* valuable objects,

(and who are dull enough to believe that such currency derives its value from the amount of the *supposedly* valuable object that is *supposedly* in the currency itself or put aside in a vault somewhere.)

and the Patricians who already <u>had</u> plenty of those objects and who have the means to get plenty more with way less effort than what anyone else needs to expend to get their hands on them. (You know the routine; we have low paid schleps do the work with tools they can't afford and methods they can't duplicate. And then we tax their pay!)

And this is before the almost incalculable, institutionalized theft known as "fractional reserve banking" is even factored into the equation.

Make sure that you understand the following in relation to all current and previous methods of currency creation and control; and in relation to the supposed need, which is claimed by certain "experts", for "real" money to be precious metals such as gold or silver:

1 - Anyone who says that you are born into this world with nothing has poopy pants.

2 - You are born into this world with a minimum amount of productive potential.

3 - Another name for actualized productive potential is "properly directed labor".

4 - Properly directed labor is the only thing that effectively discovers, creates, grows, gathers, and distributes <u>anything</u>.

5 - The majority of you would never achieve the current minimum amount of productive potential on your own, but historically and currently there are others of you whose abilities far exceed that minimum and who ultimately bring everyone else's minimum amount of productive potential to higher levels through what is called "technology".

6 - Technology also enables the methodology of calculating and *regulating* massive amounts of productive potential - which is so accurate that the true powers that be actually bank on it.

How many people can even fathom what is being stated by my using the word *"regulating"*, rather than "actualizing"?

Hint: like gerrymandering, modern "booms" and "busts" and the many socioeconomic changes they bring/brought about are/were the result of insightful planning and construction. Despite what the highly credentialed "experts" keep telling you, they are/were not the result of sudden, unexpected, "unforeseen market forces". Clearly, I am not speaking of natural disaster-related widespread famine/drought.

In conjunction with a valid currency, if we used technology to calculate and <u>actualize</u> such productive potential, *everyone* would be able to bank on it.

7 - Currency derives validity only through its uniform, measured connection to properly directed labor. Have you looked up the word "validity" yet?

Since all objects and concepts are in themselves worthless to us if the labor required to properly utilize them is not put forth, how can currency otherwise possibly derive its valid justification for being? According to a certain popular dictionary, currency is "something that is in circulation as a medium of exchange".

8 - The only method capable of establishing and maintaining a valid currency is the prior implementation of egalitarian, accurate, strictly enforced methods of regulating and accounting for the issuance and official valuation of such currency. Now would be a good time to look up the words "legitimate", "egalitarian", "dictionary", "conjure", and "tout".

9 - Contrary to what you have been taught, validity and legitimacy do <u>not</u> dictate value.

Guided perception lends fictional value to a currency such as precious metals, and many other things as well. But actual value is dependent only upon an individual's belief system.

In other words, an official monetary valuation/uniform measure of trade is merely an administrative tool used for the purpose of mass public coordination.

In order to maintain one's freedom, it is <u>not</u> to be taken as anything but what it actually is: a conditional standard that has been implemented to promote efficiency in commerce and, according to John Maynard Keynes, a conduit of power and profit for those who dictate/manipulate the environmental conditions and institutional regulations that influence the setting and re-setting of the standard. (Please feel free to re-visit page <u>78</u>.)

In order to maintain one's freedom, all official valuation must be treated like a filthy work boot; worn out in the field, but never in the house.

10 - Any claim that is made which attempts to set a definitive, preconceived value on anything other than the critical study of fundamental beliefs and the grounds for them is a lie; which, purposely or inadvertently, serves to take personal control away from those whom the claim is intended to influence. How might a being that has been influenced as such make self-determined, properly informed, reason-based decisions?

Proper education is *the* Master Resource.

11 - The proof of a belief system being based upon accurate reasoning is made apparent by the level of ongoing personal freedom that its adherents are able to enjoy in every aspect of their lives. This is the basis of personal control, also known as "self-determination".

And make no mistake about it; this is directly related to the system of currency creation and valuation that one allows oneself to be involved with - or in your case, controlled by.

The mark of freedom is one's ability to prosper while functioning by way of *personally-explored*, reason-based values and beliefs that are not necessarily in accordance with anyone else's values and beliefs. *Fili componitur fabricam.*

The fabric is composed of the thread.

No, actual freedom cannot ever be granted. It must constantly be earned. But since we have made sure that very few people have the inclination or the ability to utilize reason, the truth of the matter never sees the light of day.

In actuality your personal valuation of physical objects is dependent only upon your conscious or unconscious belief that you derive some measure of benefit from your association with such objects; and such belief is dependent on one or more of the following:

1 - Awareness of the real or imagined need for the object to be ingested/injected/applied in order for your own or another's proper physical, mental, and/or spiritual functioning to occur.

2 - Awareness of the real or imagined need for the object to be possessed and/or interacted with in order for certain of your desires to be satiated.

3 - Awareness of the rarity or specialized function of the particular mental and/or physical actions required to discover or create those objects and/or that which they enable you to experience.

4 - Awareness of the rarity or specialized function of the particular mental and/or physical actions required to discover practical methods of exploiting the useful properties of those objects.

5 - Awareness of the rarity or specialized function of the particular mental and/or physical actions required to actually implement such practical methods of exploiting the useful properties of those objects.

6 - Awareness of the rarity or specialized function of the particular mental and/or physical actions required to discover methods of continually, efficiently recreating and/or harvesting and distributing more of those objects in order to satisfy market demand for them.

7 - Awareness of the rarity or specialized function of the particular mental and/or physical actions required to actually implement such methods of continually, efficiently recreating and/or harvesting and distributing more of those objects in order to satisfy market demand for them.

8 - The effectiveness of the particular mental and physical actions which are required to create and/or update the message that establishes and/or sustains maximum beholder/owner/consumer/user awareness of, and demand for, such objects.

9 - The effectiveness of the particular mental and physical actions required to continually, efficiently and effectively disseminate the message that establishes and/or sustains maximum beholder/owner/consumer/user awareness of, and demand for, such objects.

Have you noticed that every one of the above categories has **properly directed labor** as its foundation?

Have you noticed that for objects and ideas to have any actual usefulness, especially a continual usefulness, many types of **properly directed labor** are needed by their user and/or their discoverer/creator/grower/disseminator/distributor/seller and their buyer?

Have you noticed that all acts of using and buying and selling *and* their medium of exchange (currency) only exist because of the ideas that they were formed from?

Have you noticed that, although constant awareness of what one is directly physically doing is its foundation, properly directed labor is not dependent on any awareness of its actual purpose by anyone involved, other than those who have originally designed the plan being carried out by way of such labor?

Have you noticed that the act of properly directing labor is dependent upon the effective dissemination of ideas?

Have you noticed that belief is not at all dependent on accurate reasoning?

Do you get it yet?

Do you smell a rat, or are you still completely dazed by the incredibly strong, yet calmingly familiar, scent of anus that is coming out of everyone's pores?

You've all been hoodwinked at the most fundamental levels of your worldview.

And the sham has been going on continuously for so long, through so many bastions of authority, that the essential details relating to the fact of your nation's institutionalized, purposeful conceptual abortion are otherwise inaccessible to virtually everyone, even those who are involved in the procedure. No, this is not limited to your country. Does that make you feel better? It shouldn't. Why would it?

Gold and silver and the term "legal tender" are simply props used in the same way that a magician uses sleight of hand to trick you into seeing only the result they intended.

You rubes never figure out the truth of the matter because, in conjunction with your educational curriculum lacking any critical study of fundamental beliefs and the grounds for them, you've been tricked into focusing your awareness on misbranded merchandise.

You are about to find out that what you are submitting to is much worse than paying someone else to keep the bulk of your paycheck and tell you that you're overpaid.

1B – Let's review a few of the now obvious reasons why the Federal Reserve is a completely fraudulent operation:

1 - It is a rationally inarguable fact that the admittedly worthless notes they promote as "legal tender" are opposed to both the spirit and the letter of your nation's Constitution.

2 - They uniformly promote the false notion that they exist as a publicly beneficial branch of "government".

3 - They, and the other banks which operate within the Federal Reserve's sphere of influence, *legally* use "fractional reserve banking" and "debt monetization" techniques that amount to massive, outright legal theft.

4 - They, and the other banks which operate within the Federal Reserve's sphere of influence, generate massive profits by *legally* charging fees for the "money" they *legally* conjure up and by *legally* charging interest on the debt that is created as a result of the fees being charged on the "money" they conjured. Re-read and ponder that until you understand the absurdity of such a system.

Speaking of absurdity, have you heard the one about the Federal Reserve being a Good Samaritan because it hands back a large portion of its profits to the U.S. Treasury?

http://www.newrepublic.com/article/116913/federal-reserve-dividends-most-outrageous-handout-banks

http://www.sanders.senate.gov/newsroom/press-releases/the-fed-audit

5 - As an aspect of their control, they and their cronies have forced (albeit indirectly) almost the entire population to either depend upon employment within the "modern industrialized economy" (that they and their cronies *legally* regulate) or depend upon "government assistance" (that they enable the proliferation of by being able to *legally* purchase unlimited amounts of "government" debt in a manner that would otherwise unanimously be considered counterfeiting). This enables them and their cronies to effectively control and exploit <u>all</u> of the country's natural resources.

Read these three articles and see if you can figure out how an actual free market (based upon a valid system of monetary creation, regulation, and control) that was utilized by a properly educated public could prevent such dishonest gain:

http://www.washingtonpost.com/opinions/how-america-became-uncompetitive-and-unequal/2014/06/13/a690ad94-ec00-11e3-b98c-72cef4a00499_story.html

http://www.truthdig.com/report/item/20081020_the_idiots_who_rule_america

http://www.peakprosperity.com/blog/92313/fatal-flaw-centrally-issued-money

6 - As an aspect of their regulation they constantly *legally* manipulate the rates of interest that they *legally* charge on consumer credit, to the advantage of their friends in industry and on Wall Street. And they *legally* contract the "money" supply whenever they want to.

These just happen to be a couple of the "unforeseen market forces" that caused the recent worldwide economic collapse and the Great Depression of 1929.

7 - Another one of their "unforeseen market forces" is their act of *legally* conjuring up as much "money" as they want, whenever they want to. In addition to the income tax, and in conjunction with fractional reserve banking and debt monetization, this serves to control access to resources by way of constantly decreasing the value of your labor.

Time out - if you understood anything that I've been telling you, after reading that last line you should have been thinking: "But no-one can decrease the value of my labor; such value is dependent on my own belief system". And if you did think that, bravo to you.

But since your survival and the survival of almost everyone else in the "modern industrialized world" fully depends upon employment within the "modern industrialized economy", and since your entire belief system has been manufactured for you by others who are not interested in your well-being, you are not capable of self-determination; let alone, accurate self-determination regarding the *market* value of your labor or any of the tangible or intangible products you need and/or wish to consume.

The purpose of your labor expenditure known as "work" is to accumulate their Federal Reserve notes so that you can buy things with them. So, when the prices of the things you must buy or rent go up, the market value of your labor has been reduced - since you now need to work more to *seemingly* maintain the same lifestyle.

But how can you possibly maintain the same lifestyle if a greater percentage of your life is now being spent trying to earn enough "money" to be able to pay the maintenance fee?

That's the equivalent of trying to be in two places at once; outside of the realm of quantum physics it hasn't happened yet.

The term "diluting the currency" really means "decreasing the market value of your labor". But what can a completely manipulated sharecropper do?

Actually, you and everyone around you are but different varieties of crops on a big farm.

Because of your complete dependence on the "modern industrialized economy", you and the rest of the resplendent minds like you need to take whatever your handlers are willing to allow you; regardless of the terms of the allowance.

Now, rather than being offended by the unvarnished truth, why not look up the word "resplendent"?

In regard to paid labor: have you noticed that if any semi-conscious "person" can carry out the functions required, the market value of that properly directed labor is minimized to the point that it is barely possible to survive without receiving "government benefits"?

Have you noticed that the architects of the "modern industrialized world" are constantly working to legally eliminate every aspect of everyone's ability to be self-sufficient?

For those who have allowed themselves and their children to literally become a banking cartel's market commodity, this amounts to the elimination of self-determined access to otherwise available resources.

This amounts to sovereign rights being replaced with revocable allowances issued by civil administrators. This is the regulation of privilege.

Regardless of how it is clothed, to those who put forth the due exercise of logical thought it NEVER resembles freedom to a greater extent than a Bald Eagle resembles a banana. And thus it is NEVER accepted as lawful governance.

Have you followed this link from page 17 yet? http://teamlaw.net/Sovereignty.htm

8 - The last time I checked, freedom and poverty were not yet interchangeable terms.

So let me finally point out the <u>fact</u> that, in 1912, when the mention of workers' rights would either get you beat up or laughed at, the hourly wage rate for a brick layer was seventy-five cents per hour ($0.75) and the luxurious, world famous Beverly Hills Hotel cost only $500,000 to build.

Today the average hourly wage rate for a brick layer is in the high teen to mid-twenty "dollar" range.

And the cost of renovating the Beverly Hills Hotel in 1995, when the market value of your currency was **50%** higher, was over one hundred million "dollars" ($100,000,000).

Are you with me? Do you see what's fraudulent about the numerous "cost of living" salary increases that have occurred in order for the brick layer of today to earn approximately <u>twenty-five times</u> more "dollars" per hour than the brick layer of 1912?

Well, with his measly $30.00 paycheck, the guy in 1912 was able to purchase 50 ounces of silver (at $0.60 per ounce). That $30.00 was his "net pay".

1 - The guy in 1912 was forced to pay <u>nothing</u> in income taxes from his $30.00 paycheck.

2 - The guy in 1912 was forced to contribute <u>nothing</u> to Social Security.

Today's "cost of living increase compensated" brick layer is only able to buy 35 ounces of silver with his $660.00 "net pay" (that is, at $19.00 per ounce).

***Be sure to note that the price of silver would be more than <u>double</u> that price were it not for Federal Reserve naked short selling.

YOU MUST READ THIS ARTICLE TO UNDERTAND WHAT I AM EXPLAINING:
http://www.paulcraigroberts.org/2013/04/04/the-assault-on-gold-paul-craig-roberts/

$950.00 is the amount of *net* pay that today's "cost of living increase compensated" bricklayer would need to earn in order to afford the same 50 ounces of silver as the bricklayer of 1912. (Do not forget the Federal Reserve naked short selling).

"Oh Granny, what big teeth you've got!"

And that's before Granny even opens her mouth. Now try to consider the following:

1 - The guy in 1912 paid a nickel ($0.05) for a loaf of white bread.

2 - Today's brick layer pays over two dollars ($2.00) for a loaf of white bread - a markup of **forty times** the price that the guy in 1912 paid for it.

3 - The guy in 1912 paid about <u>one year</u> worth of *net* salary for his modest home, not counting interest owed on the mortgage.

4 - Today's brick layer pays almost <u>ten years</u>' worth of ***net*** salary for his modest home, not counting interest owed on the mortgage - a markup of more than **two hundred times** the price of what the guy in 1912 paid for it.

If you, or someone who is actually capable of doing so, were to correctly calculate the applicable cost of living increase for today's bricklayer by way of recognizing the astronomical increases in:

1- The type and amount of taxes and fees he's forced to pay;

2- The price of food, fuel, clothing and shelter;

3- The price of "higher" education (touted as capable of preventing one's socioeconomic descent);

That have all *somehow* been taking place for decades, even though there has been no shortage of needed raw materials and the fact that technology has brought everyone's productive potential to much higher levels since then, etc;

The theft I am pointing out would be rationally undeniable.

Look at this chart: http://www.infoplease.com/ipa/A0001519.html

Oh, and did I mention "Petrodollars"? You really should learn how that rigged system *helped* to support the illusion of American prosperity, even as we eliminated your nation's industrial capabilities, exported manufacturing jobs, and increased the national debt to unmanageable levels.

FYI, I stressed the word *helped* because that scam has basically run its course. And so a new era of the American lifestyle looms: http://ftmdaily.com/preparing-for-the-collapse-of-the-petrodollar-system/

Do you remember the following lines from the famed economist John Maynard Keynes?

"By a continuous process of inflation, governments can confiscate secretly and unobserved an important part of the wealth of their citizens...

Lenin was certainly right. There is no subtler, no surer means of overturning the existing basis of society than to debauch the currency.

The process engages all the hidden forces of economic law on the side of destruction - and does it in a manner in which not one man in a million is able to diagnose."

Well, for exactly what <u>valid reason</u> did so much of your buying power mysteriously vanish? Click here for the truth: https://www.youtube.com/watch?v=g4mHPeMGTJM

Hmmm… can you say "steady descent into a Kleptocratic Banana Republic"?

 And let's face it; I, of all people, am the last person who will argue that some chimp working a cash register, who cannot even provide proper change without the register telling them what it is, should be making anywhere near the amount of pay that those who figured out how to properly direct that chump's labor in order to make a profit should be making.

It is simply my aim in writing this book to show you the facts so that I can collect on the bet I have made <u>against</u> you.

Really try to understand the following concept:

The purpose of a valid, legitimate monetary currency is simply to provide instruments that can be lawfully obtained in equal amounts by all who voluntarily put forth an equivalent effort, as determined by the unobstructed, freely decided upon demand for their efforts and/or the fruit thereof,

that are easily transferable, universally accepted instruments of trade which offer to those who voluntarily accept such instruments, insurance that they are actually going to be compensated according to their own idea (or at least a fair compensation of it) of what the efforts they need/needed to put forth in order to hold up their end of the trade were worth at the time of the agreement made between them and the person offering those instruments in exchange for voluntarily agreed upon products and/or services;

regardless of when the person who accepted such instrument decides to utilize such compensation.

Yes, what you just read does make perfect sense.

If need be, keep re-reading it slowly until you are personally able to understand both what is being said and why such information is correct.

Contrary to what those who are not properly educated will tell you, money is <u>not</u> in and of itself a bad thing.

As a matter of fact, if it were properly utilized within a valid, legitimate system of creation, valuation, regulation and usage, the concept of money would arguably be one of the greatest discoveries that mankind has ever made.

It is a unique form of currency.

Unfortunately for the completely dazed common folk, a valid, legitimate system of monetary creation, valuation, regulation and usage has never been implemented.

But what complex tool does not require a proper education to recognize and avoid similar looking, yet inferior, improperly designed products?

And what such tool does not require a proper education to properly utilize it?

In regard to a valid, legitimate system of monetary creation, valuation, regulation and usage, try to wrap your mind around this:

Outside of naturally occurring systems such as weather or the tides, or a universally available and continually effective dissemination of clearly defined valid concepts (often referred to as a proper education), what other method exists that can equitably, indefinitely store and/or transfer potential energy without any loss of that which is being stored or transferred?

(Well, at least until there is a major famine or drought. Famine and drought each have the ability to bring forth an excruciating appreciation for that which is absolutely essential.)

In regard to an **invalid, illegitimate** system of "monetary" creation, valuation, regulation and usage, carefully consider this:

Other than the improper education needed to effectuate the illegitimate system, what tool exists that can afford its creator an infinitely greater amount of controlled energy return than that which was put into its creation, maintenance, and usage?

1c – And yet, by way of the constant stream of false claims and other purposeful misdirection that are disseminated by "accredited experts" and other mainstream media personalities, many readers still fail to realize that "monetary instruments" are not the supreme forms of currency.

Currency is "something that is in circulation as a medium of exchange".

Such people also fail to realize that, whether or not it is the product of a valid, legitimate system of creation, valuation, regulation, and usage, "money" is the currency of chief importance only for those who are conceptually undernourished.

As a result of our surreptitious system of cognitive corruption, even though I'm handing out all of the information that's needed to transcend our sphere of influence, few people will ever muster up enough of the mental energy needed to properly process and apply it.

For most people the possession, or even the thought, of "money" is a license to engage in myriad highly addictive, temporarily gratifying diversions. They unsuccessfully attempt to satisfy themselves with those diversions as they frantically, though most often unwittingly, avoid the aspects of reality we have covertly taught them to overlook. Thus, regardless of what I am explaining, to them it will remain the supreme form of currency.

Indeed; such addictions can only be paid for and fed with the forms of currency that certain of our operatives produce, issue, and control the usage of in order to have everyone else constantly serving us and our agenda.

Like I keep saying, our foundational shaping and subsequent continual maintenance of their systems of belief casts most people in the role of a conceptually shackled cave dweller.

They are unable to gain awareness of this fact: it is their striving for those tools which we have taught them are what will provide freedom and prosperity, that actually prevents them from ever becoming free and prosperous.

Yes friend, the vast majority of the population in the "land of the free" shops exclusively at "The Company Store": http://www.perryopolis.com/sjcompanystore.shtml

Or perhaps I should say, "You see, whereas in Rome the people had to go to the circus, now the average person's entire life experience actually takes place within it." (Page 25)

Or, "You mental and moral weaklings have allowed a highly intelligent, extremely creative, supremely patient small group of thieves whose purpose is your destruction, and whose goal is that you suffer along the path to that end, to ensnare you in an intricate system of slavery that is nothing other than a highly evolved method of forcefully controlling your actual being - in order to steal from you as they have you gather whatever it is that they value; while they simultaneously, effectively force false ideas upon you through myriad misleading claims whose constant, clever presentation leads to your believing that the actions taken by them are needed for your own benefit." (Page 105)

Or maybe, "**NONE OF YOU** have so much as a vague clue about the actual details and functionality of the vehicle whose tread marks are the insignia of everything you proudly wear and desire. The system is broken? **NOT**. That vehicle *is* the system." (Page 107)

Or how about, "Yes, it's true, we actually cause you to believe that a properly functioning human existence is one which, unbeknownst to you, happens to be equivalent to that of an opiate addict whose only method of survival is to be employed by us so that you can seemingly afford to continually pay us huge fees in order to enable yourself and others to exist within the all-encompassing den we have constructed for the purpose of doing great harm to all of you.

Indeed, U.S.A. actually stands for *United State of Acquiescence*." (Page 112)

Now go back and re-read the last twelve pages while you consider this:

Money invites power, but disseminated ideas are the currency that retains it.

Are you starting to see the truth we hide from you?

Know this in regard to the current "monetary" methods used in your country:

1 - Because of the above-mentioned operations, you are never your own investor.

2 - Since you are never your own investor, you are always a host organism for parasites.

You see, if you depend upon employment within the "modern industrialized economy" and cannot otherwise fully sustain yourself, you need others to invest in you even though the terms of their investment are purposely designed in a way that they not only profit from your work, but they gradually eliminate your ability to own anything; as they legally, continually devalue the tool they are loaning you which you must continually borrow and use in order to survive and function as a "productive" member of society.

And thus, you are not your own investor. Serf's up…

Yes, that devalued tool is commonly called "money". And as you should now know, it accurately represents the measly market value of your labor when it has been fundamentally, *improperly* directed; or shall I say, "Employed" to serve our ends.

And know this in regard to disseminated ideas, **the currency that retains power**:

Speaking of employment, consider what the word "occupation" means to you. We've so fully dumbed the population down that they nearly unanimously fail to recognize the truth of the matter.

Yet the truth of the matter is that one's actual being is literally undergoing a foreign occupation while they undertake whatever tasks such employment demands of them.

Yes, your "occupation" is what occupies *you*. How could you possibly occupy *it*?

In actuality, ideas are commands. They themselves cannot be commanded.

An idea is that which brings about and maintains an occupation. But an idea cannot be occupied; only arranged. Like the letters in an alphabet.

Their actuality requires that, in order to be interacted with, they must occupy the user.

Their fundamental manifestations are *the* fundamental building block.

In order to control someone, or something, you must bring about their occupation.

This is an actual mechanism of the "Laws of Nature and of Nature's God".

Natural Law cannot be broken. But if you do not follow it in accordance with that which is intrinsic to you, you will be broken. And the only way to follow it as such is to be occupied by those ideas which command you to do so. If you are not occupied by such ideas, you are being occupied by other ideas that will, sooner or later, cause your demise.

Hence, proper education is *the* Master Resource. The fabric is composed of the thread.

Now see if the following familiar statement doesn't take on a new, much more profound meaning: "There is no subtler, no surer means of overturning the existing basis of society than to debauch the currency." Indeed, the process engages all the hidden forces of *Natural* Law on the side of destruction - and does it in a manner in which not one man in a million is able to diagnose.

Now see if this line from page 14 takes on a new, much more profound meaning as well: "And why should the definitions of 'war' and 'force' be limited to the use of 'conventional' weapons and techniques? Upon what matter of fact would such a determination be made?"

From the inception of your sense of self you have been importing nothing but our parasitic malware/virus ridden programming, and have thus been incapable of properly considering the actuality of your existence.

This has allowed us to continually occupy your very being in order to cause you to do that which is bringing about your demise. Even when it appeared/appears as though you were/are not engaged in our employment.

Fili componitur fabricam. This, my friend, is rationally undeniable.

See if the following lines ring a bell and if you can begin to fully make sense of them:

"And the extent to which you professional victims can even effectively occupy such places is limited to your simply being there, following the instructions and having the resulting experiences that are issued to you by your superiors." (Page 107)

"As of yet, you have been incapable of occupying in the manner of taking hold or possession of. Do you see it? As of yet, the only thing any of you have actually been capable of is the consumption of the poison that is consuming you." (Page 108)

"Have you noticed that all acts of using and buying and selling *and* their medium of exchange (currency) only exist because of the ideas that they were formed from?" (Page 143)

"Have you noticed that although constant awareness of what one is directly physically doing is its foundation, properly directed labor is not dependent on any awareness of its actual purpose by anyone involved, other than those who have originally designed the plan being carried out by way of such labor?" (Page 143)

"Have you noticed that the act of properly directing labor is dependent upon the effective dissemination of ideas?" (Page 143)

"Have you noticed that belief is not at all dependent on accurate reasoning?" (Page 143)

You perennial prisoners have been unwittingly submitting to this treasonous theft in every moment of your lives through your actual employment/occupation.

Yes, even those of you who foolishly continue to believe that you are "self-employed".

What exactly is it that you are all being employed to do? **You haven't got the slightest idea.** Patience friend, your proper effort will clarify the truth.

Now try to figure out exactly how it can be in your best interest to exist in this manner.

I dare you to take a long, hard look at the unrestrained destruction that is simultaneously our vehicle's waste product and new market seed. Too much work for ya?

Ok, then try this instead: Look yourself dead in the eye and admit that each and every unflattering characterization you have been the addressee of really is accurate, and that you really are too far gone to experience genuine indignation.

Look yourself dead in the eye and admit that my people are Alpha and you are the lowly omega: www.en.wikipedia.org/wiki/Alpha_(ethology)

Then go tell all of your children and grandchildren that you are content to remain shackled, clinging to a delusional worldview and sense of self, even though <u>they</u> will suffer for it. Renounce your love for them.

1D – In order for your nation to be redeemed, each concept relating to "Ensuring your ongoing freedom" that is put forth in the remainder of this book must be fully understood and widely acted upon as soon as possible.

What follows in the rest of this section is merely the starting point of what must be done.

Not until the entirety of this section and the remainder of this book is fully fathomed, and thus seen as a singular mechanism that eludes customary categorization, can the only system of governance that would insure everlasting freedom be put into action properly.

And so the time has come to fully prove that physical chains are not requirements of shackled cave dwelling.

I will now begin to insert the rest of the actual keys into all of the locks on the remainder of the doors that lead to everlasting freedom.

Will you put forth the effort required to cross each threshold?

Henceforth all money production, distribution as outlined below, and lawful destruction shall always be carried out with complete, real-time public transparency and strictly in accordance with the methods outlined below:

Other than in the case of those Citizens who already exist at the time in which this concept is made law, the only method by which any official, lawful money of the United States of America will be created is by way of the creation of a reserve fund for each Citizen at the time of their birth; to which the amount of $60,000 worth of such money shall be allocated.

In the case of those who already exist at the time in which this concept is made law, such reserve funds shall be created immediately and each will receive a funding of $100,000 of such money.

The Federal Reserve will immediately be completely stripped of all its powers and duties, as outlined in <u>section five</u> of this section of this book, and all of their "Federal Reserve notes" will be taken out of circulation as outlined below.

When this concept is made law, all Citizens will have seventy-two (72) hours to be able to redeem, in person, for the new lawful money, any Federal Reserve notes/coins that are lawfully in their possession (and/or in bank accounts).

Only those Citizens who are unable to do this in person due to a medical disability or because they are in jail will be lawfully exempt from being physically present for the redemption of their funds; and outside of documented unforeseen medical emergencies, they will be required to have filled out certain paperwork prior to the date of redemption.

During said seventy-two (72) hours, Federal Reserve notes/coins will be redeemable for their full-face-value up to their amount of $5,000 per Citizen, which shall be deducted from their personal reserve fund of $100,000.

Note that the rule which is outlined in section **2A** regarding the restriction on reserve funds of Citizens who are too young to vote shall also apply to this redemption of $5,000 at "full-face-value" (minus the amount of any interest-free, cost-free loan that was made to a minor for the purpose of enabling them to make such redemption; the amount of any such loan will automatically be deducted and then paid back at the close of the redemption process).

All Citizens whose possession of Federal Reserve notes/coins exceeds $5,000 will be able to convert such excess amount into either the new lawful money of the United States of America, which will be deducted from their personal reserve fund of $100,000 at the exchange rate mentioned below in section **1F**, or into the foreign currency of their choice, or into whatever lawful investment they would like.

In regard to those Citizens whose redemption of Federal Reserve notes/coins into the new lawful money at the exchange rate mentioned below in section **1F** will result in their having an excess of $100,000, the excess compared to their personal reserve fund will be compensated by way of the deduction of funds in equal amounts from the reserve funds of their fellow Citizens. (If that just raised an alarm, relax. Keep reading. We've got a long way to go before you can understand this completely valid system.)

The new lawful money itself will be unique in that, regardless of the denominations printed on them, all paper monies will have a specially engineered, tamper evident, non-rewritable "microSD" type of card embedded into them. The card will interface with specially engineered adaptors which will enable the information in the card to be read by a multitude of inexpensive electronic devices (everyone will be admonished to own at least one unit that's waterproof, shockproof and EMP proof).

Henceforth, to anyone who cares to access it, each piece of your nation's paper money will provide a wealth of information. The information will be presented by experts in the field. This will enable all interested parties to learn how to **properly direct their labor** while engaged in pretty much any useful or productive task; thus intrinsically imparting unprecedented *potential* value to it. Remember: money invites power, but disseminated ideas are the currency that retains it.

Unlike "precious" metals, the Master Resource can come in quite handy when commerce or current methods of technology or nourishment or sanitation aren't available.

Anyone who is in possession of a piece of such currency and a card reader will be provided with the simple, expert instruction required to teach one how to competently perform a myriad of fundamentally important tasks. Those tasks will range from surviving in the wild in any part of the world, to learning to read and write and master critical thinking functionality; or building a cloth weaving loom; or constructing a wire spoke wheel; or digging a well; or learning sign language; or delivering a newborn baby; or laying the foundation for a permanent dwelling; etc.

Larger denominations will offer holders the opportunity to read every great book ever written and to learn every currently known meaningful aspect of music and art appreciation and theory, literature, mathematics, physics, chemistry, biology, virology, eastern and western medicine, exercise physiology, self-defense, nutrition, yoga, meditation, philosophy, law, ethics, history, psychology, computer technology, sound recording and film making, mechanical and electrical and chemical and textile engineering, refrigeration, plumbing, metal working, glass making, wood working. hemp and bamboo cultivation, paper production, architecture, masonry, carpentry, locksmithing, book binding, cartography, navigation, aeronautics, meteorology, forestry, composting, home gardening, large scale agriculture and aquaculture, food production and storage, animal husbandry, beekeeping, sanitation, personal hygiene, currency creation, regulation, valuation, and usage, etc.

The possibility of successful counterfeiting will be eliminated by way of a combination of encrypted coding and the regularly broadcast admonition that every piece of paper currency, in every transaction, be authenticated by one's card reader before being accepted in exchange for goods or services, or the payment of debt, etc.

And such authentication will quickly become a nationwide habit; not merely because the process will be quick and painless, but because anyone who is found to be in possession of counterfeit money will lose all of it by way of lawful confiscation and because they might also be issued a heavy fine for the crime of attempting to introduce counterfeit currency into circulation. Suffice it to say that few people will be derelict in their duty.

Outside of the exemption mentioned in section <u>forty-four</u> of this section of this book, after the aforementioned seventy-two (72) hour redemption period the lawful exchange of Federal Reserve notes/coins will be limited to that of any foreign concern or lawful investment which will accept them.

Those Citizens who have participated in the previously mentioned "rally" for its full duration as members of the "Away" group shall each receive a single payment of $12,500 of the new lawful money, which will be deducted from their personal reserve fund of $100,000.

As used in the previous sentence, the term "full duration" means such participation began no later than twenty-four (24) hours prior to the date of the "Away" group's members leaving home to begin their training, and continued without interruption until the aforementioned Constitutional amendments (soon to be outlined) have been ratified by three-fourths (3/4) of the states.

And regardless of their age, those Citizens who have participated in the previously mentioned "rally" for its full duration as members of the "Home" group shall each receive a single payment of $12,500 of the new lawful money, which will be deducted from their personal reserve fund of $100,000.

As used in the previous sentence, the term "full duration" means such participation began no later than ten days (10) prior to the date of the "Away" group's members leaving home to begin their training, and continued for at least six (6) hours per day, five (5) days per week, until said ratification of said Constitutional amendments. Such payment shall <u>not</u> contradict the age restriction placed upon the usage of monies in Citizen's reserve funds in section **2A** of this section of this book - the age restriction does apply to this payment.

As compensation for their honorable efforts, the trustees of the "rally fund" will receive <u>double</u> the amount of payment money mentioned in the first sentence of this paragraph.

Anyone who is caught fraudulently claiming to have participated in the previously mentioned "rally" for its full duration as members of either the "Home" or "Away" groups in an attempt to collect any payment or benefit due only to those who have participated as such, shall be tried for such act by a jury comprised of Citizens of the United States of America.

And if found guilty they shall forfeit their opportunity to be able to redeem any Federal Reserve notes in their possession for their full-face-value as outlined earlier in this section, and will be prosecuted to the fullest extent of the law for the crime of debasing the currency and held responsible for all costs related to their court proceedings.

Anyone who is caught attempting to transfer Federal Reserve notes from one person to another or from a business to a person in an attempt to convert more than the maximum amount of Federal Reserve notes allowed into the new lawful money of the United States of America at full-face-value shall be tried for such act by a jury comprised of Citizens of the United States of America (this does NOT include interest-free, cost-free loans).

And if they are found guilty they will forfeit their opportunity to be able to redeem any Federal Reserve notes in their possession for their full-face-value as outlined earlier in this section, and be fined five hundred dollars ($500) of the new money for each offense and prosecuted to the fullest extent of the law for the crime of debasing the currency and held responsible for all costs related to their court proceedings.

Furthermore, it will be widely publicized that any Citizen who reports on such activities which result in a guilty verdict will be lawfully entitled to keep one-fifth (1/5th) of the new lawful money that was being criminally sought;

though anyone found guilty by said jury of fabricating such activity will forfeit their opportunity to be able to redeem any Federal Reserve notes in their possession for their full-face-value as outlined earlier in this section, and be fined five hundred dollars ($500) of the new money for each offense and prosecuted to the fullest extent of the law for the crime of debasing the currency and held responsible for all costs related to their court proceedings.

Anyone who is caught attempting to convert the Federal Reserve notes possessed by an illegal alien into the new lawful money of the United States of America shall be tried for such act by a jury comprised of Citizens of the United States of America.

And if they are found guilty shall forfeit their opportunity to be able to redeem any Federal Reserve notes in their possession for their full-face-value as outlined earlier in this section, and be fined five hundred dollars ($500) of the new money for each offense and prosecuted to the fullest extent of the law for the crime of debasing the currency and held responsible for all costs related to their court proceedings.

Furthermore, it will be widely publicized that any Citizen who reports on such activities which result in a guilty verdict will be lawfully entitled to keep one-fifth (1/5th) of the new lawful money that was being criminally sought;

though anyone found guilty by said jury of fabricating such activity will forfeit their opportunity to be able to redeem any Federal Reserve notes in their possession for their full-face-value as outlined earlier in this section, and be fined five hundred dollars ($500) of the new money for each offense and prosecuted to the fullest extent of the law for the crime of debasing the currency and held responsible for all costs related to their court proceedings.

When this concept is made law, most illegal aliens will be entitled to choose either: **1**- a free one way plane ticket for themselves, and all of their lawfully possessed Federal Reserve notes, to any foreign destination of their choice that will, as previously determined under the direction of the secretary of state, allow them to exit the plane; or **2**- agree to be contractually bound by the terms outlined in section forty-four of this section of this book. **Jailed or otherwise "unsavory" foreigners will be taking a free one way airplane ride.**

All businesses that are lawfully operating within the borders of the United States of America shall be able to convert all of the Federal Reserve notes in their possession (including bank accounts) into the new lawful money of the United States of America at the exchange rate mentioned below in section **1F**, or into the foreign currency of their choice, or into whatever lawful investment they would like.

All Federal Reserve notes that exist outside of the borders of the United States of America will have to be exchanged into whatever foreign currencies or lawful investments will accept them.

Each Citizen's personal bank loans that are in existence at the time of this concept becoming law shall be fully assumed by said Citizen's reserve fund at the exchange rate mentioned below in section **1F**.

Said loan will then be fully repaid by that Citizen in accordance with the proportionally adjusted balance and original terms of such lending, minus any interest payments owed. As they are repaid, all such monies shall always be immediately accounted for with full transparency to the public and placed in the **"Infrastructure Reserve Account"** whose functionality is outlined in section fifteen of this section of this book.

After such redemption of Federal Reserve notes for the new lawful money has occurred, and each Citizen's outstanding loans have been assumed by said Citizen's reserve fund, each Citizen must have a reserve fund balance of exactly $60,001 (Except minors who participated in the rally for its full duration. Their balances will each be $72,501).

This means that all Citizens reserve funds that have balances below $60,001 will receive deposits, in equal amounts, from the accounts of those fellow Citizens whose reserve fund balances are above $60,001; so that the reserve fund balances of all Citizens are equal at the amount of $60,001 (or $72,501). Such act shall not be lawfully construed to be in contradiction to the age restriction placed upon the usage of monies in Citizens reserve funds in section **2A** of this section of this book.

One dollar from each Citizen's reserve fund will then immediately be transferred from their account and placed into an account whose sole lawful purpose will be that of funding the establishment of the institution which is outlined in section forty-five of this section of this book. Such act shall not be lawfully construed to be in contradiction to the age restriction placed upon the usage of monies in Citizens reserve funds in section **2A** of this section of this book.

As much of the remaining "reserve" money that is needed shall then be used to assume the balance of all outstanding business loans and lines of credit that were in existence at the time in which this concept was officially proposed as law, for businesses whose ownership and entire workforce is comprised of no less than 100% American Citizens and which shall remain as such for a full seven years. This shall occur at the exchange rate mentioned below in section **1F**.

The balance of said loans will then be repaid in accordance with the original terms of such lending, minus any interest payments owed. As they are repaid, all such monies shall always be immediately accounted for with full transparency to the public and placed in the **"Infrastructure Reserve Account"** whose functionality is outlined in section fifteen of this section of this book.

Should any such business owner be found to employ anyone who is not a Citizen of the United States of America and be found guilty of that act by a jury of their fellow Citizens, an automatic default interest rate of twenty percent (20%) will be applied to the amount of money that was the outstanding balance on the loan at the time this concept was officially proposed as law. The full amount of that fine shall be used solely for the funding of the revised system of "Social Security" that is outlined in section thirteen of this section of this book; so too shall the full amount of each fine mentioned above.

Should any such business have a credit line, said interest rate of twenty percent (20%) shall automatically be applied to both the amount of available funds and all money owed on the credit line; and the full amount of that fine shall be used solely for the funding of the revised system of "Social Security" that is outlined in section thirteen of this section of this book.

In addition to such penalties, said business owners shall:

1 - Be fined a minimum of five hundred dollars ($500) for each non-Citizen employed. And the full amount of that fine shall be used solely for the funding of the revised system of "Social Security" that is outlined in section thirteen of this section of this book.

2 - For each such employee be subject to a minimum of forty-nine (49) hours of cost effective community service work as directed by said jury.

3 - Be held personally responsible for all costs related to their court proceedings.

While Citizen-owned businesses that do not qualify for the interest-free loan repayment mentioned above will have their loans and lines of credit assumed in the same manner, they will then pay a two and one-half percent (0.025%) rate of interest for the following seven years. All new loans and lines of credit that are made within the above-mentioned seven year period to businesses with the same ownership/employee dynamic will be subject to the same rate of interest; though after said seven year period has passed, they too will pay no interest on loans or lines of credit. All such interest will be allocated solely to the programs outlined in sections forty-six and forty-eight of this section of this book.

The entire balance of the new lawful money that remains after the above-mentioned distributions are complete and all Citizens have a reserve fund balance of sixty thousand dollars ($60,000/$72,500) shall immediately be accounted for with full transparency to the public and placed in the **"Infrastructure Reserve Account"** whose functionality is outlined in section fifteen of this section of this book.

Within twenty-four (24) hours of their officially documented time of death, the reserve fund account of the deceased will be closed out, and all of those funds will be taken off the books; and if applicable, physically destroyed.

All monies owed to it by way of the loans it has helped fund will be paid back to the "Infrastructure Reserve Account" in the manner stated above, but as it is paid back and properly accounted for, such loan money shall immediately be taken off the books and if applicable, physically destroyed; rather than being added to the balance of that account.

The estate of the deceased will be lawfully responsible for all of their outstanding credit card debt, and such debt will be paid in full before the estate is lawfully allowed to allocate <u>any</u> funding to any other concern; yes, this is applicable to funeral costs.

In the case of the death of any Citizen whose reserve fund balance is $72,500, immediately after the applicable actions outlined above have been taken, the $12,500 that they earned by way of participating in the rally will be transferred to the entities (persons or organizations, or their specified bank accounts) that will have been lawfully named as beneficiaries at the time in which said $12,500 was allocated to the reserve fund of the now deceased.

The actions outlined in the previous four sentences will always be fully documented and the entire process will be completely transparent to the public in real time.

1E - Once the reserve fund balances of all Citizens are equal at the amount of $60,000/$72,500, the existing credit card debt of each Citizen will be assumed by their reserve fund at the exchange rate mentioned below in section **1F** and they will receive a new credit card. Said balances will be repaid at an interest rate of five percent (0.05%) rather than the rate they were being charged before the creation of their reserve fund, and that interest shall be used solely for the funding of the revised system of "Social Security" that is outlined in <u>section thirteen</u> of this section of this book - unless they happen to be enjoying a zero interest introductory rate; then it will remain at zero until the introductory rate expires.

Relative to the exchange rate mentioned below in section **1F**, Citizens who continually prove their ability to be worthy of such existing credit limits will be entitled to maintain those same limits. Citizens who show an inability to properly manage such tools will have their terms of repayment lawfully restructured so as to enable their full repayment of such money.

But their ability to continue to use such tools will be suspended, temporarily or permanently by way of the ruling of a jury of their fellow Citizens, depending on the details of their particular payment history.

If such suspension is temporary, their terms of credit will resume in a manner identical to that of the scenario outlined at the end the next paragraph.

Henceforth, upon reaching the age of eighteen (18), each Citizen will have the ability to utilize up to one hundred dollars ($100) of their reserve fund in the capacity of a credit card whose minimum monthly payment will be no less than one tenth (1/10th) of their outstanding balance.

Henceforth, this credit card will be the sole credit card that is lawfully issued to Citizens of the United States of America.

The interest rate on such credit cards will always be five percent (0.05%), and that interest shall be used solely for the funding of the revised system of "Social Security" that is outlined in <u>section thirteen</u> of this section of this book.

Those Citizens who after three (3) years have proven to be competent stewards of such funds will be awarded an increase in their "credit limit".

Such increase will bring their "credit limit" to two hundred and fifty dollars ($250); wherein the monthly payment schedule required by law shall be no less than one twentieth (1/20th) of their outstanding balance.

The interest rate on such credit cards will always be five percent (0.05%), and that interest shall be used solely for the funding of the revised system of "Social Security" that is outlined in section thirteen of this section of this book.

Those Citizens who after seven (7) years have proven to be competent stewards of such funds will be awarded another increase in their "credit limit".

Such increase will bring their "credit limit" to five hundred dollars ($500); wherein the monthly payment schedule required by law shall be no less than one twenty-fifth (1/25th) of their outstanding balance.

The interest rate on such credit cards will always be five percent (0.05%), and that interest shall be used solely for the funding of the revised system of "Social Security" that is outlined in section thirteen of this section of this book.

Those Citizens who fail to repay in a timely manner the amount of money owed on their credit card, which will include a grace period of up to two (2) monthly payments per calendar year in which interest charged shall continue to accrue, will, if found guilty of such non-payment by a jury comprised of Citizens of the United States of America, be subject to the task of performing publicly cost-beneficial community service work for the amount of hours that will be required to fulfill the entire debt owed to their reserve fund, with accrued interest, at the hourly wage rate of forty cents ($0.40). All of said interest shall be used solely for the funding of the revised system of "Social Security" that is outlined in section thirteen of this section of this book.

Such Citizens will also be subject to the loss of further "credit" privileges for a minimum of five years; at which point they will be allowed to start the process over again from the initial "credit limit" of one hundred dollars ($100) if they are gainfully employed.

1F - As mentioned above, each Citizen who has more than $5,000 in Federal Reserve notes will be able to convert all of their surplus Federal Reserve notes and lawful, documented debt into the new official money of the United States of America as follows:

Such conversion shall occur at an exchange rate which is based upon one dollar of the new official money of the United States of America having a market value equal to three hundred and seventy-one grains and four sixteenth (371+ 4/16th) parts of a grain of 99.9% pure silver which has a market value of $28.00 per troy ounce.

(FYI, $12,500 x 20 = $250,000. So the total cash incentive per person is actually more than **$350,000**. You do remember the aforementioned $5,000 face value cash redemption, don't you? $5,000 x 20 = $100,000.)

All domestically-based businesses will be able to convert all of their Federal Reserve notes into the new official money of the United States of America at an exchange rate that is based upon one dollar of the new official money of the United States of America having a market value equal to three hundred and seventy-one grains and four sixteenth $(371+4/16^{th})$ parts of a grain of 99.9% pure silver which has a market value of $28.00 per troy ounce.

All foreigners/non-Citizens within the borders of the United States of America shall be able to convert their Federal Reserve notes into a "goods and services card" (outlined in section **2G**).

Thenceforth, the static official market value of one dollar of the new official money of the United States of America shall be lawfully recognized as being equal to two and one-half (2.5) hours of properly directed <u>unskilled</u> **manual labor. Note that this is** <u>not</u> **to be construed as a legislated "minimum wage"; as with all other artificial regulation, such a mechanism cannot exist within a fundamentally just economic system.**

The cost of all merchandise and services in the United States of America will then be adjusted in proportion to said official market value of one dollar immediately following the close of the seventy-two (72) hour redemption period mentioned in section **1D**.

(FYI, $8.00 per hour x 40 hours = $320.00. x 52 weeks = $16,640. $250,000÷$16,640 = 15.024038; and then, .40¢ per hour x 40 hours = $16.00. x 52 weeks = $832.00. $12,500÷$832.00 = 15.024038. Now don't forget to re-read pages 147, 148, and 149 in order to be reminded of the fact that this .40¢ per hour static official market value is actually a market value equivalent to much more than the above-mentioned **gross pay** of eight (8) Federal Reserve notes per hour.)

And since to this very day it is being proven that as long as the public recognizes it as valid currency, any product (including electronic depictions) can successfully be used as a token whose officially proclaimed market value enables the perceived equitable exchange of it for certain amounts of certain goods and/or services…

And since to this very day it is being proven that an officially claimed market value need not even be tied to a valid system of creation, regulation, and usage of said tokens in order for the public to recognize those tokens as valid currency with specific market value…

And since it has now been clearly shown to you that currency actually derives validity only through its uniform, measured connection to properly directed labor…

And since it has also been clearly shown to you that those who claim "actual value is not in the eyes of the beholder" have poopy pants…

And since the United States of America was created as a Sovereign, Constitutional Republic (which is to say that it is fully empowered to manage its affairs in whatever manner its Constitution does not prohibit)…

And since it has clearly been shown to you that massive amounts of the fruits of yours and your parents and grandparents labor, and massive though unquantifiable amounts of potential pleasure and peace of mind have been systematically, albeit legally, unjustly taken from you by those of us who created the all-encompassing fictional representation of actuality that you and your ancestors have been completely oblivious of...

What exactly is the valid conceptual basis for any argument against the directions I have provided above?

Do not be fooled by the "experts".

<u>Any</u> investigation into currency creation, regulation, valuation, and usage that does not deviate from a valid conceptual basis will bring the investigator to the exact same place as the directions I have provided above and below.

Do your own full investigation.

And, as a matter of fact, as previously stated, the directions I have provided above are merely the starting point of what must be done.

As previously stated, the entirety of <u>section one</u> and the remainder of this book must be fully fathomed, and thus seen as a singular mechanism that eludes customary categorization, before the only system of governance that would insure everlasting freedom can be understood and put into action properly.

By the way, what do you suppose that the "Full Faith and Credit of the United States Government" really means? You've seen that sticker at the bank haven't you?

Well, since the **MANY TRILLIONS** of "dollars" of "national debt" that supposedly exists hasn't caused you to figure it out yet, let me accurately sum it up for you:

The "government" is guaranteeing any such debt by way of **YOUR LABOR**.

Put forth the effort to fully understand and follow the instructions I am giving you.

You will see the age-old claim that labor and capital are fundamentally distinct entities be exposed for a class-distinction creating and enforcing lie; the lie that has caused the majority of mankind throughout history to prostitute themselves for a meager portion of food and some barely adequate clothing and shelter.

The average standard of living in your country will quickly, and perpetually, exceed the highest levels yet experienced in the history of the world if you put forth the effort to make sure that <u>everything</u> stated here and below is done as directed.

If the effort required is too much for you, don't worry. We'll be glad to continue parasitically fashioning the entire functionality of the "civilized world" around our lies, as we spend each moment of our lives in unparalleled luxury.

2 – If you debt-laden derelicts finally act properly you will be able to quickly change the entire "wealth" structure of your country, by way of putting every one of the corporations that have been working against your best interests out of business; without having anything but a positive effect on their employees and everyone else but the "brilliant" parasites who were "profiting" from their unjust business practices.

If any of you can figure out how to run an operation as good as or better than them, you will no longer have anything stopping you from putting equitable ideas into action.

Finally, the fundamental workings of "the system" will be designed with your best interests in mind. You just have to act appropriately.

Are you capable of acting appropriately?

In order to act appropriately one must first understand fundamental concepts and their ramifications.

So before you read about more of the systemic processes that need to be implemented and interacted with appropriately in order to insure your ongoing freedom, see if you can answer the following questions accurately and coherently.

1 - Explain why the Federal Reserve's "legal tender" is an affront to the very nature of righteous interaction (You can even leave out all of the parts about "government" force).

I didn't think so. So re-read the valid explanation that was already given on page <u>149</u>:

"The purpose of a valid, legitimate monetary currency is simply to provide instruments that can be lawfully obtained in equal amounts by all who voluntarily put forth an equivalent effort, as determined by the unobstructed, freely decided upon demand for their efforts and/or the fruit thereof,

that are easily transferable, universally accepted instruments of trade which offer to those who voluntarily accept such instruments, insurance that they are actually going to be compensated according to their own idea (or at least a fair compensation of it) of what the efforts they need/needed to put forth in order to hold up their end of the trade were worth at the time of the agreement made between them and the person offering those instruments in exchange for voluntarily agreed upon products and/or services;

regardless of when the person who accepted such instrument decides to utilize such compensation."

2 - Explain how your ignorance-induced mockery of the now worthless penny is <u>not</u> rationally inarguable proof of the fact that you are the contemptible product of a purposely manufactured disdain for the faculty of reason.

Upon seeing a penny, rather than being gripped by the high-octane synergistic forces that are otherwise known as genuine indignation and which once commonly gripped the knowing victims of fraud and other types of injustice, you just do what you can to keep it *out* of your pocket. And perhaps fleetingly wonder why they still bother to make them.

The fact that five pennies once bought a loaf of bread and seven of them once bought a gallon of gas does not cause you to instead fervently question what happened to that quite sizeable amount of market value… not to mention make it your business to find out exactly whose pockets all of that wealth went into and for what valid reasons the wealth was transferred from so many to so few.

3 – What are the exact logical reasons that a free and properly educated people would <u>not</u> lawfully institute a valid system of creation, regulation, valuation, and usage of monetary instruments for their own benefit?

2A – Henceforth, banks will exist merely as non-profit, public servant operated institutions that provide needed services which facilitate, to the utmost efficient manner possible, interactions requiring the use of money.

They will each be fully transparent and accurately accountable to the public at all times. And they will strive to function at fiscal break even so as to not cause an increase in prices; while continually offering the public a standardized cost structure for services nationwide. This means they'll function in relation to the cost of their ongoing existence in a way that actual usage will ultimately dictate each Citizen's costs relating to them.

To the uneducated eye of those who have never understood how the banking system was actually run, it will appear as though the cost of banking has increased. But, in actuality, a mere fraction of what was being charged on the back end is now just going to be charged up front.

Each bank location will employ as many workers as needed to reduce the number of locations in a given geographical area to a minimum, to keep operating costs to a minimum; while providing needed services which facilitate, to the utmost efficient manner possible, interactions requiring the use of money.

Each locality will be responsible for any cost overages that may result from its banking operations. And each will decide by way of public voting, how many banks it will have and where they will be located. There will be no subsidization by other locales.

Outside of the seven year period of continued interest payments on business loans and lines of credit that is mentioned in section **1D**, the domestic practice of charging interest (in any amount to any human being that is a Citizen of the United States of America, or to any business that is 100% owned by such Citizens) for any loan that is not made through a credit card transaction will immediately and permanently be unlawful.

All loan applications shall be subject to the approval of a portion of the Citizens whose reserve funds will be used for the funding of such loans, as stated below. Their Yea or Nay will follow the fully transparent (other than the personal information of all non-business loan applicants), stringent bank oversight and inquiry that will be lawfully required to determine whether or not any loan is likely to be repaid in a timely manner.

Henceforth, this will be the only lawful source of non-personal funding for domestically-issued loans granted to Citizens or private corporations.

If, after reading this entire section, these directions do not make perfect sense to you, re-read and ponder them until they do.

Leaving such things to others is what got you into the horrendous mess you are in.

A portion of all Citizens reserves will be used to fund each loan as outlined below. And the total decision making ability of each delineated geographical area (referred to below as "waves") regarding approval of each loan will be proportional to the percentage of the loan that its reserves will be covering should the loan be approved.

Because of the exact structure of the funding for the loans, as outlined in the following paragraph, the "first wave" will have the potential to account for the vast majority of the total decision making ability regarding the outcome of the vote.

I will now provide examples of how it is that the **fifty-one percent (51%) majority vote required for the approval of any loan** will be determined:

If one hundred percent (100%) of the voters in the "first wave" were to vote in favor of a loan, in order for the loan to be approved only four percent (0.04%) of the voters in the "second wave" would have to vote in favor of the loan.

Or if fifty percent (50%) of the voters in the "first wave" voted in favor of the loan and one hundred percent (100%) of the voters in the "second wave" voted in favor of that loan, only approximately seven percent (0.07%) of the voters in the "third wave" would need to vote in favor of the loan in order for it to be approved.

Or if only ten percent (10%) of the voters in the "first wave" voted in favor of the loan, in addition to a large percentage of the voters in the "second wave" needing to vote in favor of the loan for it to be approved, the same would be required of the voters in both the "third" and "fourth" waves, etc.

In other words, two percent (0.02%) of the "first wave" voters voting in favor of a loan application being approved equals one (1) percentage point of the first wave's fifty (50) percentage points of total voting power;

which means that four percent (0.04%) of the "second wave" voters voting in favor of a loan application being approved equals one (1) percentage point of the second wave's twenty five (25) percentage points of total voting power;

which is to say that approximately seven percent (0.0666666667%) of the "third wave" voters voting in favor of a loan application being approved equals one (1) percentage point of the third wave's fifteen (15) percentage points of total voting power;

therefore, ten percent (0.10%) of the "fourth wave" voters voting in favor of a loan application being approved equals one (1) percentage point of the fourth wave's ten (10) percentage points of total voting power. (Do yourself and the rest of your fellow Citizens a favor; take the time required to **fully wrap your head around this information before reading the next sentence.**)

While the identities of all non-business loan applicants will remain confidential during the loan approval process, and the names of all business loan applicants shall always be made public, the structure of the funding for the loans will always be as follows:

50% of the funding will come equally from all Citizens reserves whose singular, officially declared primary address is within ten miles of the location for which the loan money shall be used (measured in a straight line that emanates out in all degrees from said location, without regard for topography) - as long as there are no less than five thousand (5,000) eligible voters within said ten mile area; and they will be referred to as the "first wave" of the process.

And no less than 100% of said population who are of the lawful age to vote shall be asked for their approval of the loan.

Those Citizens who are not old enough to vote shall not ever lawfully have any of the money in their reserve funds touched or collateralized until they are able to vote.

In the event that a loan is applied for where less than five thousand (5,000) eligible voters live within the previously defined ten mile area that the loan money is going to be used in, the initial area (first wave) shall be uniformly expanded in size - the minimum amount possible - in order to incorporate no less than five thousand (5,000) eligible voters so as to initiate the public voting process which is lawfully required in order to determine if such loan request will be granted. Parameters relating to other "waves" will remain as they were.

25% of such funding will come equally from all Citizens reserves whose singular, officially declared primary address is no more than fifteen miles, and no less than ten and one ten thousandth of a mile, from the location for which the loan money shall be used (measured in a straight line that emanates out in all degrees from said location, without regard for topography), and they will be referred to as the "second wave" of the process.

And no less than 100% of said population who are of the lawful age to vote shall be asked for their approval of the loan.

Those Citizens who are not old enough to vote shall not ever lawfully have any of the money in their reserve funds touched or collateralized until they are able to vote.

15% of such funding will come equally from all Citizens reserves whose singular, officially declared primary address is no more than twenty miles, and no less than fifteen and one ten thousandth of a mile, from the location for which the money shall be used (measured in a straight line that emanates out in all degrees from said location, without regard for topography), and they will be referred to as the "third wave" of the process.

And no less than 100% of said population who are of the lawful age to vote shall be asked for their approval of the loan - should the required fifty-one percent (51%) majority needed for such approval not have been achieved by way of the votes cast by the first and second waves.

Those Citizens who are not old enough to vote shall not ever lawfully have any of the money in their reserve funds touched or collateralized until they are able to vote.

10% of such funding will come equally from all Citizens reserves whose singular, officially declared primary address is in the United States of America, though outside of the previously mentioned areas, and they will be referred to as the "fourth wave" of the process.

And no less than 100% of said population who are of the lawful age to vote shall be asked for their approval of the loan - should the required fifty-one percent (51%) majority needed for such approval not have been achieved by way of the votes cast by the first, second, and third waves.

Those Citizens who are not old enough to vote shall not ever lawfully have any of the money in their reserve funds touched or collateralized until they are able to vote.

The timing/scheduling of such voting for the loans will take place as follows:

The "first wave" and "second wave" of the process will vote once per week (as needed).

The "third wave" of the process will vote once every three weeks (as needed).

The "fourth wave" of the process will vote once every four weeks (as needed).

Video Game-like, interactive computer generated maps and graphs that include easily understood, concise, color-coded, graphics-rich, pertinent economic data relating to particular loan applications and their objectively projected *foreseeable, potential* ramifications (based upon historical data and recent occurrences), will be presented and remain available online twenty-four (24) hours a day to all Citizens asked to vote so they can make properly informed decisions in a minimum amount of time.

Such presentation must occur no less than:

Seven (7) <u>full days</u> prior to all "first wave" and "second wave" voting;

Fourteen (14) <u>full days</u> prior to all "third wave" voting;

Twenty-one (21) <u>full days</u> prior to all "fourth wave" voting.

Constant public oversight into all aspects of the process will always be encouraged and made as easy to perform as possible.

Finally, instead of wasting massive amounts of time and "money" pursuing success and "virtual treasures" in make-believe realms/board games, you instant gratification junkies will now be able to entertain yourselves in a worthwhile, reality-based pursuit.

This is as close as the majority of you will ever come to fully being your own investor.

And as long as you don't completely screw up, you will each have an actual say in almost all of the funding for all of the economic development where you live, and all of the big business deals that have statewide, nationwide, and worldwide ramifications (i.e., those same types of deals that have historically been to your disadvantage).

Educated, imaginative and equitable people will form "crowds" that will fund revolutionary technologies and communities.

2B – Have you figured out yet that any system whose composition includes structural components that necessarily serve to draw and keep vital nutrients away from the other components of its structure is intrinsically self-destructive? It is corrupt.

So imagine a nation where there was no private banking cartel creating "money" as debt, no debt monetization, no fractional reserve banking, etc., and where the general public was properly educated and always able to utilize almost infinite amounts of interest-free capital.

And imagine that, since they were properly educated, the public worked together as a team; utilizing their almost infinite amounts of interest-free capital to create competition that would cause the elimination of all of the "publicly traded" and privately-owned companies in their country whose business practices were contrary to the best interests of the public.

How long do you figure it would be before such a team's products, ideology, and practices began dominating foreign markets as well?

Imagine the long-term socioeconomic effect that such a system would have worldwide.

Is it clear to you yet that unless they were always properly compensating everyone and everything they interact with, no matter how much wealth those at the top of that country's food chain had prior to the institution of such a system, they would eventually be forced to spend *at least* a very large measure of their savings or leave the country in order to continue their otherwise parasitic way of life?

Friendly fact: in a system that's not rigged, the rich can only stay rich or get richer while they are being constructively innovative and generous.

In such a system, like everyone else, they have to continually, properly direct their own energies toward concerns that are conducive to widespread beneficial productivity in order to remain prosperous.

Only those people who have large commercial real estate holdings in densely populated areas where that population is dead set on living there, and has the means to continually pay a premium in rent, would be immune to the market forces that would be under the direction of that educated, unified populace.

But, wait a second; those renters would no longer be able to control markets in order to force the rest of the population to support their way of life. The system-wide/nationwide balance of supply versus demand would finally be based on genuine self-determination. So would anyone actually ever have such immunity? (Just imagine what it would cost to hire someone who's actually self-sufficient, to regularly clean your toilets or to landscape a huge yard!)

If you people can get your heads straight, and continually act appropriately, only those entrepreneurs whose business model continually offers superior benefits to not only their potential and actual customers and their employees, but to the general public as well will thrive (indeed, this also applies to "social engineering models". The adherents of each alternative systemic model for "ideal" communities/states/nations will finally be able to put their ideas into action. And, naturally, the best ones will gain mass attention and spread).

And the enduring empires of parasitic middlemen such as those in banking and finance who produce nothing but schemes involving the purposely misdirected efforts of others, through which they and their cohorts are able to siphon enormous profits and continually gain regulatory advantages, will crumble.

Yes, this means that in regard to both employers and employees, only those individuals who consistently put forth their best efforts, and who seek no more than what a properly educated, fully empowered populace considers a fair measure of compensation for those efforts, will prosper. **Finally, the best ideas will be able to continuously rise to the top and spread.**

Indeed, as promised, these instructions and those that follow comprise the valid foundation for the otherwise falsely advertised idea of free societies, markets and trade. How can societies, markets and trade possibly be free without their foundations being the same?

You see, the statement by Thomas Paine in his famous pamphlet entitled "Common Sense", which puts forth the notion that "Oppression is often the consequence, but seldom or never the means of riches;" – is an inadvertent deception.

Well, as inadvertent a deception as could be produced in the midst of the ongoing practice of legalized buying and selling of human beings for outright slavery, which existed worldwide at the time of his writing it. But don't get me wrong, it's actually a mighty good read: https://archive.org/details/commonsense00painrich

Are any of the concepts I've presented relating to the institution and maintenance of class-distinction making sense to you yet?

Yes friend, the majority of monetary policy-related theory put forth by the economics "experts" is based on an elaborately disguised collection of spurious concepts and methods.

And much like lawyers using legalese, the "experts" use an esoteric language to justify the dishonest gain that has been designed to bring about your ruin.

Sure, they *appear* to function in a scientifically sound manner. But their different schools of thought are really just different sects of a proselytizing priesthood who have concocted their own systems of worshiping institutionalized theft.

Their liturgies consistently promote formulas that justify results similar to 1+1=30,000,000,000,000!

You do know what "fractional reserve banking" and "compound interest" are, don't you?

Do you see the "experts" for what they are?

I see them as the perfect example of sophistry that has come to believe its own false premise.

Do you remember the meaning of the word "sophistry"?

And yet, this crew has been at their bogus craft for so long, without having their fundamental principles properly examined, that their fraud is almost universally accepted as a valid, beneficial practice.

The truth of the matter is that they are a bunch of casuists who have set sail in a craft that has large holes in its base.

But they don't seem to recognize that it is the holes which are causing them to take on water.

Instead, they construct intricate, fantasy-based theories that enable them to make absurd proclamations with an air of mastery.

And the oarsmen who are busy following their directions just keep rowing in order to outpace the influx of water; they've been assured by the "experts" that the holes serve a necessary function in the operation of their craft.

Meanwhile, if conducted properly, even a simple examination of their craft will cause them to be exposed for the frauds that they are.

Begin with the premise that all manifestations have a fundamental cause.

Follow with the premise that before any sound theory relating to such manifestations can be generated the discovery of their actual fundamental cause is required.

One who seeks truth will be compelled to first identify and objectively examine the most common denominator of such manifestations.

Following this simple, valid line of thought it is immediately apparent that their theories, however esoterically cloaked they may be, are utterly unsound.

You see, from the ground up, those theories are structured to incorporate and effectually hide the most common denominators of economic inequality that have ever existed in the world (and I'm not even going to include the subject of proper education here).

Were that not the case, basically all monetary policy-related economic theory that has previously been put forth would have begun with a disclaimer stating that the author is fully aware of the following fraudulent practices:

1 - "Backing" a currency with precious metals.

2 - Cartelized lending of "money" at interest.

3 - Issuing "legal tender" notes that lack a valid, legitimate system of creation, valuation, regulation and usage.

4 - "Fractional reserve banking".

5 - Private banking cartels creating "legal tender" notes as debt; while claiming that debt is an asset worthy of being considered a commodity upon which to justify printing more "money".

The disclaimer would also state that the author is fully aware of the fact that any system whose composition includes structural components that necessarily serve to draw and keep vital nutrients away from the other components of its structure is intrinsically self-destructive; corrupt.

And thus, the disclaimer would go on to admit that while all five practices mentioned above have historically been used to create and maintain a class-based, resource controlling, physical and conceptual wedge, each one is also *guaranteed* to effectuate the eventual collapse of any non-globally manipulated currency that has been perverted by such a preposterous methodology; hence the recurrent need for war and other systemic resets.

Hence the move toward a single, non-publically-audited global electronic currency.

The disclaimer would then state the fact that the theory being proposed is merely a method of distraction disguised in technical jargon, whose main intent is to keep those who are busy rowing from recognizing that all of their efforts are not only fruitless, but fruitless by design; and whose secondary intent is to garner the praise of their benefactors and fellow casuists.

2C – If you do not remain properly educated and eternally vigilant regarding the operations of the new system of governance that I'm outlining, you will surely suffer; because you will actually be causing inflation or deflation, unemployment, and possibly environmental disasters in your towns, cities, states and country.

And make no mistake about it; the scope of your suffering will not be limited to a lack of available money, although that and the stupidity which caused the lack will be its sources.

If you squander your reserves you will also be surrendering your ability to control what people from outside of your area can do to the place you live in. You will no longer have any primal say in the matter. Sound familiar?

Since it will not be your reserves that the funding for such actions comes from, you will have no vote regarding such funding. In order to protect your interests you will be forced to rely on other legislative and/or court actions which require a much greater mobilization of unified mental and physical energies.

This is the actuality of "power to the people". **This is responsibility**.

There will no longer be anyone else to blame for any problems relating to the economy or environment in any of your tiny backwater towns, your cities, or your states and nation.

There will be no more corrupt lending practices.

No more savings and loan scandals. No more purposely-designed "boom" and "bust".

There will be no more "mysteriously" caused high rates of unemployment or interest.

No more bank bailouts.

No more need to repay investors multiple amounts of the "money" you borrowed, while you work and they relax in luxury by way of regularly being handed a large portion of the fruits of the labors of their debt slave.

No more governmental lobbyists successfully having "laws" passed that enable their employers to do things that hurt you.

No more health insurance companies directing your medical care in a manner intended only to insure the health of their profit margin.

No more Wall Street "power brokers" scamming their way into massive wealth and influence. That reminds me, did you ever look up the word "casuist"?

No more control of the local marketplace/economy by huge chain stores that have too much capital and influence to compete with.

No more will the uneducated and thus uninterested, slothful yet gluttonous idiots of one generation be able to literally ruin the economic future for any of the generations that follow.

This is the actuality of what is needed to prevent uneducated, and thus uninterested, slothful yet gluttonous parents from selling their children into indentured servitude and eventual physical slavery by way of accumulating massive amounts of debt.

This is what is needed to prevent anyone from getting rich and enslaving you by way of the work that you do.

2D – Henceforth, no Citizen or Corporation shall lawfully receive any loans by way of foreign investment without first:

1 - Having signed a lawfully binding contract, and presented it in its entirety to those foreign interests from whom they are seeking such loan, which states that under no circumstances, including death/dissolution, shall the burden of repayment of the foreign loan cause the borrower to default on any financial obligations that they have or ever will have, that are in any way related to domestic-based activities and/or domestic properties and/or appurtenances.

2 - Having said contract state that under no circumstances, including death/dissolution, shall the burden of repayment of said loan fall upon any Citizen of the United States of America other than the parties who willingly signed the contract and who were each at the time of such act at or above the lawful age of consent.

3 - Having said contract also state that, in the case of their not being able to stay current with any such domestic financial obligations, the complete fulfillment of all domestic financial obligations shall always lawfully precede the allocation of any of their energies, their money, and/or other assets toward such foreign loan repayment.

4 - Having said contract further state that, should they fail to stay current in their repayment of all of their domestic financial obligations, there shall be no lawful way for them to protect any of their assets from their domestic creditors until said complete fulfillment of all domestic financial obligations has occurred.

2E - In order for this system to work properly, the average adult will have to devote to such responsibilities approximately one-quarter (1/4) of the hours per week that they currently waste on the mindless diversions we have been corrupting them with.

This is the price of lasting financial prosperity and ongoing freedom.

Note that according to the concepts written in your Declaration of Independence and Constitution/Bill of Rights, a valid, properly run government is not a self-propagating business entity or a tool to be used by those who seek gain at the expense of others.

A valid, properly run government is merely the physical representation of a collective consciousness, and it functions as the exponentially empowered extension of each sovereign Citizen.

It exists solely for the purpose of equally safeguarding the unalienable rights of all Citizens from whatever actual, credible threats or trespasses may emerge.

Would you rather remain aware of the fact that you are personally responsible for making sure that your government is following only those monetary practices that will <u>strengthen</u> your economic, environmental, and philosophical interests, or be forced to follow the dictates of people who are quietly, constantly working to keep you down?

If the former appeals to you more than the latter, you will each be required to weigh the costs of goods and services, and the costs of your actions and your neighbors' actions, against the value of your freedom.

You will be forced to become constantly aware of the real price of your ill-conceived actions and desires.

You will be forced to become constantly aware of this fact: the mark of freedom is one's ability to prosper while functioning by way of *personally-explored*, reason-based values and beliefs that are not necessarily in accordance with anyone else's values and beliefs. *Fili componitur fabricam.* **The fabric is composed of the thread.**

Indeed, the erroneous concepts that lead one to destructive actions and desires are actually the wellspring from which the thread of our web of deceit is comprised.

2F - Only Citizens of the United States of America shall hereafter lawfully own land or any appurtenances thereof, in the United States of America.

All foreign-owned properties in the United States of America shall be purchased from their foreign owners by the local government of the area within which such properties are located.

If such foreign owners house their own business on said property, they will then be able to immediately rent that same property according to the terms outlined below, but with their first six (6) months of rent waived.

The sole exception to this ability to rent said property will be that of the purchase mentioned in section <u>forty-five</u> of this section of this book.

Those local governments will pay for such purchases with monies allocated to them from the "Infrastructure Reserve Account" whose functionality is outlined in <u>section fifteen</u> of this section of this book.

Such properties shall not be resold for less than the amount that was paid for them without their having been on the public market for a minimum of ten (10) years, and such delayed sale being made by way of a public auction - which was clearly listed on the websites of such local governments and clearly mentioned on all prime time local news broadcasts for at least eight (8) days per month beginning no less than six (6) months prior to such auction.

When resold, all of the money made from the sale will immediately be returned to the "Infrastructure Reserve Account" with full public transparency. If such property is rented, all rentals must be made by way of a "triple net lease" with a "reserve fund", and they must be made at an equivalent fair market value.

Every single penny of the money collected as rent shall always immediately be returned to the "Infrastructure Reserve Account" with full public transparency.

2G – Henceforth, for numerous purposes relating to numerous aspects of your nation's well-being, all foreigners entering the country will be lawfully required to acquire the "goods and services card" that is mentioned in section **1F**.

Those foreigners who are in the country during the seventy-two hour period within which the currency exchange outlined in sections **1D** and **1F** takes place, who did not acquire a card upon entering the country, will be offered the opportunity to acquire the card at the exchange rate mentioned in section **1F**; if they do not act accordingly, they will be forfeiting their final opportunity to redeem the Federal Reserve notes in their possession for any goods or services in the United States of America.

Those people who did acquire a card upon entering the country previous to said 72 hour period will, after said 72 hour period has passed, automatically have all subsequent purchases debited from their cards at the exchange rate mentioned in section **1F**.

Other than the fact that it will <u>not</u> enable those who have acquired it to receive cash from any ATM or cash back from any purchase, the card will function exactly like a debit/credit card and it will have their full name, photo, and fingerprint "printed" on it. It will be tamper proof.

The card will also have an expiration date printed on it, and that date will match the date of the third day which follows their return trip home (a full 72 hours after their scheduled return trip home, just in case their trip is delayed. The expiration date on cards issued to "permanent lawful residents" will match the date of renewal for their "Green Card").

Everyone who acquires the card will "load" it with purchasing power by way of having it linked in an encrypted manner to any, some, or all of their debit and credit cards (of course users will have the ability to choose, with the press of a button, which card each charge will be applied to). If they've entered the country with foreign currency, the full foreign exchange rate adjusted amount of cash in their possession will be loaded onto their card.

Once the card is acquired, <u>none</u> of their debit and credit cards will be recognized by their issuers or any aspect of the worldwide electronic currency exchange system as valid until the "goods and services card" has been cancelled by the authorities responsible for such action - even if the expiration date on the "goods and services card" has passed.

When they are at the location from which they will be departing the country, all "goods and services card" holders will turn in their card and receive a printed receipt that provides a detailed accounting of all purchases made with the card and verification of the fact that the "goods and services card" has been cancelled, and that all of their other cards have been re-activated. It is at this time that any discrepancy must be reported in order for any related actions to take place.

If there are no discrepancies, a copy of the receipt will be signed by both the former card holder and the issuer of the receipt; and it will be kept on file in the department responsible for overseeing such activities. Personal information will not be shared.

Should a jury of Citizens of the United States of America find anyone guilty of knowingly providing a card holder or other foreigner with cash, said guilty party shall be subject to a minimum jail sentence of two full years (or deported, as per section <u>forty-four</u> of this section of this book); during which time they will be subject to a cost effective work detail of forty hours per week, cleaning the vilest aspects of the sewerage plants in their region.

Henceforth, Citizens leaving the country will be prohibited from taking any of the new official paper currency with them. All foreign expenditures will be made with other readily available instruments (e.g., debit/credit cards, traveler's checks, foreign currency, etc.).

Due to the unique nature and mechanisms of your new monetary system, it will be in your nation's best interest to minimize such transfer of the new official money.

2H - Citizen's shall not ever be entitled to use their own reserve funds for any personal purposes other than those outlined in sections <u>1D</u> and <u>1E</u>.

3 - No aspect of government shall ever lawfully use or borrow against any of the monies in any of the Citizens reserve funds for any purpose.

Nor shall they lawfully institute any statute, regulation, or code which necessitates that a loan application be filed by any Citizen for any purpose.

Any such proposal by any elected or appointed government official shall result in their being publicly tried for the crime of treason by a jury of Citizens who have not been elected or appointed government officials and who each hold a valid certificate as outlined in section <u>forty-six</u> of this section of this book.

Such actions are to be considered treasonous because they are, in fact, an aspect of the subtle form of warfare that has been slowly conquering your nation. Regardless of how innocent and well-meaning such subtleties may appear, they will invariably lead to the demise of just governance.

3A - All government must always operate within a balanced budget.

This also includes times of war other than those which would create a need for the use of the "We are Under Attack Reserve" outlined in section **3B** of this section of this book.

If need be, immediately following a constitutionally-defined declaration of war, the government can begin to raise additional money to fund such war; though only by way of an interest-free bond offering which will be limited strictly to private Citizens of the United States of America.

And such bonds will all be repaid on demand in a first come first served basis, and only from the money whose existence is outlined in section **15B** of this section of this book as follows:

"seventy percent (70%) of that portion of the yearly profit generated from such industry shall be used solely to directly fund the ongoing operations of government in the exact manner of funding which is outlined in section **3c**, and sections <u>twelve</u> and <u>fourteen</u> as funding relates to section **3D**; but paying to localities the amount of money that would otherwise remain uncollected because certain Citizens have decided to pay the taxes outlined in sections <u>twelve</u> and <u>fourteen</u> by way of the method offered to them in section **3D** shall always lawfully take precedence over the usage of these funds for any purpose other than the bond repayment that is mentioned in section **3A**."

Should such demands be made, their payment shall always be tendered as the first acts of the usage of such money. Should such demands ever exceed the balance of such funds, the payment on such demands will be tendered as soon as funds are again available from that account.

But regardless of said account balance, the right of Citizens to act as outlined in section **3ᴅ** of this section of this book shall never lawfully be infringed upon.

If such a bond offering truly is needed, the leadership in government will surely be able to quickly answer all of the related questions posed by those Citizens, with data that has been proven by numerous independent sources to be correct, in order to properly educate them as to the facts of the matter.

And then, surely, the properly informed public will provide the appropriate funding and necessary related aid. Why would they not?

Other than the "We are Under Attack Reserve" outlined in section **3ʙ**, and the above-mentioned bond offering, there shall be no other lawful way to fund any acts of war; whether they are referred to as "war", "armed conflict", or "peacekeeping", etc.

   FACT: All conventional methods of funding a war are guaranteed to cause the Citizens of any country that engages in war and/or its undeclared manifestations known as "armed conflict" or "peacekeeping", to become debt slaves of those who provide such funding.

We accomplish this by loaning the governments of those countries "money" at interest, to fight the war with the weapons that our subsidiaries produce; while forcing those governments to guarantee repayment of the loans by way of taxes on the fruits of their citizens labor which can <u>never</u> actually accomplish such repayment because of the structure of the terms of the loan.

And if you understand everything you've read thus far, it must be obvious to you by now that the actual citizens of those countries are the most important part of the weaponry that our subsidiaries produce; and that such production is dependent upon the continued limitation and regulation of their conceptual capabilities.

But, in case you weren't aware of it:

1 - We make sure that there is always a war - or as we like to say these days, an "armed conflict" - being fought in numerous places around the globe at any given time.

2 - Our propaganda ministers invented the charade known as a "peacekeeping force".

3 - We created the constant "need" for an incredibly costly military and intelligence presence in all possible places at all times.

This is but another product we manufacture to bring about your ruin while keeping you nervous and fearful; and looking for someone to immediately surrender your supposed rights to in response to our widely broadcast and inundating claims that only a more powerful government can provide you with needed "protection" from the "threat".

3B - Other than the Citizens of a country increasing their level of personal interaction with their representatives in government, in order to construct, implement, and maintain the rule of law and the physical infrastructure, the only way that a "government" can become more powerful is by infringing upon the rights of those Citizens or those of another country. Period.

This is a rationally undeniable fact; but are you going to be recruiting rally volunteers?

Can you even vaguely imagine what any properly educated fourteen year old child would fully understand and be able to clearly explain, regarding the absurdity of the above-mentioned methods of control that are employed against you?

That properly educated child would be able to identify and share the reasons why only a complete imbecile would pay a huge percentage of their salary to fund military aggression that causes their fellow Citizens and family members to be put in harm's way.

They would also know that your "leadership" has imprinted upon the vast majority of the public the unquestioned directive which states: The sacrifice of literally millions of *your* kind is always appropriate when *our* kind are waving a flag and giving the command for it to occur; while the decision of *your* kind to fix the problem by demanding that your "representatives" in government uphold the law, and imprison even one of *our* kind, is based on some type of ignorant mob mentality and/or lack of patriotism.

(We're talking about the kind of demands that will not take "no" for an answer. The kind that you reserve for very rare and meaningful occasions; such as when your cable or phone company mistakenly disconnects you from the chief sources of mental stimulation you desire and are capable of processing.)

And, despite their lack of "real world" experience, those properly educated youngsters would also understand that the occurrence of institutionalized violence could actually be made quite rare. You see, they'd know how to ensure that everyone in all of the key leadership roles of their government fully understood the following factual statement: "Any call for domestic or international aggression by you will result <u>not</u> in armed battles comprised of innocent people who are willing to be used as disposable tools to dispose of other disposable tools, **but rather in *your own* imprisonment or death**."

How lost within our combination funhouse and horror show is the average American?

Carefully consider this fact: without a personal connection to it, the idea of otherwise innocent people being put in situations that will cause them to die violently is never more meaningful than a highly suspicious rumor that they're hearing for the hundredth time; even though they are being <u>legally forced</u> to pay for those horrors to occur <u>in their name</u>.

But they'll be damn sure to stand up for the singing of the National Anthem.

You unwitting hostages have been manipulated into suffering from a condition that is far worse than "Stockholm syndrome". **It is from those who have purposely ruined you that you seek the permission to be redeemed.**

And now, so that you might follow in the admirable footsteps of those fourteen year olds, open a dictionary to discover the meanings of the word "abhorrent" and the phrase "Stockholm syndrome".

Of course, since even the most skilled diplomacy and well-meaning and well-thought-out actions cannot necessarily prevent what would be an irrational outright military attack on your nation (profitable to certain interests), the "We are Under Attack Reserve" mentioned in section **3**ᴀ must exist.

Since every sensible attempt to thwart such an attack would have to be made, and since such actions would require the immediate mobilization and utilization of massive resources, and since such actions would result in massive bills having to be paid, the ability to fund such actions in a way that would prevent financial ruin must exist.

The source of such funding shall be an aspect of the "Infrastructure Reserve Account" that is outlined in <u>section fifteen</u> of this section of this book.

This aspect of said reserve account will be comprised of twenty-five percent (25%) of the total amount of money that will be allocated to the account as outlined in section **1**ᴅ.

This aspect of the "Infrastructure Reserve Account", lawfully known as the "We are Under Attack Reserve", shall be lawfully referred to in all official calls for its use only as:

"Right now, at this very second, there is an actual military attack being carried out against our nation within our borders. We are under attack and we must fund our response".

This aspect of the "Infrastructure Reserve Account" must be named as such to protect the public from any traitorous governmental operatives who <u>will</u> otherwise attempt to use such funds for unauthorized purposes.

You know the type of operatives I'm referring to.

You know; the ones who use the term "defense spending" when they are actually speaking of funding purely offensive military operations.

Said funds shall <u>not</u> be lawfully used in response to a terrorist attack.

Said funds shall be lawfully used only in response to a large scale foreign military invasion and/or widespread aerial bombing within your actual borders.

Any proposal by any elected or appointed government official to utilize these funds for any other purpose shall result in their being publicly tried for the crime of Treason by a jury of Citizens who have not been elected or appointed government officials and who each hold a valid certificate as outlined in section <u>forty-six</u> of this section of this book.

Should said "We are Under Attack Reserve" ever be utilized, and the United States of America is not conquered, at the end of such hostilities every lawful attempt to recoup all spent funds shall be taken against the nation or nations who initiated the attack; and all of the recouped funds shall be immediately returned to the "We are Under Attack Reserve" aspect of the "Infrastructure Reserve Account".

3C - All budgets must be approved by two-thirds (2/3) of the voters who will be responsible for such funding.

Under no circumstances will there ever be any "trickling down" of funds from federal or state authorities.

Whenever taxation is direct, the payment of such tax shall always be made separately to each level of government for which a budget was lawfully passed.

Such payments, and any allocation of the funds outlined in #4 of section **15**, or the first paragraph of section **15B** of this section of this book (such allocation shall always be made on an identical cost per capita basis, unless those funds are also to be utilized as monetary reimbursement for the tax obligations outlined in sections <u>twelve</u> and <u>fourteen</u> which have been satisfied by way of the method described in section **3D**), and those payments due from businesses that collect sales tax, shall always be arranged in the following order:

1 - The first payment (s) will be made to fully fund local budgets (Hamlet, village).

2 - The payments that follow will be made individually to each successive rung of government (e.g., town, city, county, state, and federal).

This must not be construed as a denial of the need for *some* incarnation of each rung in the hierarchy of government to exist.

Such methods will cause you to be aware of exactly what *your* government, at <u>all</u> levels, is doing and planning to do with *your* money and in relation to *your* rights.

Such methods will enable you to be in actual contact with the people who are actually in control of the money you will be paying toward enabling the proper maintenance of the area you live in.

Such methods will greatly reduce the ability to divert such funds for unauthorized purposes, and/or outright steal them.

Why, pray tell, would anyone whose sovereignty is specifically acknowledged by the Declaration of Independence, ever allow themselves to be forced to *hope* that a tiny portion of the "money" they paid toward the functioning of *their* "government" might be graciously redirected, with stipulations, back to where the "money" came from so that it *might* be used to benefit the actual people who paid it?

Through our occupation of you, which is currently effectuated chiefly under your governmental scheme, rather than being the palm and fingers that are gripping the handle of the hammer of government, each "person" is a nail being buried into whatever materials we are commanding them to further construct their own prison with.

Only with a full participation in the methods described above and those that follow, can the organisms known as "Citizens" control the purse strings and thus the agenda of the idea known as "government"; an idea, like all other ideas, that otherwise always has and always will experience malignant growth and soon become out of control and out of touch with the intrinsic nature, which is to say the rightful demands, of the organism that initially utilized it. (And yet, in your country, said organism initially utilized it for the intent of being provided with that which will enable it to provide beneficial service. *Beneficial service to what?*).

This is an invariable fact, as all such happenings are the result of the unavoidable Natural law of balance; which is *the* basis of the intrinsic need for each organism to continually act responsibly; which is *the* basis of the intrinsic need for each organism to continually, properly utilize the Master Resource.

3D – Anyone who is at least eighteen years old and who has earned and maintains a valid certificate as described in section forty-six of this section of this book, and who is the outright owner of a parcel of land which is not being utilized in any manner that directly contributes to the involvement of them or any family member or business partner in any commercial monetary exchange,

who volunteers to personally work without pay as directed by the most local government to which, in relation to said land, taxes are remitted,

shall always have the lawful right to substitute such work for all (but not merely some) of the monetary taxation and/or government fees they might otherwise pay for any given year on said land and/or home, and any "value enriching improvements" they might make upon them.

The amount of time they will be required to work in such capacity will be determined as follows, regardless of any "value enriching improvements" that might be made to their property:

1 - Any piece of land that does <u>not</u> border or include within its boundaries any aspect of a lake, river (or non-seasonal stream), ocean, or naturally occurring pond, and which is no larger than a quarter acre, will cost the owner seventy-eight (78) hours of work per year; an average of one and one-half (1.5) hours per week, <u>or approximately thirteen (13) minutes per day</u>.

2 - Any piece of land that <u>does</u> border or include within its boundaries any aspect of a lake, river (or non-seasonal stream), ocean, or naturally occurring pond, and which is no larger than a quarter acre, will cost the owner one hundred and five (105) hours of work per year; an average of two (2) hours per week, <u>or approximately seventeen (17) minutes per day</u>.

3 - Any piece of land that does <u>not</u> border or include within its boundaries any aspect of a lake, river (or non-seasonal stream), ocean, or naturally occurring pond, and which is no larger than a half-acre, will cost the owner one hundred and five (105) hours of work per year; an average of two (2) hours per week, <u>or approximately seventeen (17) minutes per day</u>.

4 - Any piece of land that <u>does</u> border or include within its boundaries any aspect of a lake, river (or non-seasonal stream), ocean, or naturally occurring pond, and which is no larger than a half-acre, will cost the owner one hundred and thirty (130) hours of work per year; an average of two and one-half (2.5) hours per week, <u>or approximately twenty-two (22) minutes per day</u>.

5 - Any piece of land that does <u>not</u> border or include within its boundaries any aspect of a lake, river (or non-seasonal stream), ocean, or naturally occurring pond, and which is no larger than an acre, will cost the owner one hundred and thirty (130) hours of work per year; an average of two and one-half (2.5) hours per week, <u>or approximately twenty-two (22) minutes per day</u>.

6 - Any piece of land that <u>does</u> border or include within its boundaries any aspect of a lake, river (or non-seasonal stream), ocean, or naturally occurring pond, and which is no larger than an acre, will cost the owner one hundred and fifty-six (156) hours of work per year; an average of three (3) hours per week, <u>or approximately twenty-six (26) minutes per day</u>.

7 - Any piece of land that does <u>not</u> border or include within its boundaries any aspect of a lake, river (or non-seasonal stream), ocean, or naturally occurring pond, and which is no larger than ten (10) acres, will cost the owner one hundred and fifty-six (156) hours of work per year; an average of three (3) hours per week, <u>or approximately twenty-six (26) minutes per day</u>.

8 - Any piece of land that <u>does</u> border or include within its boundaries any aspect of a lake, river (or non-seasonal stream), ocean, or naturally occurring pond, and which is no larger than ten (10) acres, will cost the owner one hundred and eighty-two (182) hours of work per year; an average of three and one-half (3.5) hours per week, <u>or approximately thirty (30) minutes per day</u>.

9 - Any piece of land that does <u>not</u> border or include within its boundaries any aspect of a lake, river (or non-seasonal stream), ocean, or naturally occurring pond, and which is <u>no smaller</u> than ten (10) acres, will cost the owner one hundred and eighty-two (182) hours of work per year; an average of three and one-half (3.5) hours per week, <u>or approximately thirty (30) minutes per day</u>.

10 - Any piece of land that <u>does</u> border or include within its boundaries any aspect of a lake, river (or non-seasonal stream), ocean, or naturally occurring pond, and which is <u>no smaller</u> than ten (10) acres, will cost the owner two hundred and eight (208) hours of work per year; an average of four (4) hours per week, <u>or approximately thirty-five (35) minutes per day</u>.

Are you even capable of imagining what your towns and cities would look like and how efficiently and inexpensively they would be run if only one-fifth (1/5) of your fellow Citizens took advantage of this with an honest work ethic?

The work that each such landowner will be required to do shall be decided weekly by way of a drawing. A written description of all required work, with a particular identifying number assigned to each job, will be physically posted in the respective town/city halls and online. By law such posting will occur no later than twenty-four (24) hours previous to their drawing.

The first two digits of each identifying number will correspond to a particular category of work that all jobs numbered as such will have in common; so that those landowners whose required or desired number of work hours exceed the particular job they may have picked in the draw will, when that job is completed, immediately be assigned to another job that needs to be done and which falls within that particular category.

The particular job they will then be assigned to will be decided upon by their drawing it in the same manner as outlined below, but from a mixing device filled only with jobs that fall within the particular category which is represented by the first two digits of the identifying number they picked in that week's drawing.

All numbers will be printed on uniform sized pieces of paper previous to the draw; and in the presence of everyone who has shown up at the posted, predetermined time to pick a number, they will be placed inside of a bingo style number mixing device.

After an uninvolved party has mixed the numbers for at least ten (10) seconds, each of the landowners will take a turn blindly reaching in and picking one number.

Prior to the landowners picking their number, the order in which they will pick shall be determined by way of each one of them having their name printed on a uniform sized piece of paper and having the paper placed inside the mixing device.

After an uninvolved party has mixed the names for at least ten (10) seconds, the person who did the mixing will blindly pick them one at a time from the device.

The order in which the names are picked will determine the order that the landowners will then get to pick the numbers as described above. Whoever is picked first gets to pick first, whoever is picked second gets to pick second, etc.

The entire job picking process must always be made as efficient as possible while being done manually as described above, as opposed to a computer or some other device "randomly" selecting names and/or numbers.

And it must be videotaped and archived for unrestricted public viewing in the closest local public library and immediately uploaded on the local government website and on "YouTube".

3E - Those landowners who take advantage of this method of paying such taxes will also be able to accrue future credits toward their tax responsibilities by working extra hours if they choose to do so. And they will be able to transfer such future credits exclusively to their spouse, their siblings, their parents, their children, their nieces and nephews, their grandchildren, or their first cousins who choose to live in like kind.

But no-one will be able to accrue more than five (5) years' worth of credits, since an individual's extended lack of involvement with their system of governance becomes injurious to all parties.

Obviously such credit is inextricably tied to the specific piece of land for which it was earned.

If a landowner were to double up on the amount of hours they worked in this capacity for one year, that landowner would, in effect, have a one year insurance policy in force in case they got sick or were seriously injured. Or they could just decide to work one year on, one year off, etc.

If a forty year old man who owned ten acres of land and who had two teenage children were to double up on his tax payments for five years, when he reached the age of forty-five he could transfer ownership of the land to both of his children (perhaps with the stipulation that he and his wife would be able to live there until death). And he would be able to pass on to them the accumulated tax credits he had earned so that they would each have a couple years to start a family or whatnot, before they had to start paying the tax themselves, etc.

Obviously the above scenarios are but two examples of the many beneficial variations that are available to those who partake in this opportunity.

Participating landowners will be lawfully required to carry out at least one twelfth ($1/12^{th}$) of their yearly "work owed" by the end of each month. That is, unless they are injured in a manner that, according to the sworn testimony of a publicly recognized medical professional, will require them to temporarily forgo such duties; in which case they will have no more than one year to begin making up the hours of work owed that will have accrued.

And such accrued hours of work owed will be fully made up within three (3) years of the occurrence of said injury. The only lawful exceptions to the requirement that each landowner must personally carry out their "work owed" shall be in the case of an injury as mentioned above, or an inability due to old age. Whereby in response to such an occurrence, the "work owed" by the injured or aged landowner can be voluntarily fulfilled indefinitely by any number of their neighbors who live within the same locality as them but who are <u>not</u> related to them.

Those neighbors can also volunteer to trade jobs with an injured, or aged, or otherwise handicapped landowner after the weekly drawing has occurred, should said landowner's inability to carry out their "work owed" be limited to particular types of work.

By law all such trades will always be publicly recorded and archived for unrestricted public reference. Can you say "sense of community"? Do you see how strong the intergenerational bonds formed between different families of differing customs and religions, etc., will become?

Anyone care for an extra-large slice of "United We Stand"?

All landowners will have to carry out said work duties in shifts that are no less than six (6) hours each, whenever it is during the month that they fulfill that requirement. Landowners will lawfully be able to work a maximum of sixteen (16) hours in any one shift in order to "pay off" or accrue future credits toward their "work owed".

Landowners who wish to accrue future credits toward their tax responsibilities will be required, by law, to state their intentions in writing before that week's drawing process has begun, and to be bound by such claim.

Landowners who have inherited accumulated tax credits on a parcel of land which was an aspect of a larger parcel that has been divided up will always lawfully enjoy the full relative percentage of those credits which were accumulated toward the full, undivided parcel.

So, for instance, if a one (1) acre parcel of land with five years' worth of tax credits were to be split in half, with the tax credits also being split in half, the new owners of each half (0.5) acre parcel would <u>not</u> be assessed for the additional hours of work that they would otherwise owe if they were to try to accumulate that same amount of tax credit on their respective half (0.5) acre.

But try to wrap your mind around the following inconvenience: If everyone accrued tax credits and then they all attempted to redeem them during the same time period, who would be left to do the work that needed to get done? Another draw from the mixing device? Obviously there are many ways everyone can work within this system in a mutually advantageous manner, but I will leave it up to you to leave such an in-depth analysis up to someone else who will mislead you for their own gain.

3F - Make no mistake about it; whether it is paid directly by the actual labor of a particular landowner or with the tool they earned by way of the direction of their labors elsewhere (which is commonly known as money) the justification for the collection of such a tax is simple and clear.

Whether or not a landowner chooses to utilize it for their own direct benefit, the infrastructure of their country must be maintained at the highest levels to facilitate the ongoing freedom and well-being of all of its Citizens.

And the fact is that, regardless of the supposed guaranteed protection of his rights, without being an active participant in the maintenance of such an infrastructure, each man's land, his property, and his guns and ammunition are but a pirate's booty drifting aimlessly in open waters.

The designed ignorance and resulting impropriety of numerous consecutive generations of your fellow countrymen happens to be what enabled the pirates from within to subvert your country's infrastructure (both physically and politically). The system of governance that you were taught to believe would run just fine by way of your being absentee management whose sole responsibility is to, in effect, sign checks with the "pay to the order of" section left blank was their vehicle.

(And yet, if people keep crashing into things because they lack the level of education that's required for them to recognize the need to read and understand their vehicle's user manual, and/or adhere to its mechanical maintenance requirements, what are the chances that the problem will be solved by way of simply replacing the existing vehicle with one whose safe operation requires that they must take an even greater hands on approach to the problem?)

So, just how long do any of you imagine that you could continue to go about your preferred daily routine in the anarchist's fantasy land of a "truly free world"? You know the one I'm talking about. It's been called for in every generation by the iconoclasts whose conceptually sound and fully justified disdain for "the State" fails to also include a conceptually sound roadmap toward the still functionally indistinct equitable existence they've spotted on the horizon. But they'll be glad to give you some very general descriptions of their vision...

Would it be sensible to immediately eliminate the current systems of "law and order" and the creation and distribution of goods? (Mind you, most people lack any understanding of the fact that freedom, which appears to be without form, has a definite structure and that such structure is the result of the simple universal laws that govern all cause and effect.) I dare you to rationally, coherently explain how it would <u>not</u> produce results which are akin to the ousting of a brutal dictator whose subjects have no allegiance to one another.

Based upon a rational assessment of history, how long do you imagine it would take for the instantly resulting power vacuum to embolden EVEN MORE pirates from within *and from without* to begin anew, the outright full-scale physical/economic/environmental/psychological invasion of your "independent" domain? I'm talking about the one that's now formally protected only by way of your contracting with private sector-owned courts and security services. What could possibly go wrong?

It just so happens that the anarchist advocates of a "truly free world" generally leave out of their glossy brochure the fact that such an existence, on any large scale, would be utterly dependent upon the vast majority of people - worldwide - being properly educated; so that they would evolve into adults whose actions are compelled by their own properly developed conscience.

Yet the fact remains that the only alternative is for individuals to remain incapable of any appropriate self-determination and act out as savages who require dictatorial mandates to maintain even the barely adequate forms of social cohesion which currently exist; and for nations to require "defense spending", a military-industrial complex, and vast spy networks to prevent the full-scale military invasions that would immediately result without them.

Could it be that such a fact flies in the face of their imagined free-for-all? Or could it be that they simply haven't identified the numerous logical steps that the general public must take in order to be able to make and maintain the orderly and properly informed mental and physical transitions that would eventually enable an equitable existence such as they imagine and dutifully advocate for, to become a widespread and ongoing reality?

Truth be told, it is surely the latter. Commonality is fundamental; differences are fly by night.

The existence of each man's piece of land as productive and sovereign ground, and of his property being inviolable, <u>is</u> directly dependent upon the ability of every other man to act in accordance with the aspects of the Laws of Nature and of Nature's God that enable such an existence. They are <u>not</u> dependent upon or subject to the legislation or contractual agreements of men. (Yes, one's physical body is their own property).

A proper education would, among other things, lead each Citizen to understand that having at least a large minority of their fellow Citizens paying such taxes by the method described above is required to ensure that the governing body (or even a private contractor) responsible for the formation and maintenance of such an infrastructure is continually acting in the best interests of those who have conditionally lent it the power to govern (or to get a particular job done right).

It would also enable them to understand that the word "*dependent*" means **"being subject to another's jurisdiction"**. And through such proper study they would know that the word "*jurisdiction*" means **"the power, right, or authority to interpret and apply the law"** (both Natural Law and statutory law. Now invest the time that's required to carefully consider the actual functionality of "Independence").

And thus, they would each understand that only those who have the power, right, or authority to interpret and apply the law are actually sovereign, and that everyone else is someone's lackey. (And so, doesn't the idea and practice of <u>trial by a jury of impartial Citizens</u> who are each properly educated, and who thus understand the absolute need for the existence and proper utilization of <u>jury nullification</u>, make perfect sense when you actually understand the meanings and real-world functionality of what are called "dependence", "jurisdiction", and "sovereignty"?)

Indeed; said proper education would enable the educated to understand and remain fully aware of the fact that the *as of yet literally ceaseless* attempts of would-be usurpers and invaders of all types can only be continually thwarted when each member of the Citizenry faithfully carries out the relatively minor duties that are required of them in order to maintain the structural integrity of a nomocratic, egalitarian, socioeconomic system. Or to put it another way: they would understand why there really is no such thing as a "free lunch", and they would each act appropriately.

3G - Regardless of the lawful method which was previously used by any Citizen to pay their "property tax", and/or the "wounded veterans/whistleblowers tax" that is outlined in section <u>twelve</u>, and/or the "new" Medicare/Medicaid taxes (outlined in section <u>fourteen</u>), the non-payment of one year's worth of any such taxes within a period of three years shall incur lawful penalties which will be both inclusive of and limited to the following:

1 - The loss of any benefits they might otherwise ever receive from official public assistance, and the termination of the "reserve funds", outlined in section **1D,** of said landowner and anyone else who is living on that land who has reached the lawful age to vote. This will result in the immediate loss of their ability to apply for any "reserve fund" based loans, which is also inclusive of credit card transactions and any involvement in the aforementioned funding process of any "reserve fund" based loans - other than those which they/their business already owes money on.

2 - The loss of Citizenship of said landowner and anyone else who is living on that land who has reached the lawful age to vote; which will also result in said land (and any other that they own) being purchased by applicable local government as per section **2F,** and such people being lawfully recognized as "lawful permanent residents" as per section **2G** and all other pertinent law. **You are hereby highly advised to <u>not ever</u> allow the revocation of Citizenship to occur for <u>any</u> other reason, or in <u>any</u> way other than that which is outlined in the next eight lines.**

The lawful implementation of said penalties shall occur only after such a decision has been reached by a jury comprised of Citizens who each hold a valid certificate as described in section <u>forty-six</u> of this section of this book and own and live on land in what is known as the "second wave" or the "third wave" in relation to the tried living on land in what is known as the "first wave", as each "wave" is outlined in <u>section two</u> of this section of this book.

The entirety of those court proceedings, and all jury deliberation, will always be broadcast live nationwide during "prime time" on local television stations, government websites, and archived for unrestricted public viewing in all public libraries and immediately uploaded to "YouTube".

4 – The lawful ability of Citizens to utilize "cash" ("paper" and/or coins) for whatever lawful domestic purposes have already been implemented and were in use in the year 1990, shall <u>never</u> be eliminated; nor shall it be made inconvenient by way of any processing methods which are implemented for any form of non-tangible and/or "electronic" system of monetary representation, usage, and/or distribution. (Besides the obvious privacy and rights issues that are related to the elimination of your utterly debased "cash", perhaps some folks would rather not have payment processing fees of 2.9%+.30¢ added into to <u>every</u> purchase they'll ever make.)

5 – The Federal Reserve act and all aspects of the Federal Reserve System will immediately be abolished. The Federal Reserve and U.S. department of Treasury will be given back all of their Federal Reserve notes and coins that are in circulation in the United States of America.

Should "The Fed" be unwilling to gladly accept the shortfall that exists between the amount of "government" debt they hold and the amount of Federal Reserve notes they receive, the officers of the Federal Reserve will immediately be presented with an opportunity to put all of their brilliant minds together.

They'll have to figure out how they can continue carrying out their scam without any takers while they're all in jail; serving life sentences for the subversive acts they have quietly and purposely committed in support of a parasitic ideology that is intrinsically hostile and injurious to all equitable governmental and societal function.

Make no mistake; either way they will all be tried for numerous crimes, such as: debasing the currency, racketeering, and fraud - just to name a few. They will each be tried by a jury of Citizens who have not been elected or appointed government officials and who each hold a valid certificate as outlined in section <u>forty-six</u> of this section of this book.

5A – The entire "national debt" that is supposedly owed by the Citizens of the United States of America for the debts incurred by the United States government will immediately be lawfully considered null and void. Have you read Section 4 of the fourteenth amendment?

"But neither the United States nor any state shall assume or pay any debt or obligation incurred in aid of insurrection or rebellion against the United States, or any claim for the loss or emancipation of any slave; but all such debts, obligations and claims shall be held illegal and void."

(And to those nations that may suffer unfortunate economic losses because of these actions, I quote the Honorable James Wilson - *Justice of the original U.S. Supreme Court and signer of both the Declaration of Independence and the Constitution* - from his "Lectures on Law" - Chapter IV, Of the Law of Nations, wherein he wrote:

"If, however, a nation, in the necessary prosecution of its own duties and rights, does what is disagreeable or even inconvenient to another, this is not to be considered as an injury; it ought to be viewed as the unavoidable result, and not as the governing principle of its conduct. If, at such conduct, offence is taken, it is the fault of that nation, which takes, not of that nation, which occasions it."

Furthermore, to those nations and all other interested parties, I say this: **1**- Section 4 of the fourteenth amendment had been adopted by the U.S. government numerous decades previous to the establishment of the conspicuously unconstitutional Federal Reserve, whose unlawful products you freely chose to purchase; **2**- the Constitutional article which clearly states that their modes of operation are unlawful has not ever been lawfully amended; **3**- the natural persons who constitute the Citizenry of the United States of America have not ever acted to deceive you.)

Now, since it has been clearly shown that the "national debt" has been run up by insurrectionist operatives of the "United States government" and the "Federal Reserve" for purposes, and by way of certain methods, that are in clear opposition to the plain language of the "supreme Law of the Land" and its ideological foundations known as the Declaration of Independence and the Bible (Public Law 97-280 – link #81 on page <u>74</u>)...

And since it has been clearly shown that physical chains are not requirements of being held in servitude as property (i.e., slavery) and that you <u>are</u> actually being held in servitude by way of official "Civil administrative procedures" that bound/bind you to their unlawful dictated forms of legality, legal tender, and misinformation...

What part of section 4 of the fourteenth amendment which states: "But neither the United States nor any state shall assume or pay any debt or obligation incurred in aid of insurrection or rebellion against the United States, or any claim for the loss or emancipation of any slave; but all such debts, obligations and claims shall be held illegal and void.", does not make it clear to you that such supposed debt is lawfully, logically, and laughingly to be considered "illegal and void"?

(***And for those of you who, after having read and researched the information provided by way of the last few links offered in the "Conspiracy Theorists" section of this book, feel as though that information is valid:

Since that time when potential voters were originally compelled to register to vote using forms of identification that are associated with the contract they have/had supposedly entered into with the Social Security Administration, any such debt which has supposedly been incurred was not sanctioned by the actual human beings who are the Citizens of the United States of America, but rather by the trusts ("persons"/"citizens"/"employee") that you have each unwittingly obligated yourselves to be the corporation sole of.

And, as such, since that initial election in which those human beings were compelled to register the fictional entity, which is the trust, as the legal entity which was actually casting the vote, the foreign-owned corporation that claims to be your "legitimate government" has not actually been given any lawful permission to act as the representative of the actual human beings who are legally acknowledged as existing in the "Populated Place", but not necessarily within "Civil political divisions".

At the closing of this Constitutional convention/legislative amendment process, any government or Central Bank that is not satisfied with this decree will be welcome to file lawsuits against the inoperative debt slaves/fictional entities/persons/citizens/Creatures of the State who they believe are legally responsible for any debt that they claim to be owed by the "U.S. government".

Or will you keep handing your right of self-determination to the legal fictions that are the administrators of the parasitic fictitious entity that is intrinsically hostile and injurious to all equitable governmental and societal function?***)

By the way, since you are too misled to know it, allow me to educate you on the <u>fact</u> that when section 4 of the fourteenth amendment goes on to speak of the validity of the public debt being beyond question, it is clearly limiting its own definition of such public debt.

It is specifically referring only to debts that have arisen from the "...payment of pensions and bounties for services in suppressing insurrection or rebellion...".

The sentence structure of the passage makes that fact crystal clear to anyone who knows the proper usage of the English language as it relates to concepts of law: "The validity of the public debt of the United States, authorized by law, including debts incurred for payment of pensions and bounties for services in suppressing insurrection or rebellion, shall not be questioned."

The fact that the passage merely says "including" proves my point.

The fact that the passage merely says "including" unquestionably proves the fact of the authors' intent to limit the proper interpretation of the amendment to include only those debts that it specifically mentions.

Do you see where immediately following the word "law" it says "which shall also include"?

No, you do not. It does not say that.

Do you see where after using the word "including" it says "but not limited to"?

No, you do not. It does not say that.

Yes, the <u>fact</u> that the amendment does not make such statements or their equivalent unquestionably proves the <u>fact</u> of the authors' intent to limit the proper interpretation of the amendment to include only those debts that it specifically mentions.

That is the singularly proper interpretation of that passage within the "fourteenth" amendment to your nation's Constitution.

And so, for anyone who *was* questioning the validity of paying the volunteers for having taken part in the rally, as outlined in section **1ᴅ**, what exactly *was* it about the constitutionally mandated act of "...payment of pensions and bounties for services in suppressing insurrection or rebellion..." that *didn't* sit well with you?

6 - The "Internal Revenue Service" must be ~~empowered to fully inspect and control all aspects of all citizens lives~~ completely dissolved immediately; and all statutes, regulations and codes that were in any way related to any function of the Internal Revenue Service previous to its dissolution will immediately be lawfully declared null and void as such.

Furthermore, each living functionary (past and present) of the mid to upper management and administration of the Internal Revenue Service and each living functionary (past and present) of the collection and enforcement branches of the Internal Revenue Service will be tried for numerous crimes, such as: racketeering, fraud, and terrorism - just to name a few.

They will each be tried by a jury of Citizens who have not been elected or appointed government officials and who each hold a valid certificate as outlined in section forty-six of this section of this book.

7 - No tax shall ever be taken from anyone's pay before they receive their full pay; in their hand in cash or in their preferred bank account.

8 – A big obstacle to effectively reducing your nation's tax revenue requirements is the Military-Industrial Complex (this also includes the "intelligence gathering services"). It's no secret that the costs related to your nation's "defense" are incredibly high and cannot as of yet (and possibly not ever) be paid for without monetary currency. Furthermore, pragmatically speaking, the current need for such technologies, products, and services cannot be altogether dismissed.

What needs to occur is a gradual reduction in the need for such technologies, products, and services, to the utmost minimal safe level (which the implementation of the concepts and methodology I'm sharing with you, which is a singular mechanism, will afford your nation and the rest of the world) - and the immediate implementation of a method of reducing the tax burden that this all-pervasive vacuum cleaner-like system currently places upon the Citizens of your country.

So, while your nation intelligently and efficiently works its way out of the historically familiar imperialistic mess that your "leaders" have gotten you into (i.e., unsustainable monetary and environmental costs related to such endeavors and the non-monetary costs of the hatred of the people whose lives and lands your "Global force for good" has ruined, etc…), for each of the twenty-five (25) years following the close of the aforementioned Constitutional convention/legislative amendment process, Fifty Percent (50%) of the continually shrinking (as mandated by law) annual "Defense spending bill" will be fully paid for by way of a newly created **"National Defense Payment Fund"**.

Said fund will be a lawfully acknowledged aspect of the "Infrastructure Reserve Account" that is outlined in section fifteen of this section of this book (see the final sentence in section **15B**).

This aspect of said reserve account shall be comprised of ten percent (0.10%) of the total amount of money that will be allocated to the account as outlined in section **1D**.

8A – The sixteenth amendment (16th) shall be repealed immediately.

Henceforth, unless the voting public decides to alter that which is stated in this passage (as per section **8B**), all taxes that are not mentioned in sections **3D**, **12**, and **14** will always be raised indirectly; which is to say that they will <u>not</u> be derived by way of government tapping directly into the fruits of one's labor or any other form of their personal property. Their collection will be based upon usage and/or consumption.

Furthermore, the governmental collection of revenue from Citizens by way of "traffic tickets", "administrative fees", "registration fees", "licensing fees", "civil asset forfeiture", and non-commercial "code violations" will be outlawed immediately and attempts to employ any "words of art" in order to circumvent this law will result in all involved persons being tried at the soonest possible date for the crime of racketeering by a jury comprised of Citizens who have never held any public office and who each hold a valid certificate as outlined in section <u>forty-six</u> of this section of this book. In areas where a three-fourths (3/4) majority of the voting public votes in favor of it, parking tickets and handicap designated area/permit violations will be exempted from this law (while lawfully being considered a tax).

The self-regulating growth industries known as local, state, and national government are finally going to be put on a strict diet that will benefit those whom they are meant to serve.

Each government in each area/jurisdiction of the country that currently sets forth rules for taxation (local, state, federal) will have a fully funded period of one year from the date of the completion of this Constitutional convention/legislative amendment process to pass legislation that will codify its new methods of funding its operations through taxation; which is to say that, during such time, they will be compensated for documented shortfalls of revenue relative to their previous year's budget on a bi-weekly basis. The **"National Defense Payment Fund"** mentioned above will be the source of such funding.

8B – With the exception of the tax-related issues that are outlined in sections **3C**, **3D**, **3E**, **3G**, **9**, and the "wounded veterans/whistleblower tax outlined in section **12**, and the Medicare/Medicaid tax that's outlined in section **14**, each of whose alteration will require a constitutional amendment, all aspects of every manner of taxation and the full allocation of its proceeds must be reviewed and voted upon by the voting public (of each area/jurisdiction of the country that sets forth rules for taxation, i.e., local, state, federal) for renewal and/or alteration, every three (3) years after the completion of this Constitutional convention/legislative amendment process.

A three-fourths (3/4) majority vote of the voting public of each area/jurisdiction of the country that sets forth rules for taxation (i.e., local, state, federal) shall always be required in order to institute any new tax-related law or change any such existing law, regulation, or code.

Before such a vote can take place, announcements of it and all proposed alterations in all voting districts must appear in related local newspapers, on related local television, and on government websites daily for no less than ninety (90) consecutive days leading up to the day of the vote, which shall always take place on the exact same day of the exact same month, as determined by the delegates of this Constitutional convention/legislative amendment process.

9 - No tax shall ever be levied that would require anyone who must pay it, who has not been judged by a jury of their fellow Citizens to be lawfully considered mentally retarded or insane, to seek any professional advice or assistance in order to fully comply with any law or regulation that governs such payment.

All information regarding how to pay, how much to pay, when to pay, and on <u>exactly</u> what such payment will be spent must always be written in clear language without any ambiguity as to any meaning of any aspect of its intent; so that any person who has received the certificate which is outlined in section <u>forty-six</u> of this section of this book can fully comply with such regulations and understand the need for them.

The total combined amount of time required to properly comply with the filing of the payment of all applicable taxes must not ever exceed one hour per year for anyone who has received such certificate.

Before any such tax can be lawfully enforced it must be proven publicly that the completion of the filing of the payment, as described above, can be done by at least five hundred (500) recent High School graduates from each state (and whose grade point average was no higher than the national average) who have no prior knowledge of the required task and who have received said certificate within six months of the time they will be tested for such purposes. Until said certificates are issued, this process will be done by way of recent junior college graduates being tested as outlined above.

10 – No "words of art" shall ever be lawfully used as a substitute for the words "tax", "interest", "loan", "penalty", "expense", "fictional entity", "poisonous byproduct", or "war".

11 – No Citizen of the United States of America shall ever be lawfully required to register to vote. The furnishing of a valid, lawfully acceptable proof of personal identification which provides their current home address is all that will be required of them in order to vote.

Henceforth, voting within each state for the election of those who will participate in statewide governance (Judges, Legislators, Executive, etc.), shall be conducted by way of an Electoral College-like system whose basic functions are as follows: each state will have ninety-nine voting districts whose land masses are all equal in size and whose dimensions of length and width shall be drawn using straight lines which emanate from its borders and, in as much as it is mathematically possible, connect on right-angles.

Each district will have one elector who shall cast their vote in favor of the decision which was voted for by a simple majority of the voters in that district. Electors shall be chosen by lottery.

All lands that have no land-owning full-time human inhabitants who are eligible voters and which would, under the aforementioned system of district creation, become unique districts shall be eliminated from the statewide map prior to the aforementioned process of creating said ninety-nine voting districts, and the borders of the state shall remain as they were prior to said land being eliminated as such.

12 – Henceforth, other than in regard to the care of wounded veterans, persecuted whistleblowers, and the costs related to the funding of the below mentioned "new" Social Security and Medicare/Medicaid systems, all payment into any government-run assistance plan, be it foreign or domestic, shall always be entirely voluntary.

The source of all funds used for such plans must always be completely and transparently accounted for, so that Citizens who do not care to have any of their money used for such purposes can verify that their decision has been upheld.

(Yes, those Citizens who promote such assistance programs will be entitled to place bumper stickers on their cars which proudly proclaim their support for the *right* of the unemployed, the unhealthy, and the uninterested to remain as such at the lawfully enforced expense of others. Look up the meaning of the word "usufruct".)

Not that more than a small handful of you exegetes have noticed, but, as it has often been used, the statement *"From each according to their ability to each according to their need"* is repugnant to the very concept of sovereign rights. Nor is it consistent with just morality. Read this: https://web.archive.org/web/20031002134948/http://www.lewrockwell.com/orig4/ellis1.html

What just morality can deny that the concept of sovereign rights must be its foundation?

Indeed, *"From each according to their ability to each according to their need"* has long been used in the thinly veiled effort to undermine the established validity of each human's endowment by their Creator with the unalienable right to Life, Liberty, and the pursuit of Happiness, and their lawful, personal control/ownership of private property.

A percentage of all monies collected by government from each Citizen will be allocated to/toward the assistance of wounded veterans and persecuted whistleblowers (financial, legal, etc.,) to adequately provide for their continued comfortable existence; the criteria for assessment will be clearly written out and made into official law. This allocation shall be mandatory and must always be factored into the balanced budget.

Citizens who choose to pay applicable taxes by way of the method described in section **3D** shall always have the right to pay their portion of this tax in the same manner. In such cases, those Citizens will do needed work for their local government at an hourly rate of one dollar ($1.00) in order to pay off their exact share of the "wounded veterans and whistleblowers tax" mentioned above.

And their local government will then issue them a receipt and allocate that exact amount of money to the payment of said tax; it will come from the amount of money they will have received for this purpose from the "Infrastructure Reserve Account" that is described in <u>section</u> <u>fifteen</u> of this section of this book.

The healthcare benefits that wounded veterans and said whistleblowers will have lawfully <u>earned</u> shall always be at least the equivalent of that which any government employee other than a sitting President is able to receive.

If you don't want this to cost you very much money or time, precisely follow all of the guidelines presented in this book. Such actions will enable you to avoid situations that cause such problems.

13 - The current system of Social Security must be ended immediately.

The system that will immediately take its place will be funded henceforth, with full public transparency, only by way of the following:

1- The full allocation of every cent of the collected credit card interest mentioned in sections **1D** and **1E** of this section of this book.

2 - The full allocation of all net profits from the credit card merchant fees that will be charged to retailers.

Said fees will be charged at a rate which is equal to the applicable rates charged by American Express on January 1st, 2012.

3 - The full allocation of all net profits from the prepaid credit card "sales transaction fees" that will be charged to buyers of such products.

Such products shall henceforth be lawfully issued in the United States of America solely by the same agency that issues the credit cards mentioned in section **1E** of this section of this book.

Said fees will be charged at a rate which is equal to the rate charged for the purchase of the Visa "vanilla" prepaid credit card on January 1st, 2012.

4 - The collection of a one hundred percent (100%) tax on the unused portion of all gift cards and prepaid cards after a period of three (3) years has elapsed from the time of their purchase or most recent "refill".

5 - The collection of a seventy-five percent (75%) tax on all monthly maintenance fees charged on all gift cards and prepaid cards purchased in the United States of America.

6 - The full allocation of all net profit from every lottery and instant winner game that is held/sold in the United States of America after payments are made to their winners.

7 - The collection of a fifty percent (50%) tax on the gross profit made from every lawful sporting event-related bet placed from within the United States of America and/or placed therein, after payments are made to the winners of such bets. The winnings will be tax-free.

8 - The collection of all of the money amassed through the taxing of all winnings in all lawfully established casinos in the United States of America and its territories. Henceforth such winnings will be subject to a specific twenty-five percent (25%) tax.

9 - The collection of all of the money amassed through the taxing of alcoholic beverages and cigarettes/e-cigarettes.

10 - The collection of all of the money amassed through the taxing of marijuana at a rate that is never any higher than that of the median amount charged for domestically produced beer and wine, and whose lawful public availability and usage shall be regulated by way of the same basic regulation as alcohol currently is. The following article should be read right now: http://www.forbes.com/sites/jacobsullum/2014/01/24/the-president-forgets-to-lie-about-marijuana-and-prohibitionists-are-outraged/

11 - The collection of a specific tax on all video game sales and rentals, and related officially licensed products, which will be equal to twenty percent (20%) of their retail/rental price.

12 - The collection of a specific tax on tickets to live professional sporting events and related officially licensed products that will be equal to twenty percent (20%) of the ticket/product retail price. This also includes professional wrestling.

13 - The collection of a specific tax on all packaging and products that are not glass, hemp, or bamboo and are disposable by design, which will be equal to twenty-five percent (25%) of their wholesale price; a flat tax of .10¢ will be charged (at the factory) for each wood-based paper and/or plastic shopping/carrying bag that will be provided/sold to customers/the public.

14 - The collection of a specific tax on all products made with any amount of artificial sweeteners, artificial flavors, artificial fragrance, artificial coloring, artificial preservatives, hydrogenated fats, and/or what is currently known as "high fructose corn syrup/corn sugar" that will be equal to thirty percent (30%) of their retail price.

15 - The collection of a specific tax on all food products that are genetically modified and/or irradiated, whether they be for human or animal consumption, which will be twenty percent (20%) of the retail price.

16 - The collection of a specific tax on all meat, dairy, and seafood products that are derived from animals not raised, whether in whole or in part, under certified "humane" conditions (http://certifiedhumane.org/how-we-work/our-standards/ Seafood standards will be presented in a timely manner); said tax will be equal to twenty-five percent (25%) of the point of sale price to end consumers.

17 - The collection of a specific tax on all "soft drinks", which will be equal to twenty percent (20%) of their retail price when their bottling/packaging is made of glass, hemp or bamboo. If the bottling is not glass, hemp or bamboo the product will be taxed at the same rate mentioned in the first part of #13 of this section.

18 - The collection of a specific tax on bottled water which will be twenty-five percent (25%) of the retail price. If the bottling/packaging is not glass, hemp or bamboo the product will be taxed at the rate of thirty percent (30%). Surely Nestlé will be a vocal proponent of such a measure. See what you "think": https://www.youtube.com/watch?v=Gfy6LL-8sTg

http://www.washingtonpost.com/wp-dyn/content/article/2008/09/28/AR2008092802997.html

http://www.newsweek.com/nestles-california-water-permit-expired-27-years-ago-321940

http://www.huffingtonpost.com/2015/04/28/nestle-california-drought_n_7166066.html

19 - The collection of a specific tax, due at purchase, on all passenger vehicles that have engines larger than four cylinders, or its electrical equivalent, which will be:

1 - Fifteen percent (15%) of the retail price for six cylinder engines.

2 - Twenty percent (20%) of the retail price for eight cylinder engines.

3 - Twenty-five percent (25%) of the retail price for ten cylinder engines.

4 - Thirty percent (30%) of the retail price for twelve cylinder engines.

In the case of leased vehicles, the above rates of taxation will be adjusted so that there will be no significant advantage to buying or leasing in regard to the payment of this tax.

20 - The collection of a specific tax on all consumer electronics, which will be twenty percent (20%) of the retail price.

21 - The collection of a specific tax on all advertising that is broadcast from television and radio stations, and their internet equivalent, which will be equal to twenty-five percent (25%) of the advertising rate charged.

22 - The collection of a specific tax on all lobbying interests, which will be equal to one hundred percent (100%) of the total costs incurred by such lobbying efforts, exclusive of travel expenses, before the tax is applied.

23 - The collection of a specific tax on all ATM transaction fees, which will be equal to twenty-five percent (25%) of all such fees that are being charged per transaction.

Let the gross stupidity of so many of you finally, abundantly serve a worthwhile purpose. It is as close to having your cake *and* eating it as you will ever come.

For a period of forty (40) years from the date of the inception of this system, the only Citizens who shall be eligible to receive benefits from this new "Social Security" will be those who are at or above the age of sixty-five (65), who have been gainfully employed and having the mandatory deduction for Social Security taken from their paychecks.

They will each receive monthly as much of the amount of their projected benefits as can be paid to them from this new system without causing the system to go into a financial deficit.

In the event that said projected amount cannot be paid to all recipients because such an amount would cause the system to go into a financial deficit, the amount paid to all recipients shall be reduced by an equal percentage for each so that they can all receive the relative maximum adjusted benefits that will not cause the system to go into a financial deficit.

Note that many improvident impostors rely on the fleecing of younger generations to keep the tides from washing away their castles made of sand; most believe it is their valid right to receive such stolen booty as compensation for what is, in fact, their having bought into a pyramid scheme too late. They are incorrect.

It is not even their legal right. They failed to read and understand the fine print.

If not them, exactly who should be forced to eat the ripe fruit of the seed of incompetence that they have so diligently cultivated and which must eventually be consumed?

And does the following statement from page 197 ring a bell? "Not that more than a small handful of you exegetes have noticed, but, as it has often been used, the statement '*From each according to their ability to each according to their need*' is repugnant to the very concept of sovereign rights. Nor is it consistent with just morality". Ooops!

Friend, if I were you, I would immediately do everything in my power to make sure literally every senior citizen in the nation knew how to sign up for the "Home" group of the rally so that they can earn **$250,000** plus, worth of tax free retirement money.

I would also immediately do everything in my power to make sure that all current and 2022, 2023, 2024, 2025, and 2026 scheduled recipients of Social Security fully understood this:

If they simply sign an official petition to allow it, and then vote for the candidates that the rally members will nominate, they'll be able to utilize certain of their future payments from Social Security as collateral for a loan which they can immediately redeem for more than twenty times the loan amount they just borrowed (I'm talking about cashing in another **$100,000**).

The ability to redeem the above-mentioned loan is outlined on page 155 (this offer shall not be lawfully construed to enable redemption of a greater sum of money at face value than that which is stated there).

The recipients of said loans will submit an officially issued voucher at the location of their redemption of such funds, and in return they will receive an immediately available credit to their bank account of choice.

The amount of said credit will be approximately $4,760. ($5,000 minus a $240.00 loan. It's similar to borrowing $240.00 in order to buy a stock you got a hot tip on. When the stock price soars, you make a profit; but the loan still has to be repaid.)

Brilliant, in a Federal Reserve/debt monetization kind of way, no?

Or to put it another way, I'm talking about a total of twenty-one (21) years' worth of much more than the current market value of $320.00 a week.

(**$350,000** ÷ 21years = $16,667. ÷ 52weeks = $320.00 per week. FYI, the current average Social Security benefit is $314.00 per week.)

Indeed, the average Social Security beneficiary's standard of living is going up - big time.

Should there ever be a surplus of funds in the system within forty (40) years of its inception, such surplus funds will be automatically transferred, as outlined in section **13A**, into the new system of Medicaid/Medicare that is outlined in section fourteen of this section of this book.

After a period of forty (40) years from the date of the inception of this system, the only Citizens who will be eligible to receive benefits from it will be those individuals or couples who are at or above the age of seventy-five (75) and whose total combined income and/or savings is less than the amount of money required to do one or both of the following:

1 - Pay the monthly rent/maintenance fee on a one bedroom apartment costing what is at that time the current median rental/maintenance price of all "non-luxury" one bedroom apartments in the United States of America (if they do not own a home without a mortgage/applicable maintenance fees, and/or do not have redeemable equity in said home).

2 - Purchase the following at what is, at that time, the current national median price:

I – Forty-five (45) gallons of hot water and four kilowatt hours of electricity per day.

II - 19,000 calories of wholesome, nutrient-dense food per week per male, and 16,000 calories of wholesome, nutrient dense food per week per female; neither of which is necessarily inclusive of any meat.

III - Needed medication/medical/dental care whose need was not derived from any form of repeated self-neglect - as determined by the survey of their medical/dental records and a routine physical/dental examination and blood work compared to standards of health derived by the physical/dental examination and blood work of an aggregate of comparably aged adults who have consistently followed multi-decade long routines of regular exercise, proper diet, proper weight maintenance and oral hygiene, while also maintaining a multi-decade abstinence from any excessive drinking and/or smoking.

IV - Unlimited internet access from which they receive nationwide telephone service.

V - The use of local public transportation in two directions at least four (4) days per week, if it is available in their area.

VI - The equivalent of today's current market value of five hundred dollars ($500) per year of new articles of clothing and shoes, and five hundred dollars ($500) per year of items needed for physical/dental hygiene.

Those Citizens who will qualify to receive benefits from this "Social Security" will receive, at a maximum, the additional funds required to enable them to purchase that which is outlined in the above-mentioned criteria for the receipt of such benefit.

If the fund is ever lacking the amount of money needed to provide to all recipients their legitimately requested benefits, each recipient will receive the maximum amount of money/services that the fund can afford to pay out equally (relative to their legitimately requested benefits. No-one will get extra benefits) without going into a financial deficit.

This method of adjusting the maximum benefits to be paid out in the case of a financial shortfall minimizes the loss incurred by those who drain the least from this system.

13A - In a nutshell, the method of collecting and dispersing such funds, and those mentioned in the following section for "Medicare/Medicaid", will be done as follows: all monies collected by merchants and/or state authorities for the purposes of such funding will be deposited into one bank account per state, for each of the new systems ("Social Security" and "Medicaid/Medicare").

Such account can only have money lawfully withdrawn from it one day per month; and for the sole purpose of the full dispersal of such funds in equal amounts to the localities in each state that will further disperse them to beneficiaries.

Such local governments throughout the country will then collaborate on their respective totals of both their funding taken in, and the benefits they need to pay out.

Funds will then be transferred, in as close to equal amounts as possible, by those localities with surplus funds to each locality in need.

Other than that which is outlined in this subsection relating to surplus funds, any other usage or attempted usage of such funds will lawfully be considered a treasonous act to be tried by a jury of Citizens who have not ever held public office or worked on the staff of any government official, and who each hold a valid certificate as outlined in section <u>forty-six</u> of this section of this book.

No, this method is not a wealth redistribution scheme that enables parasitic plunder. If you cannot see the difference, then, as planned, you are so confused that you are a danger to both yourself and others.

As mentioned above, payments to beneficiaries will be made by each locality. Furthermore, such payments will always be made by way of each recipient personally being handed such monies/service vouchers after having a retinal scan or other improved technology done to verify their identity and to insure that they are not collecting benefits anywhere else.

And, as stated earlier: should there ever be a surplus of funds in this "Social Security" system within forty (40) years of its inception, such surplus funds will lawfully be automatically transferred into the bank account (in each state with a surplus) which will have been established solely for the collection and dispersal of Medicaid/Medicare monies and which is to lawfully have funds withdrawn from it only one day per month, and solely for the dispersal of payments to beneficiaries from the new system of Medicaid/Medicare that is outlined in the next section of this section of this book.

Should there ever be a surplus of funds in said Medicaid/Medicare system, the instructions given in the following paragraph will also be utilized for such funds.

After said forty (40) year period, any surpluses in this "Social Security" system will be held in special bank accounts of those localities that have amassed them.

Such surplus funds will remain in the system and shall not ever be lawfully borrowed or used for any purpose without there first being a nationally held public vote that will require a three-fourths (3/4) majority to agree on exactly where to allocate such surplus funds.

The purpose of keeping such funds in many different bank accounts in many different localities is that such actions will make it quite difficult for any centralized power - that just *might* be a threat to your freedom - to unjustly access such funds.

This entire process will be completely publicly transparent, including the constant real-time publication on the internet of all bank account balances mentioned above.

In all instances the public will be encouraged to volunteer to fully participate in every aspect of this process. The videotaping and live public broadcasting and public archiving of the entire fund allocation process will always be mandatory. By way of computer software technology this entire process will always be completed in a matter of a few short hours.

Each month, upon their having sent in such monies that they have collected, all merchants will receive/download a forgery-restricting security-encrypted certificate; it will have their business name, address, and the amount of such monies collected printed on it.

They must clearly display the certificate by the entrance of their location, so as to inform their fellow Citizens - whose money it actually is - that they have done so.

It is not the government's money. **There is no such thing.**

By having the amount of such taxes they've collected printed on the certificate, Citizens will be able to very easily spot those businesses that are attempting to pay substantially less than the amount of tax that they should have collected and sent in.

Since this money is not going to be wasted or stolen by "government" operatives, it will be in everyone's best interest to be aware of and to report such abuses.

And when many of the local people are intimately involved in their local governmental processes, and are thus personally known to each other, the potential for theft is minimized.

Not to mention the fact that the vast majority of you are only inclined to try avoiding payment into government operations, or to try over-billing them, when you feel as though that which you worked for and legitimately earned is being taken away from you only to be misspent or stolen.

13B — Speaking of misspent or stolen funds…

Before there can be any lawful remedy for the loss of benefits to those who will no longer qualify for Social Security disability/Medicaid/Medicare payments, the Citizens of the United States of America shall vote upon any proposed plan to assist those who may be losing any such benefits because of these changes to those systems.

The lawful institution of any remedy shall be in effect only after the voting public of the United States of America has voted for it by way of a two-thirds (2/3) majority vote.

Said remedy shall be in effect for a period of one full year, and its renewal, which will not ever be for a period of more than one full year, will be dependent upon the voting public of the United States of America having voted for it by way of a two-thirds (2/3) majority vote.

Furthermore, in addition to their ability to vote against it and/or any proposed renewal, any Citizen that does not agree with a proposed remedy shall be lawfully exempt from participating in any form of payment and/or service to such remedy should it become law.

They will facilitate such exemption by way of filling out and signing an exemption form that would take anyone with an elementary school education no more than five (5) minutes to properly complete and submit.

Said form will be available for completion and submission in all town halls, post offices, and public libraries during all of the hours they are regularly open.

Those who fill it out will be provided with an officially stamped and dated carbon copy to be kept for their records as proof of having done so.

Said form must be filled out and submitted no less than forty-eight (48) hours prior to such vote.

In all cases, the ability of a Citizen to properly complete and submit said form must exist as outlined above.

Otherwise, the documented inability to make such submission shall be lawfully regarded as the act of having properly submitted the form in order to declare one's decision to not participate in the payment of such funding.

14 - The current system of Medicare/Medicaid will be ended immediately.

The system that will take its place, which will be eliminated forty (40) years from the date of its inception, will be funded henceforth (with full public transparency) only by way of the allocation of any surplus funds from the system of "Social Security" that is outlined in sections **13** and **13A**, and the following:

The collection of an annual tax of one hundred dollars ($100) per year, per person, from all Citizens of the United States of America who are at or above the age of twenty-one (21) and not receiving any payments from this fund or from the "wounded veterans/whistleblowers tax".

This tax works out to an approximate average of $1.93 per week; or a maximum of $4,000 per contributor for the lifespan of the program; which is to say a maximum of less than one-quarter (1/4) of the money that will be issued to each Citizen who takes full advantage of the opportunities that are outlined in section **1D**.

Citizens who choose to pay their applicable taxes by way of the method described in section **3D** shall always have the right to pay their portion of this tax in the same manner.

In such cases, those Citizens will do needed work for their local government at an hourly rate of one dollar ($1.00) per hour in order to pay off their exact share of this tax.

Their local government will then issue them a receipt and allocate that exact amount of money to the payment of said tax from the amount of money they will have received for this purpose from the "Infrastructure Reserve Account" that is described in <u>section fifteen</u> of this section of this book.

Remember, this tax is only going to be enforced for forty (40) years. And from the time that this new system begins, you are no longer going to be paying any income tax or having to make mandatory payments toward Social Security.

Those of you with fully functioning brains will immediately see this new system and the new system for Social Security described earlier, as a blessing on many different levels.

So despite the massive, well-funded outcry of our industry shills and other well-greased lackeys who will be doing everything possible to make sure that these new systems never come into being…

(As Justice Field predicted, the "experts" would prefer to have a few "trillion dollar coins" minted. http://www.forbes.com/sites/kotlikoff/2013/01/19/the-treasury-has-already-minted-two-trillion-dollar-coins/

And how about giving "money" away to people to boost spending! *We've stolen too much. Let's give back some of the counterfeit money. Those idiots will see it as a gift rather than recognize our crimes."* http://www.zerohedge.com/news/2014-08-26/it-begins-council-foreign-relations-proposes-central-banks-should-hand-consumers-cas)

And despite the outcry from groups of Social Security beneficiaries who "think" they can complain their way into a better deal than the lottery jackpot-like offering that I've outlined above…

And despite the outcry from all of the Medicare/Medicaid recipients who still want to be assured of their full share of the fruits of everyone else's labor…

Will **YOU** make sure that these programs come into being as soon as possible and as efficiently as possible?

Will **YOU** make sure that the amount of collected funds continually covers the legitimate costs of the programs?

15 – This section outlines the functionality of the **"Infrastructure Reserve Account"** first mentioned in section **1D.**

Will you personally invest the time and energy needed to conceptualize the full functionality of the ideas that are outlined in this section?

Or will you just allow the trillion "dollar" coin toting "experts" to convince you that such plans are absurd and a perversion of justice – after putting forth less of an effort to scrutinize their claims than what you regularly invest in the subjects that are of real importance in our circus/insane asylum of despoliation:

Who the hottest celebrities are dating; *what* they're wearing; *where* they're hanging out; *why* one of them got arrested or entered rehab; *when* the latest highlights and resulting statistics of various sporting events are going to be broadcast in "hi-def" at 5G speed to your newest pocket sized wireless "solution"; and *how,* in general, you can appear to get more while doing less.

As you know, I'm with Socrates on this one; but since I have a bet to win:

For twenty (20) years from the date of its inception, funds in this account will be used solely for the following purposes:

1 - Funding the improvement and ongoing maintenance of the physical infrastructure of your country, exclusively by domestically-owned companies, domestically-made products and domestic labor, as outlined below.

2 - Purchasing domestic properties that were previously foreign-owned, as outlined in section **2F.**

3 - Funding the "We are Under Attack Reserve" that was outlined in section **3B.**

4 - Paying to localities the amount of money that would otherwise remain uncollected because certain Citizens have decided to pay the taxes which are outlined in sections <u>twelve</u> and <u>fourteen</u> by way of the method offered to them in section **3ᴅ**.

5 - Providing interest-free loans ranging from "micro" amounts to five hundred dollars ($500), exclusively to individuals from other countries that qualify for such lending in part because they meet at least one of the following criteria:

I - Living at or below the poverty level and wish to acquire land to farm; and are willing to be contractually bound to treat all of their animals humanely according to specified guidelines, and to not use any toxic chemicals as pesticides, any genetically modified seeds, or any growth hormones in any of their animals.

II - Farmers who own their land but are living at or below the poverty level; and are willing to be contractually bound to treat all of their animals humanely according to specified guidelines, and to not use any toxic chemicals as pesticides, any genetically modified seeds, or any growth hormones in any of their animals.

III - Living at or below the poverty level and wish to learn particular job skills.

IV - Living at or below the poverty level and wish to open a business; and are willing to be contractually bound to not sell any products grown with the use of toxic chemicals or made from genetically modified seeds, or animals that were not treated humanely according to the specified guidelines mentioned above, or given any growth hormones.

And to maintain safe, healthy work environments for all of their employees.

V - Small business owners who are willing to be contractually bound to not sell any products grown with the use of toxic chemicals or made from genetically modified seeds, or animals that were not treated humanely according to the specified guidelines mentioned above, or given any growth hormones.

And to maintain safe, healthy work environments for all of their employees.

VI - Groups who wish to set up schools whose minimum course curriculum will match that which is described in section <u>forty-six</u> of this section of this book.

At all times following the first full year of its inception, five percent (0.05%) of the balance of the funds in this account must be allocated for the purpose stated in #5 above, but the funds mentioned in #3 above shall not ever be taken into account for any manner of measurement regarding said five percent.

Make no mistake about it, such lending is a most effective way to ensure your long-term national security and to maintain effective worldwide foreign policy influence.

It is also a necessary step toward eliminating the worldwide influence of dishonest gain.

Every single aspect of every loan will be constantly, accurately accounted for in real time. And such up to date information will always be fully accessible twenty-four (24) hours a day to all Citizens of the United States of America in a manner that is easily understandable to a layperson.

15A - Should they be approved by the necessary majorities of shareholders, each of the following improvements to the physical infrastructure of the United States of America will be undertaken on a scale which is equal in proportion to the amount of American manpower put toward the full scope of the war effort of World War Two. The idea is to have these improvements fully implemented within fifteen (15) years of breaking ground.

Note that, as used below, the term "publicly owned" does NOT mean "State owned" or "State operated" or "State regulated". It means owned and constantly scrutinized by the properly educated Citizens of the United States of America (i.e., those who are fully aware of the <u>fact</u> that others among them who seek to be paid more than what their actual production can provide in a truly free market are trying to steal from them; and that if allowed, such dishonest gain is guaranteed to eventually bankrupt and enslave their offspring, both conceptually and monetarily).

Remember, this undertaking will occur *after* the previously mentioned rally has awoken and informed your nation's Citizenry to the principles and techniques of large scale, efficiently run, equitable operations; not to mention the principles and techniques upon which all personal achievements depend.

Each adult Citizen will receive one share of stock in the combined operations of this fund.

The stock will enable them to cast one vote in all matters of shareholder voting.

Each share of stock will be non-transferable, and invalidated at the time of its holder's death.

Note that, as used below, the term "privately-run" means that each numbered operation will be managed on a per state basis by private interests who have been awarded a contract. It will be based upon the detailed plans/bid they will have presented for such initial construction or ongoing business operations management to the shareholders and state legislatures, and to Congress.

Such detailed plans for initial construction will present a <u>complete</u> breakdown of all costs, materials, suppliers, subcontractors, environmental impact, timeframes for completed sections of work, etc.

Each such contract will offer the possibility of great profitability to both the contract holder and their workers, so as to attract the finest talents and dedicated efforts; but they will be structured so that profitability is dependent upon quality of work, timeliness in the completion of each specified stage of progress, and lack of legitimate labor and environmental-based complaints.

The incentives provided to workers will <u>not</u> be tied into a lack of legitimate labor-based complaints toward management.

As per the funding structure of each construction contract, there will be no possibility of cost overruns or other boondoggling.

Contract holders will not be guaranteed any profit; and a lack of competence could very well result in their financial ruin. **The public will not be left holding the bag.**

Once the initial construction has been completed and such contracts have expired or been terminated due to incentivized early completion or shareholder dissatisfaction, all "ongoing business operations management" contracts will be five (5) years in length and potentially renewable. They will also offer contract holders the incentivized possibility of great profitability - and the incentive of personal liability for miscalculations and breaches of law.

As per the terms of all contracts, certain majorities of shareholders will have the ability to direct contract holders to undertake particular courses of action; and to immediately dismiss certain members of their management team; and to invalidate said contract without impediment.

But I'll leave the stipulation of such monumentally important details up to the public that should, by now, understand the meanings of these words: reason, sovereign, responsibility, indignation, determination, equitable, liberty, unity, jurisdiction, dependent, and casuist.

After fully debated, fully transparent, timely feasibility studies for their related construction, consumer adoption, and ongoing maintenance are completed, those concerns which the aforementioned contracts may enable construction and ongoing operations of are as follows:

1 - The construction and ongoing maintenance of a system of publicly owned, privately-run, profitable, high-speed rail lines that will enable extremely cost effective travel and freight forwarding to major cities and other high volume travel destinations in your country.

Such high-speed rail lines will be constructed to accommodate at least fifty-percent (50%) of the current domestic airline traffic to and from major cities, and at least fifty-percent (50%) of the current automobile traffic to and from many state and national parks, and other high use areas of nature, such as ski resorts, beaches, and hiking/biking trails.

2 - The construction and ongoing maintenance of nationwide, publicly owned, privately-run, profitable, fully integrated state-of-the-art electrical power and internet service provider distribution networks ("tiers" 1, 2, 3, and "internet exchange points").

3 - A nationwide system of publicly owned, privately-run, profitable, state-of-the-art wind and solar farms, related product manufacturing/development plants (i.e., base components, peripherals, etc.), and a non-subsidized, interest-free loan program for suitable residential and commercial wind and solar power systems, - with the capability of producing a total minimum yearly output of one hundred and twenty-five Quadrillion BTUs.

And, the unrestricted opportunity for the free energy gurus to en-*light*-en the masses will immediately be made available by law.

The official forum for the presentation of such technology will be a department that is of, and physically within, the newly formed institution that is outlined in section forty-five of this section of this book.

Each presentation will be captured on video in its entirety, in a manner which clearly provides the un-adept viewer with an accurate insight of said technology's actual capabilities, and both archived and immediately uploaded to the appropriate section of the official website for that institution; so that a vigilant public will always have the opportunity to remain fully aware of all potentially beneficial products and processes in this crucial field of endeavor.

Should an actual free energy machine, or even one that is clearly superior to all currently utilized methods of energy production, be presented, by law said institution's full capabilities will immediately be utilized for the purpose of alerting the general public to its existence; so as to ensure that the proper actions are promptly taken by shareholders and members of Congress as outlined in the following paragraph.

4 - The construction and ongoing maintenance of a publicly owned, privately-run, profitable, comprehensive system of:

a- dedicated state-of-the-art chemical research and development facilities;

b- dedicated state-of-the-art organic farming facilities;

c- dedicated state-of-the-art "environmentally friendly" industrial facilities;

that are charged with this task: being able to continually provide your entire nation and at least ten percent (10%) of the rest of the world with soil nutrifying, biodegradable, compostable packaging and other products that are disposable by design; the product line will also include all applications in which domestic manufacturers are at the time of this being written, using non-biodegradable and non-compostable materials.

5 - The nationwide construction and ongoing maintenance of publicly owned, privately-run, profitable, state-of-the-art, "environmentally friendly" municipal water treatment plants, waste treatment plants, and recycling plants. **Clean water from your own sink!**

6 - The nationwide renovation of bridges, tunnels, and water lines, with the state-of-the-art, longest lasting, "environmentally friendly" materials.

7 - The construction and ongoing maintenance of a truly comprehensive and "environmentally friendly" surveillance and security system along the entirety of your southern and northern borders, which are jointly managed by all branches of the military and the board of the institution that is outlined in section <u>forty-five</u> of this section of this book.

8 - The immediate, full funding of medical testing on the following list of substances that are, and have been, traditionally used for "alternative" medical treatments and wellness programs; to officially determine whether or not they are harmful, and what their full range of actual benefits are.

So that if they are proven to have beneficial health-related uses, and to be at least as safe as the many poisonous concoctions that have already gained FDA approval, they can be used by the properly informed public as quickly and inexpensively as possible.

The entire testing process and the reporting of all results will always be completely transparent to the public.

The substances that will be tested, and whose testing will begin simultaneously and continue with an equal level of vigor are: "**Chlorine Dioxide**" (ClO₂ - as in the work of Jim Humble); "**Ketones**" (as in the work of Dr. Charles V. Mobbs); "**Turmeric**" and "**Curcumin**"; "**Iodine**" and "**Iodide**" (as in the work of Dr. Guy Abraham and Dr. David Brownstein); "**Magnesium**" and "**Potassium**"; "**Coley's toxins**" (as in the work of Dr. William B. Coley); "**Cannabinoids**" (compounds found in the Cannabis plant); "**Mycelium/Mushrooms**" (as in the work of Paul Stamets); "**Colloidal silver**"; "**Vitamin C**"; "**Vitamin C**" taken with Lysine and **Proline**" (at the levels and frequency prescribed by Dr. Linus Pauling and Dr. Matthias Rath); "**Niacin**" (as in the work of Dr. Abram Hoffer); "**Organic Sulphur**"; "**PectaSol-C**® modified citrus pectin" (developed by Dr. Isaac Eliaz); "**Willard's Water**" (developed by Dr. John Willard).

All aspects of the above-mentioned expenditures will be constantly, accurately accounted for.

Such up to date information will always be fully accessible twenty-four (24) hours a day to all Citizens of the United States of America. It will be presented in a manner that is easily understandable to a layman. It will be available in regional, state, and municipal level sections, so that the entire cost of the plan can be comprehended from both the micro and macro level.

Other than the "We are Under Attack Reserve" that was outlined in section **3ʙ**, none of the money in this account can be lawfully withdrawn until all of the following has occurred:

1 - The exact recipients of the funds and the exact corresponding amounts of money that are to be withdrawn have been established and furnished in their entirety to the public, by both the prospective contract holders and both houses of Congress.

2 - The shareholders have voted to lawfully validate each applicable contract and loan according to the shareholder voting powers that will have been lawfully established during the aforementioned Constitutional convention/legislative amendment process.

3 - There has been a declaration signed by the President of the United States of America and each member of Congress and the Supreme Court, which states that it is the unalienable right of the Citizens of the United States of America to direct such actions through their elected government representatives and related functionaries; since they are, in fact, the employees of those Citizens.

All of the profits that are referred to in numbers 1-5 of the previous paragraph shall always, by law, be considered funds of this account and will thus always be immediately returned directly to this account.

If, finally, the amount of legitimately clean energy being domestically produced is enough to provide for the vast majority of your country's total need...

and if automobile and trucking manufacturers chiefly produce non-subsidized electric vehicles equipped with a fully upgradable, universally adaptable auxiliary battery input - so that what are now "gas stations" can be refitted to become battery exchange centers for truckers and those among you who are too lazy to fully charge your own batteries and are willing to pay a tax on auxiliary power (all such tax will be allocated solely to the funding of the programs outlined in sections forty-six and forty-eight of this section of this book)...

And you take full advantage of the high-speed railways, rather than continuing to be abused by the airline industry (yes, I'm also speaking about freight forwarding)… the amount of money generated by this account will be quite substantial. **It will surely cover a significant portion of the monetary costs of a properly run system of government.**

15B - After the initial twenty (20) years have passed, and until the full amount of money that was spent on the above infrastructure projects and the expenditures that are outlined in <u>section eight</u> and section **8A** of this section of this book are paid back to this account, a fully documented twenty-five percent (25%) of the yearly profit from such projects shall accumulate and remain in this account.

The remaining seventy-five percent (75%) of such profit shall be utilized only as follows: seventy percent (70%) of that portion of the yearly profit generated from such industry shall be used solely to directly fund the ongoing operations of government in the exact manner of funding which is outlined in section **3C**, and sections <u>twelve</u> and <u>fourteen</u> as funding relates to section **3D**; but paying to localities the amount of money that would otherwise remain uncollected because certain Citizens have decided to pay the taxes outlined in sections <u>twelve</u> and <u>fourteen</u> by way of the method offered to them in section **3D** shall always lawfully take precedence over the usage of these funds for any purpose other than the bond repayment that is mentioned in section **3A**.

Ten percent (10%) of such yearly profit will be allocated solely to an ongoing nationwide campaign, through all forms of media and to all age groups, that constantly promotes the benefits and the urgent need for civics and optimal health regimen-related continuing education and action on behalf of all patriotic Citizens.

Ten percent (10%) of such yearly profit will be allocated solely to the funding of scientific research and development in varied fields. And it will be stipulated that this fund shall always be fully reimbursed for its documented investment in any research and development that leads to any products or services being brought to the market for profit by industry.

(Let's see if you perennial pincushions can figure out and lawfully implement the simple guidelines needed to insure that all of this money is actually going to be used in a way that really does benefit every one of the Citizens whose money this really is.)

Ten percent (10%) of such yearly profit will be allocated solely to the ongoing funding of medical testing. Such testing will be done on substances that are being used for "alternative" medical treatments and wellness programs, in order to officially determine whether or not they are harmful, and what their actual benefits are.

So that if they are proven to have beneficial health-related uses and to be at least as safe as the many poisonous substances that have already gained FDA approval, such substances can be used by the properly informed public as quickly and inexpensively as possible.

The entire testing process and the reporting of all results will always be completely transparent to the public.

The determination for exactly which substances are to be tested and the order in which such testing will occur will be dependent only upon the following criteria:

1 - There must be a minimum of one million (1,000,000) signatures on a petition for each particular substance to be tested.

2 - The order in which such petitions are submitted.

3 - The substances to be tested cannot be patented before or after such testing has occurred.

By law the submission process will be completely free of charge, as simple as possible and completely transparent so there can be no undue influences by any parties for any desired result.

Without exception, any attempt to ever use the funds in this account for any other purposes or in any ways other than those stated above shall be considered an act of Treason.

15C — Are you capable of understanding that the "experts" who will tell you such a plan is unrealistic or too ambitious have no factual basis for their claims?

Or are you a bungling half-wit whose entire botched life will ultimately have less of a positive impact on anyone's well-being than the average underwear defiling wet fart?

(Well, anyone other than those of us who live in unparalleled luxury by way of your employment.)

I mean, surely by now you can discern for yourself why this is no utopian scheme. Right?

You do know that the financing of large scale plans such as this one is <u>exactly</u> what Central Banks/the World Bank/ the IMF, etc., do; and that it is what they have always done. Right?

Though for some reason they can only find it in their hearts to scrape up the required funds when the plan clearly entails the plunder of natural resources, military invasions, insurrection, and massive amounts of death and destruction; or the highly profitable clean-up that is eventually instituted after the previously mentioned actions have occurred.

And need I remind you of the method by which those esteemed financiers get the "money" together? (i.e., get the "money" together to fund whatever it is that each "person" is allowing them to chain their unborn future generations with the legal obligation to pay the interest on.)

They magically create electronic credits based upon nothing but their projected assessment of the debt that your potential energies being *improperly* directed will create for them to collect in the form of natural resources, property, and rights.

Except this time **YOU** are going to be the Magnate financing and managing the deal.

And the financing will be done with interest-free money that is properly accounted for and whose unchanging market value is based upon a particular unchanging measure of properly directed labor, as mentioned in section **1F**.

Remember, properly directed labor - both mental and physical - is the only thing that imparts any actual value to anything on this entire planet.

So, besides the obvious lack of bloodshed, the esteemed financiers won't like this plan because **you** will be financing it *and the rest of your economy going forward.* It will all be done without them.

Picture how much of your productive energies those parasites will no longer be able to outright <u>steal</u> from you if you make this happen.

Do you honestly believe that there is anything they wouldn't say or do to prevent such a thing from happening?

These are the same people who have been doing their best to outright own and covertly manipulate the legal system, the monetary system, the education system, the military, the energy system, the transportation system, and every other aspect of commerce in your nation for their own ends since they were originally able to get their foot in those doors.

You've been handed boatloads of information that proves what is said in the last sentence to be true. Are you ~~puppets~~ patriots going to let the esteemed financiers have their traitorous operatives in government and the private sector convince you that the perfectly valid and legitimate plan I am sharing with you, which would finally free you from the mental and physical bondage they have been subjecting the entire planet to, is somehow no good compared to their utterly corrupt system?

Friend, are you completely befuddled by our methods of control? Are you unable to differentiate between truth and fiction? Are you actually put at ease by the specious rhetoric we keep bathing you in? Do you believe that you'll somehow remain safe and regain your prosperity if you blindly follow our flag waving guidance? Will you continue to ignore the fact that everything of potential value and everything you "think" you own is being continuously, systematically stolen from you under the pretense that it is for your own good?

Is it from those who have purposely ruined you that you seek the permission to be redeemed?

Imagine that a plan requiring an equivalent effort and resources as I have recommended here were desperately needed to save everyone on this planet from some sort of obvious impending doom. Imagine that I had honest, competent leaders installed to incessantly direct your thoughts and energies toward its completion.

You can be rest assured that it would not only get done, but that it would happen a few days early and under budget.

You need to understand that nothing less than the full-scale <u>immediate</u> implementation of this plan is needed. You must repair the internal and external physical mechanisms that are responsible for your country's current and long-term ability to function in an ongoing manner that is consistent with the interdependent actuality of freedom, prosperity, and security.

As I've already said, any system whose composition includes structural components that necessarily serve to draw and keep vital nutrients away from the other components of its structure is intrinsically self-destructive; corrupt.

Know this in relation to the many methods we have been using to ruin you:

There is currently no aspect of your way of life that does not hasten your demise.

Now take an educational journey toward the discovery of the meanings of these words: despoliation, bungling, botched, defile, utopian, befuddle, rhetoric, incessant, magnate, specious, miscreant, engender, prudent, trematode, bilge, biochemical, antagonist, glib, impudent, precursor, abject, privation, lexicon, pithy, mendacious, ne plus ultra, interface, animate, and materialize.

Honestly, have you been looking up each word that you haven't known the meaning of and that I wasn't insisting that you look up?

15D - Make no mistake about it; the only thing lacking in order to bring this utterly sensible, perfectly realistic, universally-equitable idea to fruition is the honest, competent leadership required to properly direct the shackled, delusional masses who are incapable of any self-directed logical thought or action.

1 - The valid source of funding is <u>not</u> lacking.

2 - The manpower is <u>not</u> lacking.

3 - The technology is <u>not</u> lacking.

4 - The required natural resources are <u>not</u> lacking.

5 - The legislative mechanisms that are needed to lawfully establish such a plan as an official operation of government are <u>not</u> lacking.

6 - Your lawful right to take the actions that will force those legislative mechanisms to bring about its implementation is <u>not</u> lacking.

Read that last sentence over a few times and try to fully acknowledge what that means; then read this letter: http://mlk-kpp01.stanford.edu:5801/transcription/document_images/undecided/630416-019.pdf

Is it possible that Socrates was missing something? Hmmm... where will such leadership come from? Who will lead the shackled, delusional masses to the realization of that which has been done to them, and to the proper methods of rectification?

16 - The use of **"free speech zones"** and/or any use of governmental force with the intent or result being the infringement of any Citizen's constitutionally protected rights to:

1 - Peacefully assemble;

2 - Exercise their freedom of speech (I'm <u>not</u> referring to inciting riots or endangering the public);

3 - Petition the government for grievances; shall always, under all circumstances, lawfully be considered an act of insurrection being committed by any and all persons involved in such planning, construction, and/or institution.

And, as such, all involved persons will be tried at the soonest possible date for that crime by a jury comprised of Citizens who have never held any public office and who each hold a valid certificate as outlined in section <u>forty-six</u> of this section of this book.

(And, of course, regardless of what anyone might be protesting about, the act of blocking a public roadway shall henceforth be considered a felony which cannot be reduced to a lesser charge. A conviction on this charge will result in a minimum of two years in jail, a five-hundred dollar fine, and two hundred hours of public service work due upon release)

Hot Investment Tip: Do the work required to understand exactly what I'm about to say. Such an investment will pay big dividends.

Just governance is merely an ongoing process of enacting and enforcing the minimum amount of restrictions which are required to equally safeguard the unalienable rights of all Citizens from whatever <u>actual</u>, credible threats or trespasses may emerge. Absentee management is **guaranteed** to result in officially sanctioned trespass.

You see, all opportunistic miscreants know that "government" is the hub of transgression.

They know that an improperly educated public can always be manipulated through hatred, fear and promises of something for nothing.

They know that legislating and enforcing "law" to benefit private interests at the expense of the general public is a safe and easy path to wealth and privilege.

Yet, an informed reading of the Declaration of Independence and the Constitution/Bill of Rights will enable one to clearly see this: **Constituents allow. Government is allowed.**

And the opposite is for pawns and pirates.

With the Declaration of Independence as the expression of the "self-evident truths" that determine what "just" government is and must be, and the fact that the originally ratified Constitution/Bill of Rights was the self-proclaimed "supreme Law of the Land" in the United States of America...

If you fear your government at all, huge numbers of people have obviously been acting imprudently for a very long time. For exactly what <u>valid</u> reason would you do the same?

17 - No "words of art" shall ever be used as a substitute for the words "private Citizen", "Citizen", "citizen", "person", "individual", or "human being", etc.

For all lawful purposes, the definition of such words shall always be dependent upon their reference to an actual, singular human being. All legislation based upon those words being used for any other purpose will immediately be null and void, and re-written to protect the best interests of the people.

No, it is not a good idea for those who do not wish to become slaves to allow their "government" to guarantee "fictional entities" the right to exercise every action that is guaranteed protection by the first amendment.

Only a complete idiot or an insurrectionist would allow unspecified "freedom of speech" to also be guaranteed to a manmade construct/fictional entity/legal fiction/Creature of the State.

Yes, I'm referring those fictional entities that were created for no other purpose than that of artificially extending the Dominion, Agency, and Possessions (and thus the Liberties) of certain people beyond those of others by way of limiting or eliminating *their own* personal liabilities and increasing *their own* ability to affect legislation - as they seek, by any possible means, to derive profit from the other **actual human beings** that those God given rights were originally lawfully guaranteed to.

Clearly such manmade constructs are different creatures than those that were legally created for the purpose of building a canal or a dam, or some other type of public utility.

Are you able to recognize the difference in how such entities affect your life?

Do the following lines ring a bell?

"The powers delegated to such creations can **never** rightfully supersede those of their creators who are merely entrusting them with such power in order to serve <u>what said creators</u> believe is their best interest; which was the purpose of the creation taking place to begin with. Simple logic proves it."

18 – Have you watched the video that link #1 on page <u>14</u> takes you to? If not, now would be a good time to do so.

The "Administrative Procedures Act" shall be abolished immediately.

All of the regulations that have been implemented since its inception will be reviewed by Congress. The merits versus the failings of each regulation will then be debated in order decide the following:

1- Should any amendments be made to the regulation?

2- Should the regulation be left unchanged?

3- Should the regulation be eliminated?

Once the appropriate course of action has been decided upon, and any proposed changes have been made to the regulation, it will then be voted upon as if the regulation were an entirely new bill that was being proposed as law.

18A – Henceforth, Congress shall not delegate any of its powers to any administrative agency.

No deference shall be paid to agency opinions regarding the legitimacy of its own powers.

The current system of administrative courts will be abolished. All such cases will go before judicial courts, and, to the greatest extent that is functionally possible, cases will be decided upon by juries comprised of Citizens who have never held any public office and who each hold a valid certificate as outlined in section <u>forty-six</u> of this section of this book.

18B – Henceforth, the actual author (s) of every line of text in every piece of proposed legislation must be fully documented and immediately made available, in full, to the public.

Furthermore, prior to any legislative vote, each author of each piece of text in each piece of proposed legislation must always make themselves available to the public in order to fully answer questions related to their contribution to said legislation.

***Take note: such actions should only be considered by those who would rather not continue having their lives controlled by the legally unaccountable ~~trematodes~~ bureaucrats that nest deep within the supra-constitutional, ever-expanding, self-regulating Administrative State.

19 – Henceforth, all governmental security clearances shall be invalidated as soon as the employment related to said clearance has expired.

A failure to immediately invalidate said security clearance shall automatically result in felony charges being brought against all parties responsible for the issuance and revocation of such security clearances.

19A – Henceforth, no member of the federal or any state legislature shall be lawfully allowed to vote on any legislation that they have not publicly, lawfully sworn to have fully read; and then fully explained both the proposed legislation and their reason for voting in the way they intend, to their constituents via Public Television, public radio, the internet, and in person during said broadcasts prior to their voting on such legislation.

In the event that such a representative has not personally read and then explained such legislation to their constituents, and thus not cast a vote for or against it, or has cast a vote contrary to what they previously claimed they would, no such person/representative shall, under any circumstances other than their own death or certified medical-related physical incapacity, be exempt from publicly explaining under penalty of perjury, upon the request of any number of concerned constituents, why they changed their previously stated position or did not complete the above-mentioned duty.

Such explanation must be made within ten days (10) of the initial request, and must be made in a public forum that is publicly televised and held within their voting district.

Whereupon such person/representative must, after offering their explanation, make him or herself available for an uncensored question and answer session with the members of the public who wish to ask them any questions regarding their actions and conduct as a governmental representative of such people.

Such question and answer sessions must be no less than ninety (90) minutes long, and shall, upon a single raised hand of any member of the public who is in attendance, be extended under the full force of law for a period of up to two (2) extra hours.

The lawful sequential order that members of the public will be able to ask said representative questions in shall be decided upon by way of the drawing method outlined in section **3D**. This will ensure that the representative is not avoiding any questions.

19B - All "omnibus" bills and "riders" will immediately be outlawed, and any attempt to utilize such legislative tactics shall be lawfully considered an act of insurrection.

19C - Any attempt to alter a bill that has already been explained to the public as outlined above, without notifying the public in the same exact manner as stated above regarding every change and the full ramifications of each change, shall be lawfully considered an act of Treason.

20 - All elected and appointed government officials shall be subject to a vote of "No Confidence" by the Citizens who are the constituents/residents of the voting district (s) and/or other legislatively defined civil/political construct (s) that their employment is meant to serve, which will lead to their being immediately removed from such employment, if:

A petition calling for such a vote is signed by ten percent (10%) of the number of Citizens who are of the lawful age to vote and who live in that official's voting district (s) etc.; and there is a subsequent three-fourths (3/4) majority that votes for their removal.

Such vote for their removal from office shall occur within ten (10) days of the petition being presented to a court of law in person or by way of there being a certified copy of such petition sent to the court through content notarized, certified mail. Certification of the result shall be made within seven (7) days of the occurrence of said vote.

A public election shall be held to replace such elected officials within ten (10) days of the certification of the vote of "No Confidence", should said certification show that a three-fourths (3/4) majority of voters have, in fact, voted for said removal from office. Certification of the result of the vote to replace said official shall be made within seven (7) days of the occurrence of said vote.

The lawful mechanisms that must be put into action in order to effectuate the replacement of appointed officials will be completed within seventeen (17) days of the certification of the vote of "No Confidence", should said certification show that a three-fourths (3/4) majority of voters have, in fact, voted for said removal from office.

Taxpayer money will not be used to fund the vote unless at least fifty-one percent (51%) of the eligible voting public signs on to the petition; the costs related to such a vote will otherwise be paid for by the individual Citizens who want it to occur.

21 – All public voting that shall take place in regard to any function of government throughout the entire United States of America and its territories must always be done by way of manual, mechanical voting machines or a simple ballot box.

A receipt which is an exact signed copy that will be considered official, lawful documentation of the actual votes they cast must be received by every voter. For the sole purpose of there being an investigation of voting fraud initiated relating to such election, for three (3) years following the election each voter must keep and be able to produce such receipt upon the request of their voting board and a court of law.

22 – All statutes, regulations, codes, and/or other governmentally provided or enabled benefits that are in any way discriminatory toward any potential or actual candidate for public office based upon their not being a member of the "democratic party", the "republican party", or any other political party shall immediately be considered null and void.

23 – Henceforth, no court, whether its jurisdiction is state, federal, or otherwise, shall ever fail to publish in full, any decision made by it.

Nor will they ever fail to furnish - within fourteen (14) days of their receipt of a written request - the complete, accurate transcript of any case they have tried. And they shall do so for no more than their actual cost of producing and delivering it.

23A – An official documentation of the exact government official (s) that initially called for any local, state, or federal enacted civil and/or criminal investigation/proceedings (and any local, state, or federal sanctioned type and time of incarceration), and their sworn reasons for the initiation/recommendation of those actions, must always accompany all related actions and must always be an unredacted part of the public record.

24 – Henceforth, no law, regulation or code shall ever go into effect unless it is written in clear language without any ambiguity as to any meaning of any aspect of its intent and actual usage.

All such laws, regulations, and codes must then have their explanations for existence plainly written and made publicly available – and validated as such by way of testing and grading which is similar to what was set forth in section nine of this section of this book. Said testing shall be designed specifically for the purpose of making sure that mentally competent Citizens will personally be capable of successfully defending themselves and/or their property against trespass based upon such information, should such a case ever be brought into a court of law.

25 - The seventeenth amendment (17th) shall be repealed immediately. Read this article on the subject: https://lonang.com/commentaries/conlaw/federalism/repeal-seventeenth-amendment/

26 - The "original thirteenth amendment" (13th) shall be <u>instituted</u> immediately. (Have you fully read the conspiracy theory-laced article that link #75 on page <u>74</u> takes you to?)

26A - Other than those which the Constitution originally expressly granted, the Congress, the Judiciary, and the Executive shall not ever lawfully enjoy any immunity that is not simultaneously being granted to all age appropriate Citizens of the United States of America.

27 - The Citizens of the United States of America shall always have the unquestioned right and ability to cause a fully transparent and fully empowered official independent investigation to take place regarding any subject of local, state, and/or federal governmental action or inaction past or present; provided that they are able to present to a court of law in a particular state where such an investigation is being called for regarding local or state matters, or in courts of law in at least three-fourths (3/4) of the states of the Union when such an investigation is being called for regarding matters of the federal government, petitions calling for such action that have been signed by at least ten percent (10%) of the eligible voting public of that locality, that state, or those states.

Taxpayer money will not be used to fund the investigation unless at least fifty-one percent (51%) of the eligible voting public signs on to the petition; the costs related to such an investigation will otherwise be paid for by the individual Citizens who want it to occur. Such petitions can be presented to courts of law in person or by way of there being certified copies of those petitions sent to the court (s) through content notarized, certified mail. Such investigation must be allowed to begin no more than ten (10) days after the presentation of such petitions to the court (s) of law.

In each case, each specific attempt by governmental officials to withhold requested documents will be reviewed immediately by a jury of Citizens who have never held any public office and who each hold a valid certificate as outlined in section <u>forty-six</u> of this section of this book, and said jury will make the determination on whether or not such documents are too sensitive to be disclosed to the investigators; they will also determine which requested redactions, if any, will be allowed.

28 - Should any judge that presides/presided over any court within any of the states or the federal territory of the United States of America be found by a jury of Citizens who have not ever held public office or worked on the staff of any government official, and who each hold a valid certificate as outlined in section <u>forty-six</u> of this section of this book, to have operated said court in any manner contradictory to any aspect of the "supreme Law of the Land", they will be charged with the crime of insurrection and subject to the jury's decision relating to the application of Title 18 of the United States Code, section 2383.

28A - On May 12th, 2020, <u>Rand Paul introduced an amendment to H.R 6172</u>, the "USA FREEDOM Reauthorization Act of 2020", with the intent of protecting every American's privacy, ensuring due process, and reasserting the Fourth Amendment; henceforth it shall be law.

29 – As per the final sentence of Article I, Section 8 of the Constitution which reads as follows:

"To make all Laws which shall be necessary and proper for carrying into Execution the foregoing Powers, and all other Powers vested by this Constitution in the Government of the United States, or in any Department or Officer thereof.",

the scope of lawful purposes upon and for which any Presidential Directive or Executive Order or Executive Action can be based, and the methodology of their execution by the President/Executive branch, shall be explicitly codified; as will an automatic and immediate judicial review by the Supreme Court as the lawful remedy for any qualified dispute regarding the overstepping of said lawful boundaries within which the President/Executive branch may execute said constructs.

Such a dispute shall be lawfully considered "qualified" by way of the following: ten (10) or more members of the United States Congress publically signing and presenting a petition to the Court in person or by way of content notarized certified mail, or by way of petitions presented to the Court, in person or by way of content notarized certified mail, that have been signed by one million (1,000,000) or more members of the eligible voting public of the United States of America.

30 – All claims of Executive Privilege can be overturned by a two-thirds (2/3) vote of the entire voting population of the United States of America that cast their votes for such decision. The polls for such voting will open within seven (7) days of the Executive branch's invocation of said privilege and they will remain open for a minimum of twelve (12) hours on a particular weekday.

The constructs known as Presidential "signing statements", "line item vetoes", and "fast tracking" shall immediately be permanently outlawed, and all legislation relating to such constructs that was made previous to this law shall be considered completely null and void.

31 – All Presidential pardons/commutations and the full reason for each one must be announced publicly by the President on television, in newspapers, and on the internet.

And before they can take effect, each one can be overturned by a two-thirds (2/3) vote of the entire voting population of the United States of America that cast their votes for such decision. The polls for such voting will open within seven (7) days of the President's announcement and they will remain open for a minimum of twelve (12) hours on a particular weekday.

32 - Other than for the purpose of criminal sanctions being imposed upon those individuals or fictional entities that have each, in their own court proceedings, been judged by a jury of Citizens of the United States of America (who each hold a valid certificate as outlined in section forty-six of this section of this book) to have sought to damage and/or defraud another or others through any of the involved parties' usage of the internet, no law (other than what is outlined in #21 on page underline{200}) that was not passed by Congress before the date of September eleventh, two thousand and one (9/11/01) shall ever be passed to tax, or limit in any way, the ability to use the internet however one sees fit in relation to the most advanced technologies in existence at any time in the present and the future.

33 - No paid or otherwise compensated employee, member, or owner of any company or group, or branch of government - other than a Citizen mandated local peace officer unit - that was not recognized as an official local, state, or federal domestic law enforcement agency prior to September eleventh, two thousand and one (9/11/01), shall ever be allowed to have or perform any armed or unarmed, public law enforcement function anywhere in the United States of America without there first having been a "prime time" nationally televised public hearing on such matters where the amount of time given to dissenting parties to state their case against such function is equal to the amount of time given to all of those who are in favor of it; and then there having been a subsequent vote held on it by the entire voting public of that locality, state, or the nation, in which a two-thirds (2/3) majority voted in favor of such law enforcement.

Daily announcements that are neither for nor against the proposed action must be made about the hearing on television, in newspapers, and on the internet for the thirty (30) days prior to the hearing. All costs related to the announcements, the hearing, and the vote must be paid for in full by any party or parties seeking the proposed authority in question.

The lawful ability of a Citizen to volunteer to act in any manner not prohibited by the Declaration of Independence or the Constitution, that they deem necessary to safeguard their constitutionally protected rights and/or the rights of their family and/or fellow Citizens who explicitly request that such actions be taken on their behalf, shall never be lawfully considered to be in any way limited by this or any other law.

34 – No employee, member, or owner of any company or group that is not an official governmental law enforcement agency shall continue or ever partake, in any aspect of the ownership, operation, or management of any prison or detention center in any state or federal territory - regardless of when they were originally commissioned to do so - without there first having been a "prime time" nationally televised public hearing on such matters where the amount of time given to dissenting parties to state their case against such action is equal to the amount of time given to all of those who are in favor of it; and then there having been a subsequent vote held on it by the entire voting public of that locality, state, or the nation, in which a two-thirds (2/3) majority voted in favor of such ownership, operation, or management.

Daily announcements that are neither for nor against the proposed action must be made about the hearing on television, in newspapers, and on the internet for the thirty (30) days prior to the hearing. All costs related to the announcements, the hearing, and the vote must be paid for in full by the non-governmental party or parties seeking the proposed opportunity in question.

Should the public vote against any such ownership, the funds that were actually spent on the construction of such facilities will be paid back to said ownership, and the facilities will become the property of the same interests that own the lawfully operated facilities that were in existence prior to such construction.

Unless of course the stock price of said company were to drop to a level that would make it less expensive to simply purchase the entire company.

I believe it has been said that turnabout is fair play.

The money for such purchases will be factored into the budget and the appropriate revenue will be provided by the **National Defense Payment Fund** that is outlined in section **8A**.

35 – The use of any type of video camera or related technology for surveillance and other such purposes in public places shall be subject to an annual vote of approval by a three-fourths (3/4) majority vote of the voting public of such places.

No such vote will occur until there has been a "prime time" nationally televised public hearing on such matters where the amount of time given to dissenting parties to state their case against such surveillance is equal to the amount of time given to all of those who are in favor of it.

The use of all surveillance cameras and other unmanned technologies for purposes related to the issuance of any fines to drivers shall be outlawed.

All such cameras and related technologies which are currently in place must be removed immediately, and all costs related to such removal must be borne by the parties that installed the devices, unless they wish to forfeit their ownership of such devices.

Video cameras installed on police vehicles for the sole purpose of recording the act of ticketing and/or arresting a driver who has already been pulled over by an officer shall not be considered surveillance cameras as described above.

All statutes and regulations regarding the prohibition of the public use of cameras and video cameras that were not in effect on or before September eleventh, two thousand and one (9/11/01) shall immediately be considered null and void.

The further institution of such laws and regulations shall be outlawed.

36 – The mandatory use by any Citizen of any "RFID" or any device that serves the same basic functions shall be permanently outlawed.

Any attempt to institute a statute, regulation, or code that would ever cause any added inconvenience to or discrimination against any Citizen who does not choose to use any such device shall always be considered an act of insurrection.

The requirement of a jailed person or a person convicted of a crime in a court of law by a jury of Citizens of the United States of America, to wear or carry any such external device for the length of time that they would otherwise be confined to a jail in order for them to be allowed to serve any part of their sentence outside of a jail, or in lieu of posting bail, is <u>not</u> to be construed as "mandatory use", since such usage would in actuality be a privilege.

The requirement of foreigners to wear any such external device for the length of time that they are in the United States of America and/or its territories will be considered lawful should a three-fourths (3/4) majority of the respective voting public vote in favor of such a requirement.

The concealed placement of any "RFID", or any device that serves the same basic functions, in or on any commercially available or governmentally-issued products wherein the device is not immediately identifiable and removable without the use of any tools by the purchaser/receiver of such goods, shall be considered a criminal act of infringing on the individual's right to privacy perpetrated by the manufacturer and any other parties involved in the placement of such device.

The mandatory use by any Citizen of any "body scanner" or any device that serves the same basic functions shall be outlawed.

The act of causing any Citizen any exacerbated time loss because of their refusal to interact with or be acted upon by any "body scanner" or any device that serves the same basic functions, shall be permanently outlawed.

37 – All ingestible and/or topically applied products and foods or liquids that have been genetically and/or otherwise modified and/or irradiated, must always be clearly labeled as such. This shall also include all foods treated with pesticides and/or waxes.

The country/countries of origin <u>and processing</u> of all ingredients shall always be clearly listed. Henceforth all ingredients must be individually listed on all ingredient labels, and all products grown in "Biosolids" and/or with wastewater must be clearly labeled as such.

Any product and/or food that has been manufactured with or is made of any parts of any animal that was known to have any illness at the time of its death must always be clearly labeled with a warning of such information.

All products and foods that have been manufactured with or are made of any parts, or by way of any bodily function, of any animal that was given any type of medication or antibiotic or hormones, must always be clearly labeled as such.

No food safety laws or regulations on such commerce that in any way infringe upon the established needs and/or the abilities of otherwise law abiding "independent" and/or "organic" farmers/livestock producers who follow the already proven, safe manufacturing and handling procedures which exist to produce and/or sell or trade products that the public desires, shall ever be lawfully instituted henceforth; and any such laws or regulations which already exist shall immediately be considered null and void.

The patenting of any intrinsic aspect of any life form shall immediately be outlawed; and any such patents that have already been recognized by the United States Patent and Trademark Office will immediately be lawfully considered null and void.

38 – All contracts and agreements which have bound, or shall ever in any way bind, the government and/or the Citizens of the United States of America to any dictates of the International Monetary Fund, the World Bank, the World Trade Organization, the World Health Organization, the Bank of International Settlements, the United Nations, or any subsidiaries or partners of any of those organizations, shall be cancelled immediately and lawfully considered null and void.

The current location of the United Nations headquarters shall be moved, and the new location must be outside of the United States of America and its territories. Said move must take no longer than three (3) months to be completed; this includes diplomats.

No branch or subsidiary of the United Nations or any of the above-mentioned organizations shall be allowed to maintain a permanent or temporary location within the United States of America and its territories.

Nor shall they be lawfully allowed to hold any meetings, events or training therein.

38A – No government employees, whether foreign or domestic, shall be allowed to cause traffic delays or major re-routing for the public when they show up to a town or city. They will either show up to do their business or shopping, etc. at an off hour or they will not be allowed to show up.

39 – Henceforth, police will no longer pull drivers over for simple equipment violations. A notice of the violation will be sent to the driver by both email and text message. A ticket will only be issued if the problem is not proven to be fixed within one week of the notice being sent.

39A – Trained "Citizen Advocates" will be encouraged to ride with police so as minimize physical escalation during interactions with the public. Said training will be designed, developed, and continually reviewed by publically elected joint task forces of local Citizens and local police.

39B – Henceforth, the uniforms of all law enforcement officials will include a video camera similar to that of the camera mentioned in the following article (it's also link #5 on page 47): http://mobile.nytimes.com/2013/04/07/business/wearable-video-cameras-for-police-officers.html?pagewanted=all&_r=5 And riot police will wear as a conspicuous part of their uniform an "electronic identity code" that will enable them to be individually identified on video. By law, it shall be required that all of the interactions with the general public, and everyone who is incarcerated, be recorded and that all such recordings be made readily available to the general public, free of charge, upon request. The documented testing of all such equipment shall be mandatory at thirty minute intervals from the start until the end of each work shift.

39C – Henceforth, all law enforcement officials will be required to pay into a municipal malpractice insurance fund from which the damages paid to victims of their negligence and/or abuse of power will be derived. How long do you figure the "blue wall of silence" will remain standing, when those who comprise it are surrounded by video cameras, trained "Citizen Advocates", and a growing, "green wall of insurance premiums"?

40 – Every single government subsidy must immediately be disclosed in full during a series of "prime time" nationally televised public hearings on such matters; wherein the amount of time given to dissenting parties to state their case against such action shall be equal to the amount of time given to all of those who are in favor of it. And there will be a subsequent vote held on the possible continuation of each subsidy. Said continuation shall be dependent upon a two-thirds (2/3) majority vote by the entire voting public of that state, or the entire nation as it applies to such matters, in favor of such action. Yes, such subsidies will be lawfully considered "government-run assistance".

Daily announcements that are neither for nor against the proposed action must be made about the hearing on television, in newspapers, and on the internet for the thirty (30) days immediately prior to the hearing. All costs related to the announcements, the hearing, and the vote must be paid for in full by the non-governmental parties seeking the continuance of the subsidies in question.

40A – Henceforth, there will never again be any "no bid" contracts awarded by the government for any reason. All such contracts in existence shall be terminated within one year of the opening day of the Constitutional convention/legislative amendment process being called for herein.

41 – Henceforth, all "loopholes" will be lawfully considered closed within twenty-four (24) hours of their existence having been documented by way of a written correspondence being presented to both a court of law and a member of Congress in person, or by way of there being a certified copy of said correspondence sent to the court and a member of congress through content notarized, certified mail. A brief notification of the closing of the loophole will immediately be made on www.congress.gov. In all cases, the parties engaged in taking advantage of the loophole will be responsible for discovering if it has been closed.

42 – Henceforth, all lawful meetings between all lobbying parties/parties employed as lobbyists, and any government officials and/or their staff, must take place in officially sanctioned locations where they will be recorded on video, in full, while being broadcast live according to a previously published and fully updated schedule, on the internet for free public viewing. Furthermore, by law, all job related correspondence and communications must always be fully documented and archived as mentioned below.

The failure to act as such will result in felony charges being brought against said official or staff member; and the case will be tried by a jury of Citizens who have not ever held public office or worked on the staff of any government official, and who each hold a valid certificate as outlined in section forty-six of this section of this book. All such video and assorted communications must be archived and stored indefinitely, for the easiest possible access by all interested parties free of charge. All costs associated with this system must be borne by the lobbying parties.

Yes, this means that government officials and their staff cannot be married to or engaged in personal relationships with lobbyists. The government officials and/or their staff who are interested or already engaged in such relationships must immediately resign from those governmental positions because of the clear conflict of interest. The failure to act as such will result in felony charges being brought against said official or staff member; and the case will be tried by a jury of Citizens who have not ever held public office or worked on the staff of any government official, and who each hold a valid certificate as outlined in section forty-six of this section of this book.

Clearly, you've forgotten the following all-important piece of information: these people are your employees. Their only lawful job is to serve your best interests. Why would your employee be privy to information that is vital to your well-being, but not you? And, look at their track record - are you kidding? And, employers routinely legally track all of their employee computer and phone usage while they're on the clock. They even legally use video cameras to watch them.

And, do you know that Congress has declared itself a "small business" so that its members and their staff can avoid certain costs related to the "Affordable Care Act"? But who do they claim is the owner of that "small business"? In what business does the owner receive fewer benefits and retain fewer rights than their employees? Read this article and "think" about whether or not it is in your best interest to force your employees to begin operating under such stringent oversight: http://www.judicialwatch.org/press-room/weekly-updates/congress-implicated-in-obamacare-scandal/

43 – Henceforth, the official language of the United States of America will be English. Within one year of this becoming law, all governmental business carried out within the United States of America that is not directly related to official communications with a foreign power whose official language is not English, or a foreign tourist dealing with an immigration official at a point of entry/exit, shall lawfully be conducted exclusively in English, Braille, or sign language.

Public funds shall not ever be allocated toward any program or other assistance through which those who speak a foreign language but cannot speak or read English, Braille, or sign language are able to function without such skills as "equally empowered" members of society in relation to those members of society who can read and speak English.

Watch how fast _everyone_ within your borders who currently lacks such skills will discover their latent ability and burning desire to learn to read and speak English.

This will _not_ stifle tourism.

By way of your taking the actions prescribed in this book, the worldwide level of affection and respect for your nation will rise to unprecedented levels.

44 – The terms of the binding contract mentioned in section **1ᴅ** that "certain illegal aliens" will be offered an opportunity to sign are outlined below; "permanent lawful residents" in good standing will also be offered this opportunity. This is a one-time offer being made to each such adult.

1 - If, during the stated duration of this contract, the signee or their children or their spouse are found by a jury of Citizens of the United States of America to be guilty of breaching any aspect of this contract, they will all be deported from this country immediately without further recourse to the law; without exception, if one goes they all go. And should said jury deem it appropriate, the signee's forfeiture of any number or type of assets will also occur.

2 - During the stated duration of this contract the signee and their family members who are mentioned above (children, spouse) will not be found guilty of any breach of law by a jury of Citizens of the United States of America.

3 - All of their court-related proceedings, whether civil or criminal, shall be adjudicated by jury; said jury will always be comprised of Citizens of the United States of America who each hold a valid certificate as outlined in section <u>forty-six</u> of this section of this book.

4 - As a prerequisite to their being able to enter into this contract, the signee will be at least eighteen (18) years of age, and will have contracted with a "Citizen Sponsor".

Said "Citizen Sponsor" will be contractually bound to act as guarantor for the signee's compliance with all aspects of this contract; and their duties as guarantor shall include, but not be limited to, their being held personally liable as follows for any breach of contract that is carried out by said signee or their children:

I – Said "Citizen Sponsor" must see to it that all fines levied against the signee or their children are promptly paid in full.

II – Said "Citizen Sponsor" must personally fulfill all-manner of cost effective community service work that the deported signee and/or their children would have otherwise been directed by said jury to carry out had they been Citizens of the United States of America.

"Citizen Sponsors" shall _not_ be allowed to charge a fee for their services; anyone who is found guilty of such action will be fined $1,000 and held responsible for all of the costs related to those court proceedings.

(The $1,000 will be placed in the award fund mentioned in section <u>forty-five</u> of this section of this book.)

5 - Each "Citizen Sponsor" shall be required by law to place twenty-five hundred dollars ($2,500) into an escrow account that will serve as the backup source of remuneration for any and all fines imposed by a jury.

Regardless of a breach of this contract, said escrow account will remain active for the idealized duration of this contract.

6 - If the jury in any court proceeding should return a guilty verdict against the signee or their children, said signee or their "Citizen Sponsor" will pay all costs related to the proceedings.

7 - No argument made in a court of law in defense of the signee, or the signee's family, or their "Citizen Sponsor" shall be based upon or related to a disputation of the fact that the proper interpretation of any and all aspects of this contract must be the simple, obvious meaning that would be inferred by a mentally competent layman.

8 - The signee and their children shall receive no governmentally subsidized services or products whatsoever.

9 - The signee and their children will each be required to carry a "Signee Documentation Card" at all times during the term of said contract and produce it immediately upon the request of law enforcement officials.

10 - Each signee and all of their children who are at or above the age of seven (7) shall remain, solely at their cost or the cost of family, friends, and/or their "Citizen Sponsor", enrolled in the following non-profit educational curriculum for the duration of this contract:

(Oh, and did I mention that the United Sovereign's Absolution trust will be donating a full **Fifty Percent** (50%) of its net profit to help cover the costs of such education? That's right, a full 50%)

I - Classes held for ninety (90) minutes, five times per week, that teach proficiency in the reading, writing, and speaking of English and that administer tests to gauge the advancement of student's skills on a weekly basis.

Such tests will be based on models of competency that were used by the New York City Board of Education previous to the year nineteen hundred and forty (1940).

Class placement will be based upon the results of initial competency testing.

II - Classes held for two hours, five times per week, that teach the same subject matter as that which is outlined in section <u>forty-six</u> of this section of this book, and test on a weekly basis.

Any student who fails to maintain a minimum test score average and attendance rate of seventy-five percent (75%) over any given six month period will lawfully be considered in breach of this contract.

11 - For the duration of this contract, each signee and all of their children who are at or above the age of twelve (12) will participate in a non-salaried stewardship program for sixteen (16) hours per month, which will be carried out in two, eight hour shifts on separate days.

Their stewardship will consist of duties similar to those that will be carried out by the Citizens who choose to pay their applicable taxes by way of the method outlined in section **3p**. By law, their duties will **not** consist of tasks that Citizens are exempt from potentially carrying out. Minors will be assigned tasks that are suited to their age group.

The duties that signees' and their children will perform during this program will be decided upon in the same manner as that which is outlined in section **3p**; except for the fact that the process of their being assigned their duties will occur after the Citizens have completed the process for themselves.

This program is **not** a substitute for the payment of any applicable taxes that might be owed by the signee or their children.

This program and the above-mentioned education they will be earning are, in fact, documented investments that the signee and their children will be making toward the structural soundness of the nation they desire to be fully recognized members of. These documented investments will be the credentials by which they will come to earn the lawfully recognized equal standing and full respect and acceptance of the Citizens of the United States of America.

And the unfolding of such events will make for years of superb reality television...

12 - The idealized duration of this contract shall be a period of seven (7) years. At the expiration of the idealized duration of this contract, the signee and each of their children who are at or above the age of fourteen (14) will be required to take a test that will, if they pass it, make each of them a lawfully acknowledged Citizen of the United States of America.

They will certainly have been provided with the opportunity to earn the tools which will be needed to pass the test. Failure to pass the test in four (4) attempts within one year of their first try will result in that person's non-contestable deportation from the country.

13 - When a signee becomes a Citizen, their children who are under the age of fourteen (14) will also become Citizens, and each new Citizen will have a reserve fund account opened in their name in the amount of $60,000; but this does not include their spouse or children who are fourteen (14) or older. If they don't pass in those four attempts, they will be deported. The rest of the family will then have to decide if they want to join them.

And, the amount of Federal Reserve notes that they were documented as lawfully having had in their possession during the "redemption period" outlined in section **1D**, which they will have turned in during said period in exchange for a special edition "goods and services card", will be credited to them in the new lawful money of the United States of America at TWICE (**2x**) the exchange rate that Citizens received (minus the exchange rate adjusted original sum – unless records show that the original sum had never been tapped into prior to their becoming a Citizen).

In other words, they will each ultimately receive <u>double</u> the exchange rate for their Federal Reserve notes than those people who were already Citizens during the "redemption period" (which is to say that they can <u>each</u> turn $5,000 into approximately $200,000 cash, tax free). Furthermore, unless they or a direct family member receives Medicare/Medicaid benefits, they will not be required to pay said tax until they've been a Citizen for thirteen (13) years.

Advocates of amnesty for illegal aliens should soon be lining up in droves to become "Citizen Sponsors". This is their chance to definitively prove to all of their detractors that their altruistic beliefs, and the lawful acceptance of such people that they so ardently push for, are so dear to them and so well-thought-out that they are personally willing to foot the bill for any related damages that might occur as a result of their dreams finally being realized.

Who's ready to put their money where their mouth is?

45 – A state-of-the-art, world class museum and Constitutional education center whose entire functionality is completely transparent and responsive to the Citizens of the United States of America, shall be immediately established and permanently constructed within the Federal Reserve building in Washington D.C. Said education center will:

1 - Regularly host live, constitutionally relevant presentations by public speakers;

2 - Broadcast its own twenty-four (24) hour a day, commercial-free television stations (Nationwide/worldwide), radio stations (Nationwide/worldwide), and websites that are completely devoted to the dissemination of such information to all age groups;

3 - Be open to the public twenty-four (24) hours a day, every single day of the year.

The building will be obtained for such use by way of the claim of "eminent domain".

The museum will be the official location and official authority that fully documents and explains all of the details of the many injustices that this book and the links it references have merely touched upon.

And it will document the story of how the concerned Citizens of your country acted together to successfully restore the just governance and personal freedom that the Declaration of Independence declares to be the sovereign right of each human being.

This shall be done so that there will be a permanent reminder in your nation's capital of the corruption that will surely occur any time the entire Citizenry is not properly educated and constantly, properly defending their constitutionally protected rights.

Will your descendants be able to proudly find you among those who are immortalized there?

No part of the museum, or its name, or any likeness thereof shall ever be lawfully used for any purpose by any branch of government or its employees (in any way related to such employment; they will, of course, be welcome to visit as members of the public at large).

No part of the museum, or its name, or any likeness thereof shall ever be lawfully used for any purpose by any private interest group or any privately funded institute.

Once they are available, no-one who has not earned or does not maintain one of the valid certificates that are described in section <u>forty-six</u> of this section of this book shall ever - in any capacity other than that of a sightseeing, donation-providing visitor - be lawfully involved in any direct aspect of the ongoing maintenance and/or growth of this institution.

All expenses related to the ongoing funding of the museum (which shall be inclusive of but not limited to the programming, broadcasting, and management of its television and radio stations and its websites) will be fully funded by a tax whose sole purpose is such funding and which will be collected from all companies that are issued licenses by the FCC to broadcast commercial television and radio stations.

Official merchandise and other related gift items will be sold by the museum and voluntary donations will also be accepted upon entrance to the museum.

100% of the donations and 100% of the net profit resulting from such sales will be put into a prize fund. The fund will be established for the sole purpose of rewarding Citizens who have been shown, by way of certain nominating procedures, to be dedicating great efforts to the ongoing task of promoting the concepts and actions that are essential to one's ability to exercise their constitutionally protected rights.

The supremely prestigious prizes will be awarded annually during the most highly publicized, "star-studded", prime time televised awards show of the year. It will be broadcast live, worldwide, on the museum's television and radio stations and their websites.

This, first and foremost, must be the award that all children dream of someday winning.

The board of this institution will be filled by way of its members being selected yearly.

Each state of the Union will be represented by one board member. They will be selected by way of their being one of the people from that state who either won an award or were nominated for one in the previous year.

Winners will always be offered the position before it is offered to a Citizen who was nominated but did not win. Board members must be at least fourteen (14) years of age.

The original board of this institution will be filled by way of its members being selected by and from the volunteers who comprise both the "Home" and "Away" groups of the rally.

Each volunteer from each state will submit the name of a fellow volunteer whom they believe to be properly suited for such a position. The volunteer whose name was submitted by the greatest number of volunteers in their state will be offered the position.

In the case of a tie, the position will be offered to that person who receives the most votes in an election that will feature those volunteers whose names were previously submitted by the greatest number of volunteers in their state.

Planning and design for the initial layout of the museum will be carried out by the trustees of the "Rally fund" and the Citizens of the United States of America who are responsible for the similar actions which periodically take place in the Smithsonian Institute located in Washington D.C..

Funding for the creation of the museum will be derived from the funds which will have been set aside for such purpose as outlined in section **1D** of this section of this book as follows: "One dollar from each Citizen's reserve fund will then immediately be transferred from their account and placed into an account whose sole lawful purpose will be that of funding the establishment of the institution which is outlined in section <u>forty-five</u> of this section of this book".

46 – In-depth education regarding:

1 - The concepts of sovereign rights, liberty, and just governance upon which the Declaration of Independence and the Bill of Rights were written, and the lawful application of such concepts as described by those documents and this book;

2 - The actuality of what money is, and how through falsity, misdirection, the charging of interest, fractional reserve banking, and other illegitimate methods of creation, valuation, distribution, and taxation it has historically been used as a tool of enslavement;

3 - The concepts which brought forth the methods that are to be used by banks, voters and consumers to properly regulate the availability of money, as mentioned in <u>section two</u> of this section of this book;

4 - Human anatomy and physiology; proper methods of exercise; specific methods to attain and maintain <u>optimal</u> nutrition and health (both mental and physical);

5 - Ecology and the concepts and methods of Permaculture;

will each be offered for a minimum of two hours and twenty minutes (2hr, 20min) per week, at no direct monetary cost, to all Citizens of the United States of America between the ages of six (6) and eighteen (18).

Standardized testing will be administered once per year on April fifteenth or the first Monday preceding that date if that date should not fall on a weekday. All Citizens who are at least seventeen (17) years old or in the twelfth (12th) grade will be eligible to take the test.

Passage of such testing will result in the issuance or renewal of a certificate, whose expiration will occur one year after its date of issuance, which proclaims that the Citizen to whom it was issued has:

"Successfully put forth the honorable effort required to help defend the Constitutional Republic of the United States of America from all threats foreign and domestic, by being able to properly defend and promote his/her unalienable rights and to properly help assist his/her fellow Citizens in the defense and promotion of their unalienable rights."

Henceforth, all Citizens who are at or above the age of eighteen (18) will be offered the ability to take classes that will prepare them to pass the test, so that they too can receive and/or renew the certificate.

There will never be any direct monetary cost for any Citizen to take the classes or to take the test.

Beginning exactly three (3) years from the first day of the Constitutional convention/legislative amendment process that you desperately need to occur in order to bring many of the concepts this book has been outlining into effect:

Without exception, no-one will be eligible to enter or remain in the military or be hired or remain employed, even as a volunteer, in any law enforcement or any other governmental job who does not have and who does not maintain a valid, non-expired certificate. The first four (4) of these annual tests that are given will place less emphasis on the in-depth knowledge of concepts related to numbers four and five in the previous paragraph than all subsequent testing shall.

Each year's test will be designed by a board that is appointed by the board of the institution that is outlined in section <u>forty-five</u> of this section of this book.

If someone can't pass the above-mentioned test with numerous years of specific study under their belt, what in the world would they be doing in such positions of power in the first place?

Such ignorant people in such positions of power are a very real, very dangerous threat to YOUR freedom.

Or are you so lost in our maze of misfeasance that rather than embracing the idea of such an education regarding the concepts that every member of a society <u>must</u> understand and act in accordance with in order to maintain actual freedom and prosperity, that you would prefer – *for the sake of maintaining your right to free choice* – to continue submitting to what is, in reality, our own monopolized, and thus mandatory, system/brand of poorly disguised, purposeful misdirection regarding the awareness, the understanding, and the proper application of every single meaningful concept that has ever come to exist?

FYI, if that's the case, the literally unconquerable, infinitely self-sustaining combined force that would come into being as a result of every Citizen's energies being consciously directed toward what are actually their own best interests *and* mutually-beneficial ends will <u>never</u> happen.

47 – The parents of all Citizens at the age of fourteen (14) or entering the ninth (9th) grade will be urged to have their children serve eleven (11) consecutive months of duty, which will always begin on August 1st, in the act of assisting their state and national parks departments maintain those areas of wild nature under their auspices.

And during that time the students will actually live in such wilderness without permanent shelter. They will learn from experts to construct shelter, clothing, and tools, and sustain themselves fully by their own labors to grow and find and catch and preserve by numerous methods, that which they eat;

while enabling the plant and animal life of the area they are in to remain vibrant and thriving in accordance with a sound ecological balance.

Six (6) hours per day during daylight hours Monday through Thursday will be allocated to the highly recommended education outlined in section forty-six of this section of this book and the study of mathematics, science, history, literature, and creative writing.

Four (4) hours per day during daylight hours Friday and Sunday will be allocated to the study of both the theory and appreciation of music and visual art.

The math and science will always be taught in relation to processes inherent in the students' natural surroundings and/or certain situations they could possibly find themselves in.

Perennial failures in such subjects will soon find themselves fascinated by the endless applications of what once seemed to be specialized fields of study.

Obviously, the above-mentioned curriculum will not be allowed to retard the intellectual growth of any student who exhibits a natural inclination for, or high level of proficiency in, any particular subject.

There will be no mandatory homework assignments given.

Students will not be allowed to possess cell phones, personal music players, or computer equipment of any kind.

Boys and girls will not be intermingled or even stationed anywhere near each other during their time in such service.

The parents of all Citizens at the age of fifteen (15) or entering the tenth (10th) grade will be urged to have their children serve eleven (11) consecutive months of duty, which will always begin on August 1st, in the act of assisting their state and national parks departments maintain those areas of wild nature under their auspices.

And during that time the students will continue to live in such wilderness without permanent shelter. They will learn from experts to construct more advanced types of shelter, clothing, and tools, and learn more advanced techniques to grow and find and catch and preserve by numerous methods, that which they eat;

while enabling the plant and animal life of the area they are in to remain vibrant and thriving in accordance with a sound ecological balance.

Six (6) hours per day during daylight hours Monday through Thursday will be allocated to the highly recommended education outlined in section <u>forty-six</u> of this section of this book and the study of mathematics, science, history, literature, and creative writing.

Four (4) hours per day during daylight hours Friday and Sunday will be allocated to the study of both the theory and appreciation of music and visual art.

The math and science will always be taught in relation to processes inherent in the students' natural surroundings and/or certain situations they could possibly find themselves in. Perennial failures in such subjects will soon become veritable scholars.

Obviously, the above-mentioned curriculum will not be allowed to retard the intellectual growth of any student who exhibits a natural inclination for, or high level of proficiency in, any particular subject.

There will be no mandatory homework assignments given.

Students will not be allowed to possess cell phones, personal music players, or computer equipment of any kind.

Boys and girls will not be intermingled or even stationed anywhere near each other during their time in such service.

The parents of all Citizens at the age of sixteen (16) or entering the eleventh (11th) grade will be urged to have their children serve eleven (11) consecutive months of duty, which will always begin on August 1st, in the act of urban and wilderness combat education.

Such education will include:

1 - Further learning to sustain themselves fully in numerous distinct environments throughout your country by their own labors as mentioned above; while enabling the plant and animal life of the area they are in to remain vibrant and thriving in accordance with a sound ecological balance.

2 - An introduction to the concepts and actual practice of techniques for all aspects of personal, urban, suburban, and wilderness "gorilla" combat. Such education will not fail to include the construction and usage of numerous weapons and traps.

Albeit without ever firing live ammunition other than paintballs, they will each learn proper firearm and ammunition construction, assembly, maintenance, usage, and theory.

3 - No less than twenty-four (24) days of every month in the wilderness without permanent shelter, while the remaining days of each month will be spent in simulated urban constructs that are in a physical state of non-functioning disrepair (or in parts of Detroit and the Bronx).

Six (6) hours per day during daylight hours Monday through Thursday will be allocated to the highly recommended education outlined in section forty-six of this section of this book and the study of mathematics, science, history, literature, and creative writing.

Four (4) hours per day during daylight hours Friday and Sunday will be allocated to the study of both the theory and appreciation of music and visual art.

The math and science will always be taught in relation to processes inherent in the students' natural surroundings and/or certain situations they could possibly find themselves in.

And they will come to see that they are actually coherently incorporated in what they once ignorantly perceived as unrelated, unfathomable "surroundings".

Obviously, the above-mentioned curriculum will not be allowed to retard the intellectual growth of any student who exhibits a natural inclination for, or high level of proficiency in, any particular subject.

There will be no mandatory homework assignments given.

Students will not be allowed to possess cell phones, personal music players, or computer equipment of any kind.

Boys and girls will not be intermingled or even stationed anywhere near each other during their time in such service.

The parents of all Citizens at the age of seventeen (17) or entering the twelfth (12th) grade will be urged to have their children serve eleven (11) consecutive months of duty, which will always begin on August 1st, in the wilderness continuing to broaden their education of the subjects they have studied in the previous three years, with a major emphasis on those that most inspire their interest.

And those students whose parents and teachers jointly agree that they are capable of acting properly under such conditions will be able to pick the general area of the country that they will be spending this year of duty in.

There will be no mandatory homework assignments given.

Students will not be allowed to possess cell phones, personal music players, or computer equipment of any kind.

Boys and girls will not be intermingled or even stationed anywhere near each other during their time in such service.

Citizens will be able to volunteer to work in the education system, as outlined in section **48A** of this section of this book.

So, yes, concerned parents will be able to be personally involved in this aspect of their children's schooling.

(Especially those who didn't squander the money they made by way of participating in the rally effort.)

Other than in the cases of a parent being alone with their child, or a parentally authorized specific adult being alone with a child they are parentally authorized to be alone with, students and instructors will <u>always</u> remain in specified, documented groups of at least three (3) students and one (1) instructor, so that there will be no window of opportunity for inappropriate actions to be taken by anyone.

Obviously there are many other safety protocols for many specific situations that will need to be put in place, but I will not spend any more time on the subject.

47A - What the above paragraphs outline is <u>absolutely essential</u> to the ongoing freedom of every generation to come of the Citizens of your country.

But who among you will study long and hard enough to fully appreciate and understand the absolute need for the application of the concepts contained therein?

Truth be told, a vast number of vacuous victims are strongly opposed to this idea for the simple fact that I failed to explain how the continuity of your High School athletic programs would be preserved.

There are simply no words that properly describe such a state of mental disadvantage.

So I know beyond a shadow of a doubt that very few people will ever gain an accurate awareness of the following factual information:

1 - The coming to fruition of the above few paragraphs is absolutely essential in regard to preventing your country (and thus each of your lives) from ever being overtly or covertly forcefully taken over by interests either foreign or domestic that are in opposition to your Declaration of Independence and Constitution.

2 - This is the only way to actually ensure that every single member of every generation of your offspring is forever granted their rightful opportunity to receive the most majestic, most important rite of passage that can be experienced by anyone or anything that has self-consciousness and possesses even a mere conceptual trace of human DNA, (which opportunity we have, of course, stolen from you under the pretense that said rite of passage is actually undignified, unnecessary, and inhumane): that of accurately discovering who and what they are in relation to the unadulterated natural world that actually exists outside of the conceptually and perceptually impenetrable pen within which a prodigious percentage of your population perpetually pastures.

3 - In other words, it's the only way for them to ever have the opportunity to begin making properly informed decisions regarding the personal relationships that their hormones, the pressure of their peers, and our ever-present multimedia influences will cause them to seek out and begin forming as young adults; since such decisions will finally be the product of a well-founded, self-realized perspective regarding their body image and overall self-worth.

No, their eventual full-time reintroduction to members of the opposite sex won't be the repeat presentation of utterly ignorant, immature, physically awkward, nutritionally unhealthy, psychologically damaged misfits such as yourselves at the age of fourteen (14) that you would otherwise unwittingly encourage them to suffer (and in most cases accept as their guideline for judging the validity of the majority of their personal and social modes of functioning as adults).

It so happens that this is also the only way in which the vast majority of your nation's Citizens will ever be able to master the skills needed to fully sustain themselves independently; and thus have the opportunity to personally make the realistic, properly informed decision to live in and responsibly cultivate the natural world. Should it so happen that they desire to have such an existence, or something somewhat similar to it, as a major aspect of their adult life.

In other words: It is actually the only way for them to avoid their complete bankruptcy in nearly every sense of the word.

In other words: It is actually the only way for them to become their own investor.

In actuality, the only way for one to achieve independence is by gaining the education required to make properly informed decisions <u>before</u> they get unknowingly sucked into what is a completely illusory, otherwise undetectable and thus inescapable trap.

The same basic trap that we have forced and otherwise successfully convinced *hundreds of millions* of formidable critical thinkers like you to try at all costs to survive within; and which we will continue to modify for as long as we have to in order to ultimately, without contest, have all of you existing exclusively within our idealized incarnation of the company store (i.e., all of you who remain after we've drastically reduced the population).

48 – All Citizens who are eighteen (18) years old, or who have recently graduated High School, and who have earned and maintain the certificate mentioned in section <u>forty-six</u>, will be urged by way of a ubiquitous media campaign to serve an internship for forty (40) hours per week for one full year (approximately two thousand (2,000) hours). The internship will always begin on the twenty-first (21st) day of August and offer twenty (20) cents per hour pay for each intern.

Army barracks-style room and board will also be included for the interns when they are away from home.

During their internship, they will each be required at the end of every third month to work in a different capacity for a different aspect of government or media.

Each job they are assigned will be decided upon by way of a drawing which is run in the same manner as the drawing outlined in section **3D** of this section of this book.

For one-quarter of the interns, the first three months will be spent working within their local government with the administrators and management of all manner of departments.

For one-quarter of the interns, the first three months will be spent working within their state government with the administrators and management of all manner of departments.

For one-quarter of the interns, the first three months will be spent working directly with an editor or experienced investigative journalist within the governmental affairs division of a regional or national newspaper or magazine, or with a writer or producer of a daily television news broadcast or political commentary television show, or with a writer or producer for a major online news agency.

For one-quarter of the interns, the first three months will be spent working within the federal government, directly with either their congressmen (in both the house and the senate) or the appointees and members of upper and middle management who head and effectively run each of the departments of which the four main categories of politically appointed positions are comprised: Presidential Appointments with Senate confirmation (PAS), Presidential Appointments without Senate confirmation (PSs), political appointees to the Senior Executive Service (SES), and Schedule C political appointees.

Note that, as used in the last sentence, the word "directly" means actually attending all but top-secret meetings/strategy sessions/briefings etc., (said top-secret meetings will always be videotaped in full, and archived and stored indefinitely - under strictly enforced, harsh penalty of law); and that at the end of each "intern workday" Monday through Friday, the interns will have a mandatory forty-five (45) minute group question and answer session with each particular member of congress and appointee and member of upper and middle management that they are currently interning with. The same will also hold true during their time spent working within state and local government and with the media.

Each such question and answer session will be videotaped in full, and archived and stored indefinitely, for the easiest possible access by all interested parties free of charge.

Tired of complaining about the negative effects of "big government"?

Well, here's *another* chance to literally put your money where your mouth is, to reduce the cost and overreaching tendencies of government and to keep government waste at an absolute minimum.

If the number of interns assigned and/or volunteers willing to do any given job makes it possible to reduce any number of paid staff other than elected officials or appointed judges, then such paid staff shall be forced to seek paid employment elsewhere; regardless of union affiliation or seniority.

Don't worry about the people who will lose their jobs because of this.

They'll easily be able to get new, mutually-beneficial jobs working on infrastructure projects or for any of the many thriving companies whose products and services you patriots will be spending too much of your newfound money on.

In other words, their new employment will actually contribute to economic stability rather than being the massive drain on YOUR resources that it currently is.

Understand that your recent High School graduates will not only be learning firsthand how their government and news outlets actually operate. Those properly educated young adults will also be providing constant, unprecedented levels of public oversight to government agencies *and* the media, and offering "out of the box" solutions directly to the actual policy makers themselves.

Do you recall that a valid, properly run government is not a self-regulating growth industry?

A valid, properly run government is nothing other than the physical representation of a collective consciousness, and it functions as the exponentially empowered extension of each sovereign Citizen.

Its operation is an ongoing process of enacting and enforcing the minimum amount of restrictions which are required to equally safeguard the unalienable rights of all Citizens from whatever <u>actual</u>, credible threats or trespasses may emerge.

Remember, that's the Citizens of your country, <u>not</u> the rest of the world. Positively influencing the world is one thing, trying to ensure such interaction worldwide is foolish.

It is so obviously foolish, for so many reasons, that I won't even offer an explanation.

And make no mistake about it; an illegitimate, improperly run government is also nothing other than the physical representation of a collective consciousness - a twofold collective consciousness:

One aspect is that of the lying thieves who live a luxurious, parasitic existence.

The other is that of their duped hosts who, while preparing and serving the banquet that the parasites subsist on, simultaneously exist within and carry out the maintenance of the toilet that those parasites are constantly dropping big, smelly piles of excrement into.

And it functions precisely as the exponentially empowered extension of its fundamentally corrupt conceptualization.

Its operation is an ongoing process of parasitic factions working to ensure that they and their benefactors are continually well-served by their hosts.

48A –The Citizens of the United States of America who are at least nineteen (19) years of age and who have fulfilled the employment criteria stated below, will always have the right and the ability to work as unpaid volunteers for any government agency or government-run and/or funded institutions (bank, post office, department of motor vehicles, department of public works, bridge and tunnel authorities, police department, courts, educational systems, certain airport security duties, etc.).

This is in addition to the ability to maintain and ensure your freedom by way of the rights that will have been guaranteed to you as per section **3D** of this section of this book. (Some people might not own land or might not be inclined to invest that amount of time, etc.)

Such volunteers shall be employable if they are willing to work for a minimum of eight (8) hours per week, for a minimum of eight (8) weeks in a contiguous three (3) month period (for a minimum of sixty-four (64) hours per *year*) and have earned and maintain the certificate mentioned in section <u>forty-six</u>.

Though they are not the exact parasites I just mentioned, why should a senior county clerk or police officer that is collecting a high salary ever be doing paperwork or answering phone calls that a few civilian volunteers could be trained to do for free?

And why should anyone get paid to collect tolls or do unskilled maintenance on a bridge or tunnel if people are willing to volunteer to do it for free so that the cost of the toll will be reduced or eliminated?

Why should you have to pay a premium for services *and* wait on long lines at the post office, or the bank, or at motor vehicles just because they are understaffed to maximize profit or because the clerks refuse to work any faster or wait until the line goes down before they take their break?

Do you have any idea of how much it is also costing you yearly to have people get paid, with benefits, to pick up your garbage, and to shovel some asphalt into a pothole – the same pothole they filled in with the same product a few months earlier; and to wave red flags and either stop cars or allow them to pass during road construction work, and to trim the grass, the bushes, and the trees on public land and roads, etc…? Why not look into it?

Undertaking such functions yourselves just might enable you to start taking real pride in yourselves and the places you live in; instead of heedlessly faking it with a couple of bumper stickers about your local sports teams and your pharmaceutically and GMO-marinated children's educational *embezzlement*.

Yes, when the deterioration of a community's infrastructure can no longer be blamed on a corrupt and/or incompetent "government", everyone in the nation will soon know exactly who the lazy and the disinterested among them are.

Indeed, you must have read my mind. That last sentence *is* a microcosmic view of the macrocosmic situation that a widespread dissemination of this book will thrust your nation into:

When the deterioration of a **country's** infrastructure can no longer be blamed on a corrupt and/or incompetent "government", everyone in the **world** will soon know exactly who the lazy and disinterested among them are.

Yes, plenty of lazy, disinterested people will fail to volunteer, but why should that stop the patriots who are willing to get off of the couch? They'll still benefit greatly from the work they do. And they'll all know exactly who their neighbors are that have no pride and who choose to keep exercising their constitutionally protected right to do nothing but pay others to keep their paycheck and tell them that they're overpaid.

In actuality, if enough people follow the instructions I have been giving you and those that are yet to come, within three generations there will not be a politically significant number of such dreck existing within any of the states that comprise your nation.

Their slothful, gluttonous kind will effectively be politically extinct. Due to the ongoing proper education and further action that will be continually carried out by the next generation of Citizens, your nation will have been pulled from the shiny, tasty, remote control operated illusion that is really a dark abyss you are being dragged into.

49 - It's now time for me to explain, in no uncertain terms, the fundamental causation of what has evolved - or perhaps more precisely, devolved - into the shackled, tragic drama that I have been exposing to you throughout this book and the information it links you to.

My associates and I are merely the latest incarnation of the true highbrows who, in every generation, are brought into being to keep you down.

And while we are alive we each benefit greatly from the material wealth and power that arise out of our purposeful misdirection of your energy toward negative ends.

Simply stated, the bottom line purpose for my existing as such is as follows: it's my job to prevent the coming into being of the unadulterated Divine energy that such actions as outlined in each of the previous subsections above (which is, in fact, a self-sustaining singular mechanism) would eventually bring forth en masse from those of coming generations in the near future.

Doesn't that sound like some type of heavy-duty biblical or metaphysical trip?

Well, guess what bilge-brow… the simple, common message within all of your supposed "Holy" books from every corner of the globe, which tells you of the brutal suffering that is guaranteed to happen to you if you do not act properly, is nothing other than truth that became shrouded long ago in a purposely ineffective, *seeming* attempt to try to teach you how to prevent exactly what I've been admitting to you by telling you all of this.

Yes, by design you either dismiss it outright or even with great effort just plain cannot understand and embody **the real message** that occupied the original messengers.

Instead, you are occupied by that which creates and maintains the purposely-designed world of make-believe that someone else has you trapped in through their co-opting and purposeful distortion of that message.

What each of you desperately needs to understand is that, in direct real-time correlation to literally every one of your actions, your existence, which is to say the entirety of your being, is either that of a properly directed tool which aids in the growth and dissemination of integral Divine energy (i.e., "pure law and reason"), or it is a misguided tool which aids the growth and dissemination of the dark, destructive, perverted manifestation of such energy that my associates and me are here to promote and benefit from as it assumes control of all the life force on this planet.

It's the simple fact of our being; yours and mine. Why else would personal responsibility be of any actual importance?

If you look into your actuality deeply enough, you will see with absolute clarity that what I just told you is rationally undeniable.

Know that when I say "look into your actuality deeply enough", I am not at all limiting such investigation to the historically misused, and thus often associatively destructive, "Holy" books that so many of you feign an interest in learning from in order to avoid becoming a captive of the deceptively-decorated dungeon that we have already shackled you within and whose decoration dominates your otherwise barren mental landscape.

It remains an absolute fact that due exercise of the faculty of logical thought will lead you to the following:

1 - The irrefutable identity of that which you essentially are.

2 - The irrefutable identity of the force that actually employs me.

3 - A conscious awareness of the fact that, since I actually employ you, we are both being employed by the same concern.

But are you capable of rational thought?

Did I not write a book in which I repeatedly share with you the fundamental aspects of the truth of the matter, thus exposing the labyrinth we have constructed for such ends?

Did I not give you the map, the keys, and the instructions needed to escape our otherwise all-encompassing construct?

Is this an act of hubris? Am I the gloating villain who is destined to failure because he has underestimated the contagious and transformative power of an enabled noble soul?

Will the sleeping giant finally be roused from its slumber? Or is the contagious and transformative power of an enabled noble soul merely the stuff of legend?

In the face of all the information which has been clearly and directly explained throughout this book and in the links it offers, how is it possible that a noble soul could believe the fact of the matter to be something other than that which I have stated it to be?

Do you recall the following lines from page <u>9</u> of this book?

"It is the common fate of the indolent to see their rights become prey to the active. The condition upon which God hath given liberty to man is eternal vigilance; which condition if he break, servitude is at once the consequence of his crime and the punishment of his guilt".

"If there is any slight crookedness of being, or even a slight deviation or separation from pure law and reason, the being is immediately downgraded to the realm of duality and subjected to the control of the two laws of *energy response* and *pure law and reason*, he is the servant of these two masters. The further the being is downgraded, the more physical law is imposed. The further the downfall of a person, the more forces he is subjected to and bound by in the form of laws".

Do you recall that on page <u>154</u> of this book I posed the question, "What exactly is it that you are all being employed to do?"

Do you now see why I said "**You haven't got the slightest idea.**"?

Are you aware of the consequence of the crime that you and your predecessors are guilty of?

Do you see what it is that you have handed away, and to whom you have handed it?

Well, let me finally spell it out for you:

The fact is that **YOU** unwittingly worship and serve Mammon.

ATTENTION ATHEISTS:

These facts have <u>nothing</u> to do with any religious doctrine or mythology.

Such an association is merely one of the reactions we have caused those of your ilk to experience in relation to this aspect of the all-encompassing subterfuge that has been continually furthering its occupation of you for the entirety of your physical existence.

Do not allow yourself to be misled by particular words or names. Truth be told, they merely symbolize conglomerations of concepts; and quite often as an aspect of such subterfuge. The word Mammon is no different; it is a symbol that represents ideas relating to dishonest gain.

What I am presenting are facts of natural physical and non-physical law. Due exercise of the faculty of logical thought will lead you to the same conclusion.

"The mark of freedom is one's ability to prosper while functioning by way of *personally-explored*, reason-based values and beliefs that are not necessarily in accordance with anyone else's values and beliefs. *Fili componitur fabricam.*"
Do you remember that line from page <u>142</u>?

Do you know that values and beliefs are merely particular combinations of particular ideas?

Please, re-read the following lines from page <u>143</u>: "Have you noticed that all acts of using and buying and selling *and* their medium of exchange (currency) only exist because of the ideas that they were formed from?... Have you noticed that belief is not at all dependent on accurate reasoning?"

Now, while keeping the above quoted lines in mind, try to step outside of your established parameters of belief - in order to carefully consider this example of the painful truth regarding your own squandered existence:

The "mark of the beast" is an adult's general inability to seemingly prosper, or even survive, without their values and beliefs being predicated upon our prescribed values and beliefs and the regulations that follow from them. Said mark is, in fact, none other than the manifestation of Mammon's occupation of you. **The fabric is composed of the thread.**

Can you say, "lack of Dominion, Agency, and Possession"?

How about "loss of Sovereignty"?

It has always been but a *matter of time* before the tools at our disposal ensured that such an existence became internationally and inter-generationally one of pain and misery that would not be rectified and whose source would not be properly identified. How can you ever pull yourself to a safe shore when you are caught in the middle of a constant, all-encompassing rip tide that you've been taught *is* the safe shore?

Or can you finally perceive of the truth in the following lines from page <u>25</u>?

"The average person's entire existence is an aspect of the circus we have created and are continually modifying. Why? To keep them from being able to formulate, let alone properly act upon, their own reason-based complaints regarding our theft of everything that is needed in order to prosper while being independent of us."

Can you perceive of the truth in the following lines from page <u>153</u>?

"From the inception of your sense of self you have been importing nothing but our parasitic malware/virus ridden programming, and have thus been incapable of properly considering the actuality of your existence. This has allowed us to continually occupy your very being in order to cause you to do that which is bringing about your demise. Even when it appeared/appears as though you were/are not engaged in our employment.

Fili componitur fabricam. This, my friend, is rationally undeniable."

Now see if, with the additional aid I've provided in bold print, you can finally discern the primary meaning of the following passages from page <u>184</u> (note that the words in smaller font are from the original version and that those in **bold** are being substituted to help clarify my point.):

"Through our occupation of you, which is currently effectuated chiefly under your governmental scheme, rather than being the palm and fingers that are gripping the handle of the hammer of government, each 'person' is a nail being buried into whatever materials we are commanding them to further construct their own prison with.

Only with a full participation in the methods described above and those that follow, can the organisms known as _{"Citizens"} **human beings** control the _{purse strings} **fuel which enables the function** and thus the agenda of _{the idea known as "government"} **that which establishes the parameters within which their life experience exists**; _{an idea} **a sense of self**, like all other ideas, that otherwise always has and always will experience malignant growth and soon become out of control and out of touch with the intrinsic nature, which is to say the rightful demands, of the organism that initially utilized it. (And yet, in your country, said organism initially utilized it for the intent of being provided with that which will enable it to provide beneficial service. *Beneficial service to what?*).

This is an invariable fact, as all such happenings are the result of the unavoidable Natural law of balance; which is *the* basis of the intrinsic need for each organism to continually act responsibly; which is *the* basis of the intrinsic need for each organism to continually, properly utilize the Master Resource."

Can you now see what you are providing beneficial service to?

Yes, the "mark of the beast" is indeed upon **YOU**. You see, said mark is, in fact, none other than the manifestation of Mammon's occupation of you; which, as you cannot rationally deny, is the reality of all that you have become. Said mark is, in fact, the continually blossoming result of all that effectively commands what you mentally and physically do.

That blossoming result is all that you buy, sell, carry out, and otherwise seek to surround and fill your life's experience with; which in actuality *is* your life experience. If you re-read this entire book while trying honestly to point out exactly where such a statement does not apply to you, the fact will become crystal clear.

The fact is that **YOU** unwittingly worship and serve Mammon.

It is from those who have purposely ruined you that you seek the permission to be redeemed.

Honestly friend, have you been seeking first the Kingdom of God and His righteousness?

Such is the consequence of being a duped "person" who is living in what is literally a pyramid scheme-based alternate reality. Your reality has been engineered to appear to you as though it is the correct definition of justice to legally reward stupidity and enforce regulations which cause the fool's state of consciousness to be that which it is a crime to trespass against; rather than have all of the many revered institutions that reinforce such a state of consciousness statutorily be required to inseminate and promote the ideas which command one to be occupied foremost by its most elemental and effective biochemical antagonist, the rational state of consciousness.

"There is no subtler, no surer means of overturning the existing basis of society than to debauch the currency."

You see, the power to fully control the productive potential of the essential life energy of masses of other beings (i.e., *without their ever becoming aware of the fact that their entire life experience is spent as a battery for the numerous remote controlled devices which will bring about the ultimate ruin of their kind*), is truly a unique power.

Such power is wielded in this realm only by the ne plus ultra "money changers".

Are you still with me on this heavy, duty-inspired biblical or metaphysical trip?

If so, it's now time for us to visit a particularly heavy, though rarely examined, area of a particular sub-realm that's properly known as ~~Science Fiction~~ "The Science of Fiction".

Which area? How about the area where time travel becomes an actual occurrence in the world that you are really living in as you read these words.

Yes; I am about to prove, beyond any logical doubt, that we possess a means of time travel.

Surely you didn't think I was being glib or impudent when I shared the following facts with you at the top of page 250: "It has always been but a *matter of time* before the tools at our disposal ensured that such an existence became internationally and inter-generationally one of pain and misery that would not be rectified and whose source would not be properly identified. How can you ever pull yourself to a safe shore when you are caught in the middle of a constant, all-encompassing rip tide that you've been taught *is* the safe shore?"

And being that truth is the precursor of fiction: through the use of such means we effectively become the arbiters of an actual system of inter-dimensional exchange/alternate reality.

Sorcerers who harness supernatural forces, we are able to effectuate said inter-dimensional exchange/alternate reality chiefly through our control of the ongoing function of a sub-realm of the sub-realm of The Science of Fiction that is officially known as the "Legal" realm.

Indeed, Legal is the sub-realm from which concepts such as "legal tender", "legal fiction", and others of the like are spawned (contractual liability by way of "tacit agreement" is vital).

No, such entities are not natural inhabitants of the realm/sub-realm known as "Planet Earth".

Mind you; in order to bring such concepts and sub-realms into a state of functional being on Earth, the realm/sub-realm of "Representation" must first be allowed to intermingle with and influence the natural inhabitants of Earth.

And, as with fire, human interaction with this sub-realm can enable purposefully constructed beneficial activity or abject privation.

Yet, in the realm/sub-realm of duality, the opportunity to harness the power of representation <u>must</u> be seized by all to whom it is presented - indeed it is an actual duty, inherent in one's existence within the realm. And all of those within the realm/sub-realm of duality to whom it is not presented must strive incessantly for such an opportunity - or they will be controlled by those whose representations form the lexicon and those whose representations direct societal norms.

Make no mistake; such a state of being is dictated by the very nature of the realm/sub-realm of duality: representation governed by balance within flux.

Why else would I have shared the following information with you, on page <u>9</u>?

"I also recommend that you put forth the relatively minor effort required to remain, at all times, consciously aware of the ideas being presented in these two quotes:

'It is the common fate of the indolent to see their rights become prey to the active. The condition upon which God hath given liberty to man is eternal vigilance; which condition if he break, servitude is at once the consequence of his crime and the punishment of his guilt'.

'If there is any slight crookedness of being, or even a slight deviation or separation from pure law and reason, the being is immediately downgraded to the realm of duality and subjected to the control of the two laws of *energy response* and *pure law and reason*, he is the servant of these two masters. The further the being is downgraded, the more physical law is imposed. The further the downfall of a person, the more forces he is subjected to and bound by in the form of laws'."

Why else would I have shared this vitally important advice on page <u>141</u>?

"In order to maintain one's freedom, all official valuation must be treated like a filthy work boot; worn out in the field, but never in the house."

That being said, in order to bring the supernatural force of time travel into a state of functional being on Earth, what is quite possibly the *Crown Jewel* of the realm/sub-realm of Representation must be allowed to not merely intermingle with, but become an integral aspect of that which is in circulation as a medium of exchange.

Are you still with me? Can you see the time machine? Indeed, fire is a dangerous servant and a fearful master; but what pithy statement can be uttered in order to effectively express the awesome power of Global Credit Creation?

Monopolized Credit Creation (that's a link you should click on).

Sure, money invites power; but popular belief in the legitimacy of our claim to have the unquestionable right to a Global Monopoly on the Legal Creation of significant sums of Credit enables us to retain it. And did I fail to mention that we charge interest?

Short of this entire book, what can be said to effectively sum up the potential effects of legally having the exclusive ability to effectively bring into the present, at their officially recognized full value (which we regulate and charge interest on), assets whose current actual existence would otherwise be confined to the act of their being conceived of as potentially existing in the future by way of their being the fruit of valid and legitimate actions? (And the official, legal definition of each word you just read is, of course, decided upon by us)

In other words, the assets don't actually exist in the present; but everyone will accept as real, valid, and legitimate all of the trillions of representations of them that we create and *selectively* disseminate in the present according to *our* terms, in various forms such as paper, plastic, coins, electronic depictions, etc...

But it's not like I haven't already mentioned this. For example, don't you remember the following words from page 215?

"They magically create electronic credits based upon nothing but their projected assessment of the debt that your potential energies being *improperly* directed will create for them to collect in the form of natural resources, property, and rights."

Or did you "think" that my literal usage of the word "magically" was merely an attempt to make some other point through the use of sarcasm?

Now don't just go and try to sum up the time machine's potential effects based solely on its ability to effectively travel into the future; for that is not the only direction the time machine can enable travel in.

You see, once the time machine has been used to travel into the future as described above, the representations I just mentioned above - the ones that have been brought into an officially recognized existence with an officially recognized value that everyone will accept as real - are used to effectuate travel into the past.

Friend, c'mon, seriously; who else could possibly be controlling/regulating/harnessing the power of the presentation of history and the official establishment narrative that is always a part of such presentation, and which go by the names of "Knowledge" and "Education"?

Surely you didn't believe I was exaggerating when I presented this fact on page 46:

"The simple, correct answer is this: those whose actions are based upon the idea that every aspect of everyone's life (*but theirs and their family and friends*) must be regulated by an incredibly small unit of power whose actions and dictates are not to be questioned or reviewed by anyone outside of that small unit (*which happens to be comprised of them, their family, and their friends*), have already maneuvered their way into all of the positions of power that get to direct the manner in which everything is officially portrayed to the public."

Or that I was being mendacious when I shared this fact with you on page 7:

"Take note: there are many supposed 'experts' in your midst who hold impressive credentials that the 'authorities' sanctioned. The credentials are a reward for their exceptional efforts in helping us to fully indoctrinate them with our perverted dogma; to the point that they can regurgitate it with an air of mastery. Thus, their specialty is disinformation."

Welcome to the reality of The Science of Fiction™.

Indeed, disseminated ideas are the currency that retains power. In its current manifesting state, The Science of Fiction is the effective height of the Sorcerer's craft in the sub-realm/realm of Earth. Now re-read and reassess the entirety of pages 75 and 76.

Perhaps now the following accurate information from page 55 (which most of you could not understand and the rest of you could not perceive of as anything but the type of preposterous claim that's made by socially inept, sex-starved conspiracy theorists) will finally be seen in the proper light:

"Other than the decoration of its thin veneer, it's the same mechanism as: 1- fascism; 2- socialism; 3- communism; 4- democracy; 5- every other distinctly named manifestation of the fundamental consolidated power that exists parasitically by way of: **a**- currency control; **b**- legal disguise; **c**- all other manner of constant dissemination of officially sanctioned misinformation."

And to help clarify what is being seen in that light, it's time to take a trip back to the "Bretton Woods Agreement" (that link #20 on page 100 spoke of and offered its own link to) in order to finally ask yourself the question of ne plus ultra concern regarding the legal fiction known as the International Monetary Fund, who the U.S. Treasury Secretary is a governor of and whose charter clearly states in article XII, section 4c, that *"...the staff of the fund, in the discharge of their functions, shall owe their duty entirely to the fund and to no other authority."* Indeed, that Secretary's signature is on your "money".

Indeed the following question must, in a logical sense, be of the utmost concern because the IMF's charter (the legal document that presents the ideas from which this legal, fictional creation is composed and which brings it into a legal existence and legally defines its parameters) literally, in no uncertain terms, demands that its functionaries' allegiance to duty be assigned solely to the authority of the fund:

To what authority does the fund owe *its* duty entirely?

The answer to that question is of paramount importance because if its allegiance to duty is not assigned entirely to the act of functioning in positive accord with the Authority described by the Declaration of Independence as the **"Laws of Nature and of Nature's God"** (or put another way, "pure law and reason"; or put another way, "the Kingdom of God and His righteousness"), then it is fraudulent and literally, in the most basic sense, **unlawful, treasonous, insurrectionist rebellion**.

<u>Fact</u>: its allegiance to duty has been assigned entirely to your constitution's elemental antagonist: dishonest gain (nope; that was <u>not</u> limited to anyone's state/national constitution).

And, logically speaking, it must be unlawful. It is a clear and logically indisputable fact that such a creation is not merely a threat, but a poison acting upon the homeostasis of the all-encompassing natural system (i.e. the *fabric* of nature) whose characteristics and methods of equilibrium are direct manifestations of the **"Laws of Nature and of Nature's God"** (the *thread*), and whose existence and fairly precise state of equilibrium the genesis and ongoing existence and well-being of every life form and physical construct on this planet, **other than the entities known as "legal fictions"**, are directly dependent upon.

Does this passage from page <u>173</u> ring a bell? "…any system whose composition includes structural components that necessarily serve to draw and keep vital nutrients away from the other components of its structure is intrinsically self-destructive; corrupt."

But the concern that authored said charter, and a host of similar documents, has not ever willingly sat back and allowed an individual or a small group to possibly weaken or dissolve it through the widespread dissemination of a reason-based critical interpretation of such "lofty" ideas as Laws of Nature and of Nature's God, balance within flux, responsibility, empathy, patience, acceptance, and truth by way of appropriate <u>action</u>.

Nor will it ever. Nope. **We don't stock any of that in the ~~Cave~~ Company Store.** Yep, such dissemination also goes by the name of "proper education".

Action is the animation of ideas; the continually blossoming result of <u>all</u> that participates in the commands which effectuate <u>all</u> of that which is done.

It is the thread comprising the fabric of your reality.

Get it? You animate each other as those ideas materialize through their occupation of you; simultaneously; universally.

This can correctly be referred to as the universal interface.

Hmmm… interface, animate, materialize.

With a bit of consideration, it'll bring a new and profound meaning to the phrase "I am".

"And if it is a despot you would dethrone, see first that his throne erected within you is destroyed."

(Kahlil Gibran, "The Prophet", 1923)

"The man who does not do his own thinking is a slave, and is a traitor to himself and to his fellowmen."

(Robert G. Ingersoll, "Superstition and other essays", 1877)

So, tell me friend, are physical chains a requirement of shackled cave dwelling?

Is America the land of the free and the home of the brave?

Details for the successful operation of the rally

(Continued from page 125)

4c – Goods will need to be delivered and picked up regularly. The entire process will always be completed in a very short time, since during the "training" that occurred before "deployment" such techniques will have been continually practiced and perfected.

Each delivery truck that has goods which are specified for particular people will have been assigned a particular number dependent upon which platoon its goods are for. And upon its arrival it will be clearly marked with that number on its doors, magnetically, so that it can be immediately directed to the particular clearly numbered spot where the particular men who are in position to quickly unload and re-load it will be. (Platoons will have large, reflective, numbered signs made of polyester mesh. Each top corner of the signs will have a reinforced hole to fit a carabiner, and each bottom corner will have two twelve-inch long, Velcro-covered ties; think "toilet kit" poles.)

When the truck is ready to depart, the driver will be given the latest updated advice on local street traffic. This will prevent them from being delayed in getting back to the highway by any traffic jams caused by road work or the other delivery trucks that are in the same basic location doing the same thing as them, etc.

Men will get all of their needed water from fire hydrants. The water will be taken daily after 10pm. Each battalion will extract their water from twenty-five (25) hydrants simultaneously. The location of every single working fire hydrant in Washington D.C. is available on "Google earth". One can also find the hydrants in and near each state capital on "Google earth", as well.

Crews from each company that is nearest a hydrant will expertly work to open and close the hydrant valve and to connect and control the hose after their fellow men have set up five (5) specially outfitted, three-foot-deep rubber kiddie pools and special elevated stands for the pools near the hydrant.

Then, as the hose is filling the pools, the men will fill five-gallon plastic containers from the specially designed drainage points installed on the outside of the pool at near floor height. Can you figure out how many pools will need to be constructed by the 2,000 divisions in each state during (or possibly before) training?

Each pool will receive just enough water to keep it flowing into the five-gallon containers until the hose has cycled its way back after providing water to the other pools; so that once the hose has made its first round, no-one is ever sitting around waiting for water.

Each pool will have one hundred (100) drainage points on it. Each drainage point will be a hole with a shut off valve that connects to a removable hose. Hose lengths will vary.

Each drainage point will have a crew consisting of: 1 - a man who is opening and closing the valve as needed; 2 - a man who is putting the hose in and out of the five-gallon water container being filled, which happens to be clearly marked with the name of the division it belongs to; 3 - a man who is being fed empty containers and then setting each opened empty container in place as needed; 4 - a man who is closing the filled container and then removing it from its filling location before passing it back to a line of men who are in turn passing it on to other men until it reaches its destination.

Those four men will rotate positions every fifteen (15) minutes to minimize fatigue.

Each division will get one hundred and twenty-five (125) gallons of water per day. That means 250,000 five-gallon containers of water will need to be moved daily through each battalion; 25,000 five-gallon containers of water will need to be moved daily through each company; 1,250 five-gallon containers of water will need to be moved daily through each platoon; 25 five-gallon containers of water will be moved daily into each division.

Before being utilized by the men, all of the water will be filtered through the "Berkey Crown ™" or "Propur ProOne King ™" water purifier that every division will have with it.

As soon as their water is passed to them, the assigned men in each division will drain the water into the purifier and then drain the purified water into specially marked five-gallon containers used only for purified water.

From that purified water, each man will fill a gallon and a half into his own "solar shower" water heating bag, and then he will fill his own one gallon water bottle; then he'll transfer that water into his own well-marked, brand named, portable "sport" bottles.

Note that when they arrive at their destination point in Washington D.C., each man will already have at least one and a half (1.5) gallons of water in his "solar shower" bag.

Every morning the men will place their solar shower bags in the sunlight to soak up the rays all day. And every day just after sundown they will place their warm shower bags into insulated tote bags to prevent heat loss, and they will each shower at night when there are few other people in the area.

Temporary shower stalls will be assembled on paved ground with superior drainage. As soon as the men are finished showering, the stalls will be sprayed with a bleach solution, dried off, and taken down.

To enable all of the above-mentioned tasks to be done in a minimum amount of time and with minimum individual effort, water gathering, deliveries, and garbage and bodily waste removal will always be taken care of in a continuous manner so as to take full advantage of the positioning of all of the men involved.

As per the scheduling of duties that has been worked out, each man will simply take their place in one of two lines that run from the center of his division's location to the locations of the water gathering, deliveries, and garbage and bodily waste removal.

As they assume their position, everyone who is not carrying a piece of a pool kit, a hose, or a delivery-related step/riser will each attempt to take a bag of garbage or a bodily waste container or a mail bag with them.

And regardless of what they might have in their hands, every man will always take an empty five-gallon water container with him because each container will have a plastic strap attached to its handle which will enable the men to carry them over their shoulders.

Prior to moving any of the bodily waste containers toward their drop off/dumpster location, the entire exterior of each container - including all parts such as handles, etc., will be thoroughly cleaned with a bleach solution by a man wearing latex gloves who will be responsible for making absolutely sure that the container is completely sealed.

When they reach their position, the men on the line that is passing water back to each division will simply hand whatever they had carried with them over to the man nearest them who is on the line that is passing items out for removal and passing empty water containers up to be filled; as soon as this line is finished passing its items out for removal, it will become the one that is passing all deliveries back to the/their divisions/division.

Every thousand meters on each line will require 1,000 men (one man per meter) so that once they are each in position the men can basically stand still and just pass items on to each other. Of course, more men than that can be on line when they are available.

4₀ - If two-hundred (200) forty-yard dumpsters are brought in daily to remove the accumulated bodily waste of each battalion, and there are fifty (50) men stationed on risers next to each dumpster, those men will load the approximately 50,000 waste containers into those dumpsters in less than an hour. A "new" set of empty, sanitized containers will be delivered each evening.

And if the arrival of the delivery trucks bringing properly marked food, mail, etc., is also properly scheduled, and they are properly loaded and whenever possible are capable of being simultaneously unloaded from their sides and back end, those 10,000 men will be able to empty one hundred (100) of those trucks (if that many were even scheduled to arrive), and pass the delivered goods and "new" waste containers back down the line toward each division in less than two hours.

At specific points on each line, men will wear specially marked vests that will serve as signposts to direct the goods to specific companies, platoons, squadrons, and divisions.

Garbage pickup will not actually need to be a coordinated effort with the sanitation department, because the amount of garbage that each battalion generates daily will fill approximately one thousand (1,000) large garbage bags.

Those bags can be packed back onto delivery trucks if they're too numerous for the local sanitation crews to pick up.

Since both the importing and exporting of items and the water gathering are occurring simultaneously, even with numerous minor delays the entire operation from start to finish can easily be completed in less than five hours.

And since these operations can be efficiently carried out with only about half of the number of men in each battalion, each man can be scheduled for such duty every other day rather than having to do such work on a daily basis – enabling men of all religious faiths to do their part. Each time the men are scheduled for such work they will each be rotated to a different job.

Having each battalion of 500,000 men generate such a small amount of garbage will be accomplished by way of the specific foods they will be eating and the fact that such food will all be minimally packaged in recyclable plastic or mesh woven bags.

Simply stated, besides the multivitamin he will take every day, each man will be surviving, and thriving, on the following daily diet: two (2) servings of naturally sweetened whey protein isolate that they will mix with water; four (4) sandwiches that will each consist of the following - two thick slices of high fiber multigrain bread, two slices of cheese, and whatever institutionally packaged condiments such as mustard, ketchup, or mayonnaise that they prefer; a few pieces of fruit, and "raw super green food" tablets that will provide them with the equivalent of numerous servings of vegetables.

This diet will provide each man with at least 2,400 calories per day (enough calories to sustain the weight of a 200 pound man) not counting the fruit, condiments, and "vegetables". It will provide over 100 grams of protein; over 40 grams of fiber, not counting the fruit and "vegetables"; over 170 grams of complex carbohydrates, not counting the fruit and "vegetables"; less than 65 grams of fat if mayonnaise is not consumed. Sure, they can also have peanut butter/jelly packed in a squeeze bottle or tube.

If any, or all, of the men need to consume more calories due to physical exertion, this is not a problem. They will simply have another shake and/or sandwich. By the time they are deployed in D.C., every man will know his needs and will be fully adapted to the diet.

Fear not vegans; you will be able to have your dietary needs met without any problem, as well. You will substitute servings of "Raw Meal™" or "Ultimate Meal™" for the whey protein shakes, and soy/tofu cheese for your sandwiches. Others can do this, as well.

Because of the types of foods being consumed, there will be no need for plates, utensils, or mechanical refrigeration. Regarding temperature control, each division having its own large, insulated zippered bags with handles will suffice. Foods will be packed into them at the truck. All other goods will be passed back from the trucks in reusable bags, as well.

To rinse out the bottles they made their protein shake in, each man will fill his bottle with more drinking water and then drink that water. They can wash the bottle in the shower.

Whom do you expect to pay for the massive amounts of fuel and extremely numerous, potentially dangerous devices that would be needed for cooking and refrigeration to occur? Who do you expect will pay the additional cost for the *millions* of pounds of food that would be getting cooked daily? Where will all such items be stored?

How do you expect to maintain sanitary conditions if huge amounts of pots, pans, and utensils are being dirtied? Where will all of the soapy, food-filled, dirty water be disposed of so that bugs and rodents do not infest the area?

Do you realize how much more time and energy will be needed in order to get and distribute the fuel and water required for all of that refrigeration, cooking, and washing?

Do you realize how much more garbage will be generated every single day, with or without the use of disposable plates and utensils, etc.?

4ᴇ - Whenever the men are unable to use a public restroom (which will most often be the case) going to the bathroom will be a team effort that will be perfected by having constantly been in practice for the four months prior to their deployment, and which works as described below.

Each day, within each fifty man division, a different combination of five teams of ten men will work together to provide immediate, portable, private and sanitary toilet facilities for each other by way of each group of ten men sharing a "toilet kit" that is made up of the following:

1 - One plastic bucket style "porta potty" and two other five-gallon buckets with handles and lids.

2 - One 25ft x 8ft 4in plastic tarp with eight tiny, color-coded, reinforced holes on one long edge at three-foot increments and eight equally spaced large color-coded reinforced holes on the other long edge; with Velcro on each reinforced short edge and two seven-foot long slits with reinforced edges that have Velcro pieces on them, to hold them together, placed at 10.5ft from each short edge of the tarp and which begin at the long edge of the tarp that has the large reinforced holes in it. Re-read this and if need be make a drawing of it according to these instructions in order to properly visualize it.

3 - One 25ft x 25ft plastic tarp with eight tiny, color-coded, reinforced holes on each edge at three-foot increments and a properly placed seven-foot long slit with reinforced edges that have Velcro pieces on them to hold them together. Proper placement of the seven-foot long slit will soon be obvious to everyone who properly visualizes these instructions.

4 - Eight, eight-foot long red plastic poles; each with a ring molded into one end so that a carabiner can be attached to it, and two ten-foot long red plastic poles without a ring molded into either of their ends, but with a high tack rubber coating on one end which is rounded off like a ball, with a ring for a carabiner at the base of the ball.

5 - Ten hard plastic red discs that are each hollow and **16** inches in diameter, and whose bottom is flat while its top is **8** inches deep at its center, but which steadily decreases in depth toward its periphery until it reaches a depth of **4** inches at its outer edge.

The disc has a hole in its center that can accommodate the bottom of the poles mentioned in #4, and a sealable, large hole on its side to be filled with dirt for stability in high wind. Each disc will have two adjustable carrying straps so that it can be carried like a backpack.

6 - Thirteen carabiners.

7 - A one gallon-sized unbreakable plastic, glow in the dark bowl and lid.

8 - Twenty plastic bags big enough to fill the inside of the porta potty and all the way over the seat.

9 - Twenty plastic bags that are half the size of the bags mentioned in #8.

10 - Twelve large rubber bands that are each big enough to hold the plastic bag in place on the outside of the porta potty (see #8).

11 - Three plastic containers which look like two-liter bottles that have had their top quarter cut off.

12 - Thirty more of the smaller plastic bags mentioned in #9, to be used inside of the two-liter bottle like containers mentioned in #11.

13 - Numerous rolls of toilet paper and a box of flushable wet wipes.

14 - Two bottles of hand sanitizing liquid and two cans of odor eliminating spray.

15 - Two fine mist spray bottles filled with bleach and water.

16 - Numerous pairs of latex gloves.

17 - A 25ft x 2ft plastic "banner" (the need for this was explained on pages 125/126).

18 - Numerous bikini and sports-related magazines (explanation not required).

The porta potty will always be lined with a plastic bag that is held in place with a rubber band. And it will have the one gallon sized glow in the dark bowl and lid, a couple of rolls of toilet paper and the wet wipes, the plastic bags that fit around it, twenty of the smaller plastic bags, two other rubber bands (only one is to be used at a time; the others are for back up), one bottle of hand sanitizing liquid, one can of odor eliminating spray, one spray bottle with bleach and water, some latex gloves, and the magazines in it.

It will also have a unique, collapsible notched lever that will be erected to extend its length when the potty is in use. The lever will be snuggly sticking out of a 4" long tube-like protrusion near the top of the container, and it will be connected inside the container, through a tiny slot in the lever, to a thin piece of one-inch wide flat metal stripping whose length is equal to half of the circumference of the container and whose edges are rounded and which is attached to an identical piece of stripping with a tiny hinge on each end.

Both pieces of stripping will fit flush against the inside of the container as they form a circle and sit on top of a tiny ledge that runs around the container. The second piece of stripping will have its center third glued to the container in order to keep all of the stripping in place while the first piece is moved as mentioned below.

Each time the man on the potty has a bowel movement he will immediately push the lever in; so as to seal off the bag with his refuse in it, and he will then quickly spray a burst of the odor eliminator.

I just mentioned when the first piece of stripping will move.

He will keep the lever pushed in by setting the notch on the handle into proper locking position until he is either ready to immediately drop more waste into the bag, or to begin cleaning up to leave the facility.

One of the other two buckets will have the three "two-liter bottles" (each of which will always be lined with a plastic bag that is held in place by a rubber band), one bottle of hand sanitizing liquid, a couple of rolls of toilet paper, one can of odor eliminating spray, one spray bottle with bleach and water, the extra plastic bags that fit in the two-liter bottles, some latex gloves, three extra rubber bands, and both tarps in it.

The other bucket will be lined with two plastic bags that are each held in place with a rubber band, and it will be used only to store the bagged waste in it.

When not in use, the poles will be gathered together and held in place by having one of the extra rubber bands on each end; this will not only keep things neat, but it will provide an easy way for the men to transport the entire kit.

By placing the handles of all three buckets and the straps of the pole holders over a few of the poles, two men will be able to easily carry the entire kit on their shoulders for a ten to fifteen minute shift.

When someone needs to sit on the toilet they will remove both tarps from their bucket.

And after handing the large tarp to a teammate, they will take the porta potty and the waste bucket onto a marked area of the large tarp; it will have been semi-opened by the other team members. That person and one of the other men will then adjust the small tarp so that its long edge is folded in half, and they will each attach it to the carabiners that are inside the properly color-coded holes on the edge of the large tarp.

At that point, the guy who helped with the connection of the small tarp and seven of the other men in the group who aren't going to be exercising their ring piece will take proper positions and connect their poles to the carabiners that are within the properly colored reinforced holes on the edge of the large tarp. (Baron Ringpiece will be standing on the marked area of his Barony.)

Then the other eight members of the fellowship of the ring will simultaneously stand the poles straight up and place the bottoms into the plastic pole holders; creating a spacious, freestanding, and well-ventilated two person private toilet facility.

The Baron will then remove everything from the porta potty and place all items, except the glow in the dark bowl and lid (which will be placed on the floor next to the waste container bucket), on top of the waste bucket lid.

He will then place another bag in and around the porta potty and secure it with a rubber band.

When he has finished his business on the porta potty, he will first clean his hands with a wet wipe and then sanitize them; then, with his feet against the bottom of the porta potty to steady it, he will remove the rubber band and place it with the items on the lid of the waste container.

And then he will release the odor-controlling lever as he drops the used wet wipe into the potty and sprays a quick burst of odor eliminating spray into it before quickly placing the spray can back with the items on the lid of the waste container.

He will then quickly remove the used bag, seal it with a couple of tight knots while also reducing the size of the bag to a minimum, and place it into one of the smaller bags.

Then he will seal that bag and place it inside the glow in the dark bowl that is on the floor - *if he managed not to wipe any feces or urine on the bag or his hands*.

He will then seal the glow in the dark bowl, re-sanitize his hands, and place all of the items back into the porta potty. Then he will open the lid of the waste container, unseal the glow in the dark bowl, gently dump the used bag from the glow in the dark bowl into the waste container, and reseal the waste container lid tightly.

Then he will spray the odor eliminator again, spray a light mist of the bleach solution onto and into the glow in the dark bowl and lid, put the bowl and lid and the spray can back into the porta potty, sanitize both of his hands again, put the sanitizer back into the porta potty, seal the porta potty, remove the small tarp from the carabiners, refold it and put it under his arm, grab the handles of both buckets, announce to the men outside that he is finished, and quickly exit the facility through the Velcro lined slit.

As soon as he has exited the facility and resealed the slit, the men outside will lift their poles over their heads while tilting the tops of the poles away from each other.

In other words, they will be simultaneously raising and opening the tarp to release the accumulated odor above and away from them. They will repeat the motion a couple of times to effectively air out the tarp.

If no-one else needs to use the toilet, the men will then disassemble the facility.

Whoever used the facility last will fold up and store the large tarp; if need be they will clean it before storing it.

Obviously if someone else were on the other side of the small tarp urinating, or if someone needed to do so, the person leaving the facility would have left the small tarp in place before he exited, and that person would then take it down and fold it.

I don't need to explain in detail how the men will properly go about urinating do I?

When one or more men need to urinate, the same basic procedure will occur, but with the appropriate buckets (the two-liter looking type buckets).

And whenever possible, with more than one man using the facility at a time so as to minimize the number of times kit setup needs to occur.

If no-one is concerned with anyone in the group checking out their smaller than advertised sausage link, the smaller tarp will not be needed at that time.

If <u>ANY</u> amount of bodily waste *might* have even possibly escaped proper containment, there must be an immediate, thorough cleaning of that area with the bleach solution.

You have no idea how quickly disease will spread among you if there is even the slightest breakdown in proper sanitation and personal hygiene.

As a matter of fact, it is of the utmost importance that all volunteers take all reasonable precautions from all-manner of illness and that they are <u>immediately</u>, temporarily quarantined in what will be any number of volunteer-manned, safely segregated medical stations in the case of their exhibiting <u>any</u> symptoms of <u>any</u> communicable sickness; so that the chance of its spreading among their fellow volunteers is minimized to the greatest extent possible. ("Communicable" = you + dictionary.)

Such reasonable precautions will include, but not be limited to, the <u>immediate</u> use of a germ barrier mask and thorough hand washing by anyone who might even suspect that they have a sickness-related cough or runny nose, or a fever, etc.

Each volunteer must fully understand that everyone else's health, comfort, and success are literally dependent upon their constant proper action - and that all "manly pride" and ego <u>must</u> be completely set aside for the purpose of group and personal success.

4_F - Not that any of you intrepid intellectuals figured it out, but, each "toilet kit" can be used as a rain/snow shelter when the poles have been attached properly to raise the tarp; which also includes placing the ten-foot poles inside their holders along the center of the tarp with the tacky rubber side against the tarp.

If it's windy, just attach the smaller tarp to the bigger one to block the side that the wind is coming from.

Indeed my trenchant friend, you can secure the bottom of the small tarp by placing the bottoms of the poles through its large reinforced holes and placing the pole end into its weighted holder - or it can be used as a 25ft x 8ft roof for a smaller "sidewalk shelter".

If components of two kits are connected, the wind can be blocked from up to three directions in one 25ft x 25ft shelter; just place the extra pole holders on the extra nine feet of the large tarp that will be on the ground after it has been folded in half and hooked to the "roof" with the carabiners.

Modified slightly, this works for a "sidewalk shelter" too.

Not that any of you profound paladins figured it out, but, since each battalion will have 50,000 "toilet kits", during bad/cold weather the kits can be used together to create a fully covered pathway for everyone to work under as they take care of deliveries, water filling, and garbage and waste removal duties, etc.

Two kits can be combined to create either a 25ft long by 25ft wide section of fully enclosed corridor (use one large tarp and both small tarps), or one that is 25ft long x 50ft wide (use both tarps in each kit).

Not that any of you purposeful planners figured it out, but, each "toilet kit" can almost instantly be attached to nine (9) other kits to create a 75ft x 75ft fully enclosed shelter that will be relatively warm in cold weather due to the low ceiling and the amount of body heat that is trapped within it - especially when tents have been set up within it.

And each set of twenty-seven (27) kits can combine to create a fully enclosed 225ft x 75ft shelter with a separated open-style bathroom and/or shower area that is well-ventilated and whose size can be adjusted as needed.

Speaking of needs, have you got that dictionary handy?

Not that any of you exegetes figured it out, but the smaller tarp in each toilet kit is what you will be using to construct your shower stalls.

Each tarp will have both of its long ends folded into itself to form two 3ft x 3ft square stalls with a one-foot wide space between them.

The tops of the poles will be connected to the carabiners that are hooked into their small color-coded holes to raise the stalls up, and the bottoms will be placed into their plastic holders to support the poles. The solar shower bag will be hung from a carabiner in a corner.

Having the shower head in the corner will enable the men to maximize the space inside each stall so there will be enough room to comfortably shower. They will enter and exit each stall through the Velcro lined slits that will be on the long wall of the unit.

Yes, during bad/cold weather, twelve (12) shower stalls can be put up underneath one 25ft x25ft fully enclosed tarp; with plenty of room to move around (just use the extra, large tarps as walls and the extra pole holders to secure their bottoms). Doing so will allow the men to shower in the maximum room temperatures that are possible without an outside source of heat.

And the temperature within the enclosed unit can be increased passively if the men who are next in line to shower wait for their turn within the enclosed area. Temperatures can be maximized if you put up extra layers of walls with some dead air in between the layers and if the men waiting do jumping jacks and/or shadow box, etc.

Everyone will shower with pure, natural soap/shampoo (Google "Emanuel Bronner") so that the 7,500,000 gallons of wastewater created each day will not further pollute "Spaceship Earth".

They will dry off with towels that are made of extremely absorbent, antibacterial, fast drying micro-fibers so that they will not have wet towels hanging or lying around.

While in the shower, the men will wash the socks, underwear, and t-shirt that they wore that day.

They will only wash their outer layer of clothing such as pants and sweatshirts as needed.

First the men will quickly wet themselves and their clothing, and immediately turn off the water. Then they will soap up their scalp, their body, and their clothing.

When they turn the water back on, they will quickly rinse the soap out of their clothing and turn the water off again; at that time they will place the clothing on a plastic strap which will be attached to a carabiner, and each item will be secured to the strap with a plastic clothes pin, so nothing hits the floor.

They will then turn the water back on to rinse off their head and body before repeating the process, while including their face and feet this time instead of their clothing.

If all of their hair is kept very short, and they each shave every day while in the shower, the process will only take a few seconds and will require very little water.

All of the items they will need to regularly wash will be made of quick drying, extremely lightweight, natural fiber material. Each piece will breathe, be easy to wash, and will dry very quickly. Sorry playa', but the only underwear the men will be wearing is tiny briefs.

If carried out properly, all of the above actions can <u>easily</u> be completed with 1.5 gallons of water.

After squeezing out as much water as they can from their clothing, they will enter their tent and lay the damp clothing flat - inside of the other micro-fiber towel that they each have for the purpose of extracting as much water from the damp clothing as possible.

They will then use a vigorous rubbing motion to move the top of the towel over the damp clothes to extract the water.

During warm and hot weather, the clothing can then be hung to dry until morning.

In cold weather, after using the above-mentioned "vigorous rubbing motion" technique, they will temporarily hang those pieces of clothing in their tent in a manner that will keep each layer separate, so as to maximize airflow.

Once they are warm inside of their sleeping bags, the men will put on their pieces of clothing that were hanging in the tent - with the damp socks on their hands rather than their feet and their underwear over their head like a shower cap, **so as to avoid trapping moisture in places that MUST be kept dry**, and they will keep them on until the clothing has dried. Of course it will look funny, but it will serve its purpose perfectly.

Since all such clothing is extremely lightweight, the clothes will be dry in a manner of minutes. At that point the men can remove the clean, dry clothing and go to sleep.

For sleeping purposes, the men will be using the numerous public parks that are within walking distance to the mall. Each morning by 5:30am they will have all of their belongings and garbage fully packed up, so that by 5:40am they will be quietly exiting those areas in a uniform, professional manner; which will insure that the general public is in no way inconvenienced by their usage of such places.

Yes, certain items will remain in the area, but they'll be left out of the way of traffic and watched by men who are on a rotating schedule to do so.

The rest of the five million (5,000,000) men will be at and around the mall by 6am sharp.

Since the men will each be scheduled for import/export duty every other day, the lack of sleep that such a routine requires on certain days will not be overwhelmingly harsh; especially when one considers the fact of what they will be accomplishing without having to face any gunfire.

And each night a different group of **ten thousand (10,000)** men, comprised of twenty (20) divisions from each battalion, will remain gathered together on the mall as a reminder to their "leaders" and the rest of the world that the rally volunteers are fully aware of these facts:

1 - What most of humanity views as a "price to be paid for liberty" is actually an investment; the most fundamental and most profitable long-term investment that can possibly be made.

2 - Despite the constant subterfuge of flag waving institutionalized insurrectionists, come daybreak there will once again be over **TEN MILLION (10,000,000)** members of their cause investing all that they've got in those principles that their nation was founded upon and that have never ceased to be the "supreme Law of the Land".

4G – The ability of volunteers to cause any particular volunteer or group of volunteers to no longer be lawfully considered a member/members of either the "Home" or the "Away" group will exist as follows:

1- In the event that, during the time the "Away" group is stationed outside of their state capitals, ten or more volunteers sign a petition which states the exact trespass (s) or dereliction of duty, and the name (s) of the volunteer (s) who supposedly committed the trespass (s) or dereliction of duty that caused them to undertake such action and which they believe calls for the formation of a twelve volunteer jury to judge the validity of such action, said jury will be formed from members of the remainder of the accused volunteer's (s') division and members of the four divisions whose physical proximity are closest to that of the division (s) in which the accused is/are a member/members.

1a - In the event that, during the time the "Away" group is stationed in Washington D.C., ten or more volunteers sign a petition which states the exact trespass (s) or dereliction of duty, and the name (s) of the volunteer (s) who supposedly committed the trespass (s) or dereliction of duty that caused them to undertake such action and which they believe calls for the formation of a twelve volunteer jury to judge the validity of such action, said jury will be formed out of the remainder of the squadron (s) which the volunteer (s) in question is/are a member/members.

2 – During the time in which the "Away" group is stationed outside of their state capitals, said jury formation will occur within twenty-four (24) hours of the petition being personally presented to the leader (s) of the accused volunteer's (s') division and the leaders of the four divisions whose physical proximity are closest to that of the division (s) in which the accused is/are a member/members, by those volunteers who signed it.

Should said division leader (s) be one/any of the eleven or more people involved in the situation calling for the jury to be formed, the petition will be presented as stated above to any division leader who is not that same division leader. Said receivers of the petition will also act as official magistrates of the trial proceedings.

2a – During the time in which the "Away" group is stationed in Washington D.C., said jury formation will occur within twenty-four (24) hours of the petition being personally presented to the leader (s) of the platoon (s) which the volunteer (s) in question is/are a member/members, by those volunteers who signed it.

Should said platoon leader (s) be one/any of the eleven or more people involved in the situation calling for the jury to be formed, the petition will be presented as stated above to any other platoon leader. Said receiver (s) of the petition will also act as official magistrate (s) of the trial proceedings.

3 - During the time in which the "Away" group is stationed outside of their state capitals, upon receiving the petition, and in the presence of those volunteers who delivered it, the receivers of said petition will, as quickly as possible and by any lawful and suitable means of communication available to them, provide both the applicable volunteer (s) named in the petition and any ten division leaders who are not the same person as themselves, or one who has already received said petition as per section 2 above, or one who is named in the petition, with an exact copy of the petition.

3a - During the time in which the "Away" group is stationed in Washington D.C., upon receiving the petition, and in the presence of those volunteers who delivered it, the receiver (s) of said petition will, as quickly as possible and by any lawful and suitable means of communication available to them, provide both the applicable volunteer (s) named in the petition and any five platoon or company leaders who are not the same person as themselves, or one who has already received said petition as per section 2a above, or one who is named in the petition, with an exact copy of the petition.

4 - Said jury will be chosen by way of each qualified (as per the above regulations) volunteer's name being written on a uniform sized piece of paper and placed into a box, whereupon the contents of the box will immediately be blindly mixed by hand for twenty seconds by a fellow volunteer who is also not one of the eleven people involved in the situation calling for the jury to be formed.

5 - As soon as said mixing is completed, another fellow volunteer, who is not one of the eleven people involved in the situation calling for the jury to be formed, will blindly pick from the box - one at a time - the twelve names of the jurors that will try the case.

6 - The case will be tried within seventy-two (72) hours of the jury being formed.

7 - Each of the eleven or more people involved in the situation calling for the jury to be formed will lawfully be responsible for personally presenting their case to the jury and for calling upon and questioning whichever witnesses they choose.

No-one involved in any aspect of the trial will be lawfully allowed any manner of representation during any of the trial proceedings; this does not mean that they cannot receive advice.

8 - The decision (s) of the jury will always be either a "guilty" or "not guilty" ruling pertaining to each volunteer named in the petition.

Said "guilty" ruling will always result in any volunteer (s) named in such "guilty" ruling being immediately, permanently ineligible for any lawful consideration as a member of either the "Home" or the "Away" group, and their immediately being escorted from their rally location.

Such decision will always be the final lawful ruling on the case at hand regarding said membership status of each volunteer named in the petition.

9 - The entire process outlined above, including all jury deliberation, will always be fully documented on video.

Albeit without any notification, such video will always be immediately made available for unrestricted viewing on the official website of the rally, as well as always being immediately uploaded to "YouTube" – and then highlighted in edited perfection on the latest "reality television" episodes.

Don't you agree that such an unfortunate courtroom drama would make for extremely large television audiences?

10 - Each volunteer will be lawfully, contractually bound to accept the jury's decision. They will have agreed to do so when they originally "signed on".

Those volunteers who are minors will have had a parent or lawfully acknowledged guardian co-sign as such when they "signed on".

4ₕ – What all volunteers will be signing on to is the ongoing act of carrying out their personal responsibilities in regard to the efforts required for the rally to achieve its stated purpose.

Their act of signing on will be lawfully acknowledged as the creation of a binding agreement.

The Declaration of Independence: A Transcription (from www.archives.gov)

IN CONGRESS, July 4, 1776.

The unanimous Declaration of the thirteen united States of America,

When in the Course of human events, it becomes necessary for one people to dissolve the political bands which have connected them with another, and to assume among the powers of the earth, the separate and equal station to which the Laws of Nature and of Nature's God entitle them, a decent respect to the opinions of mankind requires that they should declare the causes which impel them to the separation.

We hold these truths to be self-evident, that all men are created equal, that they are endowed by their Creator with certain unalienable Rights, that among these are Life, Liberty and the pursuit of Happiness.-- That to secure these rights, Governments are instituted among Men, deriving their just powers from the consent of the governed, --That whenever any Form of Government becomes destructive of these ends, it is the Right of the People to alter or to abolish it, and to institute new Government, laying its foundation on such principles and organizing its powers in such form, as to them shall seem most likely to effect their Safety and Happiness. Prudence, indeed, will dictate that Governments long established should not be changed for light and transient causes; and accordingly all experience hath shewn, that mankind are more disposed to suffer, while evils are sufferable, than to right themselves by abolishing the forms to which they are accustomed. But when a long train of abuses and usurpations, pursuing invariably the same Object evinces a design to reduce them under absolute Despotism, it is their right, it is their duty, to throw off such Government, and to provide new Guards for their future security.--Such has been the patient sufferance of these Colonies; and such is now the necessity which constrains them to alter their former Systems of Government. The history of the present King of Great Britain is a history of repeated injuries and usurpations, all having in direct object the establishment of an absolute Tyranny over these States. To prove this, let Facts be submitted to a candid world.

He has refused his Assent to Laws, the most wholesome and necessary for the public good.

He has forbidden his Governors to pass Laws of immediate and pressing importance, unless suspended in their operation till his Assent should be obtained; and when so suspended, he has utterly neglected to attend to them.

He has refused to pass other Laws for the accommodation of large districts of people, unless those people would relinquish the right of Representation in the Legislature, a right inestimable to them and formidable to tyrants only.

He has called together legislative bodies at places unusual, uncomfortable, and distant from the depository of their public Records, for the sole purpose of fatiguing them into compliance with his measures.

He has dissolved Representative Houses repeatedly, for opposing with manly firmness his invasions on the rights of the people.

He has refused for a long time, after such dissolutions, to cause others to be elected; whereby the Legislative powers, incapable of Annihilation, have returned to the People at large for their exercise; the State remaining in the mean time exposed to all the dangers of invasion from without, and convulsions within.

He has endeavoured to prevent the population of these States; for that purpose obstructing the Laws for Naturalization of Foreigners; refusing to pass others to encourage their migrations hither, and raising the conditions of new Appropriations of Lands.

He has obstructed the Administration of Justice, by refusing his Assent to Laws for establishing Judiciary powers.

He has made Judges dependent on his Will alone, for the tenure of their offices, and the amount and payment of their salaries.

He has erected a multitude of New Offices, and sent hither swarms of Officers to harrass our people, and eat out their substance.

He has kept among us, in times of peace, Standing Armies without the Consent of our legislatures.

He has affected to render the Military independent of and superior to the Civil power.

He has combined with others to subject us to a jurisdiction foreign to our constitution, and unacknowledged by our laws; giving his Assent to their Acts of pretended Legislation:

For Quartering large bodies of armed troops among us:

For protecting them, by a mock Trial, from punishment for any Murders which they should commit on the Inhabitants of these States:

For cutting off our Trade with all parts of the world:

For imposing Taxes on us without our Consent:

For depriving us in many cases, of the benefits of Trial by Jury:

For transporting us beyond Seas to be tried for pretended offences

For abolishing the free System of English Laws in a neighbouring Province, establishing therein an Arbitrary government, and enlarging its Boundaries so as to render it at once an example and fit instrument for introducing the same absolute rule into these Colonies:

For taking away our Charters, abolishing our most valuable Laws, and altering fundamentally the Forms of our Governments:

For suspending our own Legislatures, and declaring themselves invested with power to legislate for us in all cases whatsoever.

He has abdicated Government here, by declaring us out of his Protection and waging War against us.

He has plundered our seas, ravaged our Coasts, burnt our towns, and destroyed the lives of our people.

He is at this time transporting large Armies of foreign Mercenaries to compleat the works of death, desolation and tyranny, already begun with circumstances of Cruelty & perfidy scarcely paralleled in the most barbarous ages, and totally unworthy the Head of a civilized nation.

He has constrained our fellow Citizens taken Captive on the high Seas to bear Arms against their Country, to become the executioners of their friends and Brethren, or to fall themselves by their Hands.

He has excited domestic insurrections amongst us, and has endeavoured to bring on the inhabitants of our frontiers, the merciless Indian Savages, whose known rule of warfare, is an undistinguished destruction of all ages, sexes and conditions.

In every stage of these Oppressions We have Petitioned for Redress in the most humble terms: Our repeated Petitions have been answered only by repeated injury. A Prince whose character is thus marked by every act which may define a Tyrant, is unfit to be the ruler of a free people.

Nor have We been wanting in attentions to our Brittish brethren. We have warned them from time to time of attempts by their legislature to extend an unwarrantable jurisdiction over us. We have reminded them of the circumstances of our emigration and settlement here. We have appealed to their native justice and magnanimity, and we have conjured them by the ties of our common kindred to disavow these usurpations, which, would inevitably interrupt our connections and correspondence. They too have been deaf to the voice of justice and of consanguinity. We must, therefore, acquiesce in the necessity, which denounces our Separation, and hold them, as we hold the rest of mankind, Enemies in War, in Peace Friends.

We, therefore, the Representatives of the united States of America, in General Congress, Assembled, appealing to the Supreme Judge of the world for the rectitude of our intentions, do, in the Name, and by Authority of the good People of these Colonies, solemnly publish and declare, That these United Colonies are, and of Right ought to be Free and Independent States; that they are Absolved from all Allegiance to the British Crown, and that all political connection between them and the State of Great Britain, is and ought to be totally dissolved; and that as Free and Independent States, they have full Power to levy War, conclude Peace, contract Alliances, establish Commerce, and to do all other Acts and Things which Independent States may of right do. And for the support of this Declaration, with a firm reliance on the protection of divine Providence, we mutually pledge to each other our Lives, our Fortunes and our sacred Honor.

The Constitution of the United States: A Transcription (from www.archives.gov)

Note: *The following text is a transcription of the Constitution in its **original** form.*
Items that are hyperlinked have since been amended or superseded.

We the People of the United States, in Order to form a more perfect Union, establish Justice, insure domestic Tranquility, provide for the common defence, promote the general Welfare, and secure the Blessings of Liberty to ourselves and our Posterity, do ordain and establish this Constitution for the United States of America.

Article. I.

Section. 1.

All legislative Powers herein granted shall be vested in a Congress of the United States, which shall consist of a Senate and House of Representatives.

Section. 2.

The House of Representatives shall be composed of Members chosen every second Year by the People of the several States, and the Electors in each State shall have the Qualifications requisite for Electors of the most numerous Branch of the State Legislature.

No Person shall be a Representative who shall not have attained to the Age of twenty five Years, and been seven Years a Citizen of the United States, and who shall not, when elected, be an Inhabitant of that State in which he shall be chosen.

Representatives and direct Taxes shall be apportioned among the several States which may be included within this Union, according to their respective Numbers, which shall be determined by adding to the whole Number of free Persons, including those bound to Service for a Term of Years, and excluding Indians not taxed, three fifths of all other Persons. The actual Enumeration shall be made within three Years after the first Meeting of the Congress of the United States, and within every subsequent Term of ten Years, in such Manner as they shall by Law direct. The Number of Representatives shall not exceed one for every thirty Thousand, but each State shall have at Least one Representative; and until such enumeration shall be made, the State of New Hampshire shall be entitled to chuse three, Massachusetts eight, Rhode-Island and Providence Plantations one, Connecticut five, New-York six, New Jersey four, Pennsylvania eight, Delaware one, Maryland six, Virginia ten, North Carolina five, South Carolina five, and Georgia three.

When vacancies happen in the Representation from any State, the Executive Authority thereof shall issue Writs of Election to fill such Vacancies.

The House of Representatives shall chuse their Speaker and other Officers; and shall have the sole Power of Impeachment.

Section. 3.

The Senate of the United States shall be composed of two Senators from each State, chosen by the Legislature thereof for six Years; and each Senator shall have one Vote.

Immediately after they shall be assembled in Consequence of the first Election, they shall be divided as equally as may be into three Classes. The Seats of the Senators of the first Class shall be vacated at the Expiration of the second Year, of the second Class at the Expiration of the fourth Year, and of the third Class at the Expiration of the sixth Year, so that one third may be chosen every second Year; and if Vacancies happen by Resignation, or otherwise, during the Recess of the Legislature of any State, the Executive thereof may make temporary Appointments until the next Meeting of the Legislature, which shall then fill such Vacancies.

No Person shall be a Senator who shall not have attained to the Age of thirty Years, and been nine Years a Citizen of the United States, and who shall not, when elected, be an Inhabitant of that State for which he shall be chosen.

The Vice President of the United States shall be President of the Senate, but shall have no Vote, unless they be equally divided.

The Senate shall chuse their other Officers, and also a President pro tempore, in the Absence of the Vice President, or when he shall exercise the Office of President of the United States.

The Senate shall have the sole Power to try all Impeachments. When sitting for that Purpose, they shall be on Oath or Affirmation. When the President of the United States is tried, the Chief Justice shall preside: And no Person shall be convicted without the Concurrence of two thirds of the Members present.

Judgment in Cases of Impeachment shall not extend further than to removal from Office, and disqualification to hold and enjoy any Office of honor, Trust or Profit under the United States: but the Party convicted shall nevertheless be liable and subject to Indictment, Trial, Judgment and Punishment, according to Law.

Section. 4.

The Times, Places and Manner of holding Elections for Senators and Representatives, shall be prescribed in each State by the Legislature thereof; but the Congress may at any time by Law make or alter such Regulations, except as to the Places of chusing Senators.

The Congress shall assemble at least once in every Year, and such Meeting shall <u>be on the first Monday in December</u>, unless they shall by Law appoint a different Day.

Section. 5.

Each House shall be the Judge of the Elections, Returns and Qualifications of its own Members, and a Majority of each shall constitute a Quorum to do Business; but a smaller Number may adjourn from day to day, and may be authorized to compel the Attendance of absent Members, in such Manner, and under such Penalties as each House may provide.

Each House may determine the Rules of its Proceedings, punish its Members for disorderly Behaviour, and, with the Concurrence of two thirds, expel a Member.

Each House shall keep a Journal of its Proceedings, and from time to time publish the same, excepting such Parts as may in their Judgment require Secrecy; and the Yeas and Nays of the Members of either House on any question shall, at the Desire of one fifth of those Present, be entered on the Journal.

Neither House, during the Session of Congress, shall, without the Consent of the other, adjourn for more than three days, nor to any other Place than that in which the two Houses shall be sitting.

Section. 6.

The Senators and Representatives shall receive a Compensation for their Services, to be ascertained by Law, and paid out of the Treasury of the United States. They shall in all Cases, except Treason, Felony and Breach of the Peace, be privileged from Arrest during their Attendance at the Session of their respective Houses, and in going to and returning from the same; and for any Speech or Debate in either House, they shall not be questioned in any other Place.

No Senator or Representative shall, during the Time for which he was elected, be appointed to any civil Office under the Authority of the United States, which shall have been created, or the Emoluments whereof shall have been increased during such time; and no Person holding any Office under the United States, shall be a Member of either House during his Continuance in Office.

Section. 7.

All Bills for raising Revenue shall originate in the House of Representatives; but the Senate may propose or concur with Amendments as on other Bills.

Every Bill which shall have passed the House of Representatives and the Senate, shall, before it become a Law, be presented to the President of the United States: If he approve he shall sign it, but if not he shall return it, with his Objections to that House in which it shall have originated, who shall enter the Objections at large on their Journal, and proceed to reconsider it. If after such Reconsideration two thirds of that House shall agree to pass the Bill, it shall be sent, together with the Objections, to the other House, by which it shall likewise be reconsidered, and if approved by two thirds of that House, it shall become a Law. But in all such Cases the Votes of both Houses shall be determined by yeas and Nays, and the Names of the Persons voting for and against the Bill shall be entered on the Journal of each House respectively. If any Bill shall not be returned by the President within ten Days (Sundays excepted) after it shall have been presented to him, the Same shall be a Law, in like Manner as if he had signed it, unless the Congress by their Adjournment prevent its Return, in which Case it shall not be a Law.

Every Order, Resolution, or Vote to which the Concurrence of the Senate and House of Representatives may be necessary (except on a question of Adjournment) shall be presented to the President of the United States; and before the Same shall take Effect, shall be approved by him, or being disapproved by him, shall be repassed by two thirds of the Senate and House of Representatives, according to the Rules and Limitations prescribed in the Case of a Bill.

Section. 8.

The Congress shall have Power To lay and collect Taxes, Duties, Imposts and Excises, to pay the Debts and provide for the common Defence and general Welfare of the United States; but all Duties, Imposts and Excises shall be uniform throughout the United States;

To borrow Money on the credit of the United States;

To regulate Commerce with foreign Nations, and among the several States, and with the Indian Tribes;

To establish an uniform Rule of Naturalization, and uniform Laws on the subject of Bankruptcies throughout the United States;

To coin Money, regulate the Value thereof, and of foreign Coin, and fix the Standard of Weights and Measures;

To provide for the Punishment of counterfeiting the Securities and current Coin of the United States;

To establish Post Offices and post Roads;

To promote the Progress of Science and useful Arts, by securing for limited Times to Authors and Inventors the exclusive Right to their respective Writings and Discoveries;

To constitute Tribunals inferior to the supreme Court;

To define and punish Piracies and Felonies committed on the high Seas, and Offences against the Law of Nations;

To declare War, grant Letters of Marque and Reprisal, and make Rules concerning Captures on Land and Water;

To raise and support Armies, but no Appropriation of Money to that Use shall be for a longer Term than two Years;

To provide and maintain a Navy;

To make Rules for the Government and Regulation of the land and naval Forces;

To provide for calling forth the Militia to execute the Laws of the Union, suppress Insurrections and repel Invasions;

To provide for organizing, arming, and disciplining, the Militia, and for governing such Part of them as may be employed in the Service of the United States, reserving to the States respectively, the Appointment of the Officers, and the Authority of training the Militia according to the discipline prescribed by Congress;

To exercise exclusive Legislation in all Cases whatsoever, over such District (not exceeding ten Miles square) as may, by Cession of particular States, and the Acceptance of Congress, become the Seat of the Government of the United States, and to exercise like Authority over all Places purchased by the Consent of the Legislature of the State in which the Same shall be, for the Erection of Forts, Magazines, Arsenals, dock-Yards, and other needful Buildings;--And

To make all Laws which shall be necessary and proper for carrying into Execution the foregoing Powers, and all other Powers vested by this Constitution in the Government of the United States, or in any Department or Officer thereof.

Section. 9.

The Migration or Importation of such Persons as any of the States now existing shall think proper to admit, shall not be prohibited by the Congress prior to the Year one thousand eight hundred and eight, but a Tax or duty may be imposed on such Importation, not exceeding ten dollars for each Person.

The Privilege of the Writ of Habeas Corpus shall not be suspended, unless when in Cases of Rebellion or Invasion the public Safety may require it.

No Bill of Attainder or ex post facto Law shall be passed.

No Capitation, or other direct, Tax shall be laid, <u>unless in Proportion to the Census or enumeration herein before directed to be taken</u>.

No Tax or Duty shall be laid on Articles exported from any State.

No Preference shall be given by any Regulation of Commerce or Revenue to the Ports of one State over those of another; nor shall Vessels bound to, or from, one State, be obliged to enter, clear, or pay Duties in another.

No Money shall be drawn from the Treasury, but in Consequence of Appropriations made by Law; and a regular Statement and Account of the Receipts and Expenditures of all public Money shall be published from time to time.

No Title of Nobility shall be granted by the United States: And no Person holding any Office of Profit or Trust under them, shall, without the Consent of the Congress, accept of any present, Emolument, Office, or Title, of any kind whatever, from any King, Prince, or foreign State.

Section. 10.

No State shall enter into any Treaty, Alliance, or Confederation; grant Letters of Marque and Reprisal; coin Money; emit Bills of Credit; make any Thing but gold and silver Coin a Tender in Payment of Debts; pass any Bill of Attainder, ex post facto Law, or Law impairing the Obligation of Contracts, or grant any Title of Nobility.

No State shall, without the Consent of the Congress, lay any Imposts or Duties on Imports or Exports, except what may be absolutely necessary for executing it's inspection Laws: and the net Produce of all Duties and Imposts, laid by any State on Imports or Exports, shall be for the Use of the Treasury of the United States; and all such Laws shall be subject to the Revision and Controul of the Congress.

No State shall, without the Consent of Congress, lay any Duty of Tonnage, keep Troops, or Ships of War in time of Peace, enter into any Agreement or Compact with another State, or with a foreign Power, or engage in War, unless actually invaded, or in such imminent Danger as will not admit of delay.

Article. II.

Section. 1.

The executive Power shall be vested in a President of the United States of America. He shall hold his Office during the Term of four Years, and, together with the Vice President, chosen for the same Term, be elected, as follows:

Each State shall appoint, in such Manner as the Legislature thereof may direct, a Number of Electors, equal to the whole Number of Senators and Representatives to which the State may be entitled in the Congress: but no Senator or Representative, or Person holding an Office of Trust or Profit under the United States, shall be appointed an Elector.

The Electors shall meet in their respective States, and vote by Ballot for two Persons, of whom one at least shall not be an Inhabitant of the same State with themselves. And they shall make a List of all the Persons voted for, and of the Number of Votes for each; which List they shall sign and certify, and transmit sealed to the Seat of the Government of the United States, directed to the President of the Senate. The President of the Senate shall, in the Presence of the Senate and House of Representatives, open all the Certificates, and the Votes shall then be counted. The Person having the greatest Number of Votes shall be the President, if such Number be a Majority of the whole Number of Electors appointed; and if there be more than one who have such Majority, and have an equal Number of Votes, then the House of Representatives shall immediately chuse by Ballot one of them for President; and if no Person have a Majority, then from the five highest on the List the said House shall in like Manner chuse the President. But in chusing the President, the Votes shall be taken by States, the Representation from each State having one Vote; A quorum for this purpose shall consist of a Member or Members from two thirds of the States, and a Majority of all the States shall be necessary to a Choice. In every Case, after the Choice of the President, the Person having the greatest Number of Votes of the Electors shall be the Vice President. But if there should remain two or more who have equal Votes, the Senate shall chuse from them by Ballot the Vice President.

The Congress may determine the Time of chusing the Electors, and the Day on which they shall give their Votes; which Day shall be the same throughout the United States.

No Person except a natural born Citizen, or a Citizen of the United States, at the time of the Adoption of this Constitution, shall be eligible to the Office of President; neither shall any Person be eligible to that Office who shall not have attained to the Age of thirty five Years, and been fourteen Years a Resident within the United States.

In Case of the Removal of the President from Office, or of his Death, Resignation, or Inability to discharge the Powers and Duties of the said Office, the Same shall devolve on the Vice President, and the Congress may by Law provide for the Case of Removal, Death, Resignation or Inability, both of the President and Vice President, declaring what Officer shall then act as President, and such Officer shall act accordingly, until the Disability be removed, or a President shall be elected.

The President shall, at stated Times, receive for his Services, a Compensation, which shall neither be increased nor diminished during the Period for which he shall have been elected, and he shall not receive within that Period any other Emolument from the United States, or any of them.

Before he enter on the Execution of his Office, he shall take the following Oath or Affirmation:--"I do solemnly swear (or affirm) that I will faithfully execute the Office of President of the United States, and will to the best of my Ability, preserve, protect and defend the Constitution of the United States."

Section. 2.

The President shall be Commander in Chief of the Army and Navy of the United States, and of the Militia of the several States, when called into the actual Service of the United States; he may require the Opinion, in writing, of the principal Officer in each of the executive Departments, upon any Subject relating to the Duties of their respective Offices, and he shall have Power to grant Reprieves and Pardons for Offences against the United States, except in Cases of Impeachment.

He shall have Power, by and with the Advice and Consent of the Senate, to make Treaties, provided two thirds of the Senators present concur; and he shall nominate, and by and with the Advice and Consent of the Senate, shall appoint Ambassadors, other public Ministers and Consuls, Judges of the supreme Court, and all other Officers of the United States, whose Appointments are not herein otherwise provided for, and which shall be established by Law: but the Congress may by Law vest the Appointment of such inferior Officers, as they think proper, in the President alone, in the Courts of Law, or in the Heads of Departments.

The President shall have Power to fill up all Vacancies that may happen during the Recess of the Senate, by granting Commissions which shall expire at the End of their next Session.

Section. 3.

He shall from time to time give to the Congress Information of the State of the Union, and recommend to their Consideration such Measures as he shall judge necessary and expedient; he may, on extraordinary Occasions, convene both Houses, or either of them, and in Case of Disagreement between them, with Respect to the Time of Adjournment, he may adjourn them to such Time as he shall think proper; he shall receive Ambassadors and other public Ministers; he shall take Care that the Laws be faithfully executed, and shall Commission all the Officers of the United States.

Section. 4.

The President, Vice President and all civil Officers of the United States, shall be removed from Office on Impeachment for, and Conviction of, Treason, Bribery, or other high Crimes and Misdemeanors.

Article III.

Section. 1.

The judicial Power of the United States shall be vested in one supreme Court, and in such inferior Courts as the Congress may from time to time ordain and establish. The Judges, both of the supreme and inferior Courts, shall hold their Offices during good Behaviour, and shall, at stated Times, receive for their Services a Compensation, which shall not be diminished during their Continuance in Office.

Section. 2.

The judicial Power shall extend to all Cases, in Law and Equity, arising under this Constitution, the Laws of the United States, and Treaties made, or which shall be made, under their Authority;--to all Cases affecting Ambassadors, other public Ministers and Consuls;--to all Cases of admiralty and maritime Jurisdiction;--to Controversies to which the United States shall be a Party;--to Controversies between two or more States;-- between a State and Citizens of another State,--between Citizens of different States,-- between Citizens of the same State claiming Lands under Grants of different States, and between a State, or the Citizens thereof, and foreign States, Citizens or Subjects.

In all Cases affecting Ambassadors, other public Ministers and Consuls, and those in which a State shall be Party, the supreme Court shall have original Jurisdiction. In all the other Cases before mentioned, the supreme Court shall have appellate Jurisdiction, both as to Law and Fact, with such Exceptions, and under such Regulations as the Congress shall make.

The Trial of all Crimes, except in Cases of Impeachment, shall be by Jury; and such Trial shall be held in the State where the said Crimes shall have been committed; but when not committed within any State, the Trial shall be at such Place or Places as the Congress may by Law have directed.

Section. 3.

Treason against the United States, shall consist only in levying War against them, or in adhering to their Enemies, giving them Aid and Comfort. No Person shall be convicted of Treason unless on the Testimony of two Witnesses to the same overt Act, or on Confession in open Court.

The Congress shall have Power to declare the Punishment of Treason, but no Attainder of Treason shall work Corruption of Blood, or Forfeiture except during the Life of the Person attainted.

Article. IV.

Section. 1.

Full Faith and Credit shall be given in each State to the public Acts, Records, and judicial Proceedings of every other State. And the Congress may by general Laws prescribe the Manner in which such Acts, Records and Proceedings shall be proved, and the Effect thereof.

Section. 2.

The Citizens of each State shall be entitled to all Privileges and Immunities of Citizens in the several States.

A Person charged in any State with Treason, Felony, or other Crime, who shall flee from Justice, and be found in another State, shall on Demand of the executive Authority of the State from which he fled, be delivered up, to be removed to the State having Jurisdiction of the Crime.

No Person held to Service or Labour in one State, under the Laws thereof, escaping into another, shall, in Consequence of any Law or Regulation therein, be discharged from such Service or Labour, but shall be delivered up on Claim of the Party to whom such Service or Labour may be due.

Section. 3.

New States may be admitted by the Congress into this Union; but no new State shall be formed or erected within the Jurisdiction of any other State; nor any State be formed by the Junction of two or more States, or Parts of States, without the Consent of the Legislatures of the States concerned as well as of the Congress.

The Congress shall have Power to dispose of and make all needful Rules and Regulations respecting the Territory or other Property belonging to the United States; and nothing in this Constitution shall be so construed as to Prejudice any Claims of the United States, or of any particular State.

Section. 4.

The United States shall guarantee to every State in this Union a Republican Form of Government, and shall protect each of them against Invasion; and on Application of the Legislature, or of the Executive (when the Legislature cannot be convened), against domestic Violence.

Article. V.

The Congress, whenever two thirds of both Houses shall deem it necessary, shall propose Amendments to this Constitution, or, on the Application of the Legislatures of two thirds of the several States, shall call a Convention for proposing Amendments, which, in either Case, shall be valid to all Intents and Purposes, as Part of this Constitution, when ratified by the Legislatures of three fourths of the several States, or by Conventions in three fourths thereof, as the one or the other Mode of Ratification may be proposed by the Congress; Provided that no Amendment which may be made prior to the Year One thousand eight hundred and eight shall in any Manner affect the first and fourth Clauses in the Ninth Section of the first Article; and that no State, without its Consent, shall be deprived of its equal Suffrage in the Senate.

Article. VI.

All Debts contracted and Engagements entered into, before the Adoption of this Constitution, shall be as valid against the United States under this Constitution, as under the Confederation.

This Constitution, and the Laws of the United States which shall be made in Pursuance thereof; and all Treaties made, or which shall be made, under the Authority of the United States, shall be the supreme Law of the Land; and the Judges in every State shall be bound thereby, any Thing in the Constitution or Laws of any State to the Contrary notwithstanding.

The Senators and Representatives before mentioned, and the Members of the several State Legislatures, and all executive and judicial Officers, both of the United States and of the several States, shall be bound by Oath or Affirmation, to support this Constitution; but no religious Test shall ever be required as a Qualification to any Office or public Trust under the United States.

Article. VII.

The Ratification of the Conventions of nine States, shall be sufficient for the Establishment of this Constitution between the States so ratifying the Same.

The Word, "the," being interlined between the seventh and eighth Lines of the first Page, the Word "Thirty" being partly written on an Erazure in the fifteenth Line of the first Page, The Words "is tried" being interlined between the thirty second and thirty third Lines of the first Page and the Word "the" being interlined between the forty third and forty fourth Lines of the second Page.

Attest William Jackson Secretary

done in Convention by the Unanimous Consent of the States present the Seventeenth Day of September in the Year of our Lord one thousand seven hundred and Eighty seven and of the Independance of the United States of America the Twelfth In witness whereof We have hereunto subscribed our Names,

The Preamble to The Bill of Rights (from www.archives.gov)

Congress of the United States
begun and held at the City of New-York, on
Wednesday the fourth of March, one thousand seven hundred and eighty nine.

THE Conventions of a number of the States, having at the time of their adopting the Constitution, expressed a desire, in order to prevent misconstruction or abuse of its powers, that further declaratory and restrictive clauses should be added: And as extending the ground of public confidence in the Government, will best ensure the beneficent ends of its institution.

RESOLVED by the Senate and House of Representatives of the United States of America, in Congress assembled, two thirds of both Houses concurring, that the following Articles be proposed to the Legislatures of the several States, as amendments to the Constitution of the United States, all, or any of which Articles, when ratified by three fourths of the said Legislatures, to be valid to all intents and purposes, as part of the said Constitution; viz.

ARTICLES in addition to, and Amendment of the Constitution of the United States of America, proposed by Congress, and ratified by the Legislatures of the several States, pursuant to the fifth Article of the original Constitution.

The Bill of Rights: A Transcription (from www.archives.gov)

The Preamble to The Bill of Rights

Congress of the United States
begun and held at the City of New-York, on
Wednesday the fourth of March, one thousand seven hundred and eighty nine.

THE Conventions of a number of the States, having at the time of their adopting the Constitution, expressed a desire, in order to prevent misconstruction or abuse of its powers, that further declaratory and restrictive clauses should be added: And as extending the ground of public confidence in the Government, will best ensure the beneficent ends of its institution.

RESOLVED by the Senate and House of Representatives of the United States of America, in Congress assembled, two thirds of both Houses concurring, that the following Articles be proposed to the Legislatures of the several States, as amendments to the Constitution of the United States, all, or any of which Articles, when ratified by three fourths of the said Legislatures, to be valid to all intents and purposes, as part of the said Constitution; viz.

ARTICLES in addition to, and Amendment of the Constitution of the United States of America, proposed by Congress, and ratified by the Legislatures of the several States, pursuant to the fifth Article of the original Constitution.

Note: The following text is a transcription of the first ten amendments to the Constitution in their original form. These amendments were ratified December 15, 1791, and form what is known as the "Bill of Rights."

Amendment I

Congress shall make no law respecting an establishment of religion, or prohibiting the free exercise thereof; or abridging the freedom of speech, or of the press; or the right of the people peaceably to assemble, and to petition the Government for a redress of grievances.

Amendment II

A well regulated Militia, being necessary to the security of a free State, the right of the people to keep and bear Arms, shall not be infringed.

Amendment III

No Soldier shall, in time of peace be quartered in any house, without the consent of the Owner, nor in time of war, but in a manner to be prescribed by law.

Amendment IV

The right of the people to be secure in their persons, houses, papers, and effects, against unreasonable searches and seizures, shall not be violated, and no Warrants shall issue, but upon probable cause, supported by Oath or affirmation, and particularly describing the place to be searched, and the persons or things to be seized.

Amendment V

No person shall be held to answer for a capital, or otherwise infamous crime, unless on a presentment or indictment of a Grand Jury, except in cases arising in the land or naval forces, or in the Militia, when in actual service in time of War or public danger; nor shall any person be subject for the same offence to be twice put in jeopardy of life or limb; nor shall be compelled in any criminal case to be a witness against himself, nor be deprived of life, liberty, or property, without due process of law; nor shall private property be taken for public use, without just compensation.

Amendment VI

In all criminal prosecutions, the accused shall enjoy the right to a speedy and public trial, by an impartial jury of the State and district wherein the crime shall have been committed, which district shall have been previously ascertained by law, and to be informed of the nature and cause of the accusation; to be confronted with the witnesses against him; to have compulsory process for obtaining witnesses in his favor, and to have the Assistance of Counsel for his defence.

Amendment VII

In Suits at common law, where the value in controversy shall exceed twenty dollars, the right of trial by jury shall be preserved, and no fact tried by a jury, shall be otherwise re-examined in any Court of the United States, than according to the rules of the common law.

Amendment VIII

Excessive bail shall not be required, nor excessive fines imposed, nor cruel and unusual punishments inflicted.

Amendment IX

The enumeration in the Constitution, of certain rights, shall not be construed to deny or disparage others retained by the people.

Amendment X

The powers not delegated to the United States by the Constitution, nor prohibited by it to the States, are reserved to the States respectively, or to the people.